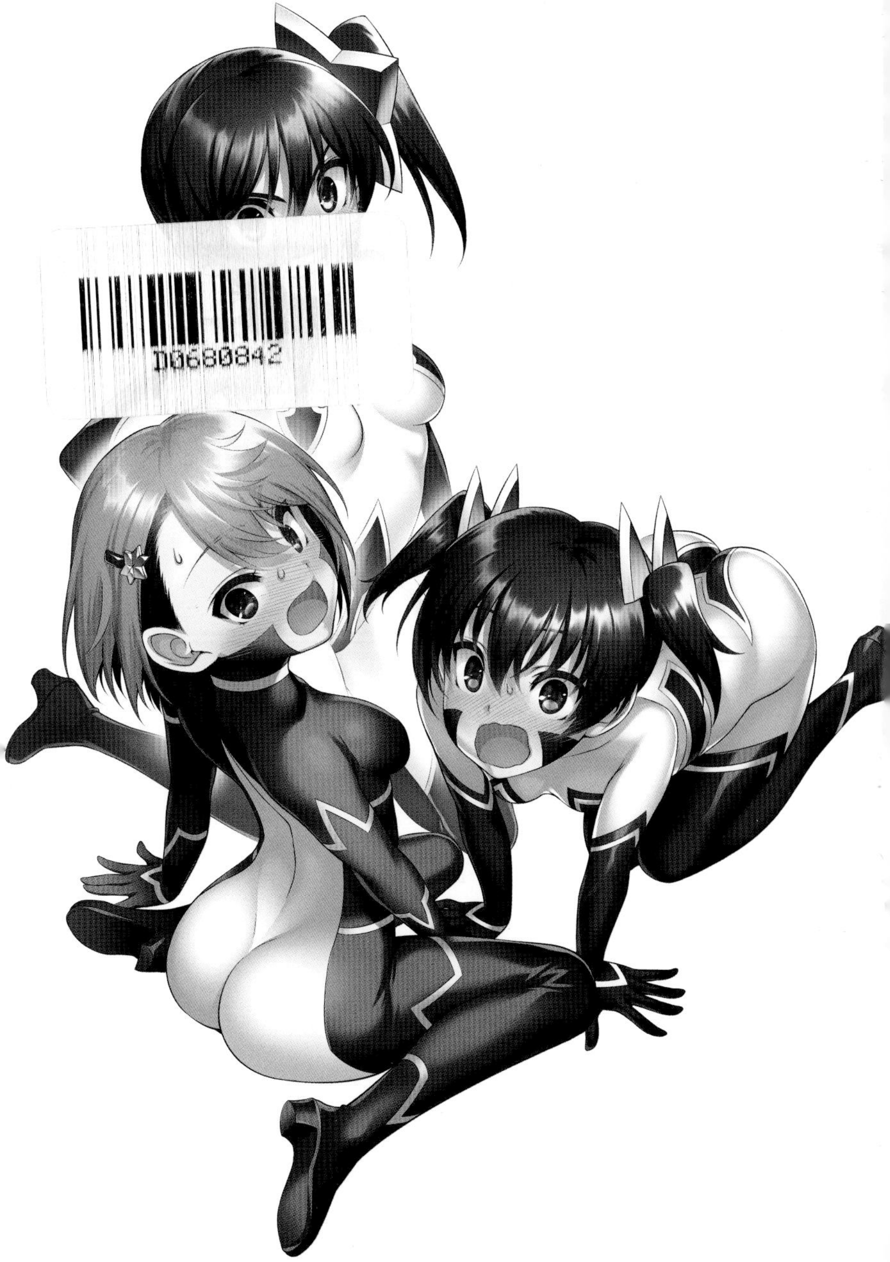

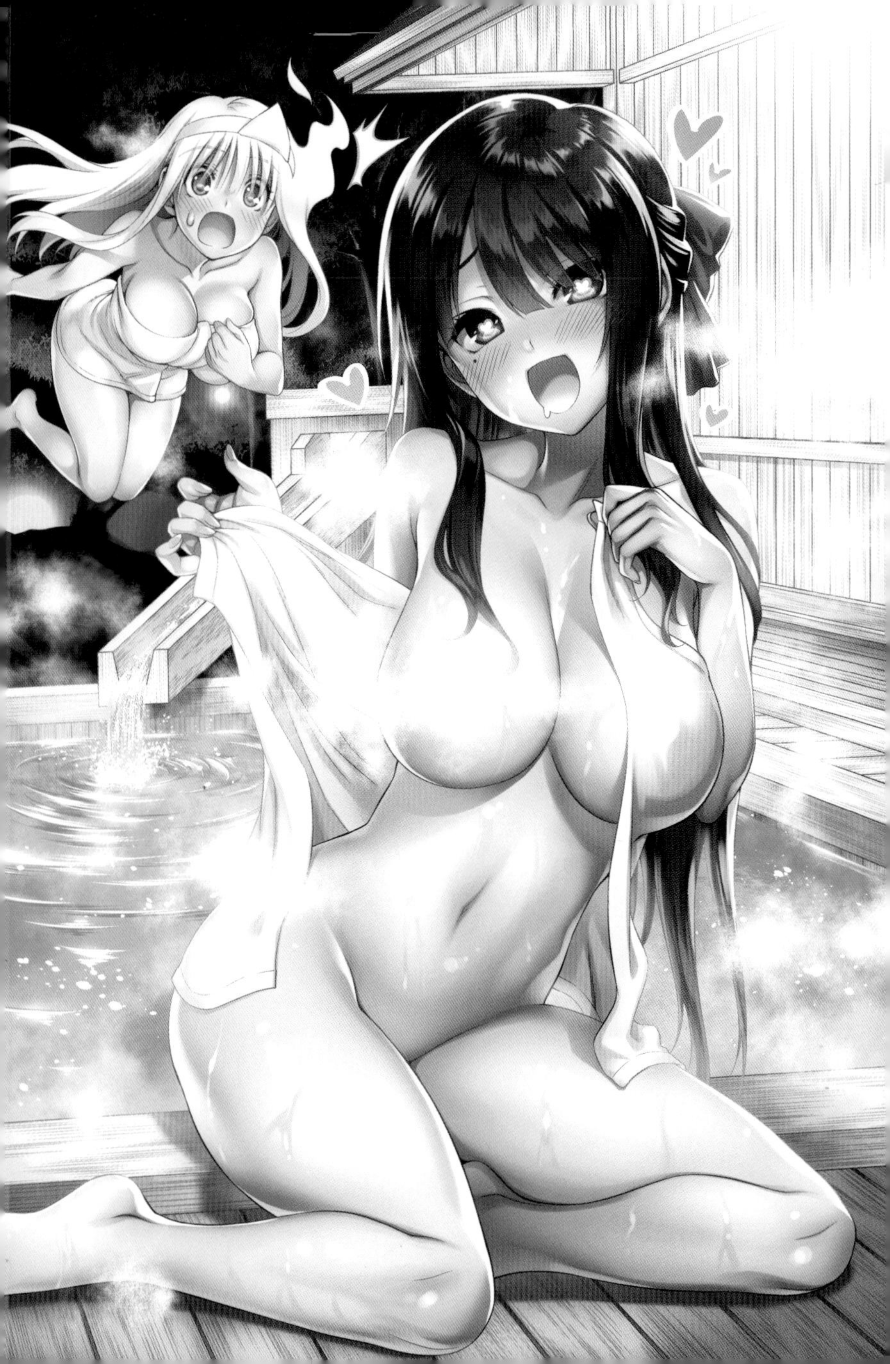

Yuuna and the Haunted Hot Springs

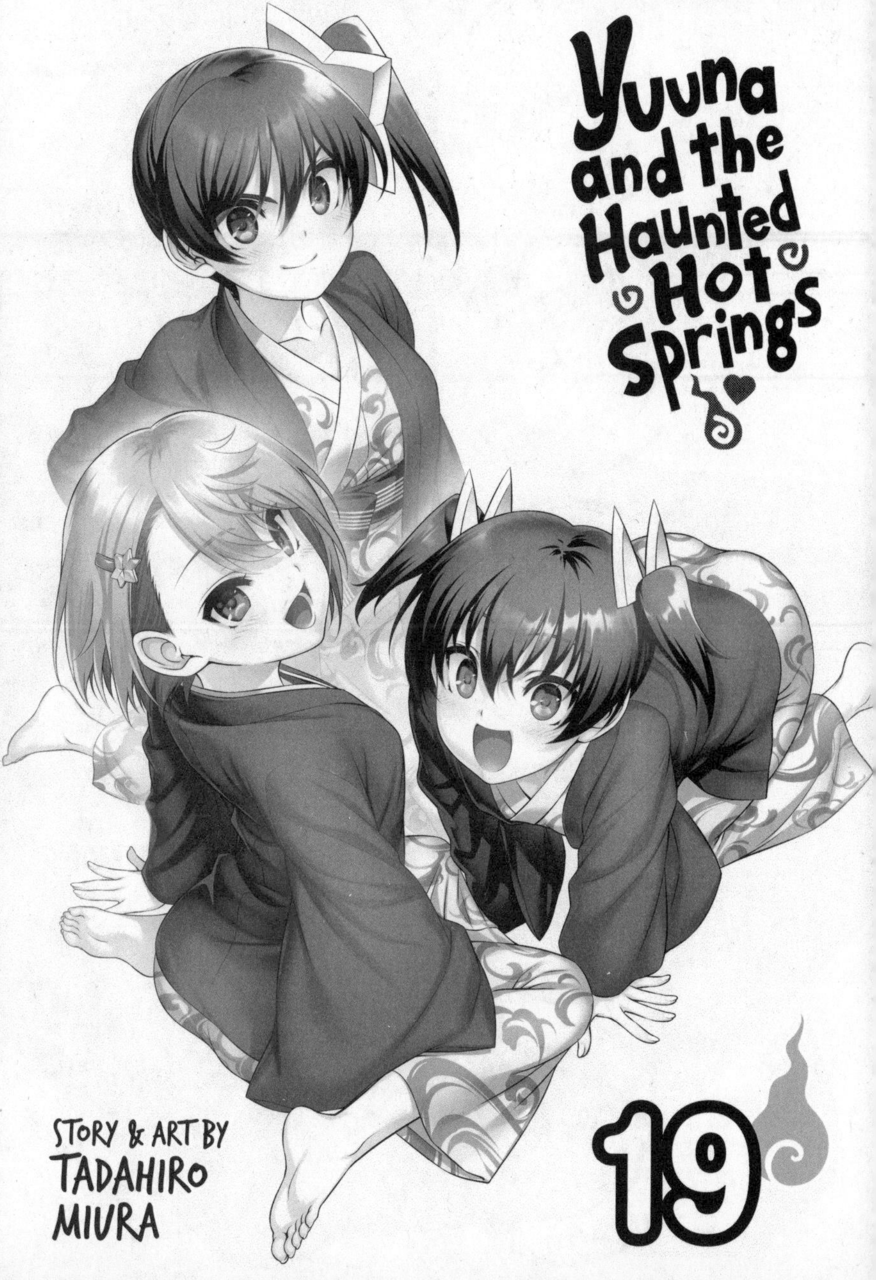

STORY & ART BY
TADAHIRO
MIURA

19

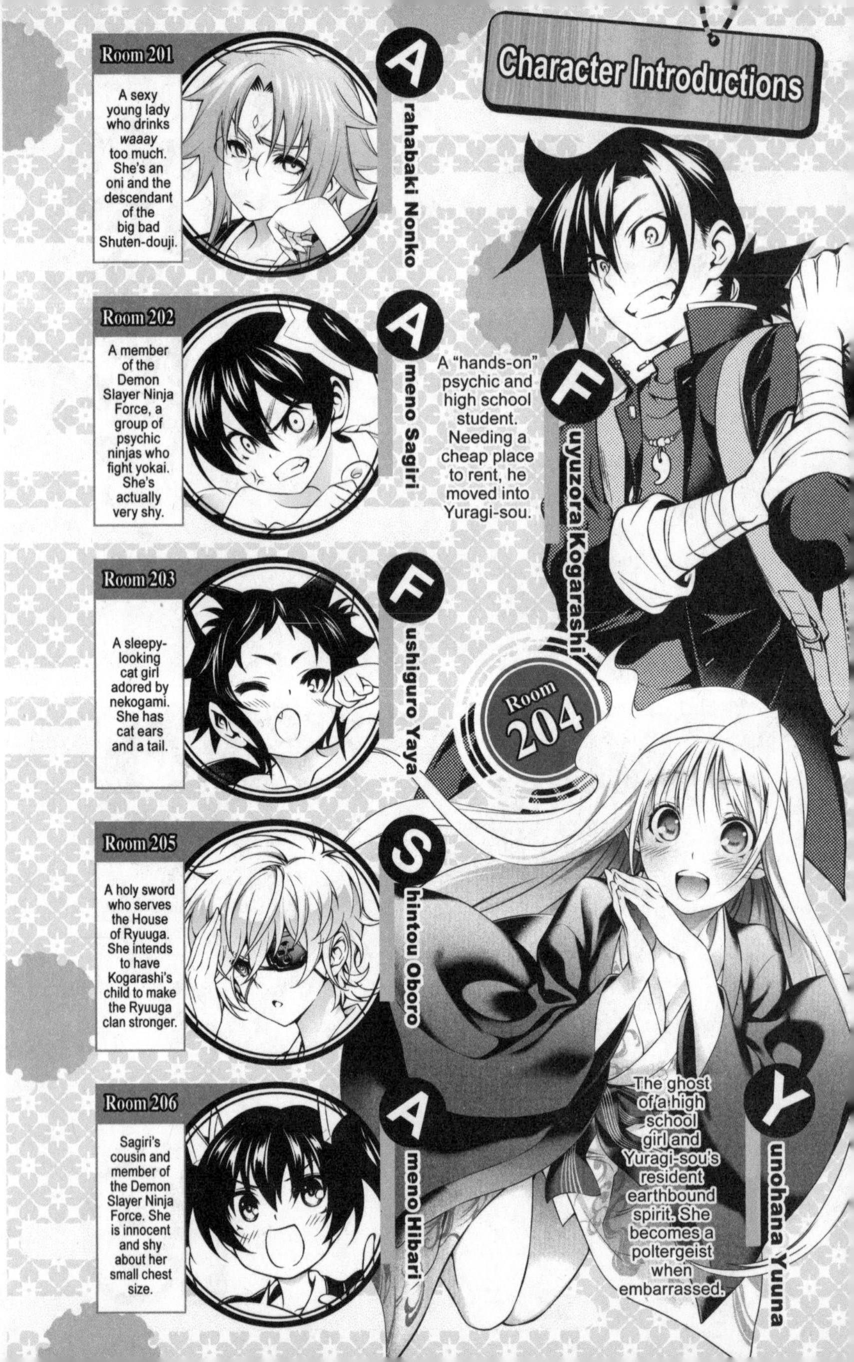
Character Introductions
Room 204
Fuyuzora Kogarashi
A "hands-on" psychic and high school student. Needing a cheap place to rent, he moved into Yuragi-sou.
Yunohana Yuuna
The ghost of a high school girl and Yuragi-sou's resident earthbound spirit. She becomes a poltergeist when embarrassed.
Room 201
Arahabaki Nonko
A sexy young lady who drinks *waaay* too much. She's an oni and the descendant of the big bad Shuten-douji.
Room 202
Ameno Sagiri
A member of the Demon Slayer Ninja Force, a group of psychic ninjas who fight yokai. She's actually very shy.
Room 203
Fushiguro Yaya
A sleepy-looking cat girl adored by nekogami. She has cat ears and a tail.
Room 205
Shintou Oboro
A holy sword who serves the House of Ryuuga. She intends to have Kogarashi's child to make the Ryuuga clan stronger.
Room 206
Ameno Hibari
Sagiri's cousin and member of the Demon Slayer Ninja Force. She is innocent and shy about her small chest size.

Nakai Chitose

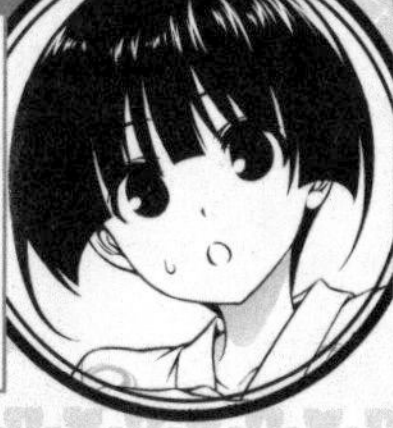

Caretaker's Room

Despite her youthful appearance, she's a zashiki-warashi and Yuragi-sou's oldest resident. She can manipulate people's luck.

Hiougi Karura

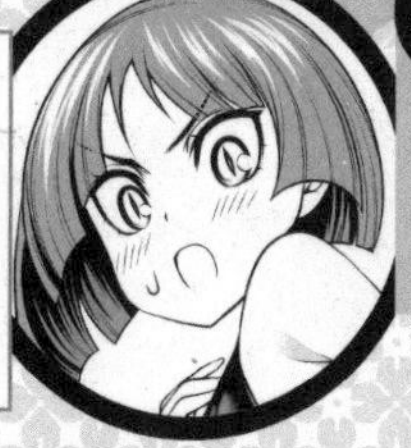

Daughter of the Dai-tengu, who governs Kyoto. Praised as a genius, she studies various magics, reviving them in the modern era.

Shigaraki Koyuzu

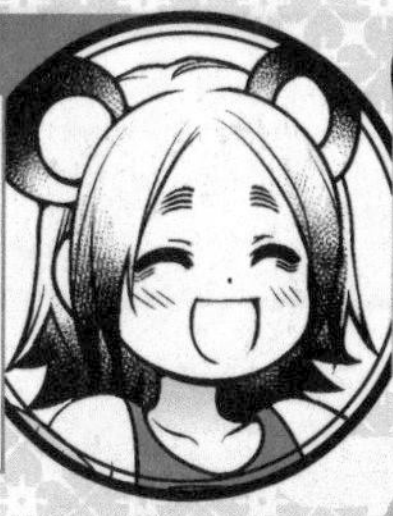

Caretaker's Room

A young bake-danuki girl. She looks up to Chisaki and is studying her boobs.

Mikogami Matora

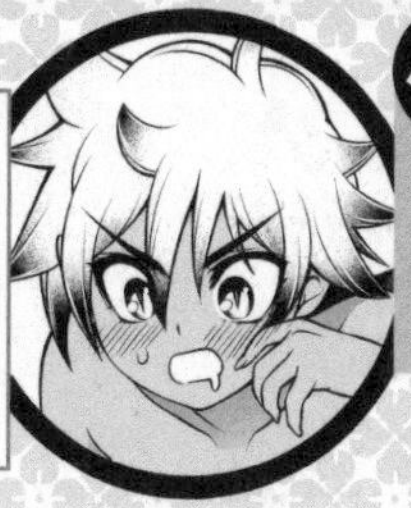

An extremely powerful yokai known as a nue. Her hobby is fighting, and she is always seeking out stronger opponents.

Miyazaki Chisaki

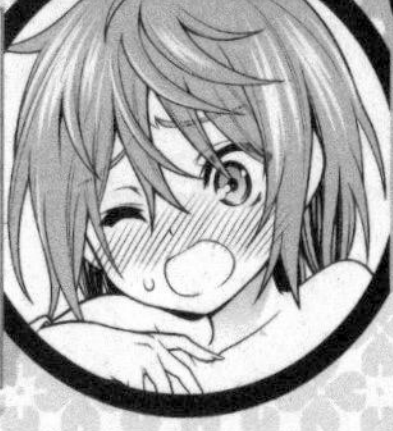

The most beautiful and popular girl in Kogarashi's class. She has a naughty imagination.

Todoroki Shion

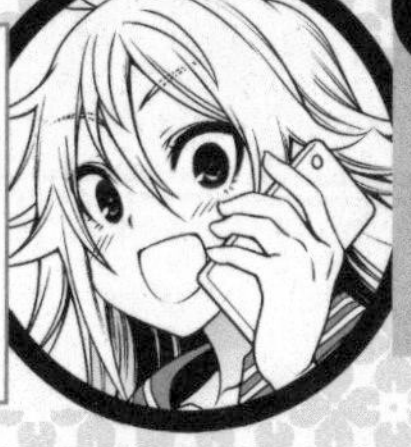

Seri's kouhai and former head delinquent in middle school. Her teddy bear panties are her favorite.

Katsuragi Miria

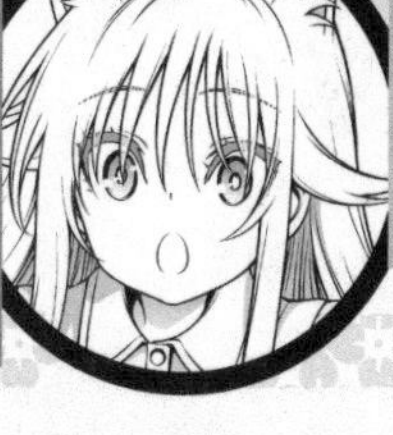

A youko girl. The Katsuragi family has long desired to be among the top of the Tenko clan, and to accomplish that she will get close to Yuuna.

Tenko Nadare

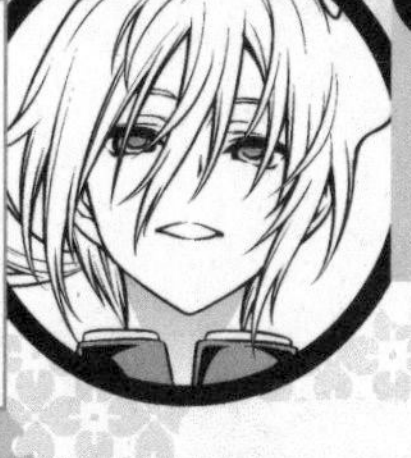

The current head of the Tenko clan. With his sights set on Yuragi-sou, he used the Water of Youth on Kogarashi and the others.

Summary

While living in Yuragi-sou, a hot spring inn turned boarding house with an unusual history, "hands-on" psychic Fuyuzora Kogarashi promised Yuuna, the earthbound spirit of a high school girl, that he would make her happy and help her pass on. Out of nowhere the members of Yuragi-sou revert to childhood. In the midst of the confusion, Nadare, the current head of the Tenko family, appears with his sights set on Kogarashi. As the members attempt to escape, Yuragi-sou is transported to another realm where Yuuna and Kogarashi begin training to boost their power, but...?!

161 Kogarashi-kun and the Replenishing Stone

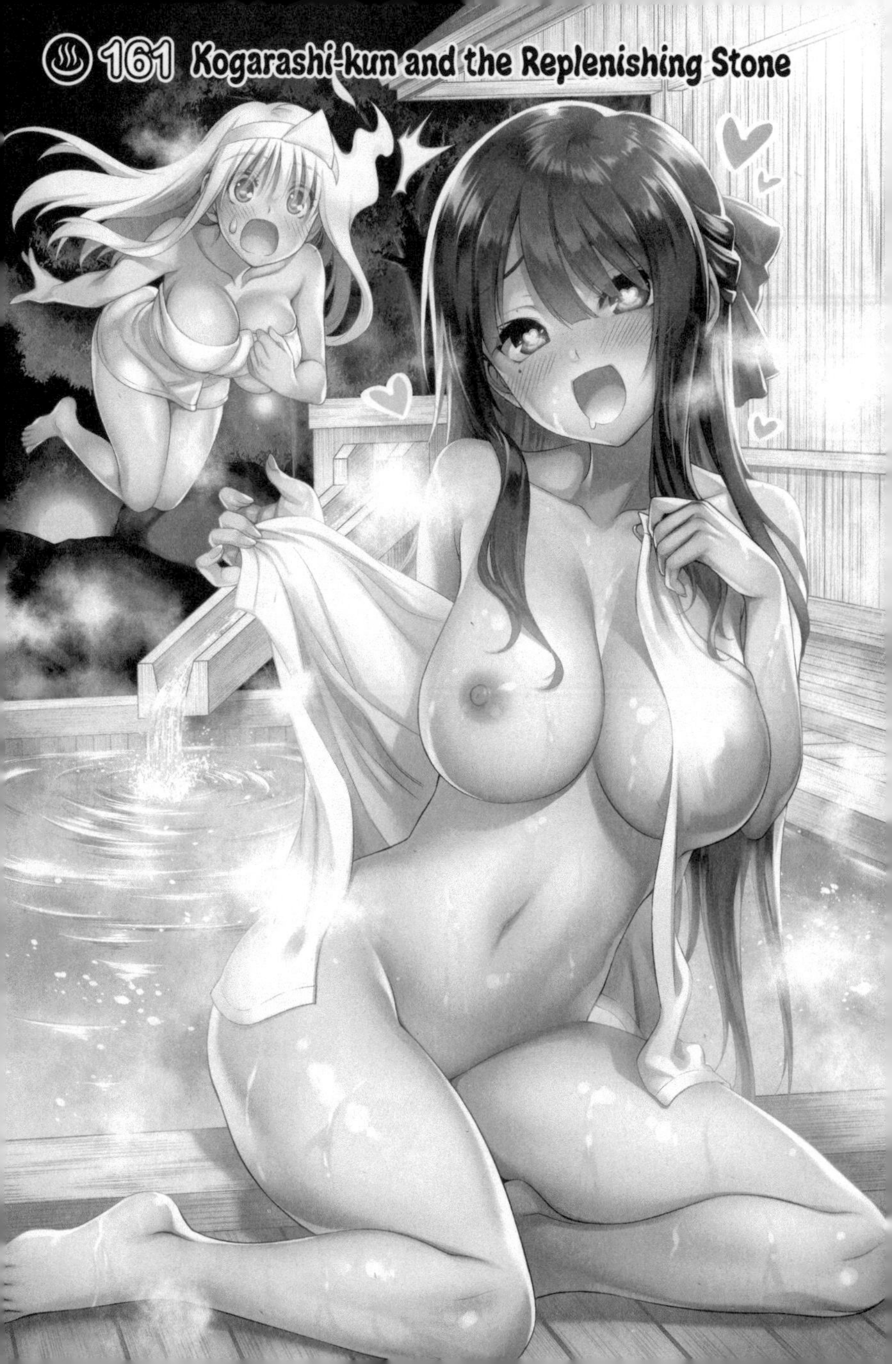

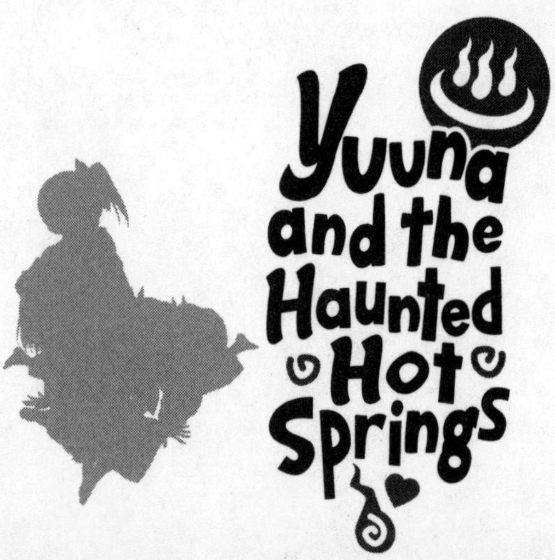

Yuuna and the Haunted Hot Springs

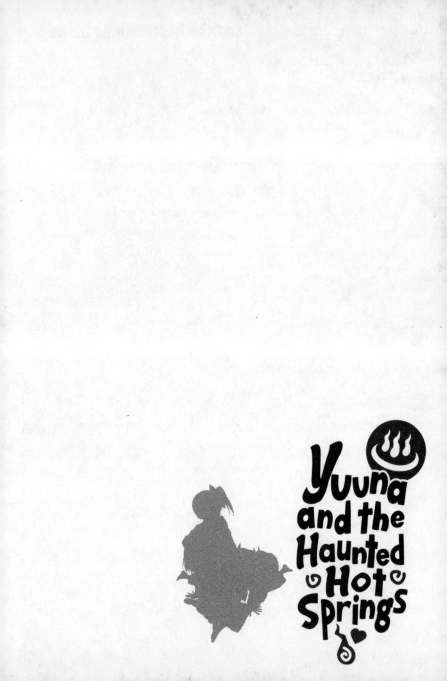

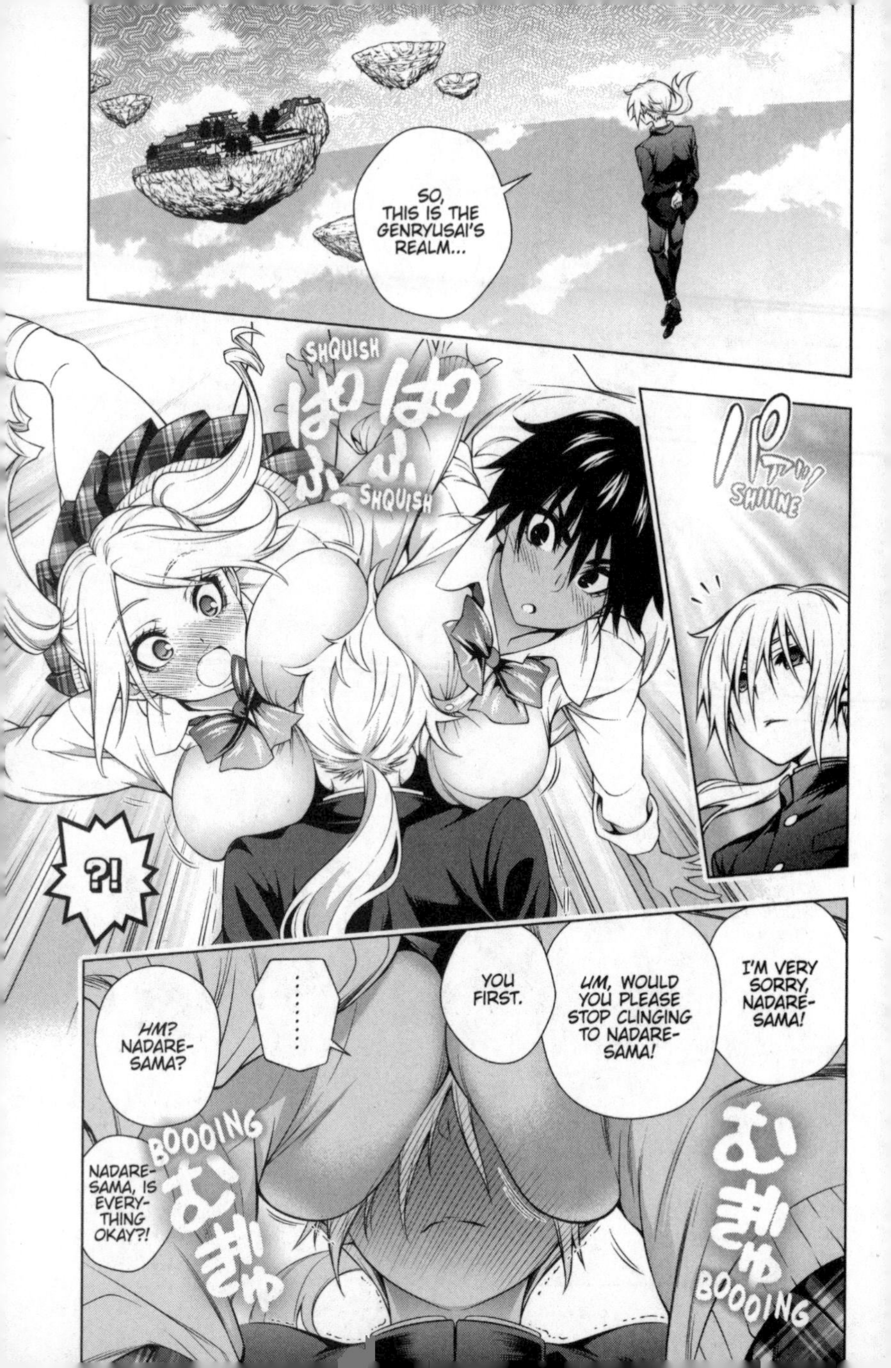
SO, THIS IS THE GENRYUSAI'S REALM...
SHIIINE
SHQUISH
SHQUISH
?!
I'M VERY SORRY, NADARE-SAMA!
UM, WOULD YOU PLEASE STOP CLINGING TO NADARE-SAMA!
YOU FIRST.
......
HM? NADARE-SAMA?
むぎゅ
BOOOING
NADARE-SAMA, IS EVERYTHING OKAY?!
BOOOING
むぎゅ

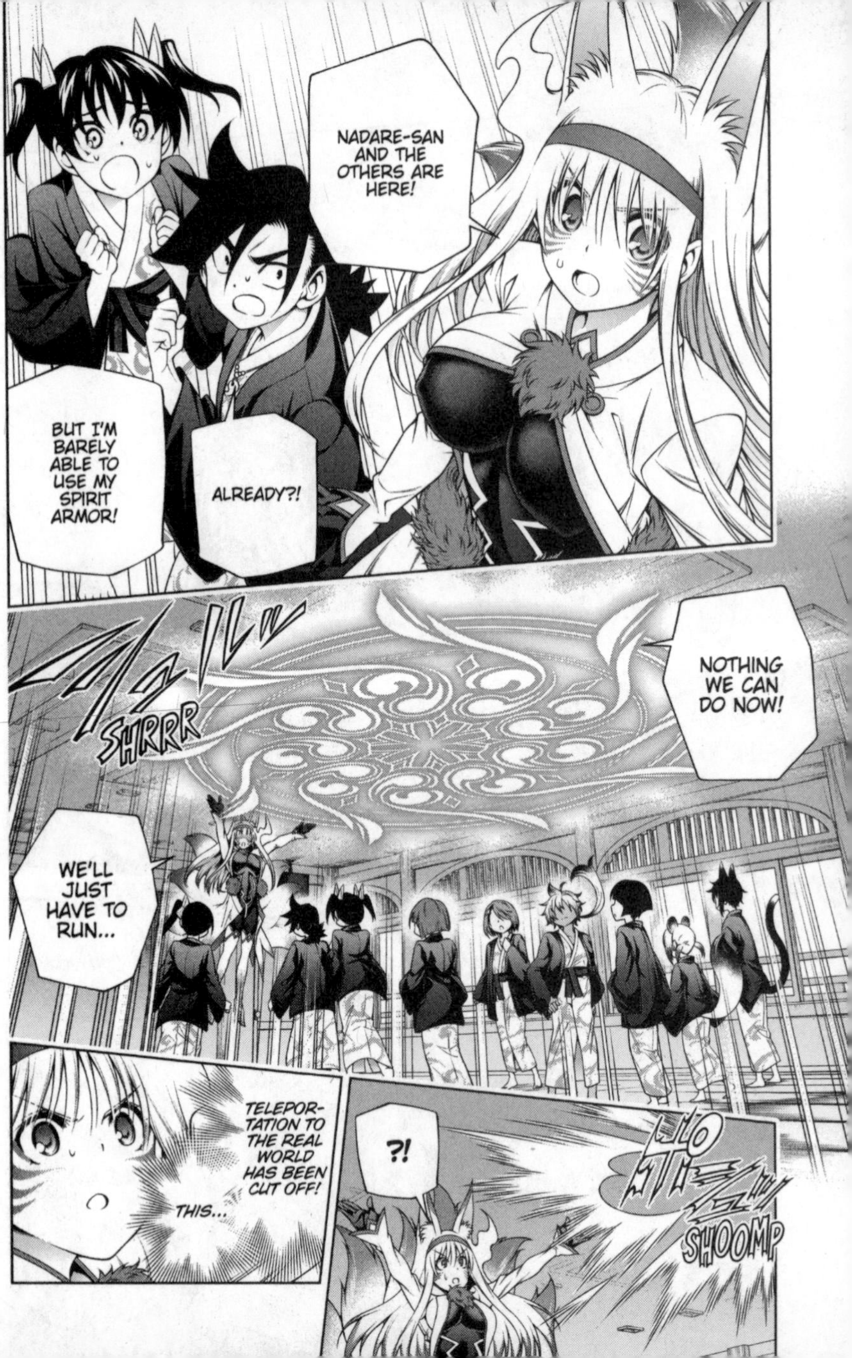
NADARE-SAN AND THE OTHERS ARE HERE!
ALREADY?!
BUT I'M BARELY ABLE TO USE MY SPIRIT ARMOR!
NOTHING WE CAN DO NOW!
SHRRR
WE'LL JUST HAVE TO RUN...
?!
SHOOMP
TELEPORTATION TO THE REAL WORLD HAS BEEN CUT OFF!
THIS...

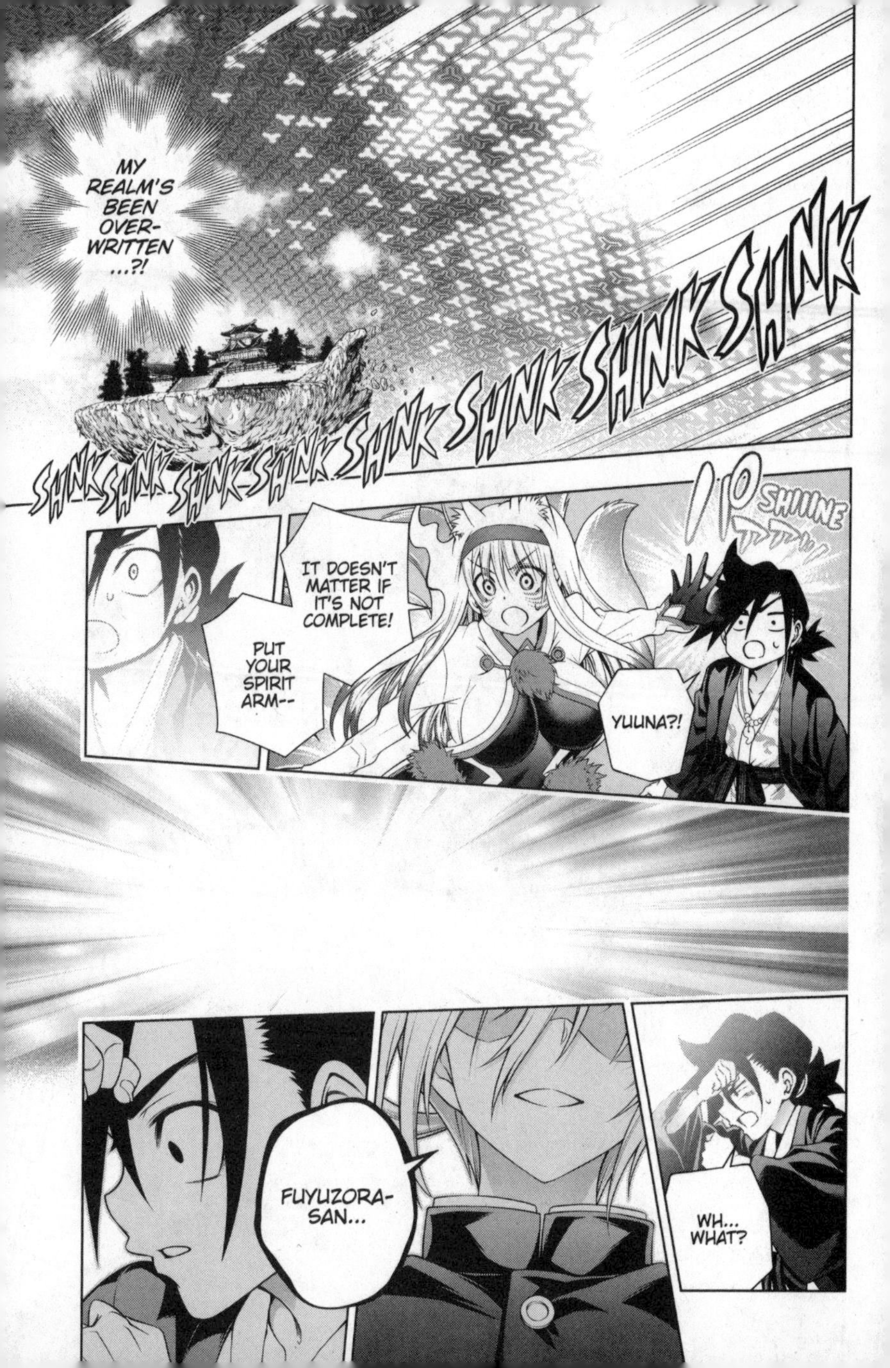
MY REALM'S BEEN OVER-WRITTEN ...?!
SHNK SHNK SHNK SHNK SHNK SHNK SHNK SHNK
SHIIINE
YUUNA?!
IT DOESN'T MATTER IF IT'S NOT COMPLETE!
PUT YOUR SPIRIT ARM--
WH... WHAT?
FUYUZORA-SAN...

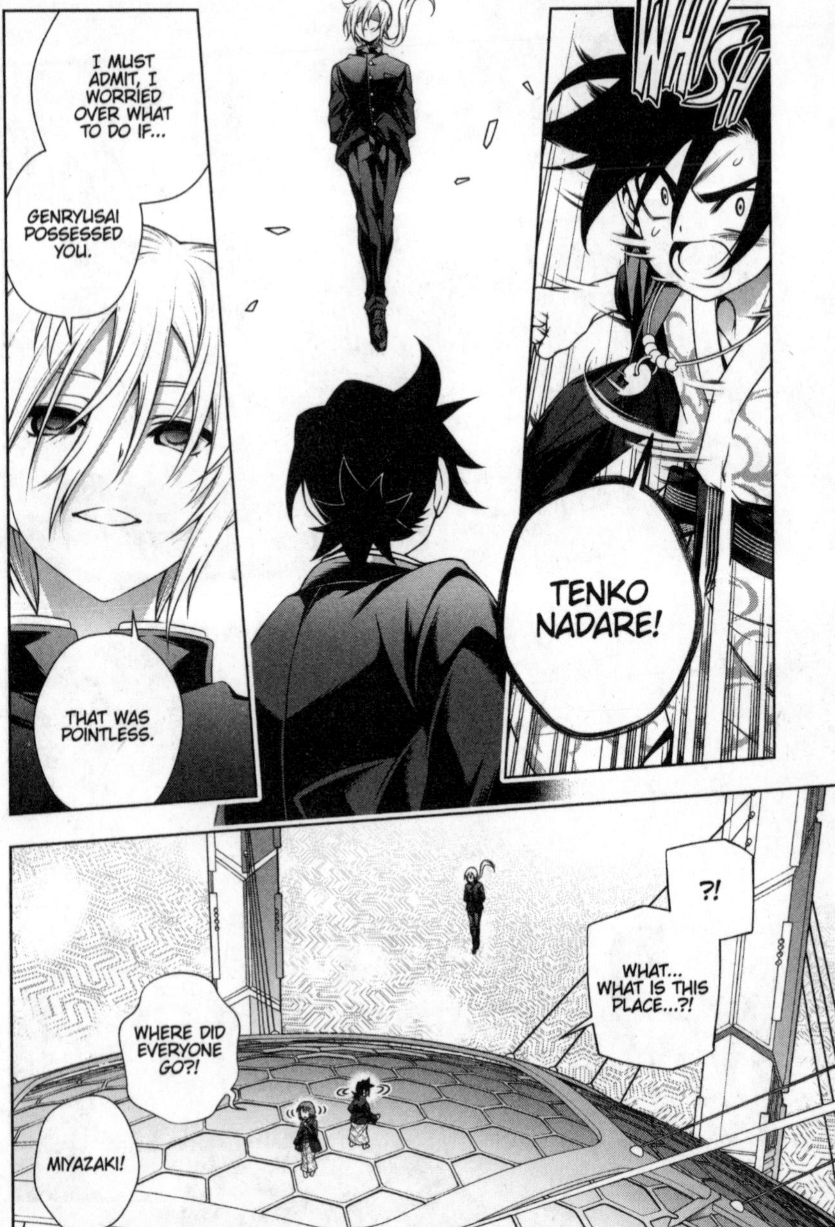
WHISH
TENKO NADARE!
I MUST ADMIT, I WORRIED OVER WHAT TO DO IF...
GENRYUSAI POSSESSED YOU.
THAT WAS POINTLESS.
?!
WHAT... WHAT IS THIS PLACE...?!
WHERE DID EVERYONE GO?!
MIYAZAKI!

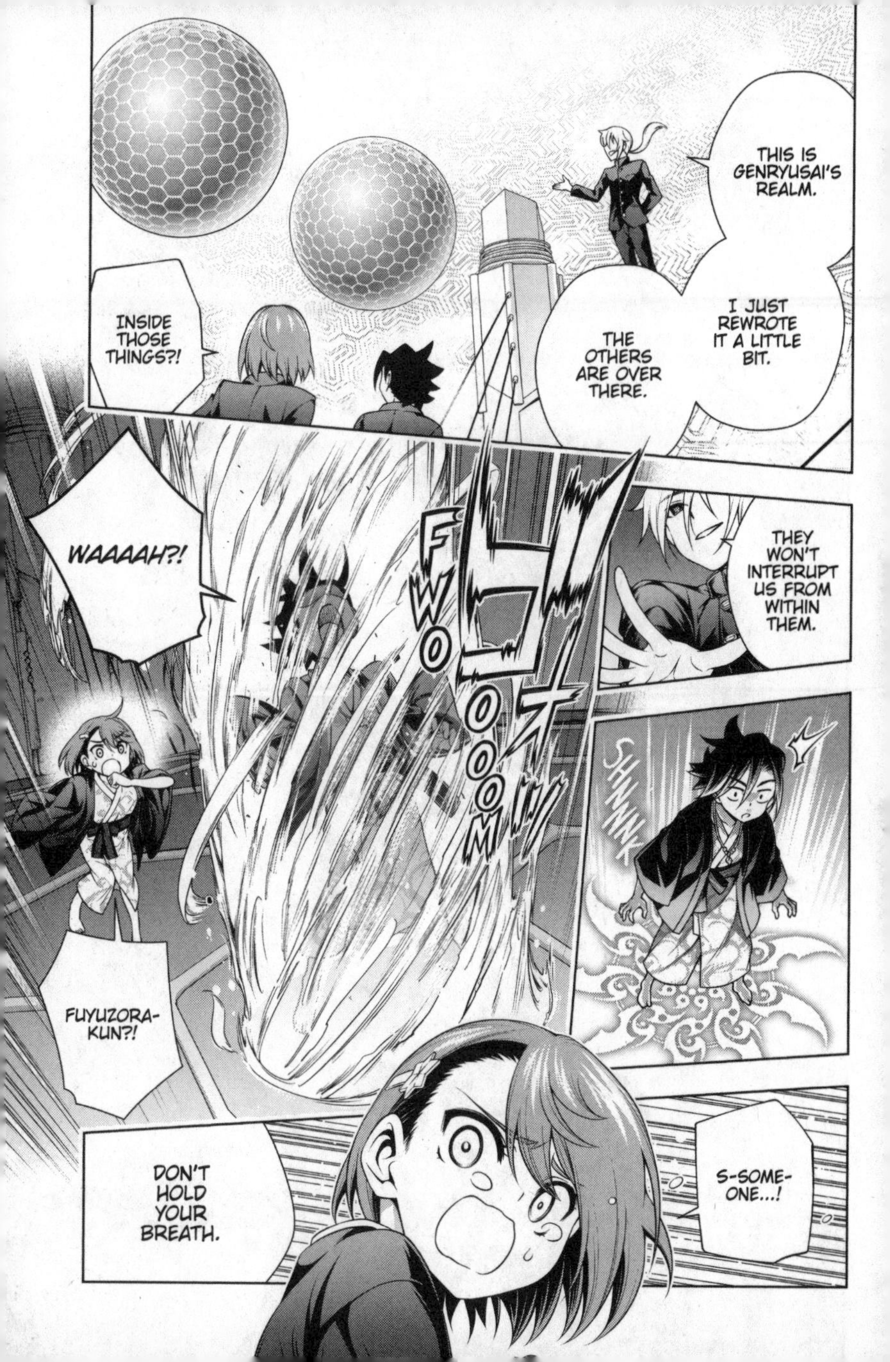
THIS IS GENRYUSAI'S REALM.
I JUST REWROTE IT A LITTLE BIT.
THE OTHERS ARE OVER THERE.
INSIDE THOSE THINGS?!
THEY WON'T INTERRUPT US FROM WITHIN THEM.
SHNNK
FWOOOOOM!!
WAAAAH?!
FUYUZORA-KUN?!
S-SOME-ONE...!
DON'T HOLD YOUR BREATH.

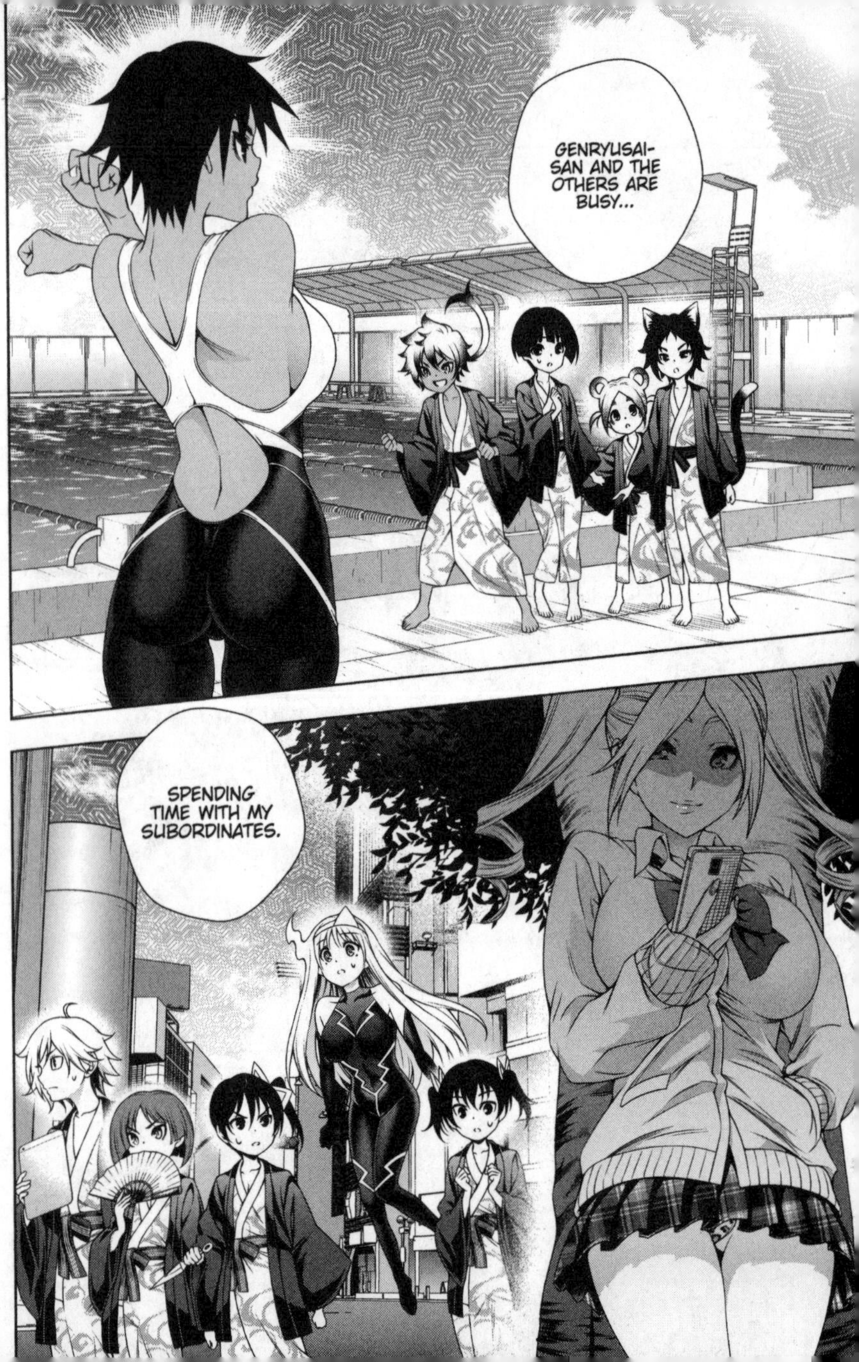
GENRYUSAI-SAN AND THE OTHERS ARE BUSY...
SPENDING TIME WITH MY SUBORDINATES.

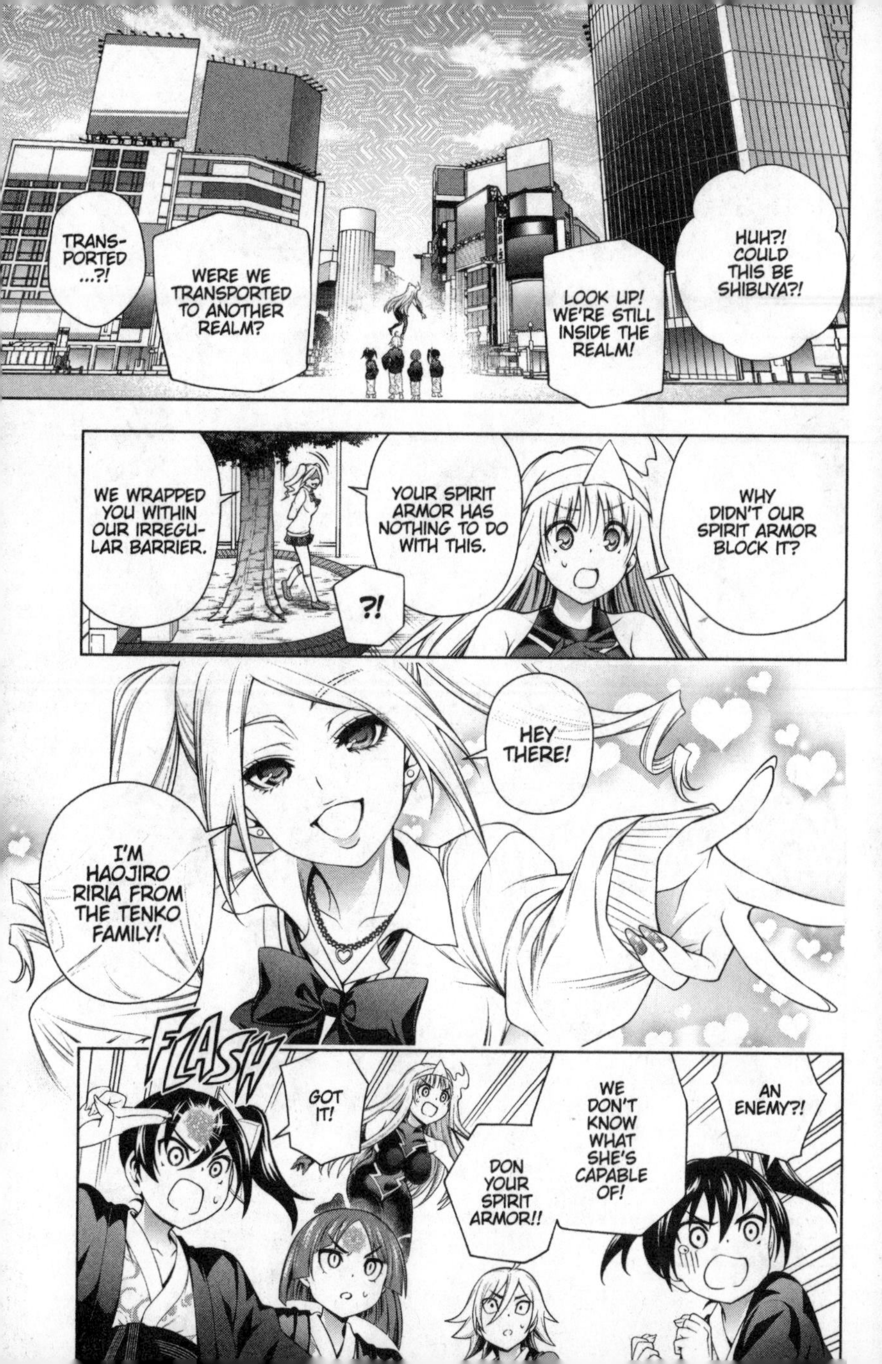
HUH?! COULD THIS BE SHIBUYA?!
LOOK UP! WE'RE STILL INSIDE THE REALM!
WERE WE TRANSPORTED TO ANOTHER REALM?
TRANS-PORTED ...?!
WHY DIDN'T OUR SPIRIT ARMOR BLOCK IT?
YOUR SPIRIT ARMOR HAS NOTHING TO DO WITH THIS.
?!
WE WRAPPED YOU WITHIN OUR IRREGU-LAR BARRIER.
HEY THERE!
I'M HAOJIRO RIRIA FROM THE TENKO FAMILY!
FLASH
AN ENEMY?!
WE DON'T KNOW WHAT SHE'S CAPABLE OF!
DON YOUR SPIRIT ARMOR!!
GOT IT!

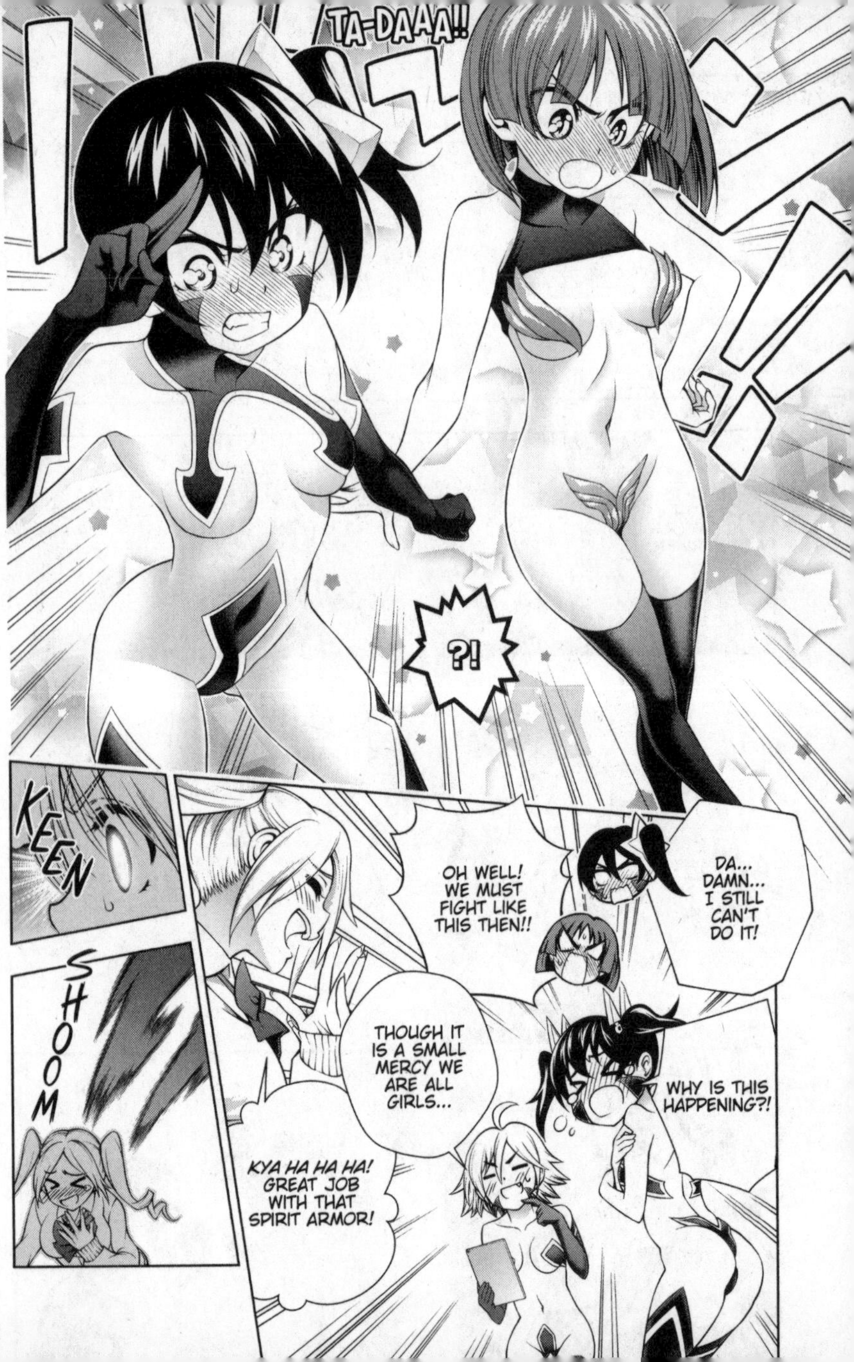
TA-DAAA!!
?!
DA... DAMN... I STILL CAN'T DO IT!
OH WELL! WE MUST FIGHT LIKE THIS THEN!!
WHY IS THIS HAPPENING?!
THOUGH IT IS A SMALL MERCY WE ARE ALL GIRLS...
KYA HA HA HA! GREAT JOB WITH THAT SPIRIT ARMOR!
KEEN
SHOOM

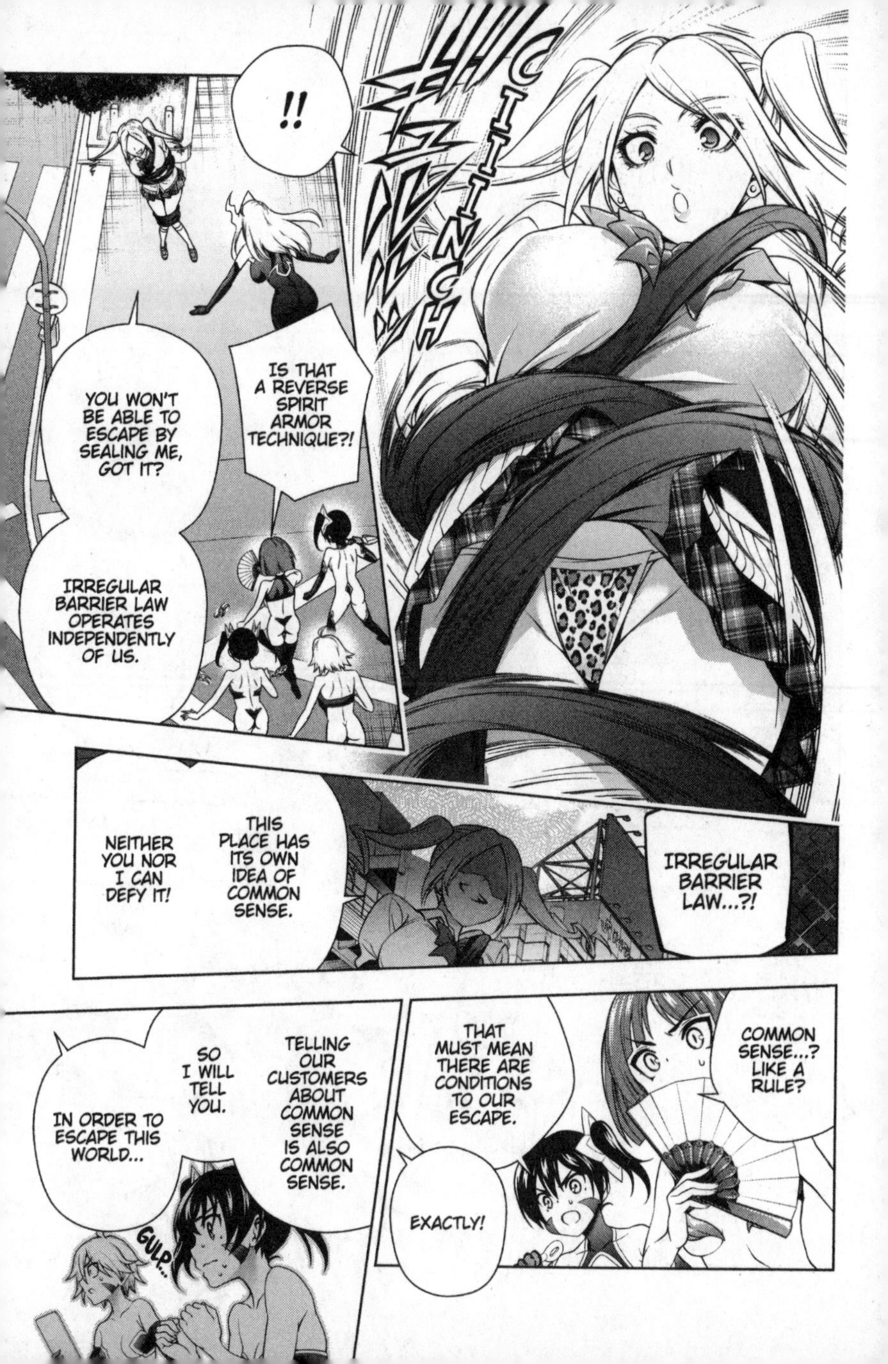
CHIIINCH
!!
IS THAT A REVERSE SPIRIT ARMOR TECHNIQUE?!
YOU WON'T BE ABLE TO ESCAPE BY SEALING ME, GOT IT?
IRREGULAR BARRIER LAW OPERATES INDEPENDENTLY OF US.
IRREGULAR BARRIER LAW...?!
THIS PLACE HAS ITS OWN IDEA OF COMMON SENSE.
NEITHER YOU NOR I CAN DEFY IT!
COMMON SENSE...? LIKE A RULE?
THAT MUST MEAN THERE ARE CONDITIONS TO OUR ESCAPE.
EXACTLY!
TELLING OUR CUSTOMERS ABOUT COMMON SENSE IS ALSO COMMON SENSE.
SO I WILL TELL YOU.
IN ORDER TO ESCAPE THIS WORLD...
GULP...

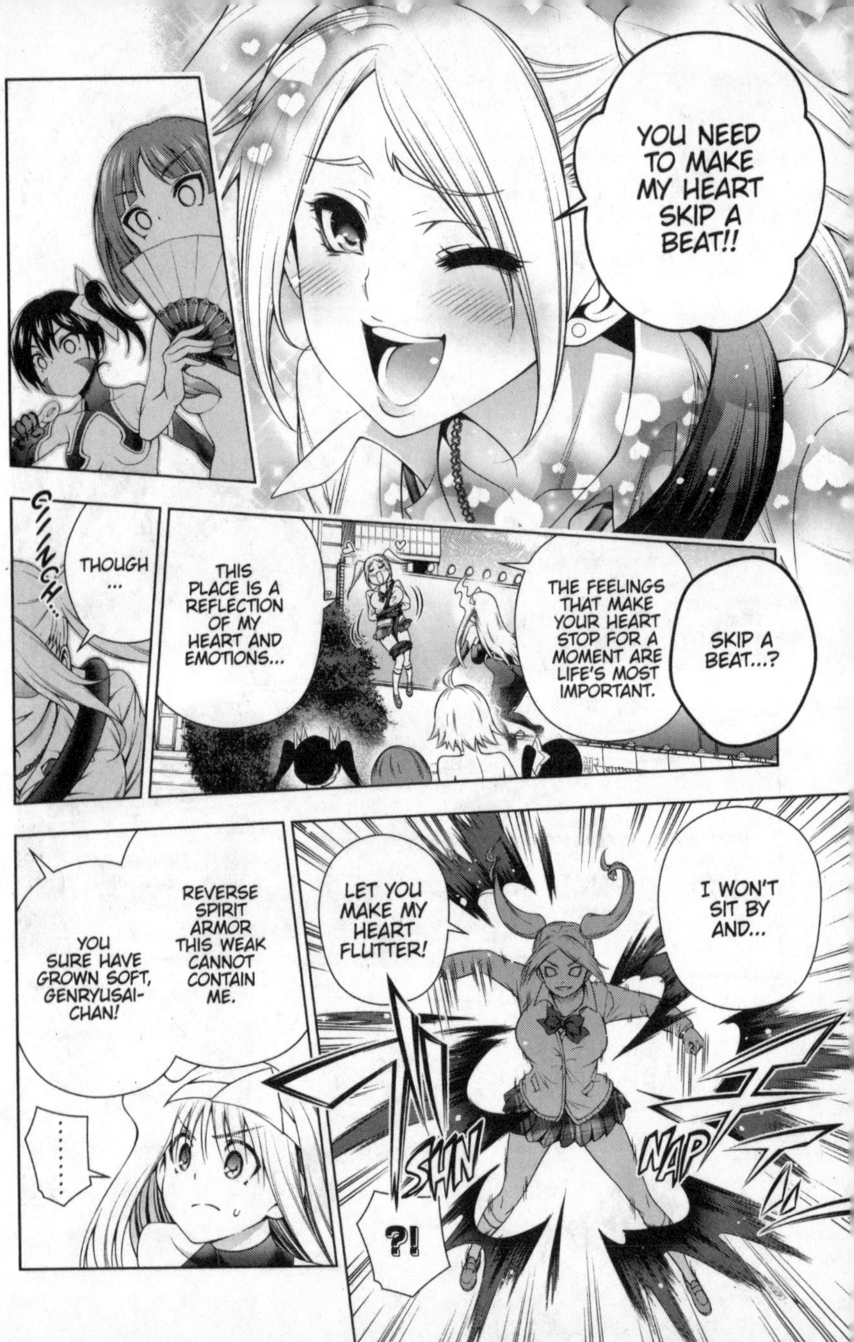
YOU NEED TO MAKE MY HEART SKIP A BEAT!!
SKIP A BEAT...?
THE FEELINGS THAT MAKE YOUR HEART STOP FOR A MOMENT ARE LIFE'S MOST IMPORTANT.
THIS PLACE IS A REFLECTION OF MY HEART AND EMOTIONS...
THOUGH ...
GIIINCH...
I WON'T SIT BY AND...
LET YOU MAKE MY HEART FLUTTER!
NAP
SHN
?!
REVERSE SPIRIT ARMOR THIS WEAK CANNOT CONTAIN ME.
YOU SURE HAVE GROWN SOFT, GENRYUSAI-CHAN!
......

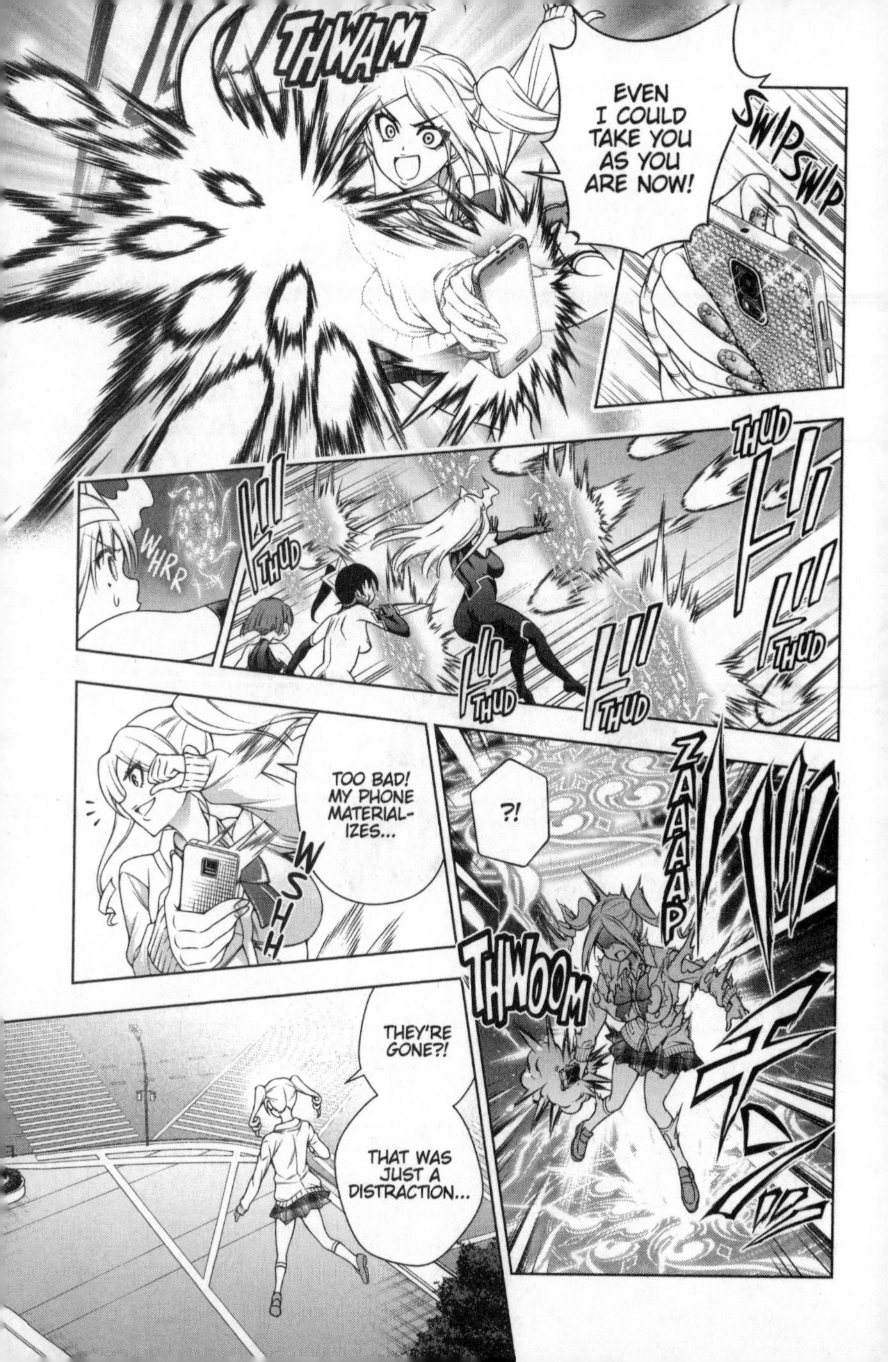
SWIPSWIP
EVEN I COULD TAKE YOU AS YOU ARE NOW!
THWAM
THUD
THUD
THUD
THUD
THUD
WHRR
?!
ZAAAAAP
THWOOM
TOO BAD! MY PHONE MATERIAL-IZES...
WSHH
THEY'RE GONE?!
THAT WAS JUST A DISTRACTION...

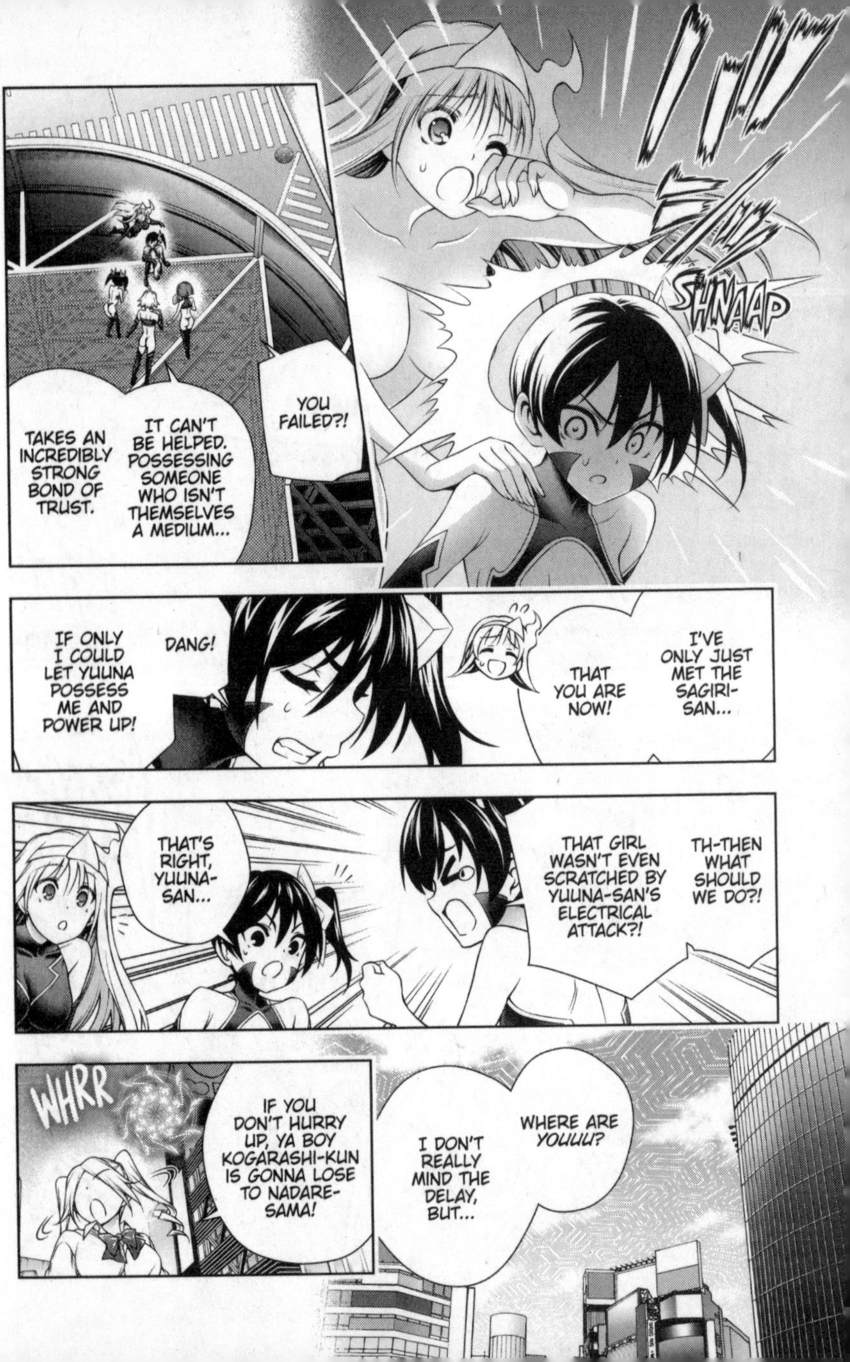
SHNAAP
YOU FAILED?!
IT CAN'T BE HELPED. POSSESSING SOMEONE WHO ISN'T THEMSELVES A MEDIUM...
TAKES AN INCREDIBLY STRONG BOND OF TRUST.
I'VE ONLY JUST MET THE SAGIRI-SAN...
THAT YOU ARE NOW!
DANG!
IF ONLY I COULD LET YUUNA POSSESS ME AND POWER UP!
TH-THEN WHAT SHOULD WE DO?!
THAT GIRL WASN'T EVEN SCRATCHED BY YUUNA-SAN'S ELECTRICAL ATTACK?!
THAT'S RIGHT, YUUNA-SAN...
WHERE ARE YOUUU?
I DON'T REALLY MIND THE DELAY, BUT...
IF YOU DON'T HURRY UP, YA BOY KOGARASHI-KUN IS GONNA LOSE TO NADARE-SAMA!
WHRR

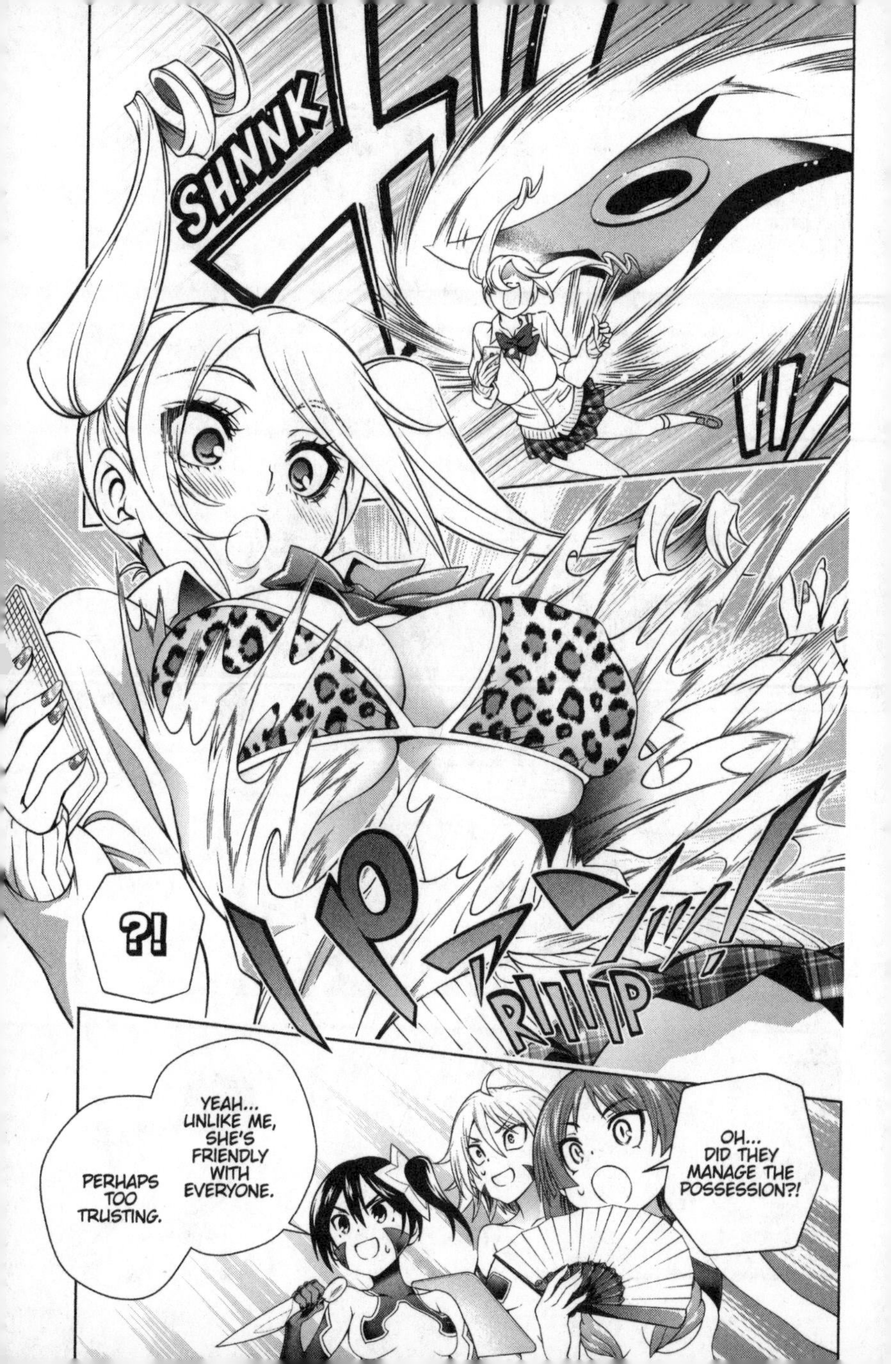
SHNNK
RIIIIP
?!
OH... DID THEY MANAGE THE POSSESSION?!
YEAH... UNLIKE ME, SHE'S FRIENDLY WITH EVERYONE.
PERHAPS TOO TRUSTING.

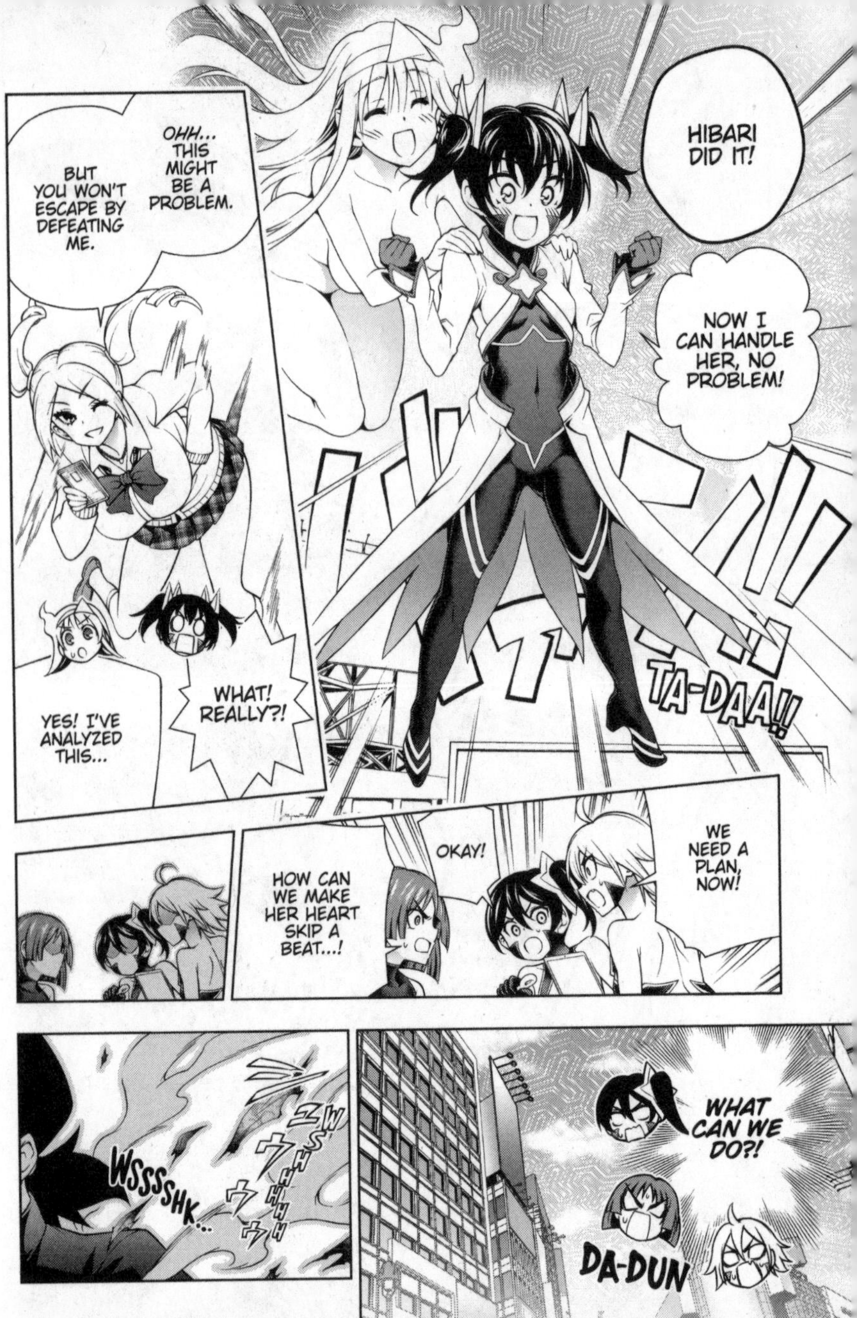
HIBARI DID IT!
NOW I CAN HANDLE HER, NO PROBLEM!
TA-DAA!!
OHH... THIS MIGHT BE A PROBLEM.
BUT YOU WON'T ESCAPE BY DEFEATING ME.
WHAT! REALLY?!
YES! I'VE ANALYZED THIS...
WE NEED A PLAN, NOW!
OKAY!
HOW CAN WE MAKE HER HEART SKIP A BEAT...!
WHAT CAN WE DO?!
DA-DUN
WSHHHHHH
WSSSSHK...

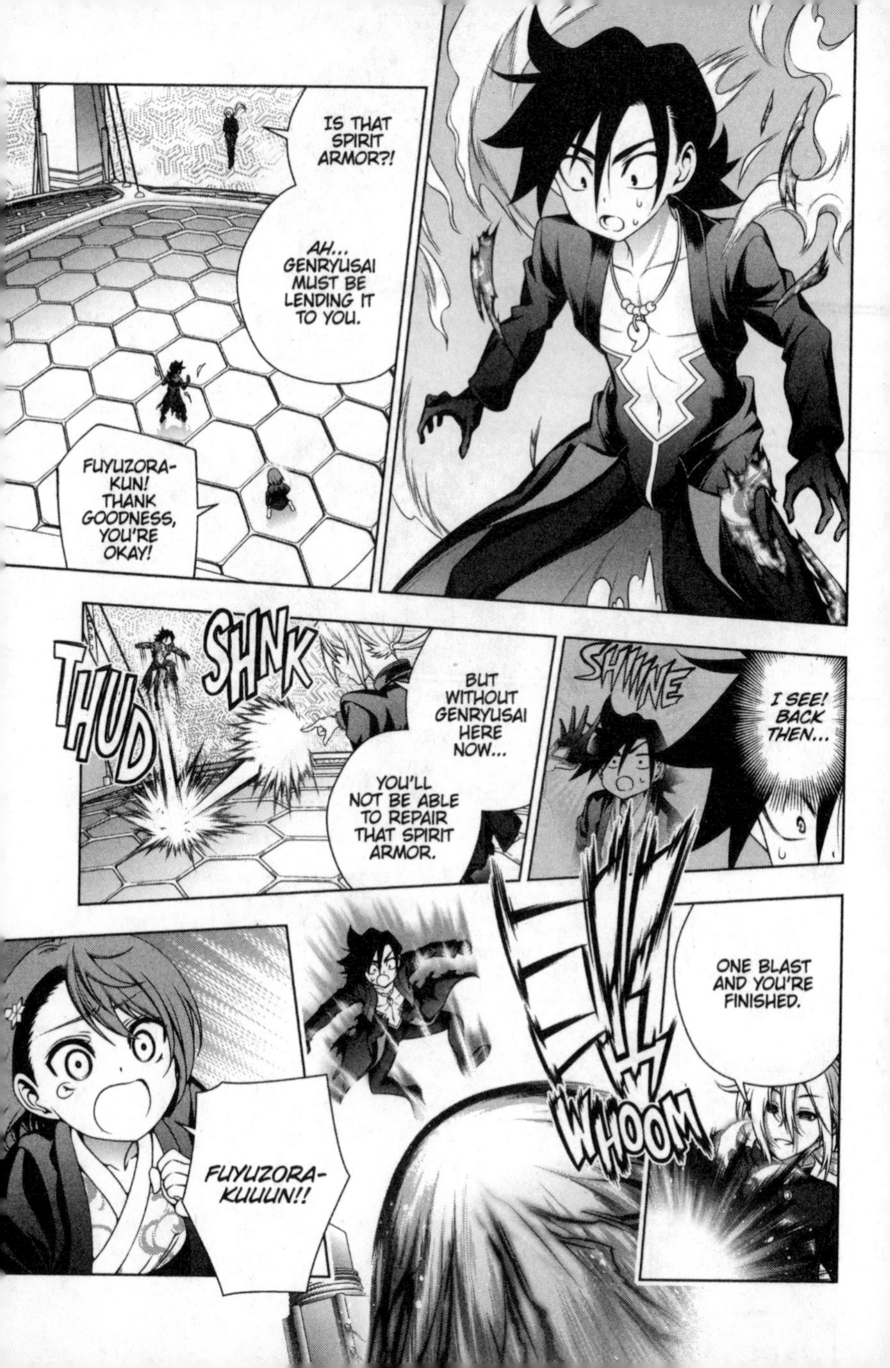
IS THAT SPIRIT ARMOR?!
AH... GENRYUSAI MUST BE LENDING IT TO YOU.
FUYUZORA-KUN! THANK GOODNESS, YOU'RE OKAY!
SHIINE
I SEE! BACK THEN...
BUT WITHOUT GENRYUSAI HERE NOW...
YOU'LL NOT BE ABLE TO REPAIR THAT SPIRIT ARMOR.
SHNK
THUD
ONE BLAST AND YOU'RE FINISHED.
WHOOM
FUYUZORA-KUUUN!!

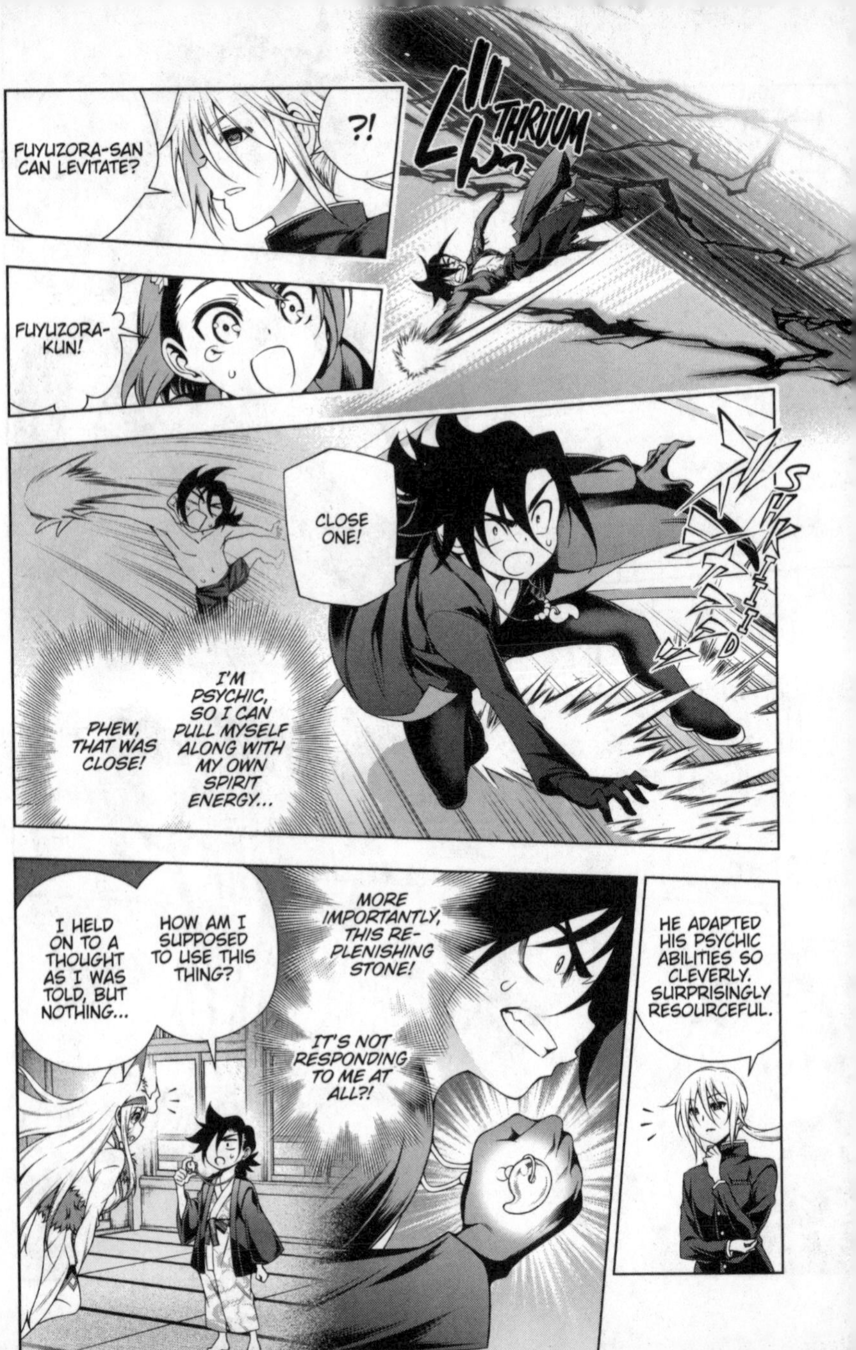
THRUUM
?!
FUYUZORA-SAN CAN LEVITATE?
FUYUZORA-KUN!
SHKIIIID
CLOSE ONE!
I'M PSYCHIC, SO I CAN PULL MYSELF ALONG WITH MY OWN SPIRIT ENERGY...
PHEW, THAT WAS CLOSE!
HE ADAPTED HIS PSYCHIC ABILITIES SO CLEVERLY. SURPRISINGLY RESOURCEFUL.
MORE IMPORTANTLY, THIS RE-PLENISHING STONE!
IT'S NOT RESPONDING TO ME AT ALL?!
HOW AM I SUPPOSED TO USE THIS THING?
I HELD ON TO A THOUGHT AS I WAS TOLD, BUT NOTHING...

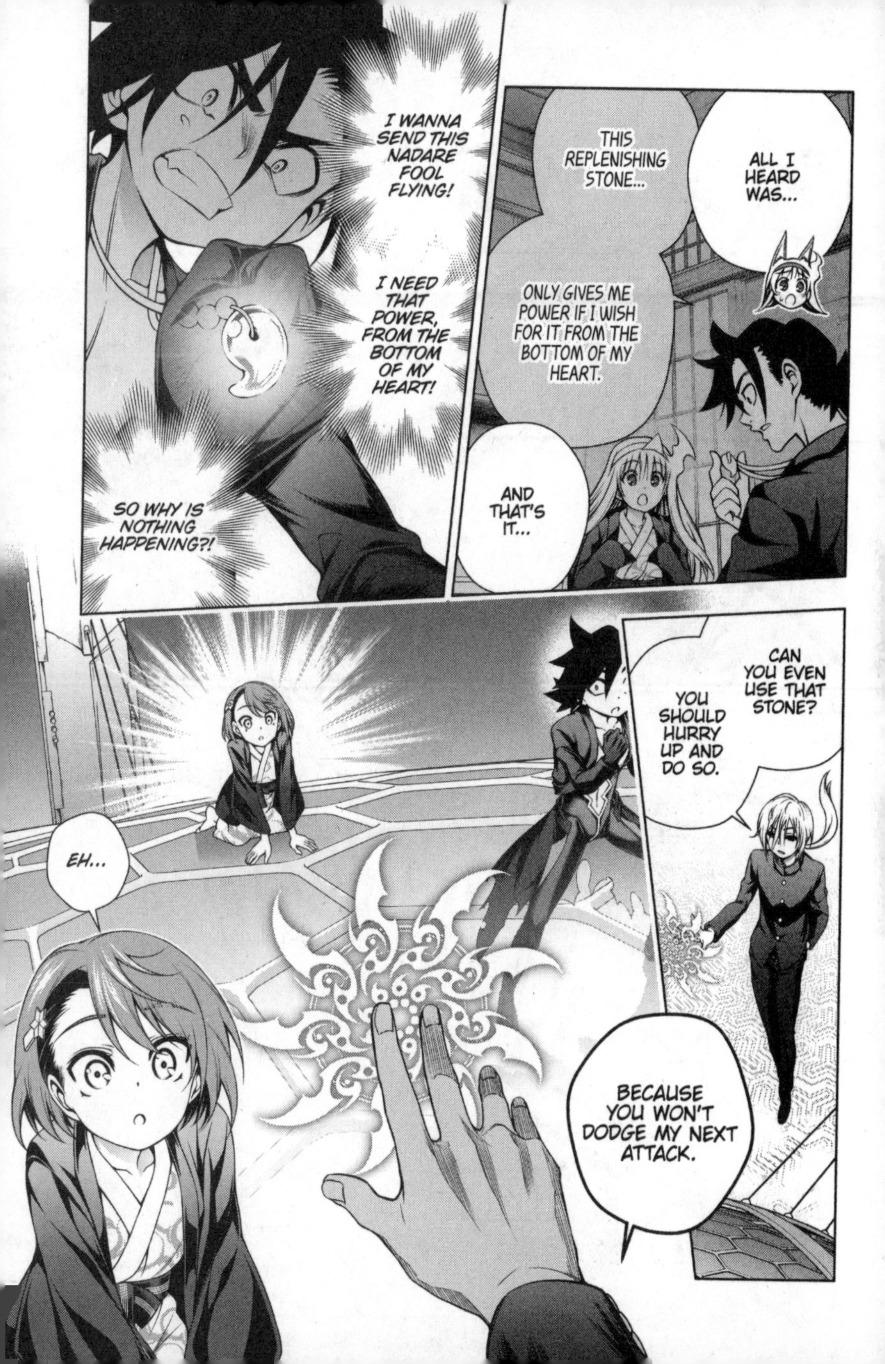
ALL I HEARD WAS...
THIS REPLENISHING STONE...
ONLY GIVES ME POWER IF I WISH FOR IT FROM THE BOTTOM OF MY HEART.
AND THAT'S IT...
I WANNA SEND THIS NADARE FOOL FLYING!
I NEED THAT POWER, FROM THE BOTTOM OF MY HEART!
SO WHY IS NOTHING HAPPENING?!
CAN YOU EVEN USE THAT STONE?
YOU SHOULD HURRY UP AND DO SO.
BECAUSE YOU WON'T DODGE MY NEXT ATTACK.
EH...

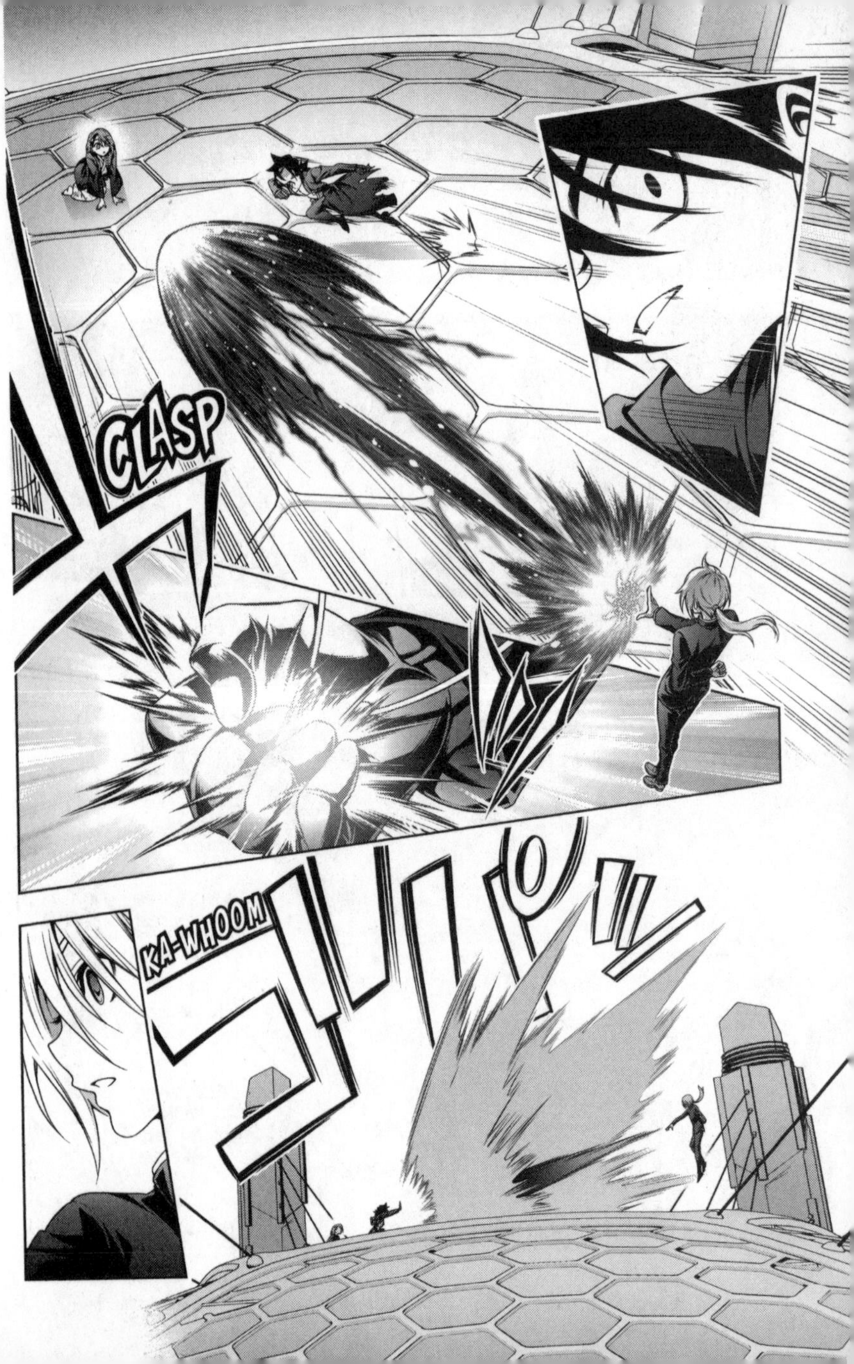
CLASP
KA-WHOOM
ゴパッ

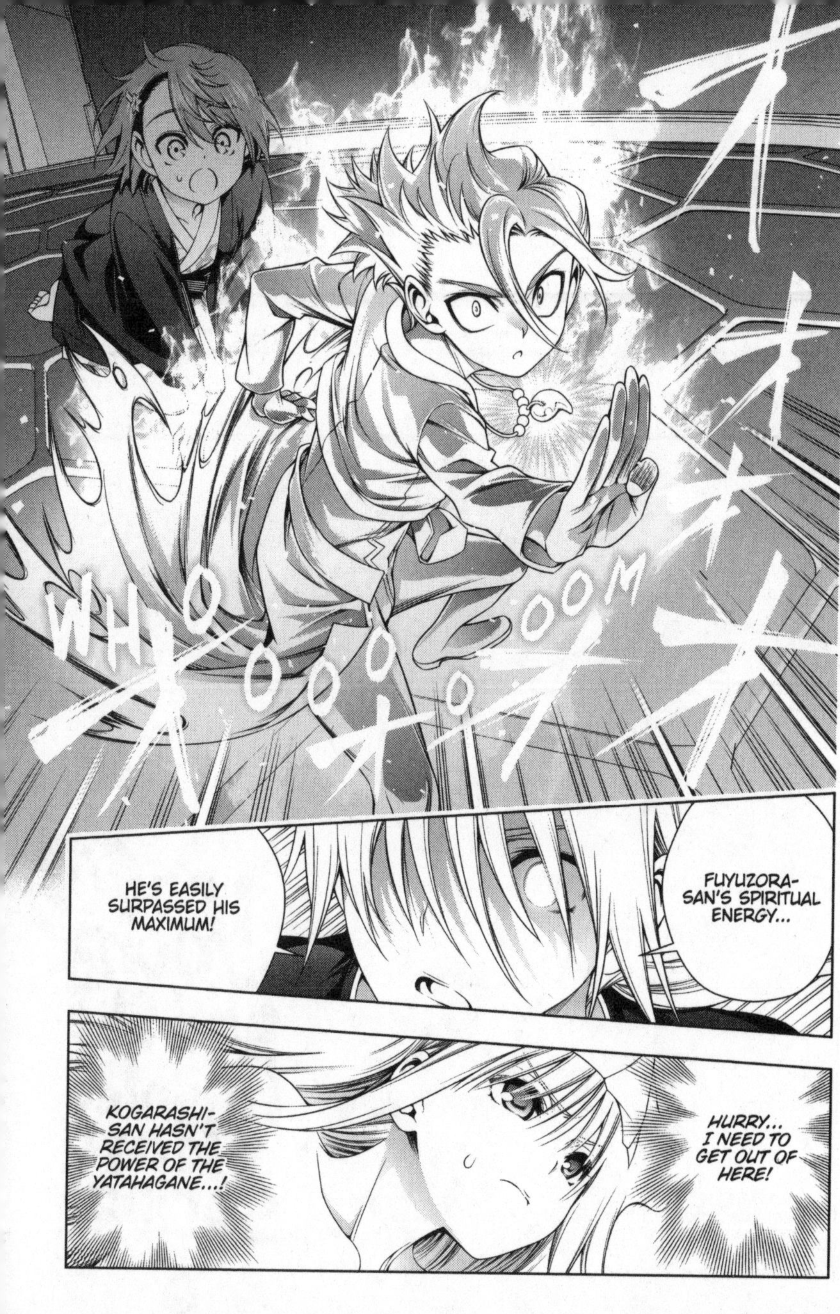
WHOOOOOOOOM
FUYUZORA-SAN'S SPIRITUAL ENERGY...
HE'S EASILY SURPASSED HIS MAXIMUM!
HURRY... I NEED TO GET OUT OF HERE!
KOGARASHI-SAN HASN'T RECEIVED THE POWER OF THE YATAHAGANE...!

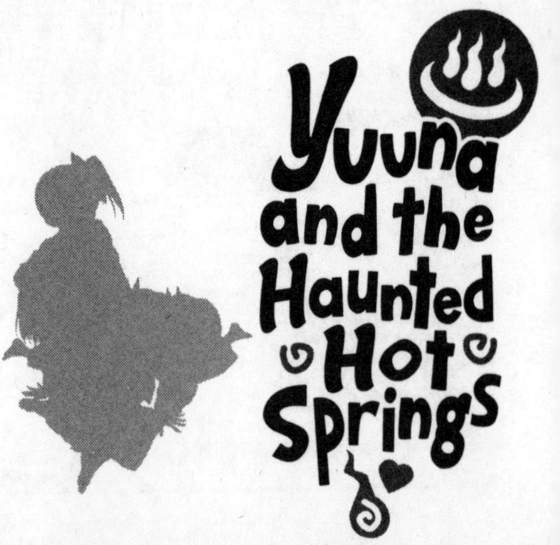

Yuuna and the Haunted Hot Springs

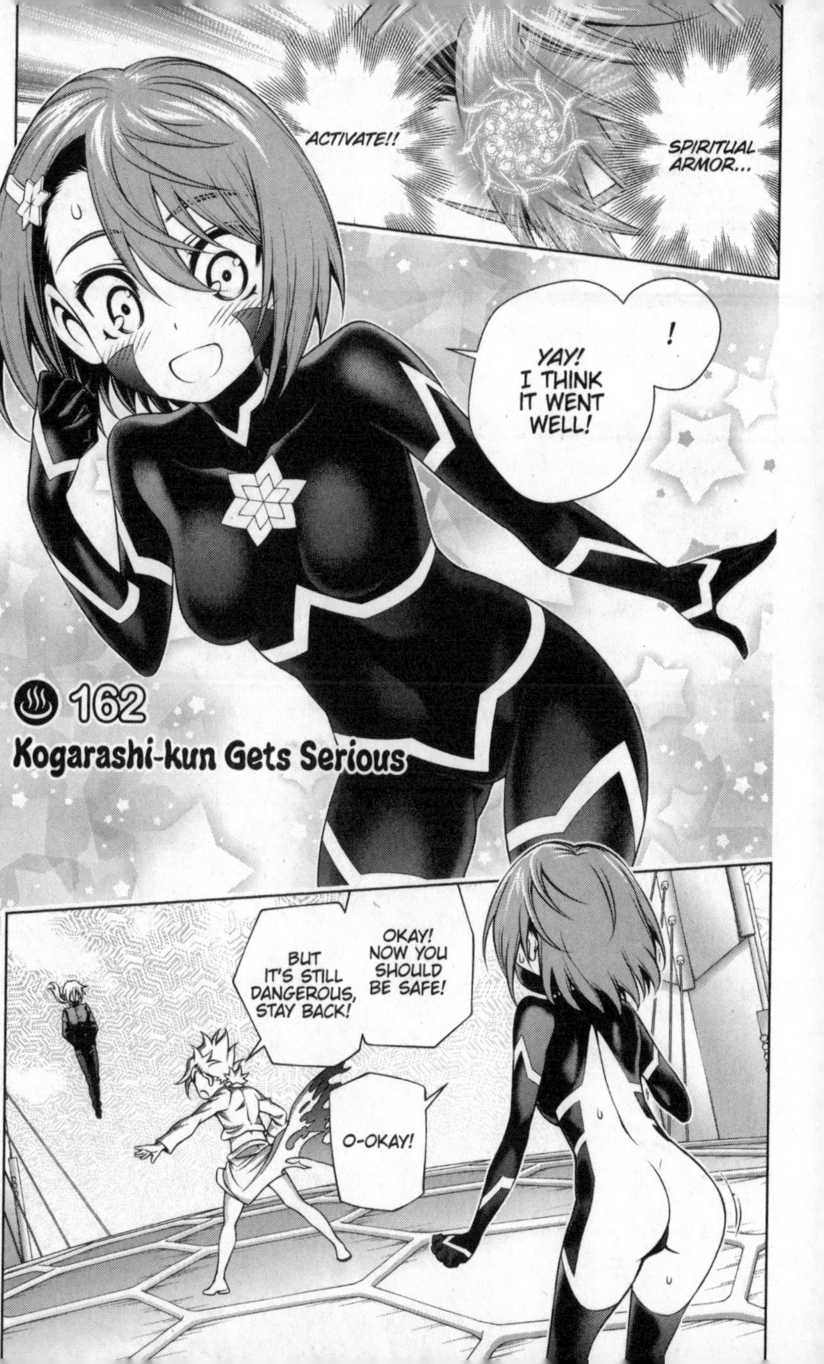
SPIRITUAL ARMOR...
ACTIVATE!!
!
YAY! I THINK IT WENT WELL!
162
Kogarashi-kun Gets Serious
OKAY! NOW YOU SHOULD BE SAFE!
BUT IT'S STILL DANGEROUS, STAY BACK!
O-OKAY!

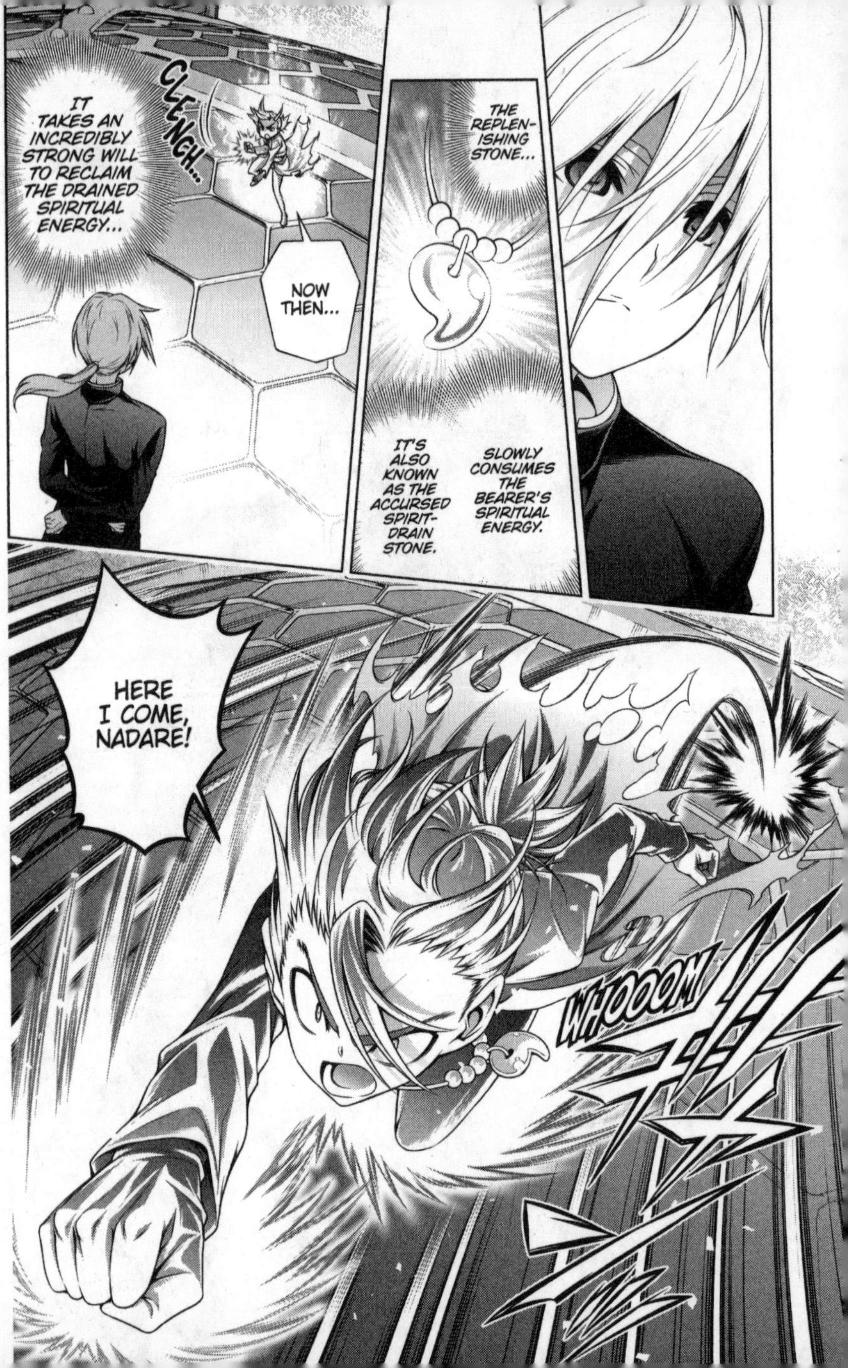
THE REPLEN-ISHING STONE...
SLOWLY CONSUMES THE BEARER'S SPIRITUAL ENERGY.
IT'S ALSO KNOWN AS THE ACCURSED SPIRIT-DRAIN STONE.
IT TAKES AN INCREDIBLY STRONG WILL TO RECLAIM THE DRAINED SPIRITUAL ENERGY...
CLENCH...
NOW THEN...
HERE I COME, NADARE!
WHOOOM

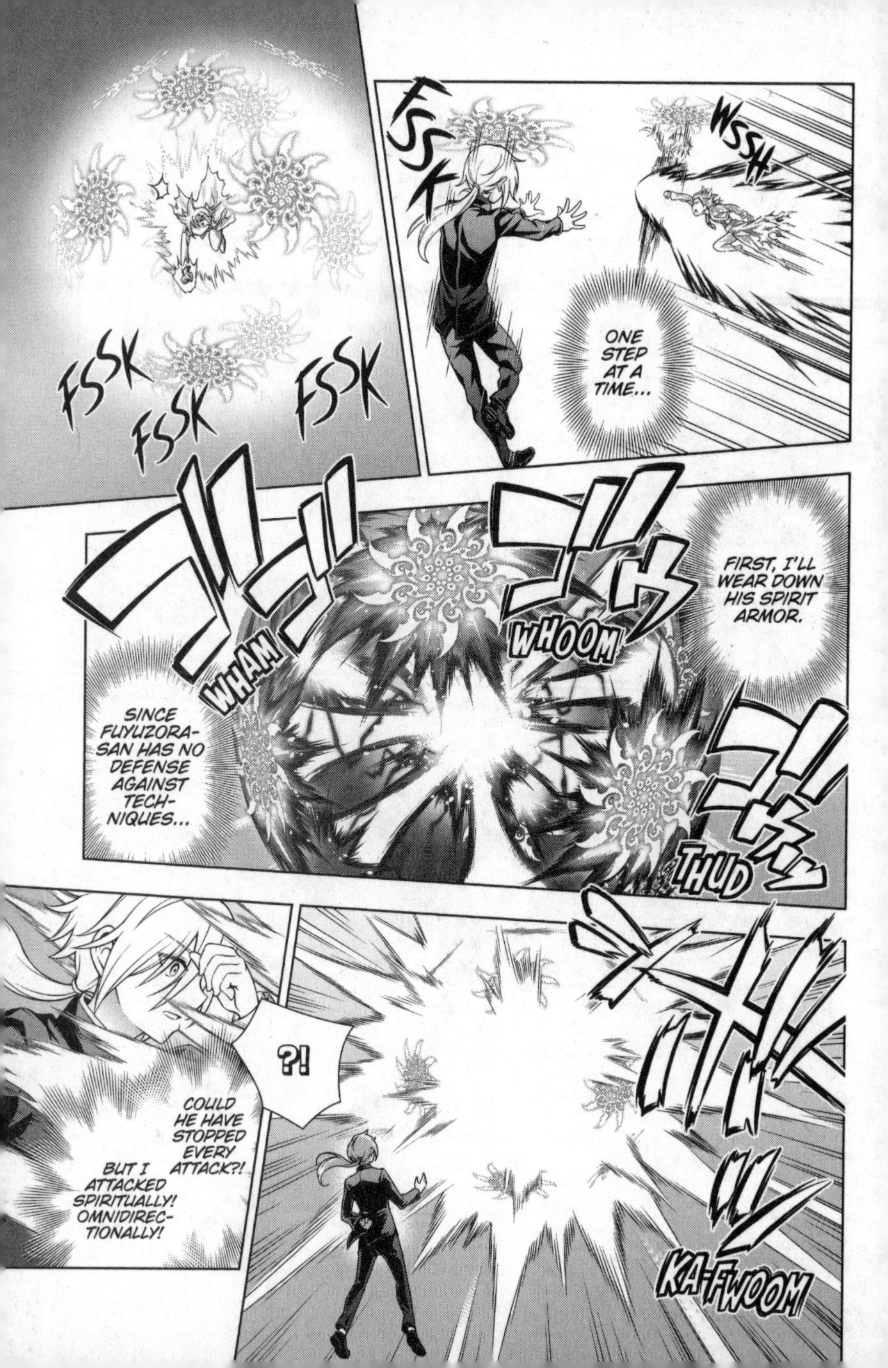

WSSH
FSSK
ONE STEP AT A TIME...
FSSK
FSSK
FSSK
FIRST, I'LL WEAR DOWN HIS SPIRIT ARMOR.
WHOOM
WHAM
SINCE FUYUZORA-SAN HAS NO DEFENSE AGAINST TECHNIQUES...
THUD
KA-FWOOM
COULD HE HAVE STOPPED EVERY ATTACK?!
BUT I ATTACKED SPIRITUALLY! OMNIDIRECTIONALLY!
?!

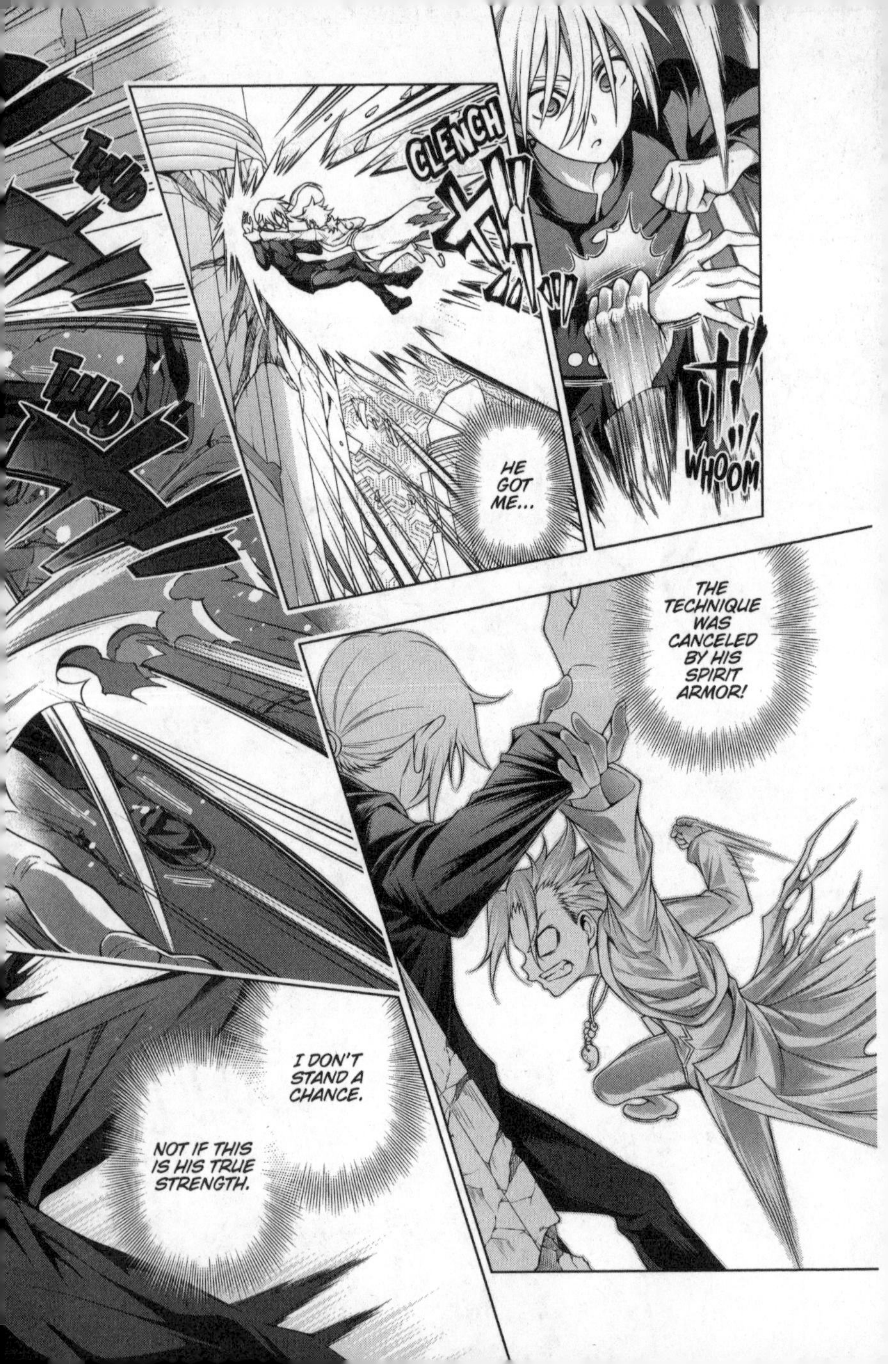
CLENCH
WHOOM
HE GOT ME...
THUD
THUD
THE TECHNIQUE WAS CANCELED BY HIS SPIRIT ARMOR!
I DON'T STAND A CHANCE.
NOT IF THIS IS HIS TRUE STRENGTH.

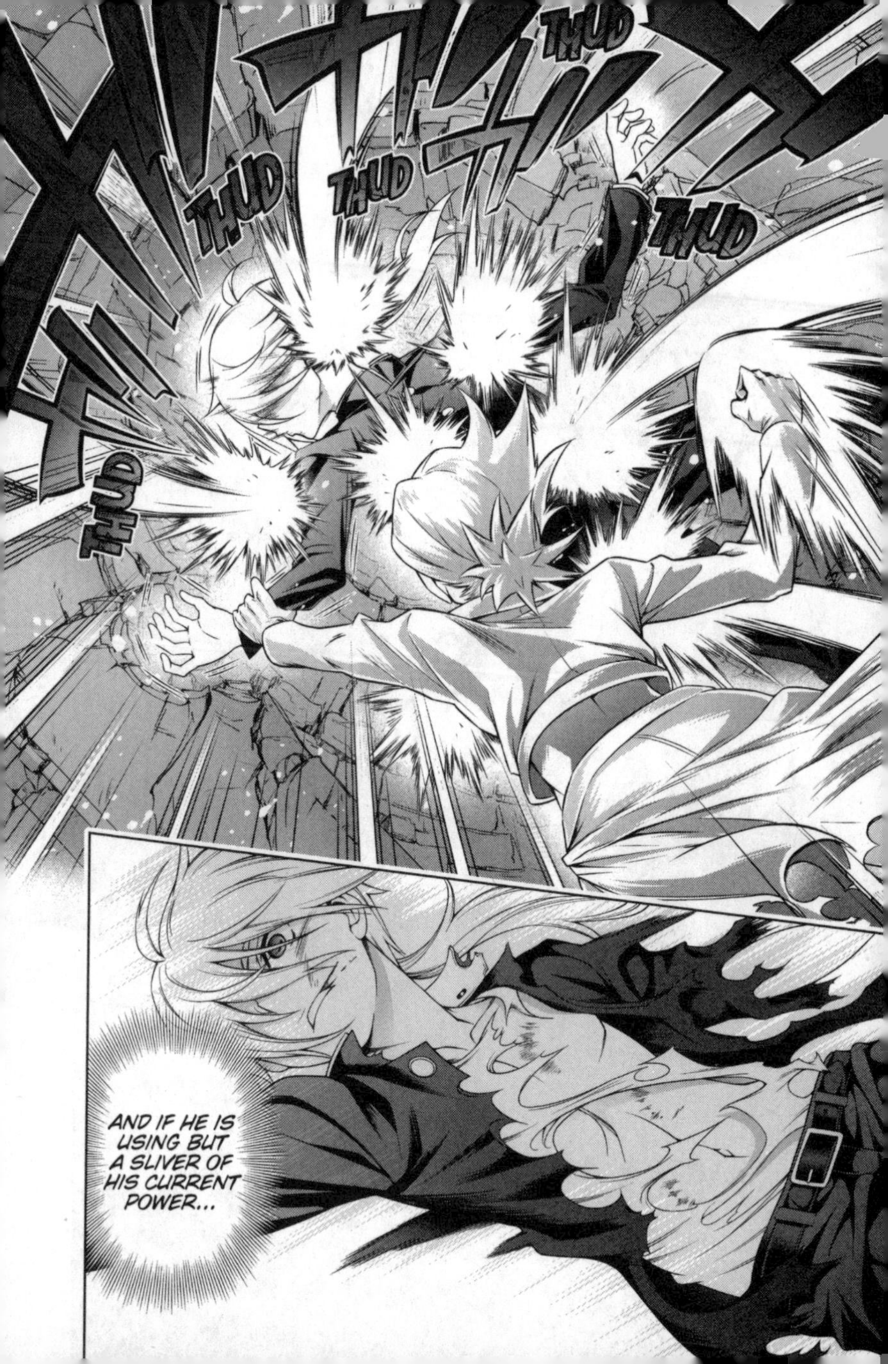
THUD
THUD
THUD
THUD
THUD
THUD
AND IF HE IS USING BUT A SLIVER OF HIS CURRENT POWER...

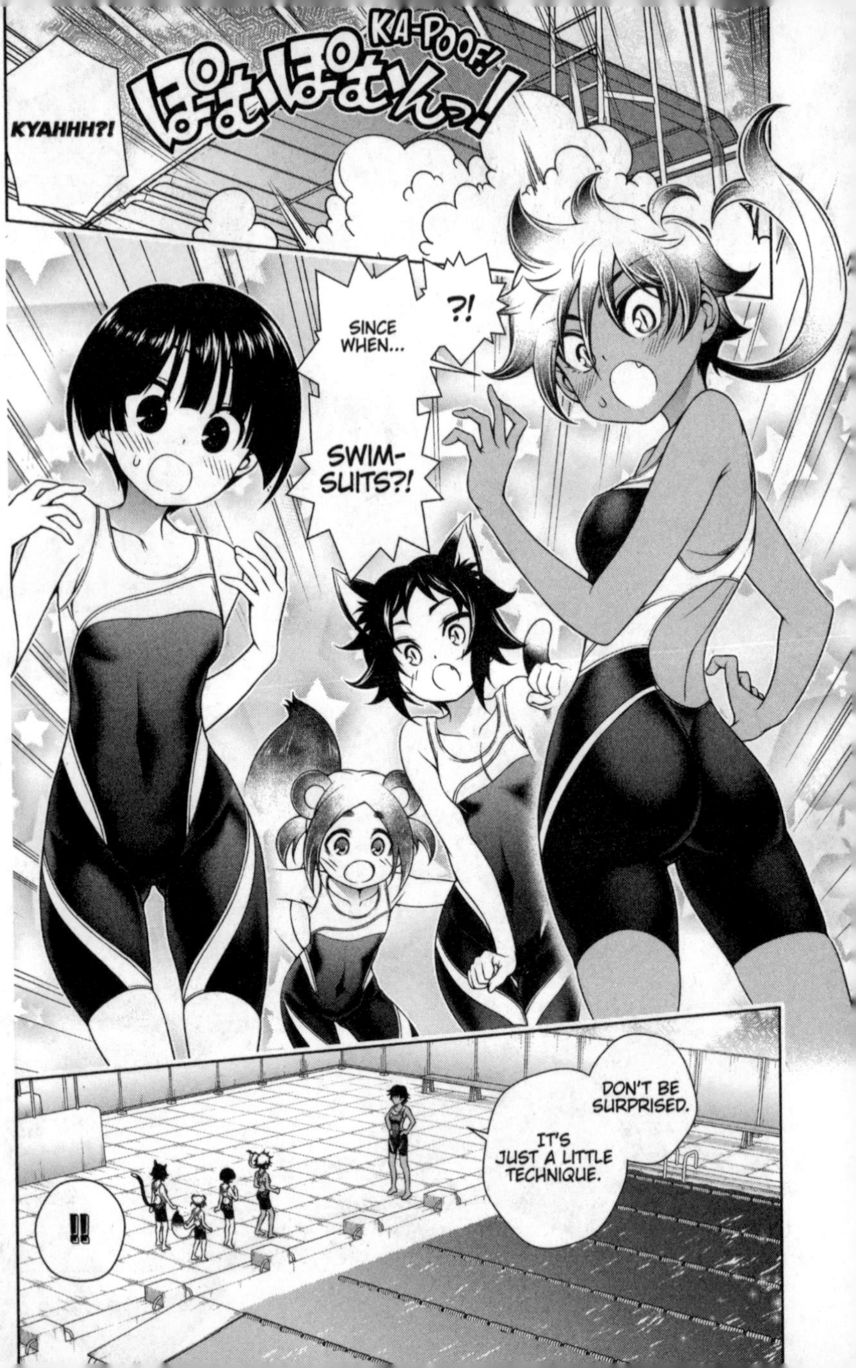
KA-POOF!
ぽむっぽむんっ!
KYAHHH?!
?!
SINCE WHEN...
SWIM-SUITS?!
DON'T BE SURPRISED.
IT'S JUST A LITTLE TECHNIQUE.
!!

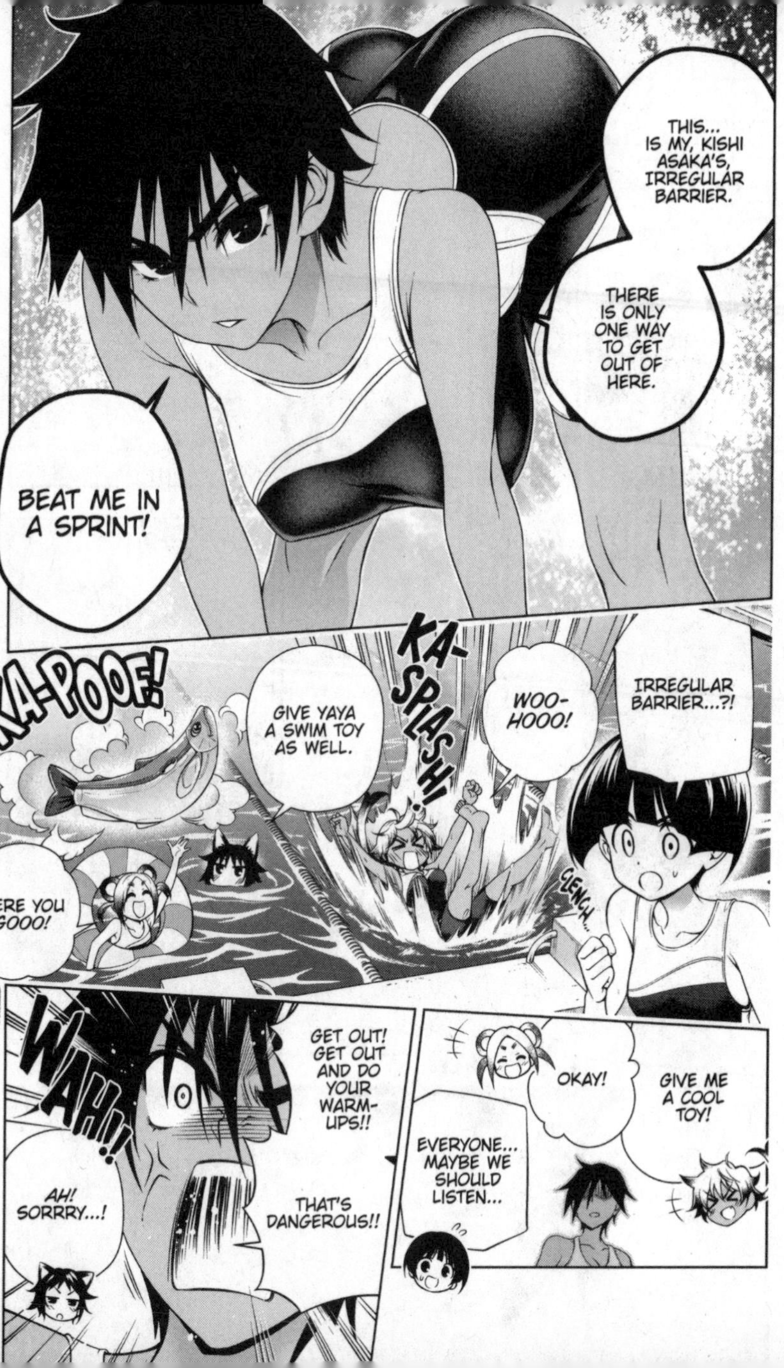
THIS... IS MY, KISHI ASAKA'S, IRREGULAR BARRIER.
THERE IS ONLY ONE WAY TO GET OUT OF HERE.
BEAT ME IN A SPRINT!
IRREGULAR BARRIER...?!
WOO-HOOO!
KA-SPLASH!
CLENCH...
GIVE YAYA A SWIM TOY AS WELL.
KA-POOF!
HERE YOU GOOO!
GIVE ME A COOL TOY!
OKAY!
EVERYONE... MAYBE WE SHOULD LISTEN...
GET OUT! GET OUT AND DO YOUR WARM-UPS!!
WAH!!
THAT'S DANGEROUS!!
AH! SORRRY...!

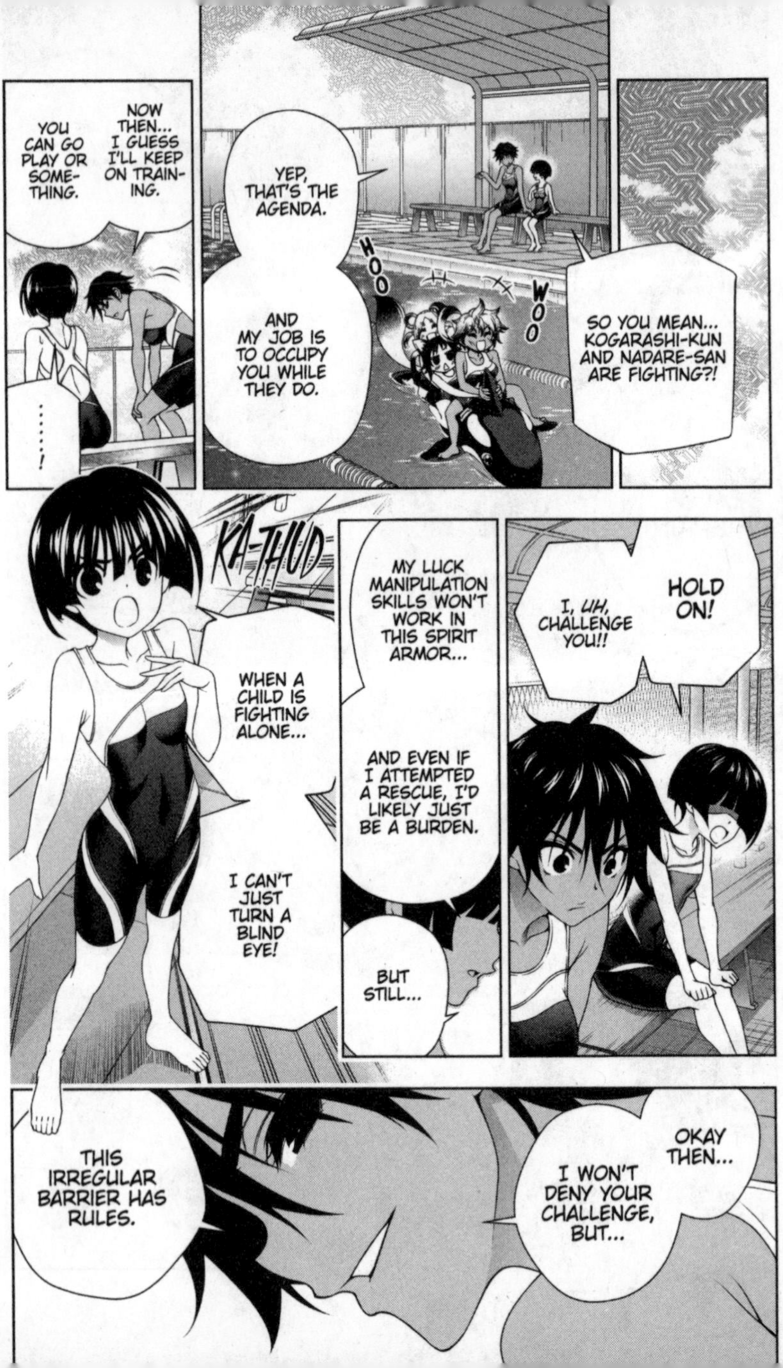
SO YOU MEAN... KOGARASHI-KUN AND NADARE-SAN ARE FIGHTING?!
WOO
HOO
YEP, THAT'S THE AGENDA.
AND MY JOB IS TO OCCUPY YOU WHILE THEY DO.
NOW THEN... I GUESS I'LL KEEP ON TRAINING.
YOU CAN GO PLAY OR SOME-THING.
......!
HOLD ON!
I, UH, CHALLENGE YOU!!
MY LUCK MANIPULATION SKILLS WON'T WORK IN THIS SPIRIT ARMOR...
AND EVEN IF I ATTEMPTED A RESCUE, I'D LIKELY JUST BE A BURDEN.
BUT STILL...
KA-THUD
WHEN A CHILD IS FIGHTING ALONE...
I CAN'T JUST TURN A BLIND EYE!
OKAY THEN...
I WON'T DENY YOUR CHALLENGE, BUT...
THIS IRREGULAR BARRIER HAS RULES.

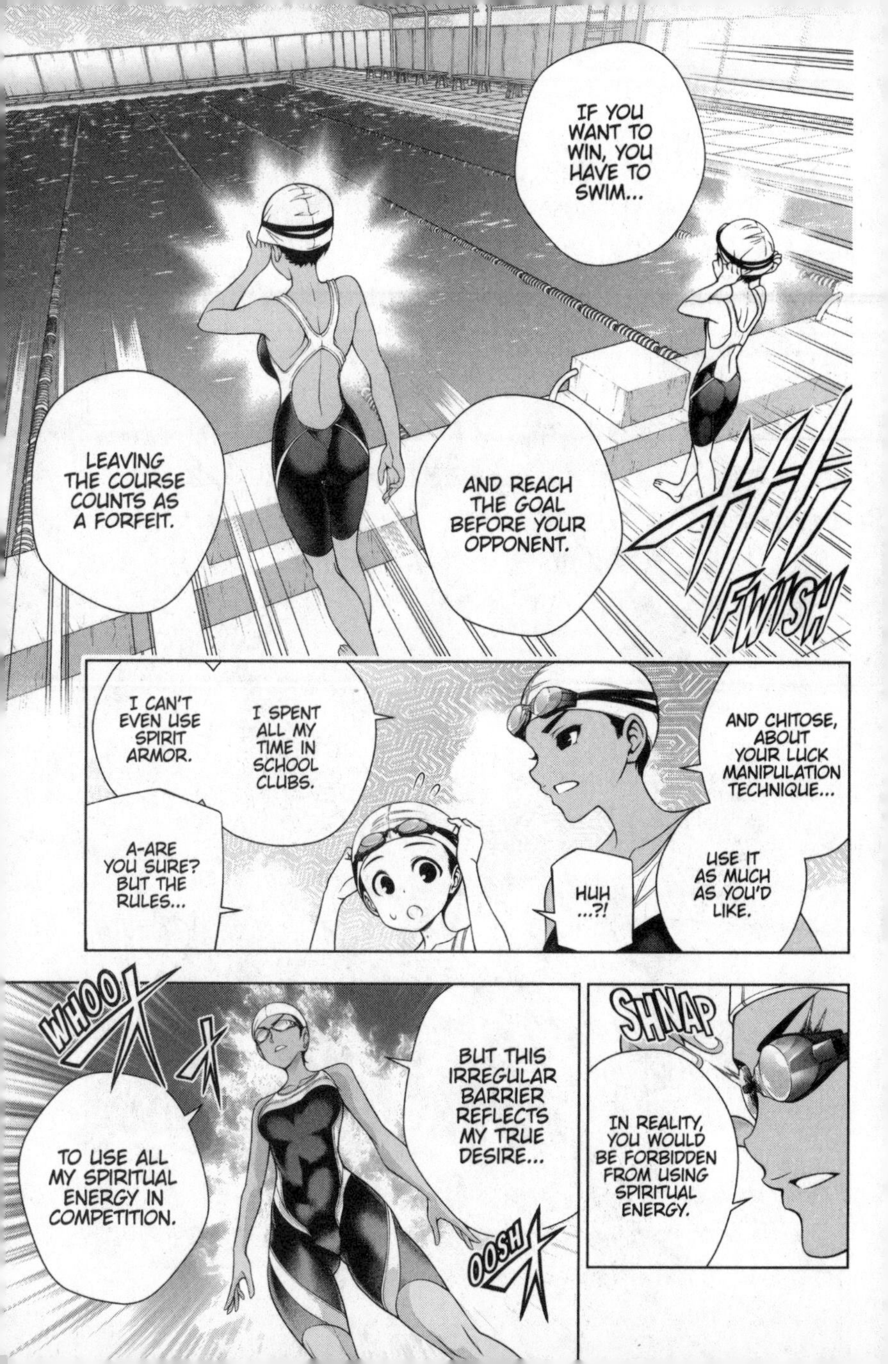
IF YOU WANT TO WIN, YOU HAVE TO SWIM...
AND REACH THE GOAL BEFORE YOUR OPPONENT.
FWISH
LEAVING THE COURSE COUNTS AS A FORFEIT.
AND CHITOSE, ABOUT YOUR LUCK MANIPULATION TECHNIQUE...
USE IT AS MUCH AS YOU'D LIKE.
HUH ...?!
I SPENT ALL MY TIME IN SCHOOL CLUBS.
I CAN'T EVEN USE SPIRIT ARMOR.
A-ARE YOU SURE? BUT THE RULES...
SHNAP
IN REALITY, YOU WOULD BE FORBIDDEN FROM USING SPIRITUAL ENERGY.
BUT THIS IRREGULAR BARRIER REFLECTS MY TRUE DESIRE...
WHOO
TO USE ALL MY SPIRITUAL ENERGY IN COMPETITION.
OOSH

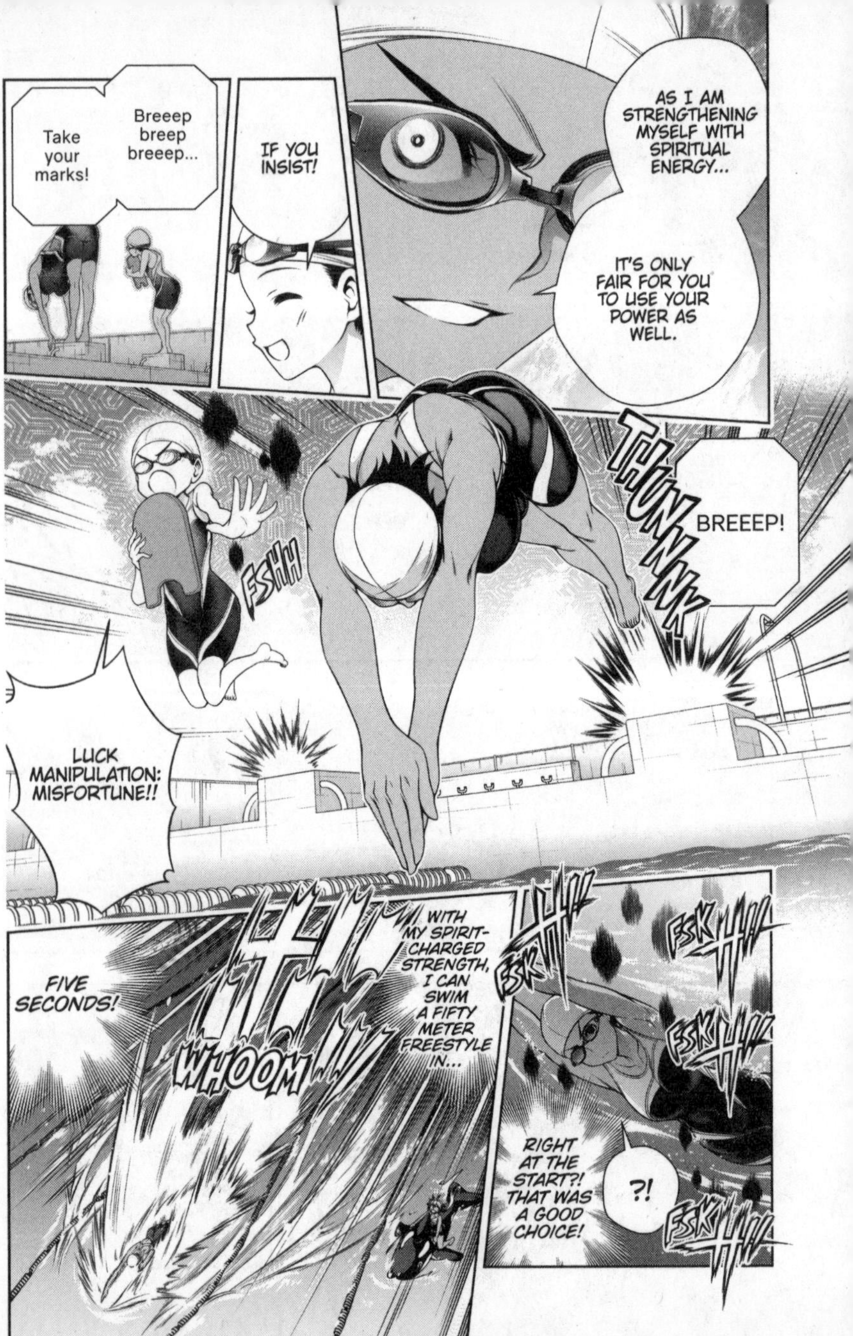
AS I AM STRENGTHENING MYSELF WITH SPIRITUAL ENERGY...
IT'S ONLY FAIR FOR YOU TO USE YOUR POWER AS WELL.
IF YOU INSIST!
Breeep breep breeep...
Take your marks!
THUNNNK
BREEEP!
FSHH
LUCK MANIPULATION: MISFORTUNE!!
FSKHH
FSKHH
FSKHH
FSKHH
?!
RIGHT AT THE START?! THAT WAS A GOOD CHOICE!
WITH MY SPIRIT-CHARGED STRENGTH, I CAN SWIM A FIFTY METER FREESTYLE IN...
FIVE SECONDS!
WHOOM

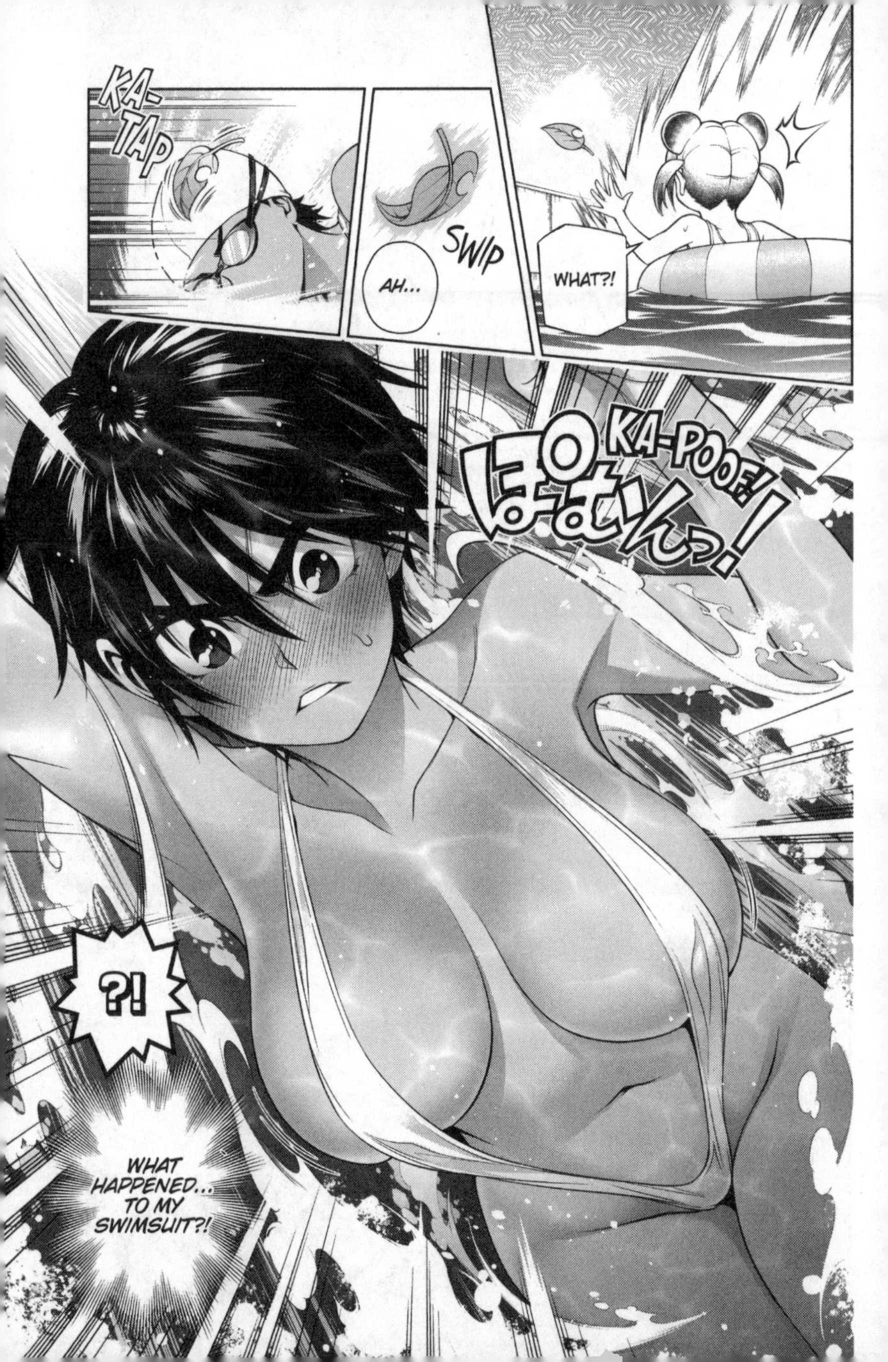
WHAT?!
AH...
SWIP
KA-TAP
KA-POOF!
ぽよんっ!
?!
WHAT HAPPENED... TO MY SWIMSUIT?!

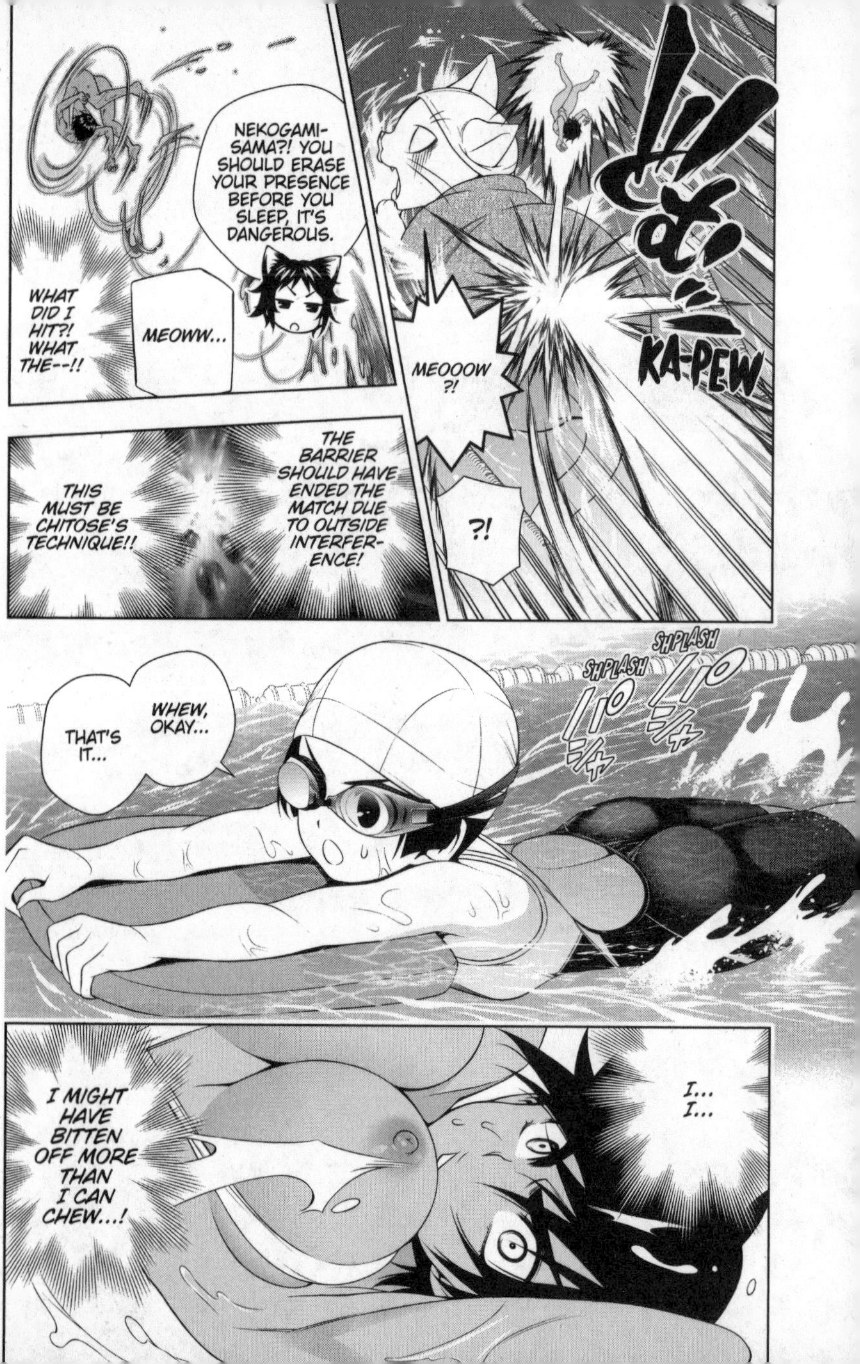

!!
KA-PEW
MEOOOW ?!
?!
NEKOGAMI-SAMA?! YOU SHOULD ERASE YOUR PRESENCE BEFORE YOU SLEEP, IT'S DANGEROUS.
MEOWW...
WHAT DID I HIT?! WHAT THE--!!
THE BARRIER SHOULD HAVE ENDED THE MATCH DUE TO OUTSIDE INTERFER-ENCE!
THIS MUST BE CHITOSE'S TECHNIQUE!!
SHPLASH
SHPLASH
WHEW, OKAY...
THAT'S IT...
I... I...
I MIGHT HAVE BITTEN OFF MORE THAN I CAN CHEW...!

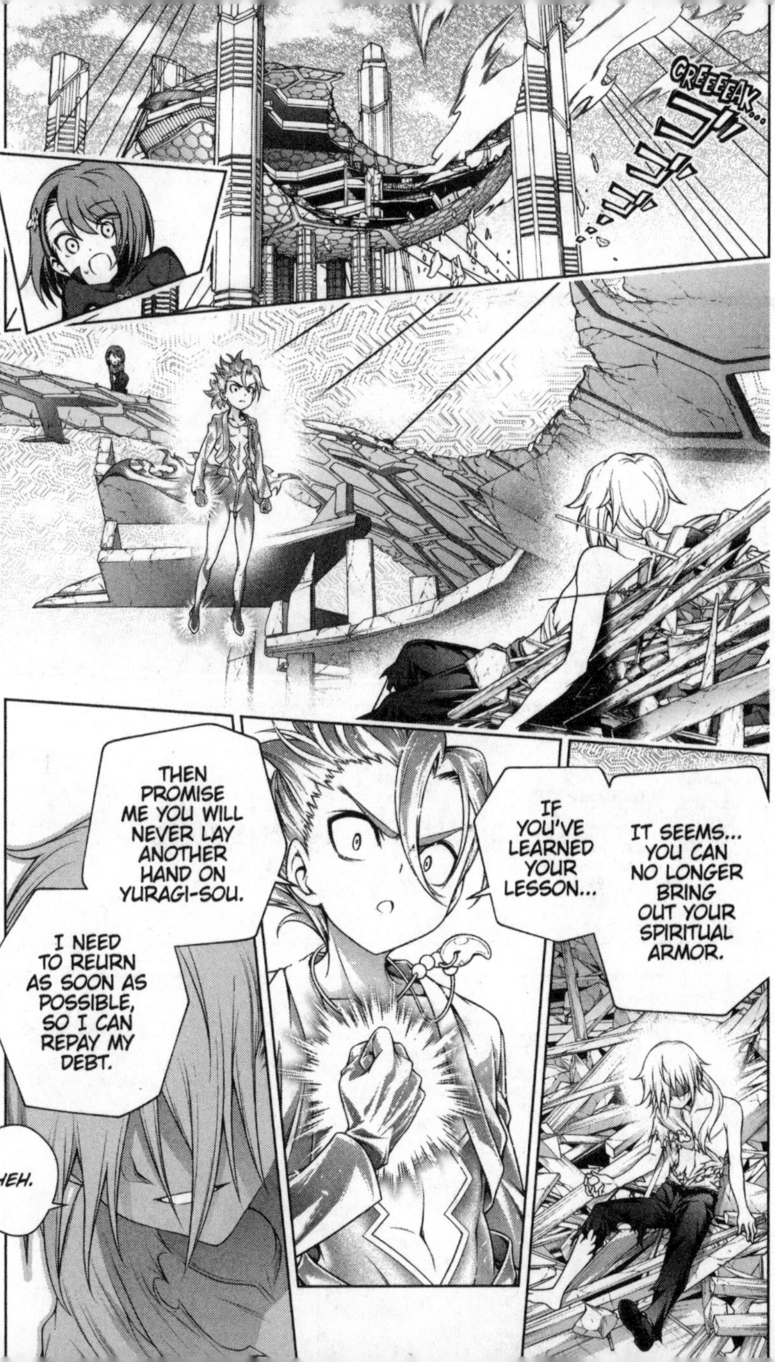
CREEEEAK...
IT SEEMS... YOU CAN NO LONGER BRING OUT YOUR SPIRITUAL ARMOR.
IF YOU'VE LEARNED YOUR LESSON...
THEN PROMISE ME YOU WILL NEVER LAY ANOTHER HAND ON YURAGI-SOU.
I NEED TO REURN AS SOON AS POSSIBLE, SO I CAN REPAY MY DEBT.
HEH.

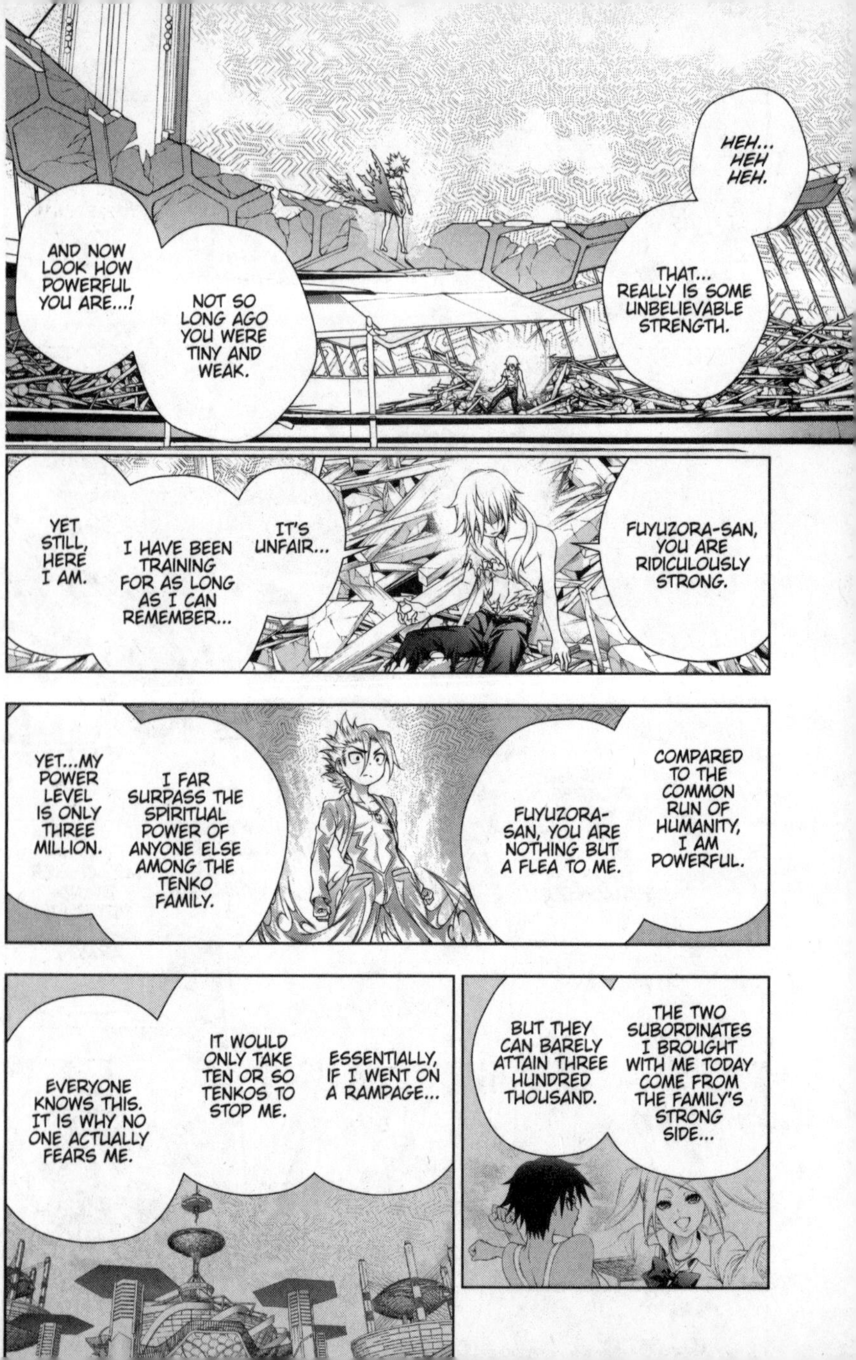
HEH... HEH HEH.
THAT... REALLY IS SOME UNBELIEVABLE STRENGTH.
NOT SO LONG AGO YOU WERE TINY AND WEAK.
AND NOW LOOK HOW POWERFUL YOU ARE...!
FUYUZORA-SAN, YOU ARE RIDICULOUSLY STRONG.
IT'S UNFAIR...
I HAVE BEEN TRAINING FOR AS LONG AS I CAN REMEMBER...
YET STILL, HERE I AM.
COMPARED TO THE COMMON RUN OF HUMANITY, I AM POWERFUL.
FUYUZORA-SAN, YOU ARE NOTHING BUT A FLEA TO ME.
I FAR SURPASS THE SPIRITUAL POWER OF ANYONE ELSE AMONG THE TENKO FAMILY.
YET...MY POWER LEVEL IS ONLY THREE MILLION.
THE TWO SUBORDINATES I BROUGHT WITH ME TODAY COME FROM THE FAMILY'S STRONG SIDE...
BUT THEY CAN BARELY ATTAIN THREE HUNDRED THOUSAND.
ESSENTIALLY, IF I WENT ON A RAMPAGE...
IT WOULD ONLY TAKE TEN OR SO TENKOS TO STOP ME.
EVERYONE KNOWS THIS. IT IS WHY NO ONE ACTUALLY FEARS ME.

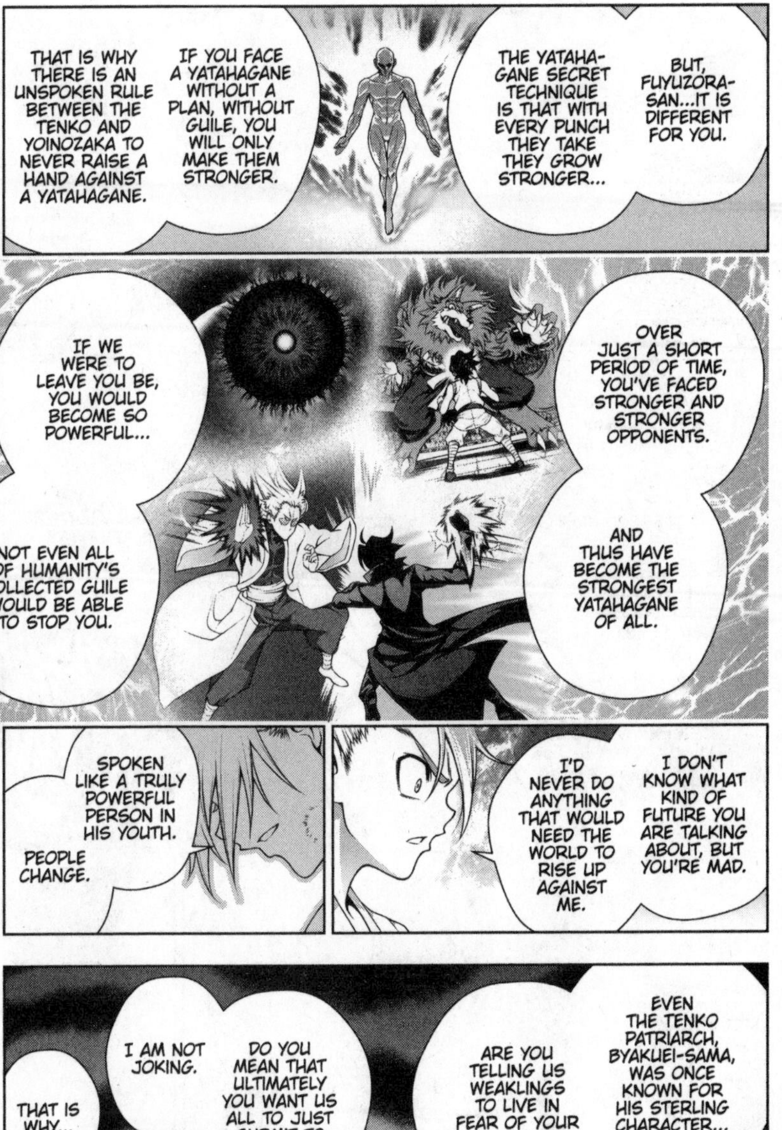
BUT, FUYUZORA-SAN...IT IS DIFFERENT FOR YOU.
THE YATAHA-GANE SECRET TECHNIQUE IS THAT WITH EVERY PUNCH THEY TAKE THEY GROW STRONGER...
IF YOU FACE A YATAHAGANE WITHOUT A PLAN, WITHOUT GUILE, YOU WILL ONLY MAKE THEM STRONGER.
THAT IS WHY THERE IS AN UNSPOKEN RULE BETWEEN THE TENKO AND YOINOZAKA TO NEVER RAISE A HAND AGAINST A YATAHAGANE.
OVER JUST A SHORT PERIOD OF TIME, YOU'VE FACED STRONGER AND STRONGER OPPONENTS.
AND THUS HAVE BECOME THE STRONGEST YATAHAGANE OF ALL.
IF WE WERE TO LEAVE YOU BE, YOU WOULD BECOME SO POWERFUL...
NOT EVEN ALL OF HUMANITY'S COLLECTED GUILE WOULD BE ABLE TO STOP YOU.
I DON'T KNOW WHAT KIND OF FUTURE YOU ARE TALKING ABOUT, BUT YOU'RE MAD.
I'D NEVER DO ANYTHING THAT WOULD NEED THE WORLD TO RISE UP AGAINST ME.
SPOKEN LIKE A TRULY POWERFUL PERSON IN HIS YOUTH.
PEOPLE CHANGE.
EVEN THE TENKO PATRIARCH, BYAKUEI-SAMA, WAS ONCE KNOWN FOR HIS STERLING CHARACTER...
ARE YOU TELLING US WEAKLINGS TO LIVE IN FEAR OF YOUR SHADOW?
DO YOU MEAN THAT ULTIMATELY YOU WANT US ALL TO JUST SUBMIT TO YOU?
I AM NOT JOKING.
THAT IS WHY...

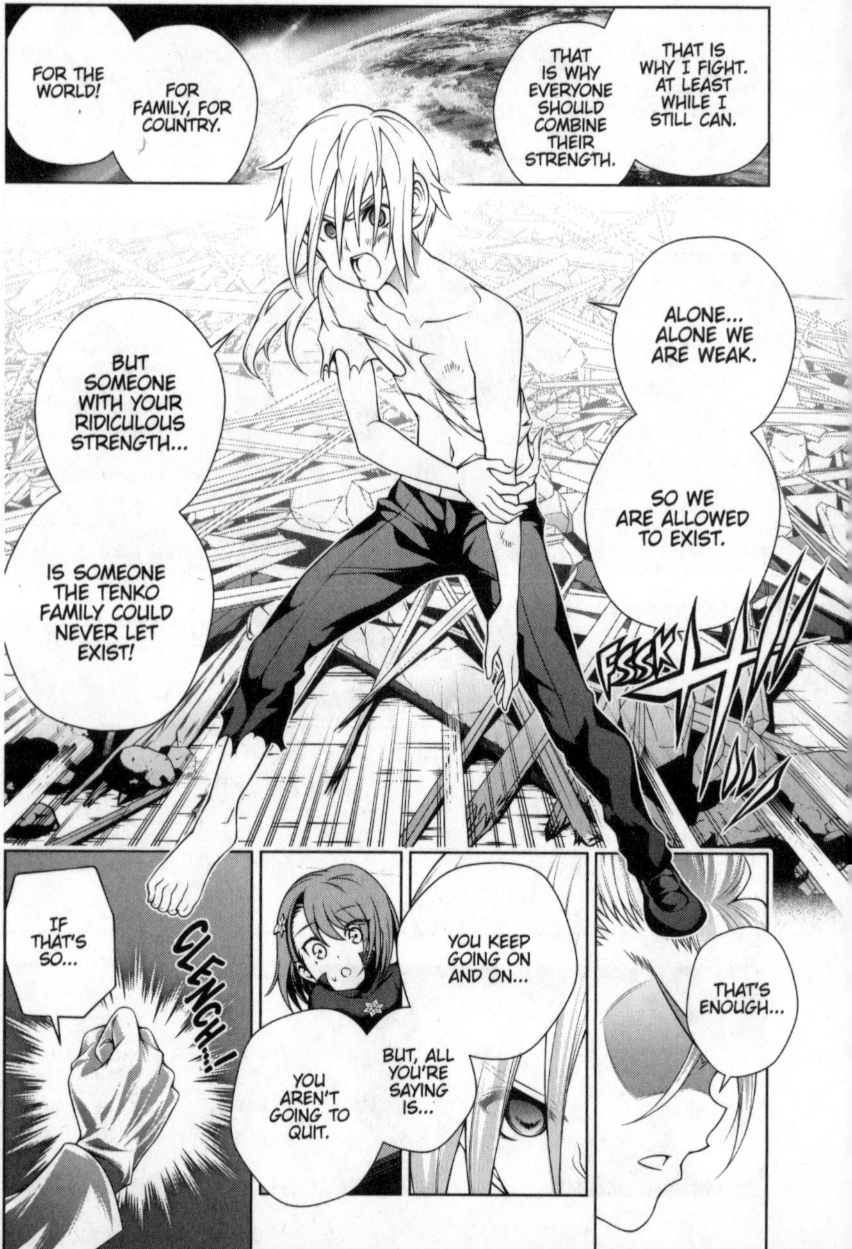
THAT IS WHY I FIGHT. AT LEAST WHILE I STILL CAN.
THAT IS WHY EVERYONE SHOULD COMBINE THEIR STRENGTH.
FOR FAMILY, FOR COUNTRY.
FOR THE WORLD!
ALONE... ALONE WE ARE WEAK.
SO WE ARE ALLOWED TO EXIST.
BUT SOMEONE WITH YOUR RIDICULOUS STRENGTH...
IS SOMEONE THE TENKO FAMILY COULD NEVER LET EXIST!
FSSK
THAT'S ENOUGH...
YOU KEEP GOING ON AND ON...
BUT, ALL YOU'RE SAYING IS...
YOU AREN'T GOING TO QUIT.
IF THAT'S SO...
CLENCH...!

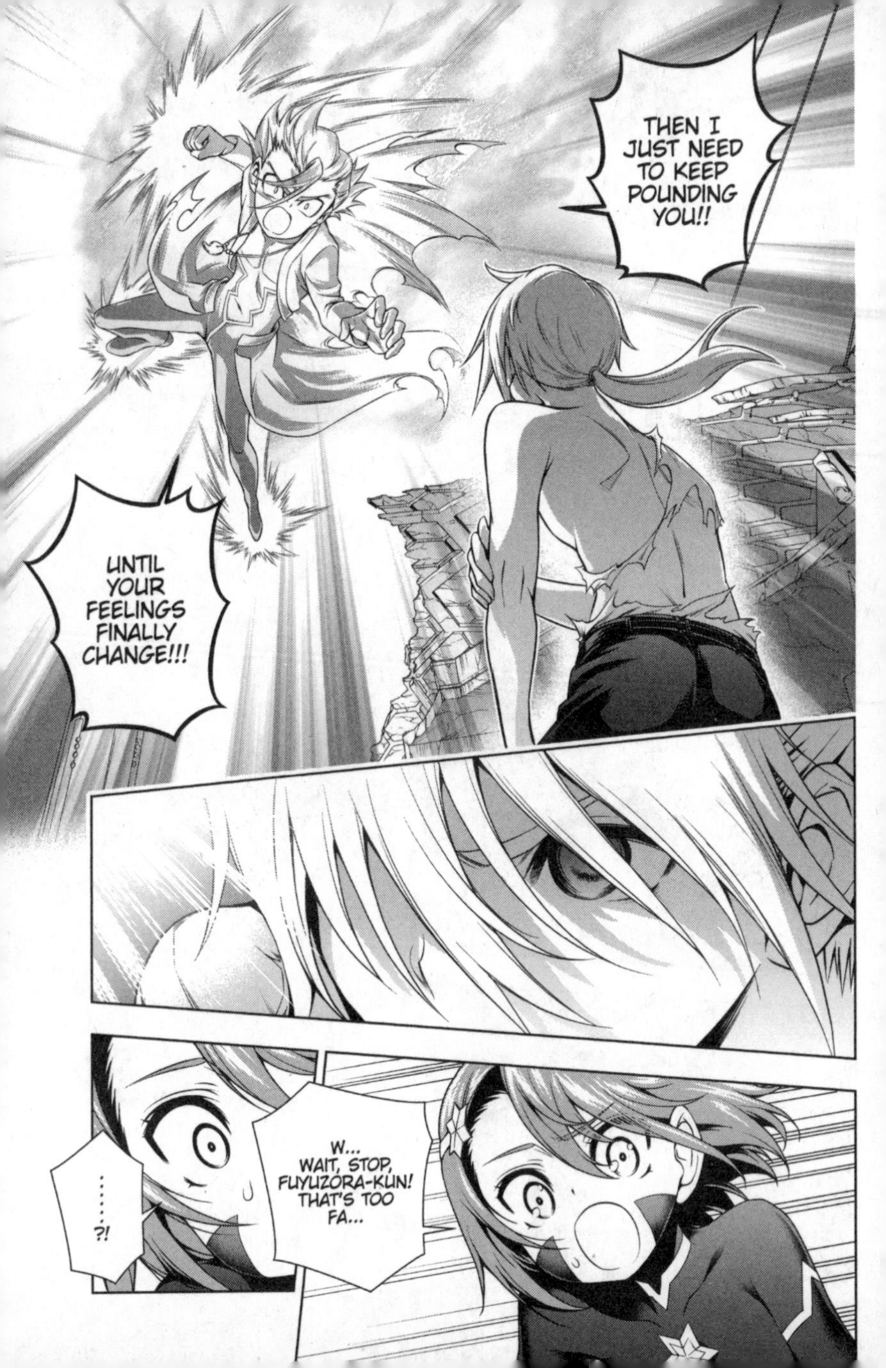
THEN I JUST NEED TO KEEP POUNDING YOU!!
UNTIL YOUR FEELINGS FINALLY CHANGE!!!
W... WAIT, STOP, FUYUZORA-KUN! THAT'S TOO FA...
......?!

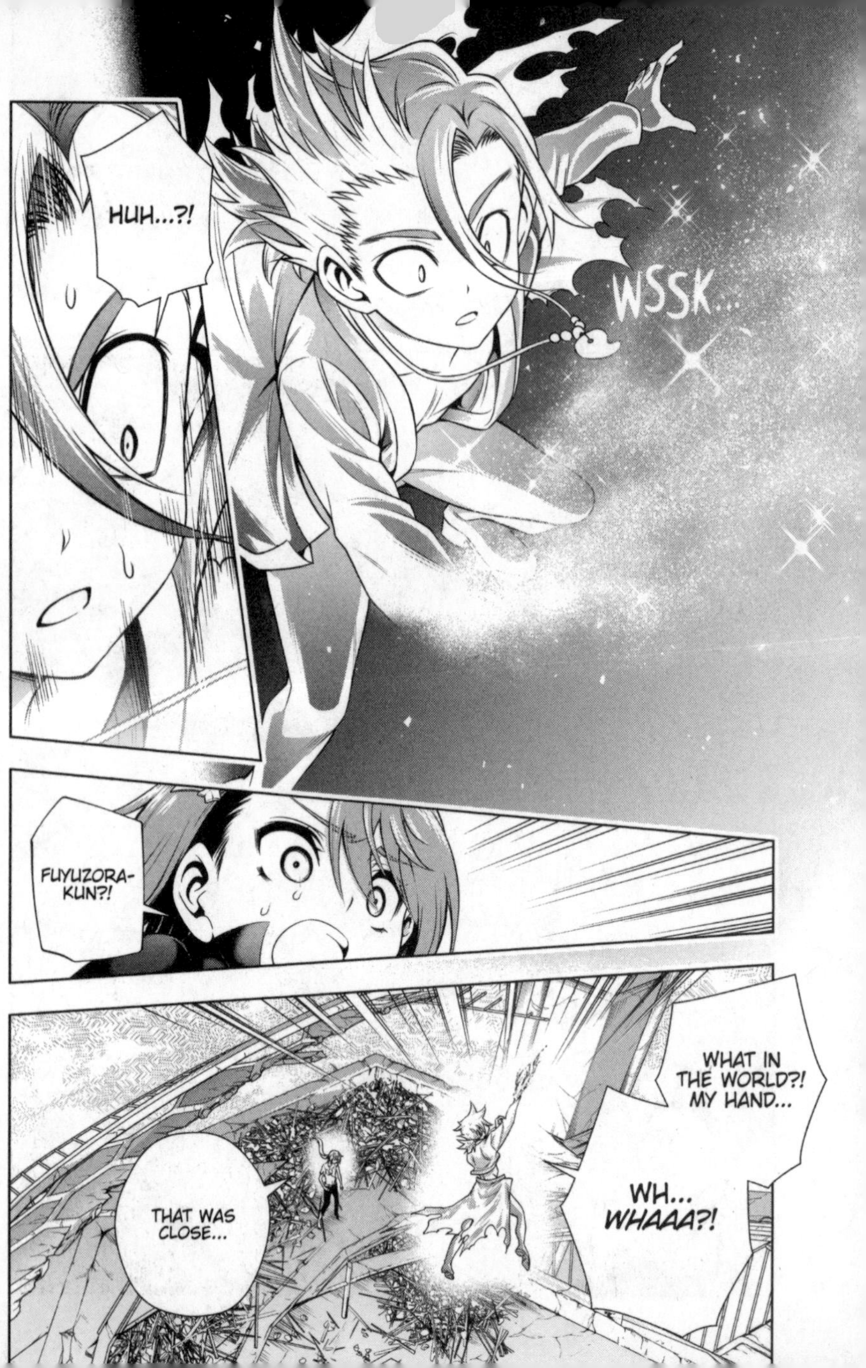
WSSK
HUH...?!
FUYUZORA-KUN?!
WHAT IN THE WORLD?! MY HAND...
WH... WHAAA?!
THAT WAS CLOSE...

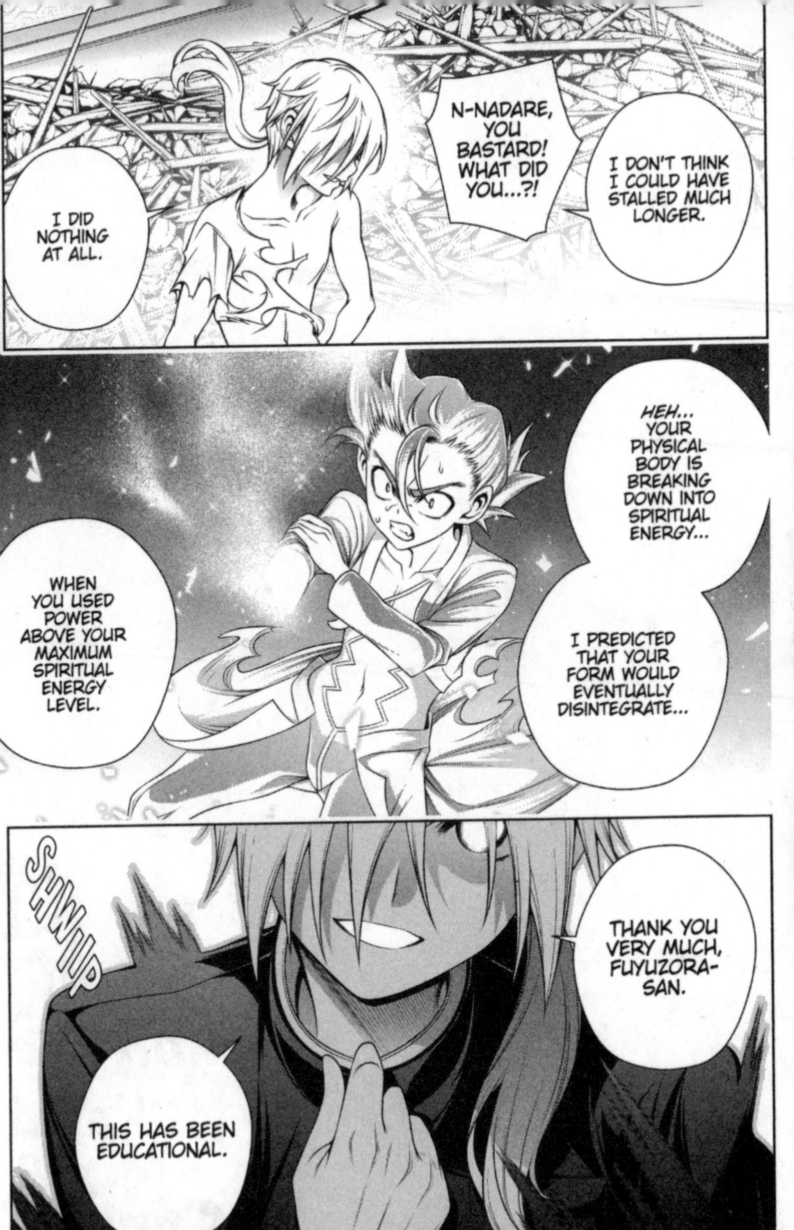
I DON'T THINK I COULD HAVE STALLED MUCH LONGER.
N-NADARE, YOU BASTARD! WHAT DID YOU...?!
I DID NOTHING AT ALL.
HEH... YOUR PHYSICAL BODY IS BREAKING DOWN INTO SPIRITUAL ENERGY...
I PREDICTED THAT YOUR FORM WOULD EVENTUALLY DISINTEGRATE...
WHEN YOU USED POWER ABOVE YOUR MAXIMUM SPIRITUAL ENERGY LEVEL.
THANK YOU VERY MUCH, FUYUZORA-SAN.
SHWIP
THIS HAS BEEN EDUCATIONAL.

Yuuna and the Haunted Hot Springs

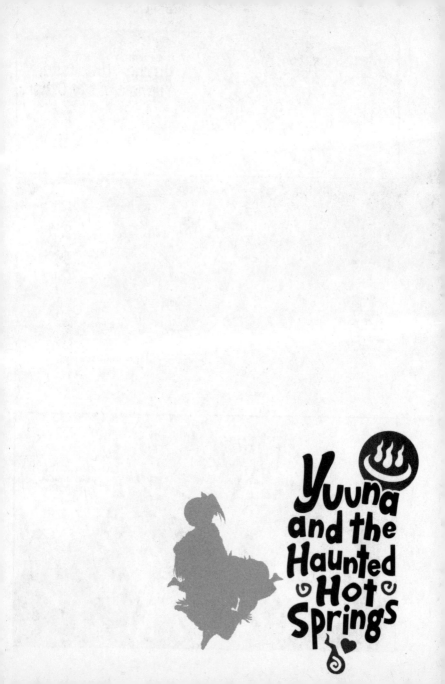

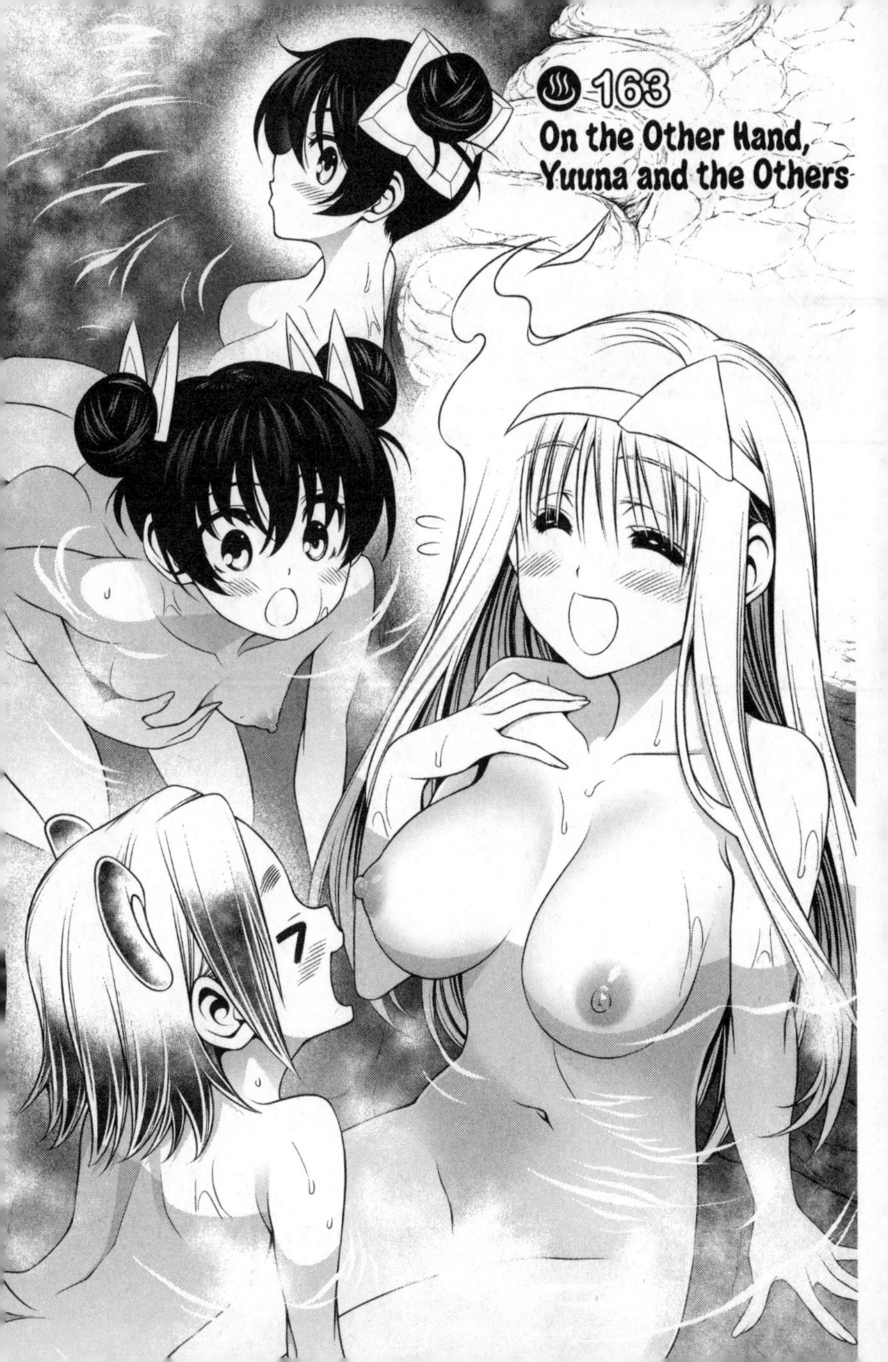
163
On the Other Hand,
Yuuna and the Others

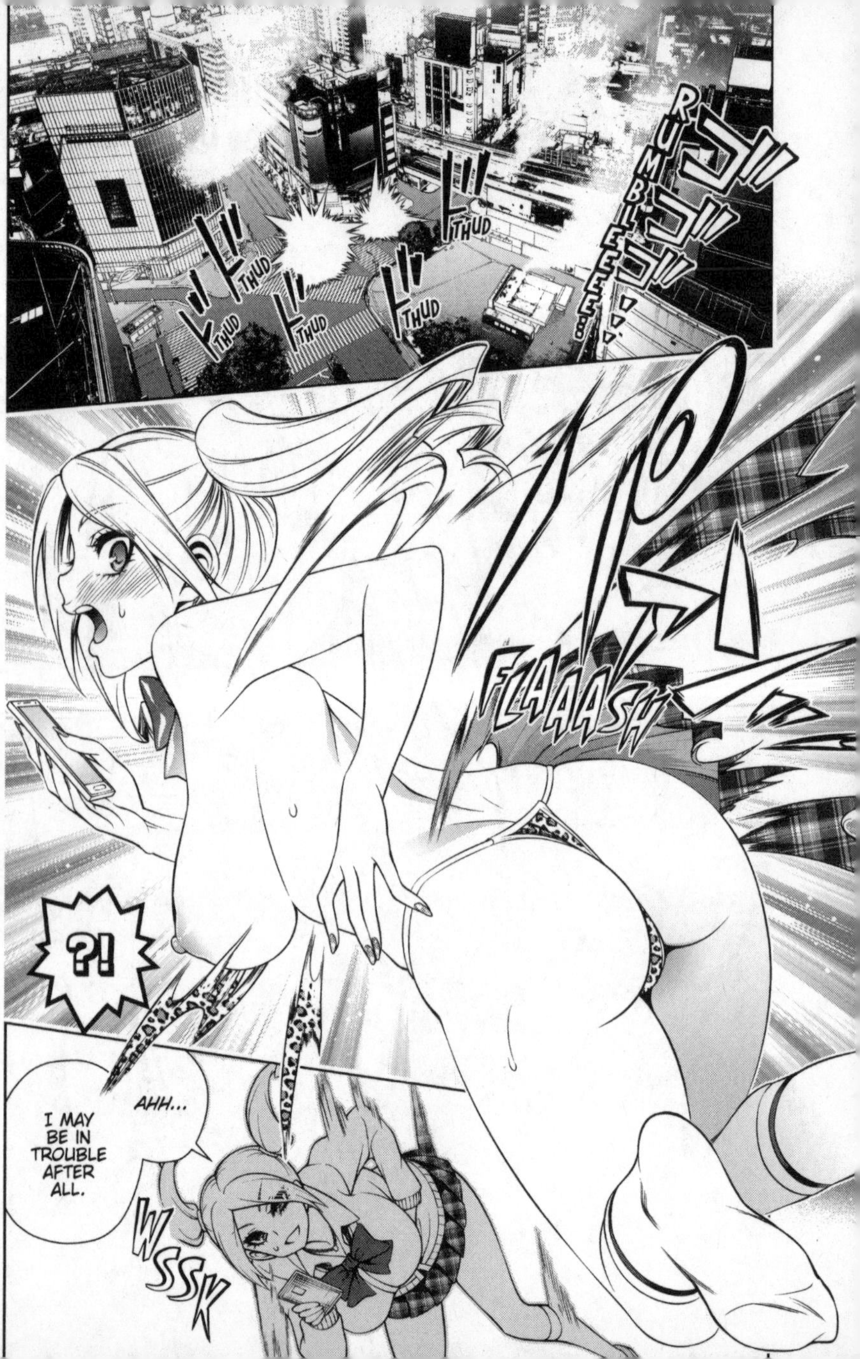
RUMBLEEEE!!
THUD
THUD
THUD
THUD
THUD
FLAAASH
?!
AHH...
I MAY BE IN TROUBLE AFTER ALL.
WSSK

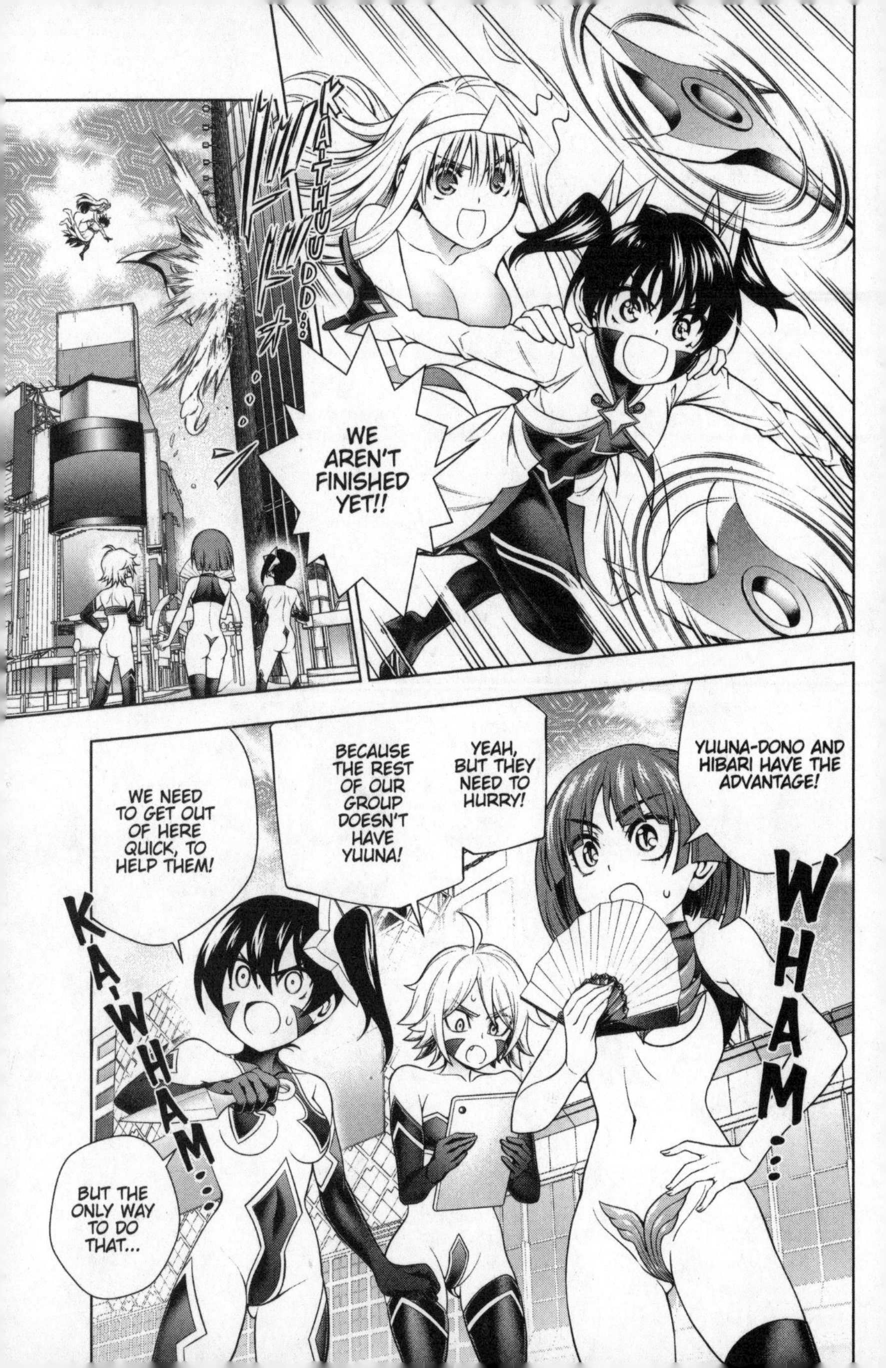
KATHUUDD...
WE AREN'T FINISHED YET!!
YUUNA-DONO AND HIBARI HAVE THE ADVANTAGE!
WHAM...
YEAH, BUT THEY NEED TO HURRY!
BECAUSE THE REST OF OUR GROUP DOESN'T HAVE YUUNA!
WE NEED TO GET OUT OF HERE QUICK, TO HELP THEM!
KA-WHAM...
BUT THE ONLY WAY TO DO THAT...

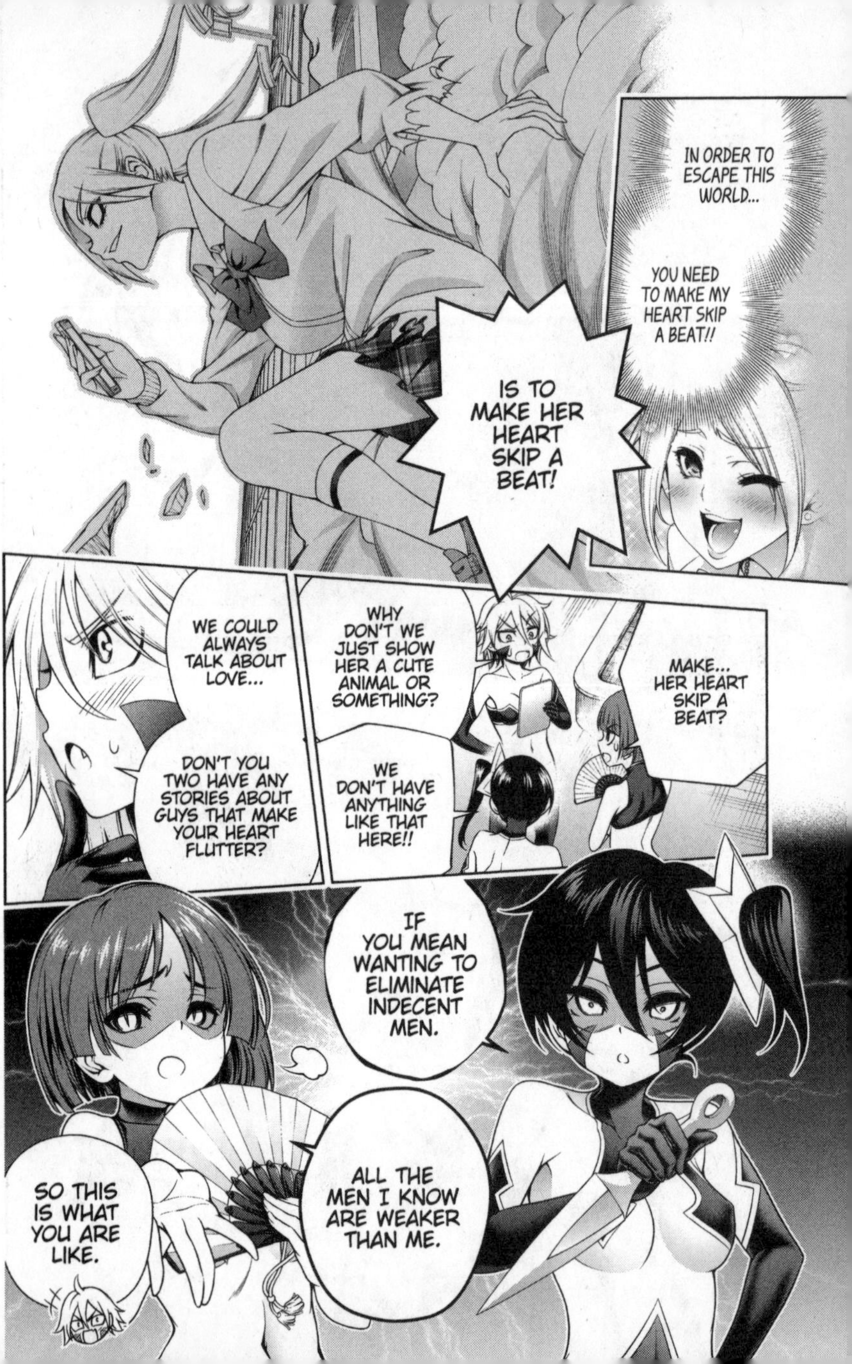
IN ORDER TO ESCAPE THIS WORLD...
YOU NEED TO MAKE MY HEART SKIP A BEAT!!
IS TO MAKE HER HEART SKIP A BEAT!
MAKE... HER HEART SKIP A BEAT?
WHY DON'T WE JUST SHOW HER A CUTE ANIMAL OR SOMETHING?
WE DON'T HAVE ANYTHING LIKE THAT HERE!!
WE COULD ALWAYS TALK ABOUT LOVE...
DON'T YOU TWO HAVE ANY STORIES ABOUT GUYS THAT MAKE YOUR HEART FLUTTER?
IF YOU MEAN WANTING TO ELIMINATE INDECENT MEN.
ALL THE MEN I KNOW ARE WEAKER THAN ME.
SO THIS IS WHAT YOU ARE LIKE.

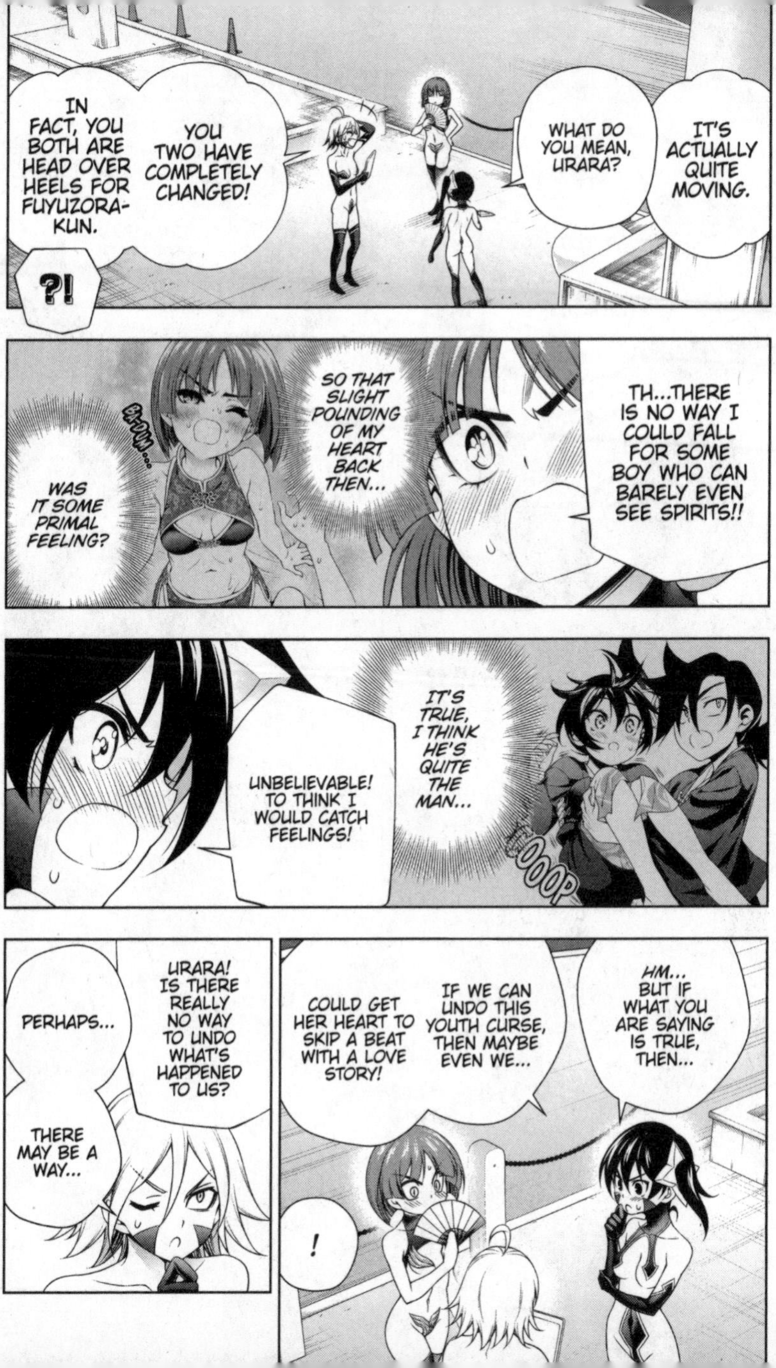
IT'S ACTUALLY QUITE MOVING.
WHAT DO YOU MEAN, URARA?
YOU TWO HAVE COMPLETELY CHANGED!
IN FACT, YOU BOTH ARE HEAD OVER HEELS FOR FUYUZORA-KUN.
?!
TH...THERE IS NO WAY I COULD FALL FOR SOME BOY WHO CAN BARELY EVEN SEE SPIRITS!!
SO THAT SLIGHT POUNDING OF MY HEART BACK THEN...
WAS IT SOME PRIMAL FEELING?
IT'S TRUE, I THINK HE'S QUITE THE MAN...
UNBELIEVABLE! TO THINK I WOULD CATCH FEELINGS!
HM... BUT IF WHAT YOU ARE SAYING IS TRUE, THEN...
IF WE CAN UNDO THIS YOUTH CURSE, THEN MAYBE EVEN WE...
COULD GET HER HEART TO SKIP A BEAT WITH A LOVE STORY!
!
URARA! IS THERE REALLY NO WAY TO UNDO WHAT'S HAPPENED TO US?
PERHAPS...
THERE MAY BE A WAY...

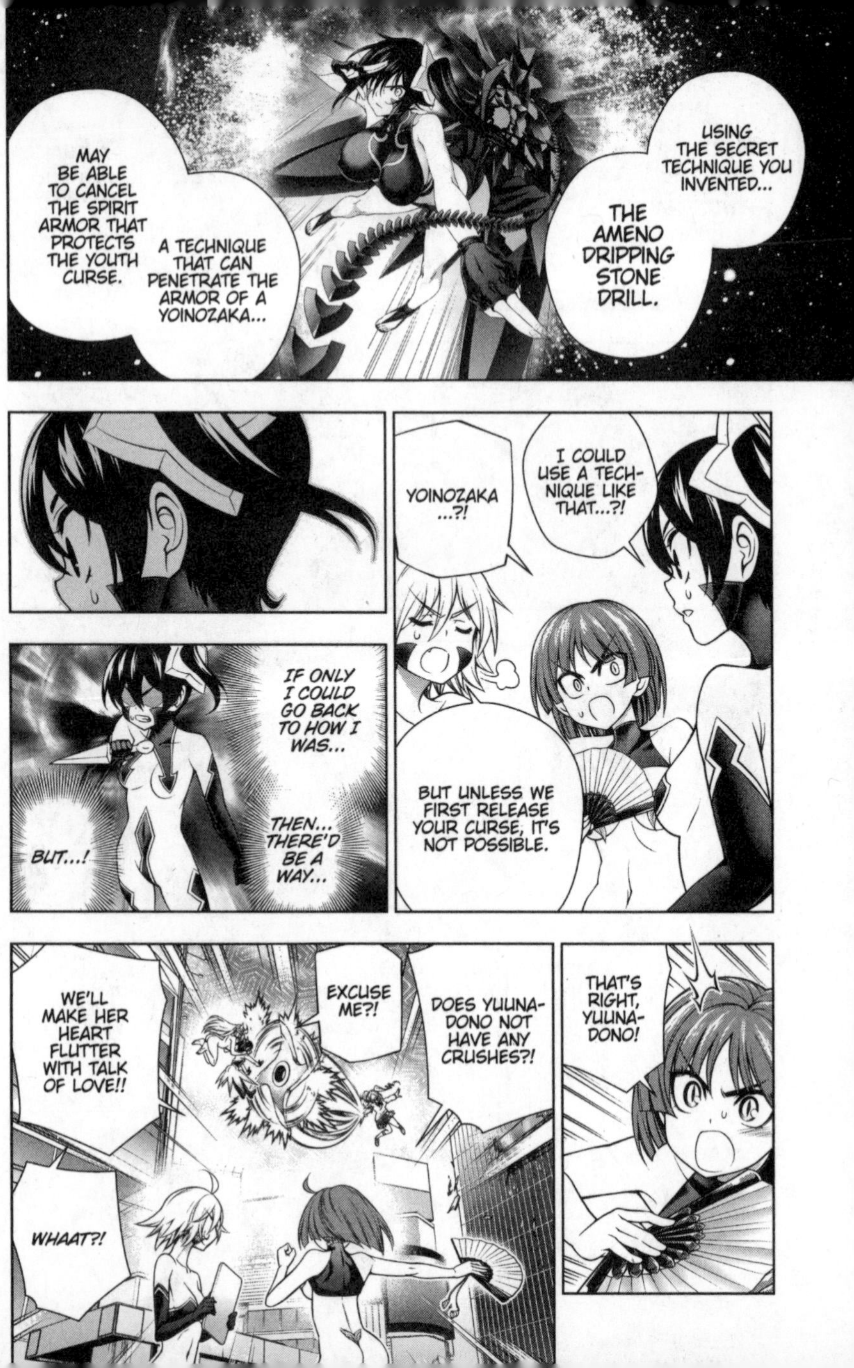
USING THE SECRET TECHNIQUE YOU INVENTED...
THE AMENO DRIPPING STONE DRILL.
A TECHNIQUE THAT CAN PENETRATE THE ARMOR OF A YOINOZAKA...
MAY BE ABLE TO CANCEL THE SPIRIT ARMOR THAT PROTECTS THE YOUTH CURSE.
I COULD USE A TECHNIQUE LIKE THAT...?!
YOINOZAKA ...?!
BUT UNLESS WE FIRST RELEASE YOUR CURSE, IT'S NOT POSSIBLE.
IF ONLY I COULD GO BACK TO HOW I WAS...
THEN... THERE'D BE A WAY...
BUT...!
THAT'S RIGHT, YUUNA-DONO!
DOES YUUNA-DONO NOT HAVE ANY CRUSHES?!
EXCUSE ME?!
WE'LL MAKE HER HEART FLUTTER WITH TALK OF LOVE!!
WHAAT?!

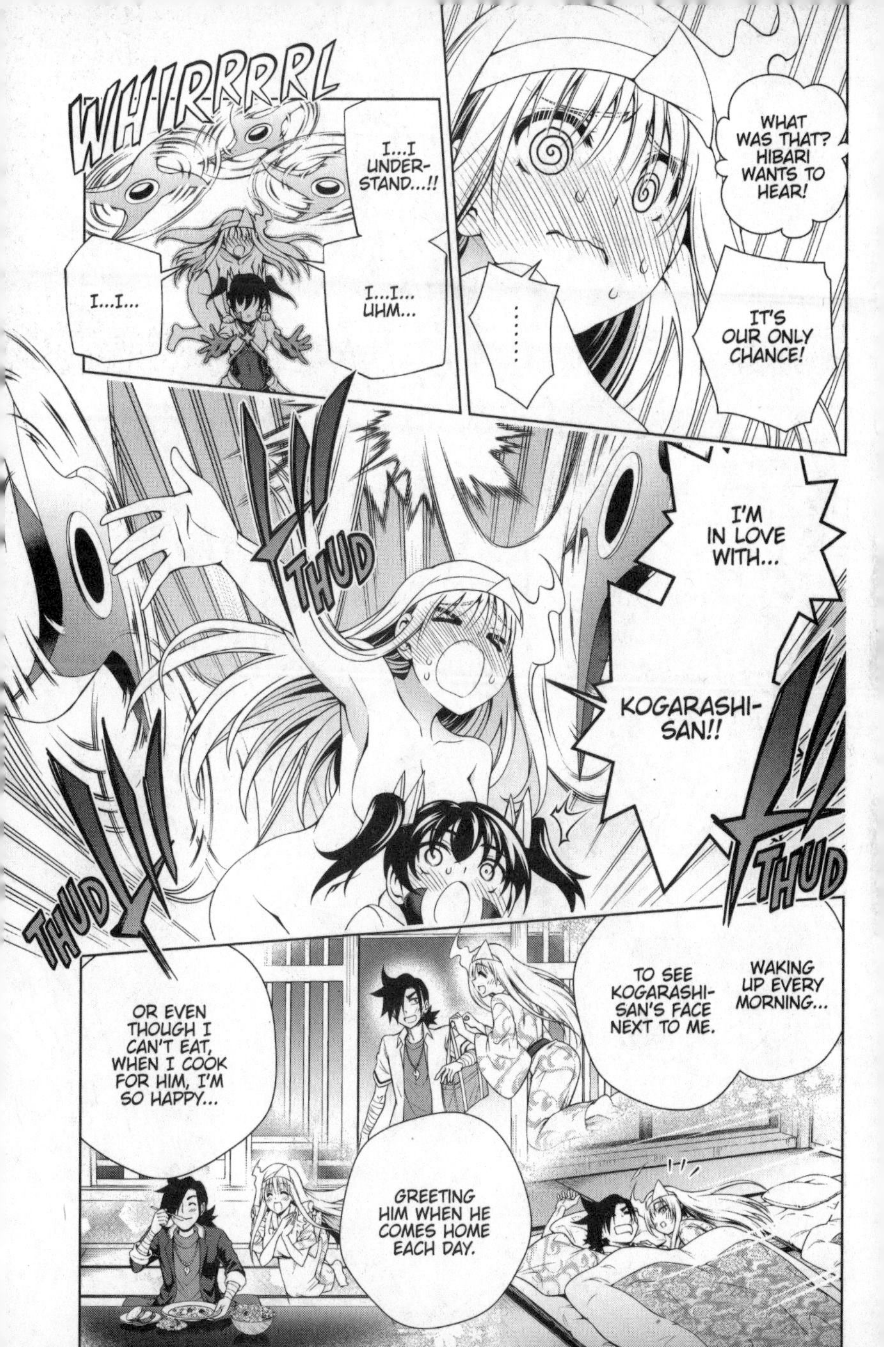
WHAT WAS THAT? HIBARI WANTS TO HEAR!
IT'S OUR ONLY CHANCE!
......
WHIRRRRL
I...I UNDER-STAND...!!
I...I... UHM...
I...I...
I'M IN LOVE WITH...
KOGARASHI-SAN!!
THUD
THUD
THUD
WAKING UP EVERY MORNING...
TO SEE KOGARASHI-SAN'S FACE NEXT TO ME.
!!
GREETING HIM WHEN HE COMES HOME EACH DAY.
OR EVEN THOUGH I CAN'T EAT, WHEN I COOK FOR HIM, I'M SO HAPPY...

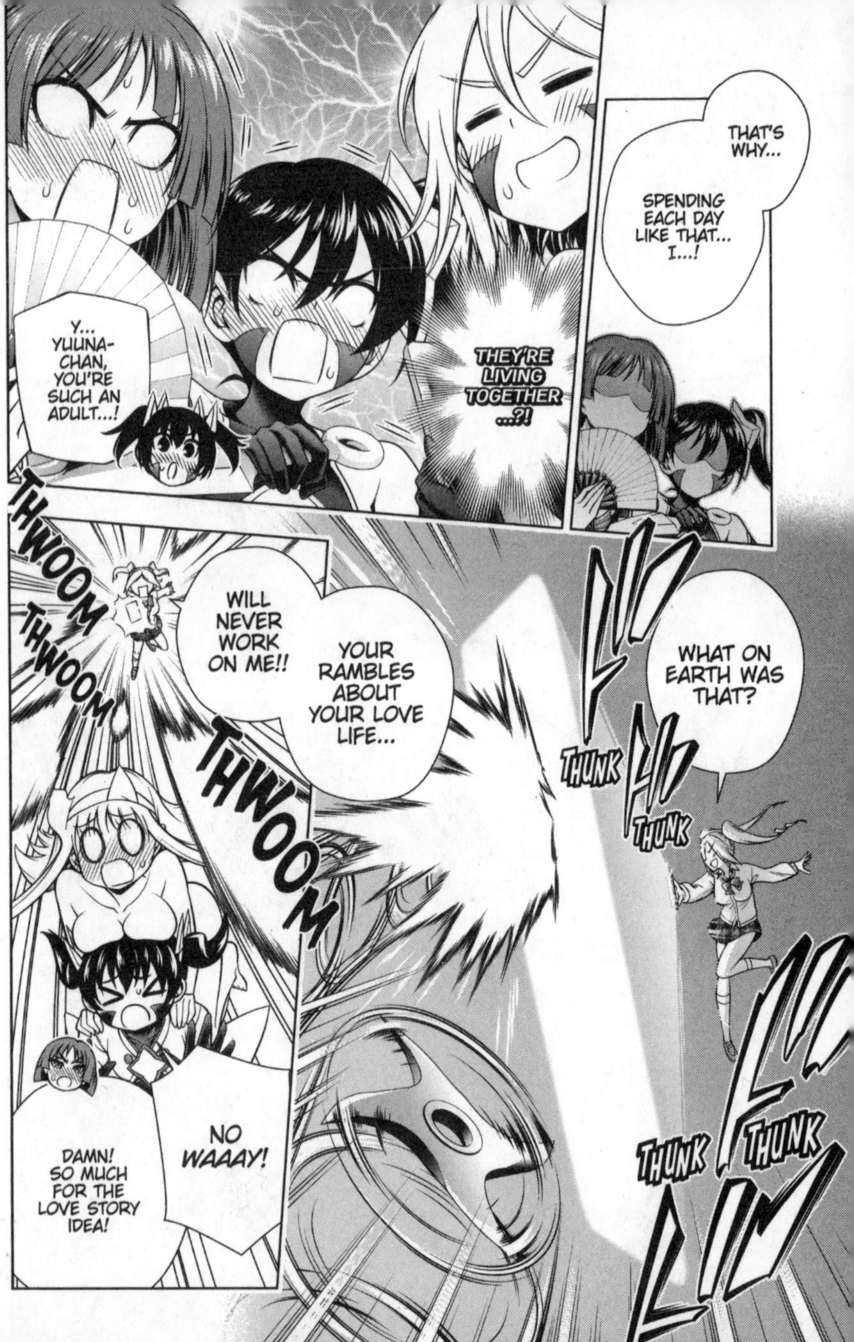
THAT'S WHY...
SPENDING EACH DAY LIKE THAT... I...!
THEY'RE LIVING TOGETHER ...?!
Y... YUUNA-CHAN, YOU'RE SUCH AN ADULT...!
WHAT ON EARTH WAS THAT?
THUNK THUNK
YOUR RAMBLES ABOUT YOUR LOVE LIFE...
WILL NEVER WORK ON ME!!
THWOOM THWOOM
THWOOOM
THUNK THUNK
NO WAAAY!
DAMN! SO MUCH FOR THE LOVE STORY IDEA!

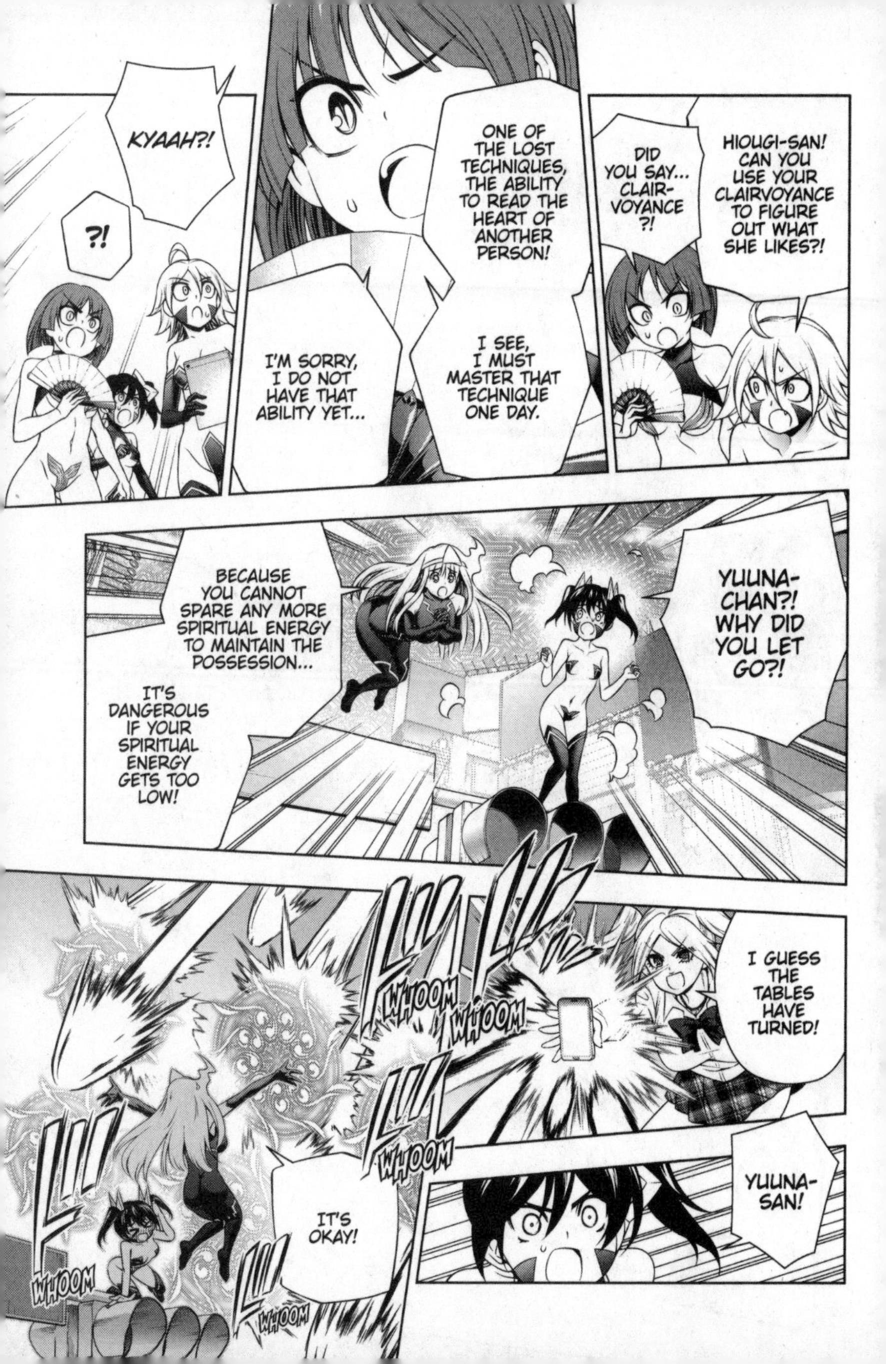
HIOUGI-SAN! CAN YOU USE YOUR CLAIRVOYANCE TO FIGURE OUT WHAT SHE LIKES?!
DID YOU SAY... CLAIR-VOYANCE ?!
ONE OF THE LOST TECHNIQUES, THE ABILITY TO READ THE HEART OF ANOTHER PERSON!
I SEE, I MUST MASTER THAT TECHNIQUE ONE DAY.
I'M SORRY, I DO NOT HAVE THAT ABILITY YET...
KYAAH?!
?!
YUUNA-CHAN?! WHY DID YOU LET GO?!
BECAUSE YOU CANNOT SPARE ANY MORE SPIRITUAL ENERGY TO MAINTAIN THE POSSESSION...
IT'S DANGEROUS IF YOUR SPIRITUAL ENERGY GETS TOO LOW!
I GUESS THE TABLES HAVE TURNED!
WHOOM
WHOOM
YUUNA-SAN!
IT'S OKAY!
WHOOM
WHOOM
WHOOM

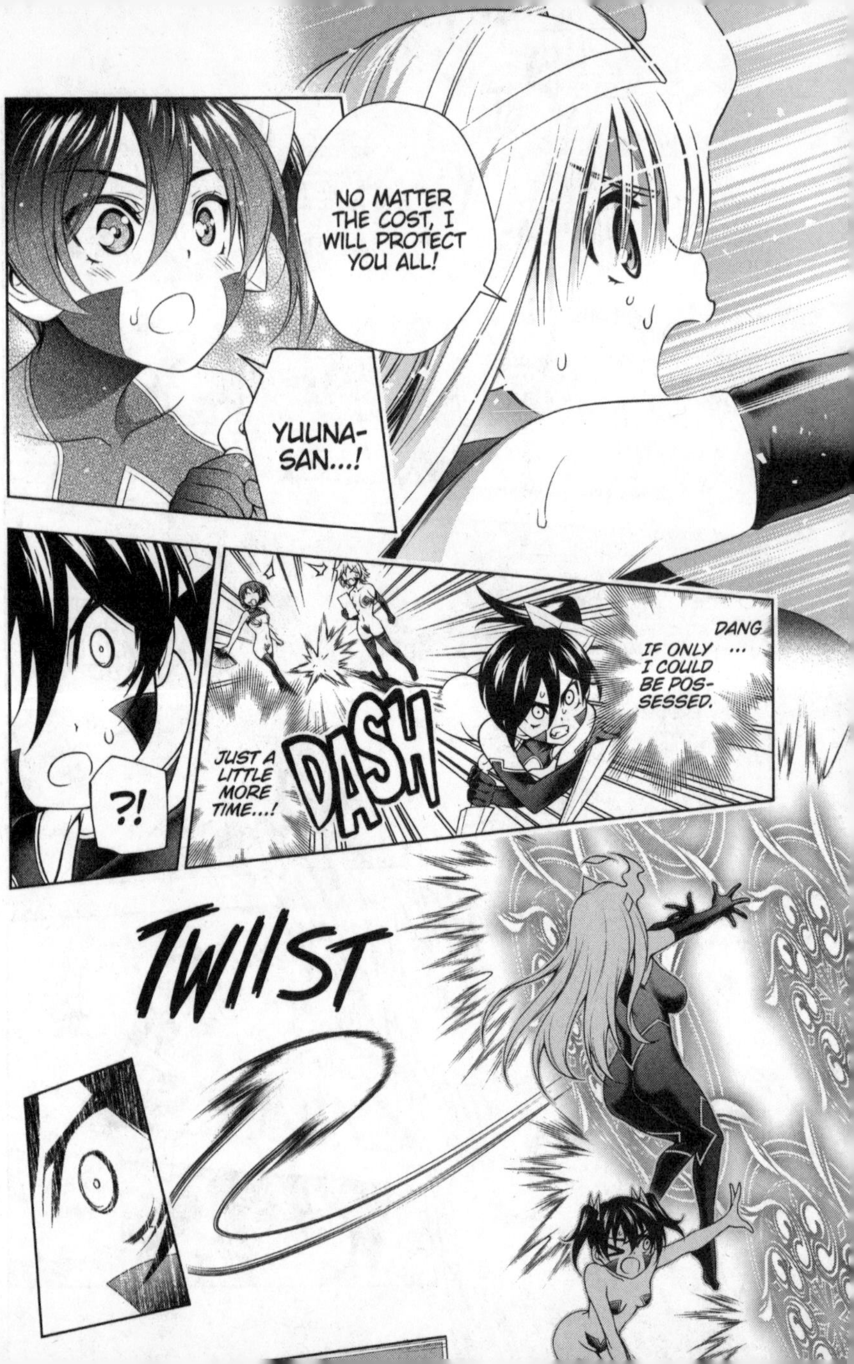

NO MATTER THE COST, I WILL PROTECT YOU ALL!
YUUNA-SAN...!
DANG ... IF ONLY I COULD BE POS-SESSED.
DASH
JUST A LITTLE MORE TIME...!
?!
TWIIST

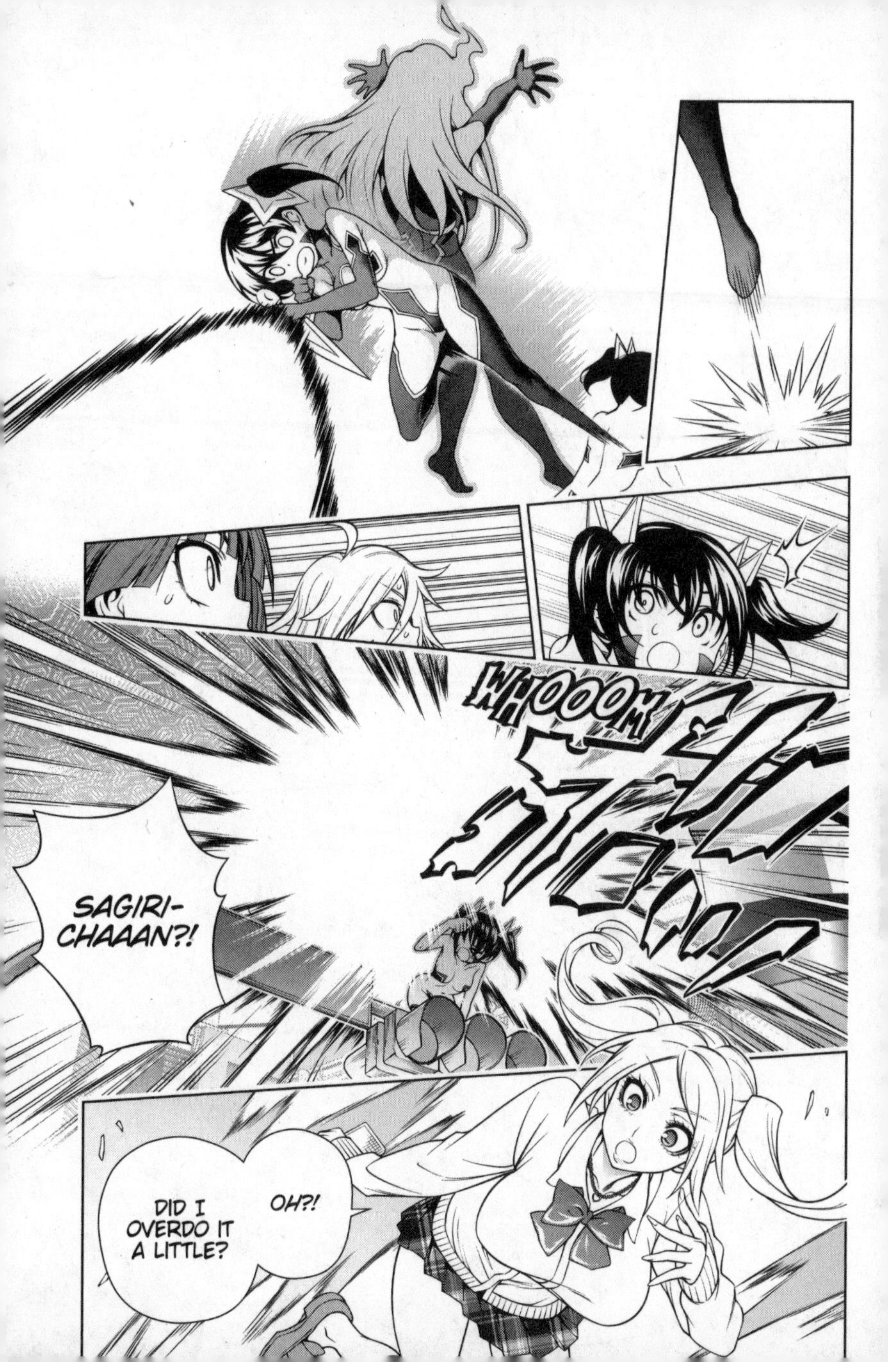
WHOOOM
SAGIRI-CHAAAN?!
OH?!
DID I OVERDO IT A LITTLE?

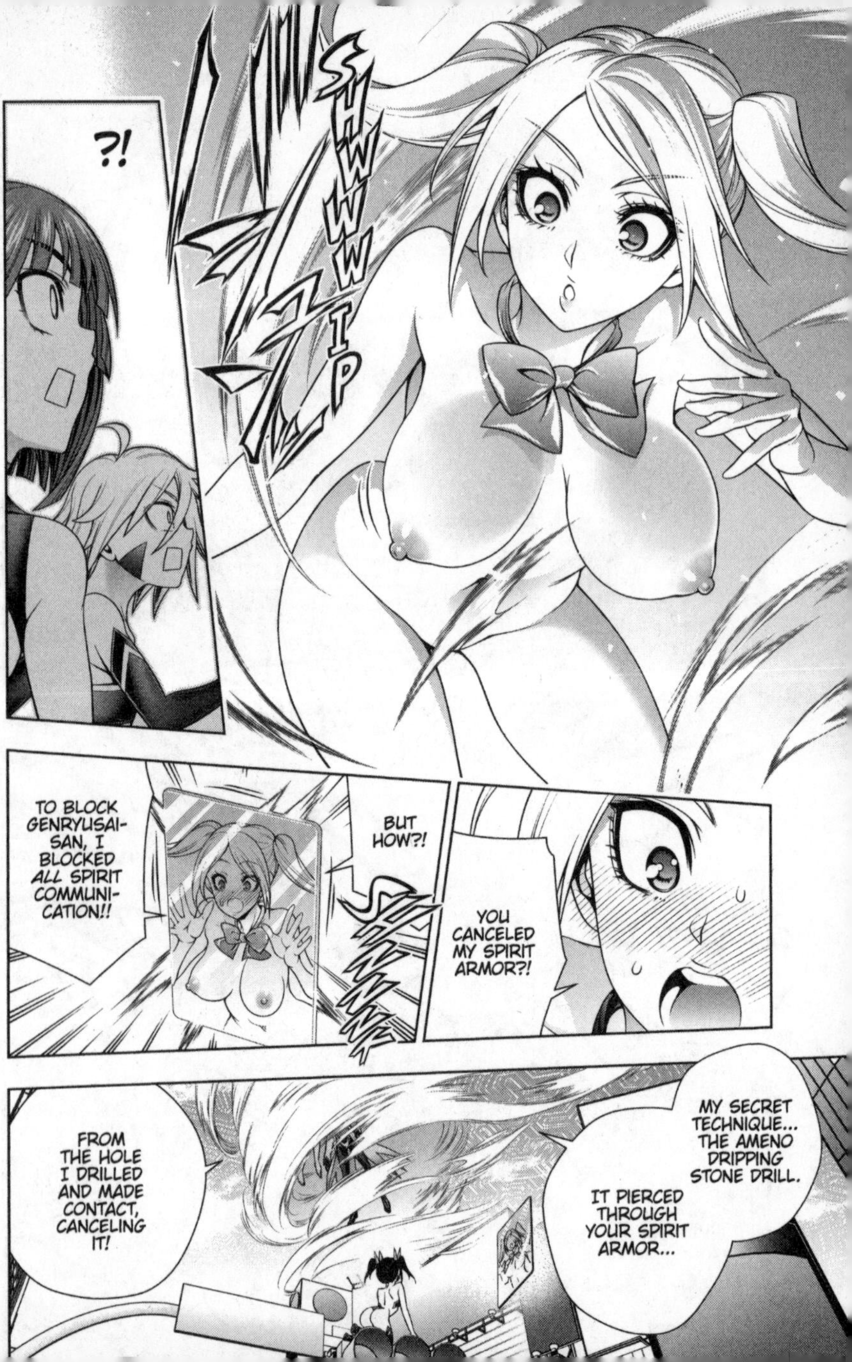
SHWWWWZIP
?!
YOU CANCELED MY SPIRIT ARMOR?!
BUT HOW?!
TO BLOCK GENRYUSAI-SAN, I BLOCKED ALL SPIRIT COMMUNICATION!!
MY SECRET TECHNIQUE... THE AMENO DRIPPING STONE DRILL.
IT PIERCED THROUGH YOUR SPIRIT ARMOR...
FROM THE HOLE I DRILLED AND MADE CONTACT, CANCELING IT!

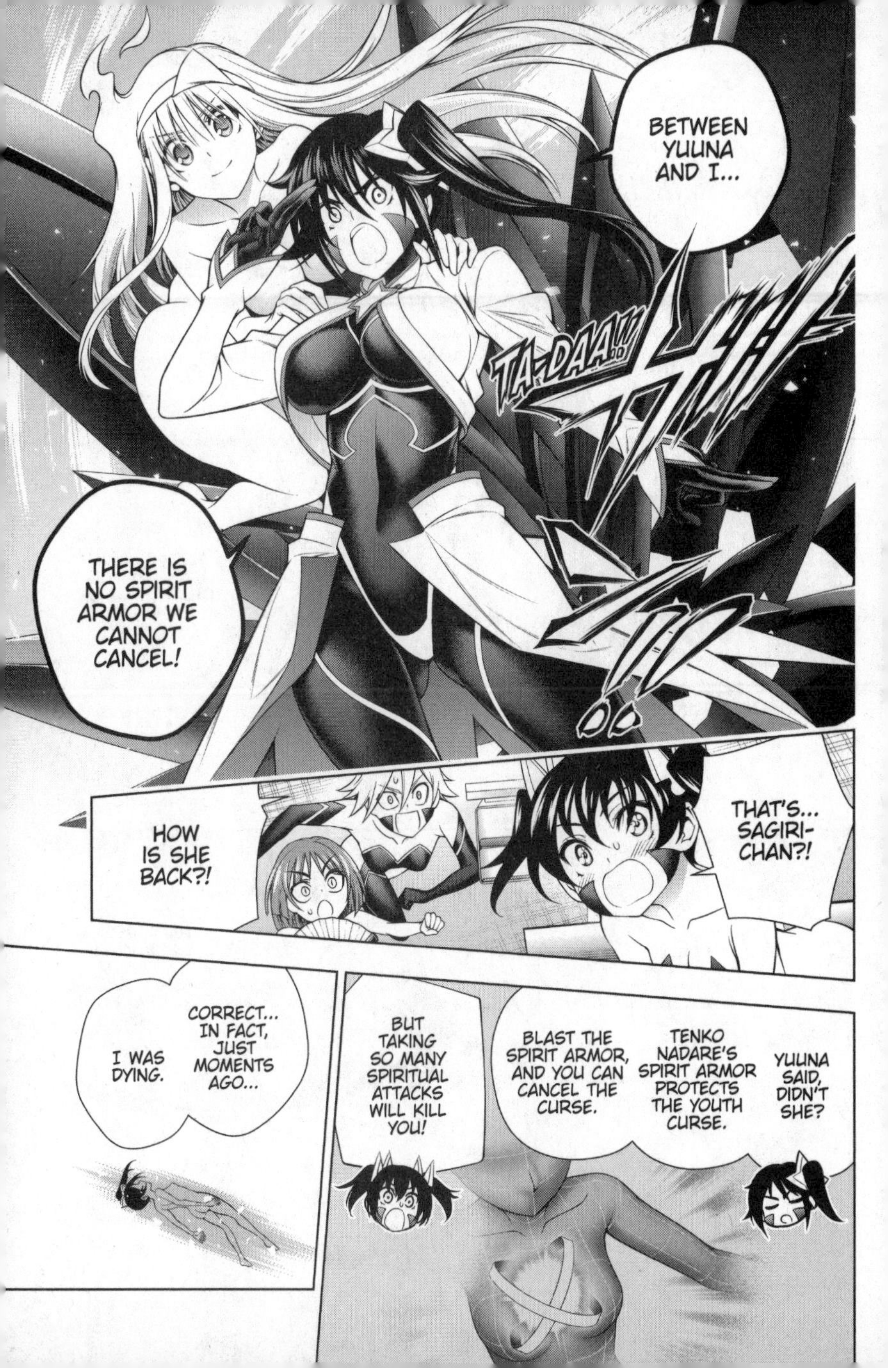
BETWEEN YUUNA AND I...
TA-DAA!!
THERE IS NO SPIRIT ARMOR WE CANNOT CANCEL!
THAT'S... SAGIRI-CHAN?!
HOW IS SHE BACK?!
YUUNA SAID, DIDN'T SHE?
TENKO NADARE'S SPIRIT ARMOR PROTECTS THE YOUTH CURSE.
BLAST THE SPIRIT ARMOR, AND YOU CAN CANCEL THE CURSE.
BUT TAKING SO MANY SPIRITUAL ATTACKS WILL KILL YOU!
CORRECT... IN FACT, JUST MOMENTS AGO...
I WAS DYING.

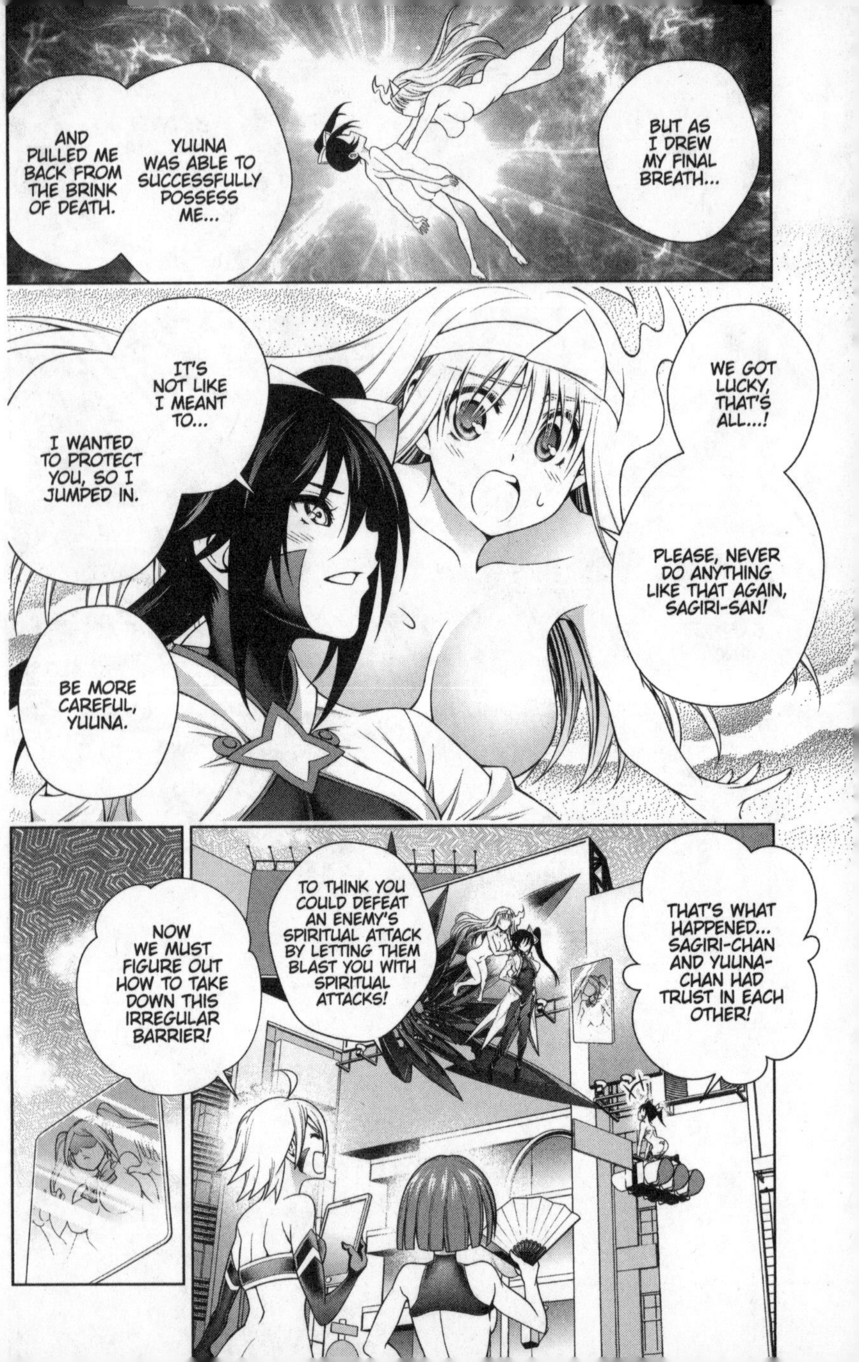
BUT AS I DREW MY FINAL BREATH...
YUUNA WAS ABLE TO SUCCESSFULLY POSSESS ME...
AND PULLED ME BACK FROM THE BRINK OF DEATH.
WE GOT LUCKY, THAT'S ALL...!
PLEASE, NEVER DO ANYTHING LIKE THAT AGAIN, SAGIRI-SAN!
IT'S NOT LIKE I MEANT TO...
I WANTED TO PROTECT YOU, SO I JUMPED IN.
BE MORE CAREFUL, YUUNA.
THAT'S WHAT HAPPENED... SAGIRI-CHAN AND YUUNA-CHAN HAD TRUST IN EACH OTHER!
TO THINK YOU COULD DEFEAT AN ENEMY'S SPIRITUAL ATTACK BY LETTING THEM BLAST YOU WITH SPIRITUAL ATTACKS!
NOW WE MUST FIGURE OUT HOW TO TAKE DOWN THIS IRREGULAR BARRIER!

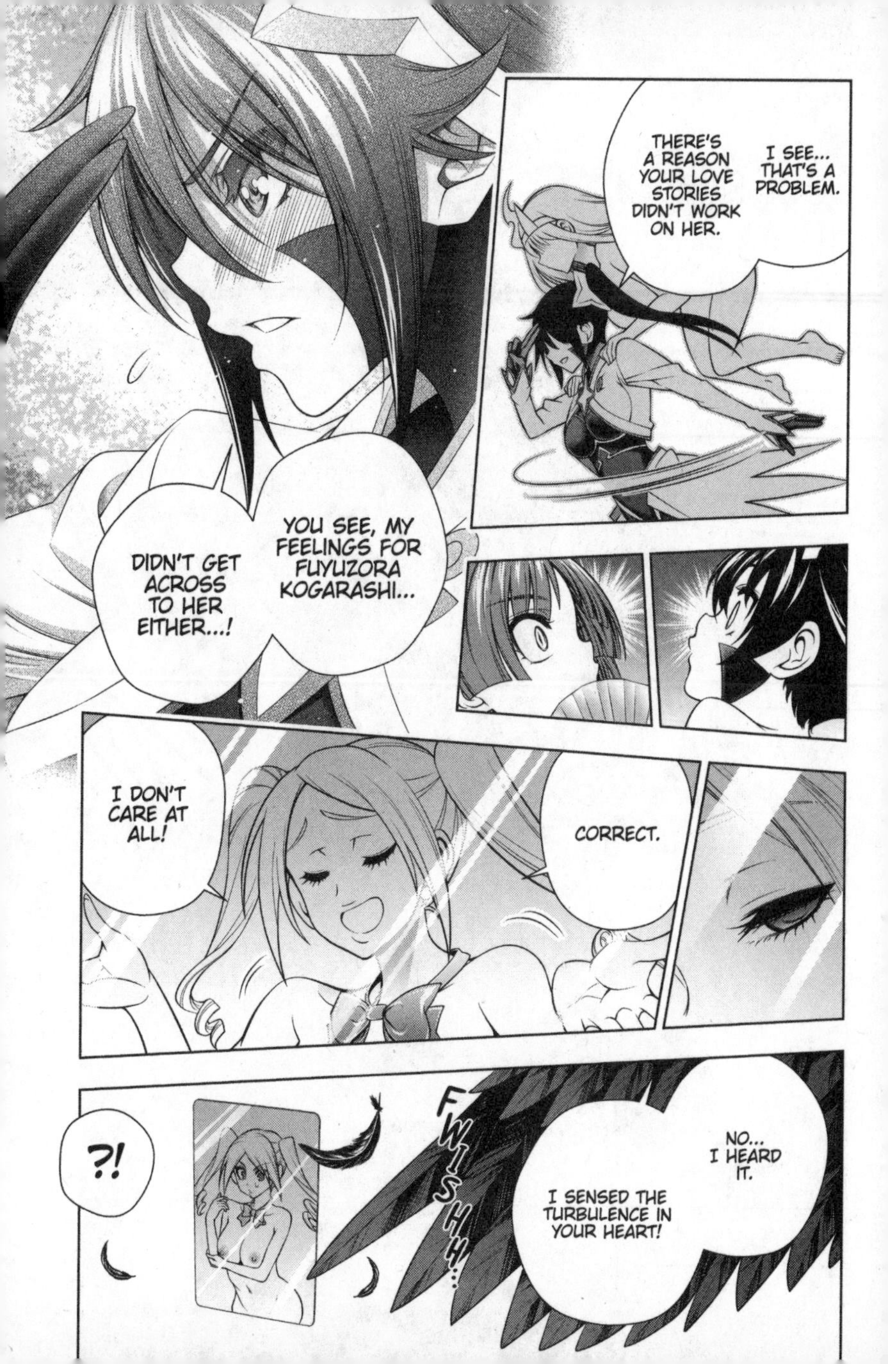
I SEE... THAT'S A PROBLEM.
THERE'S A REASON YOUR LOVE STORIES DIDN'T WORK ON HER.
YOU SEE, MY FEELINGS FOR FUYUZORA KOGARASHI...
DIDN'T GET ACROSS TO HER EITHER...!
CORRECT.
I DON'T CARE AT ALL!
NO... I HEARD IT.
I SENSED THE TURBULENCE IN YOUR HEART!
FWISHH...
?!

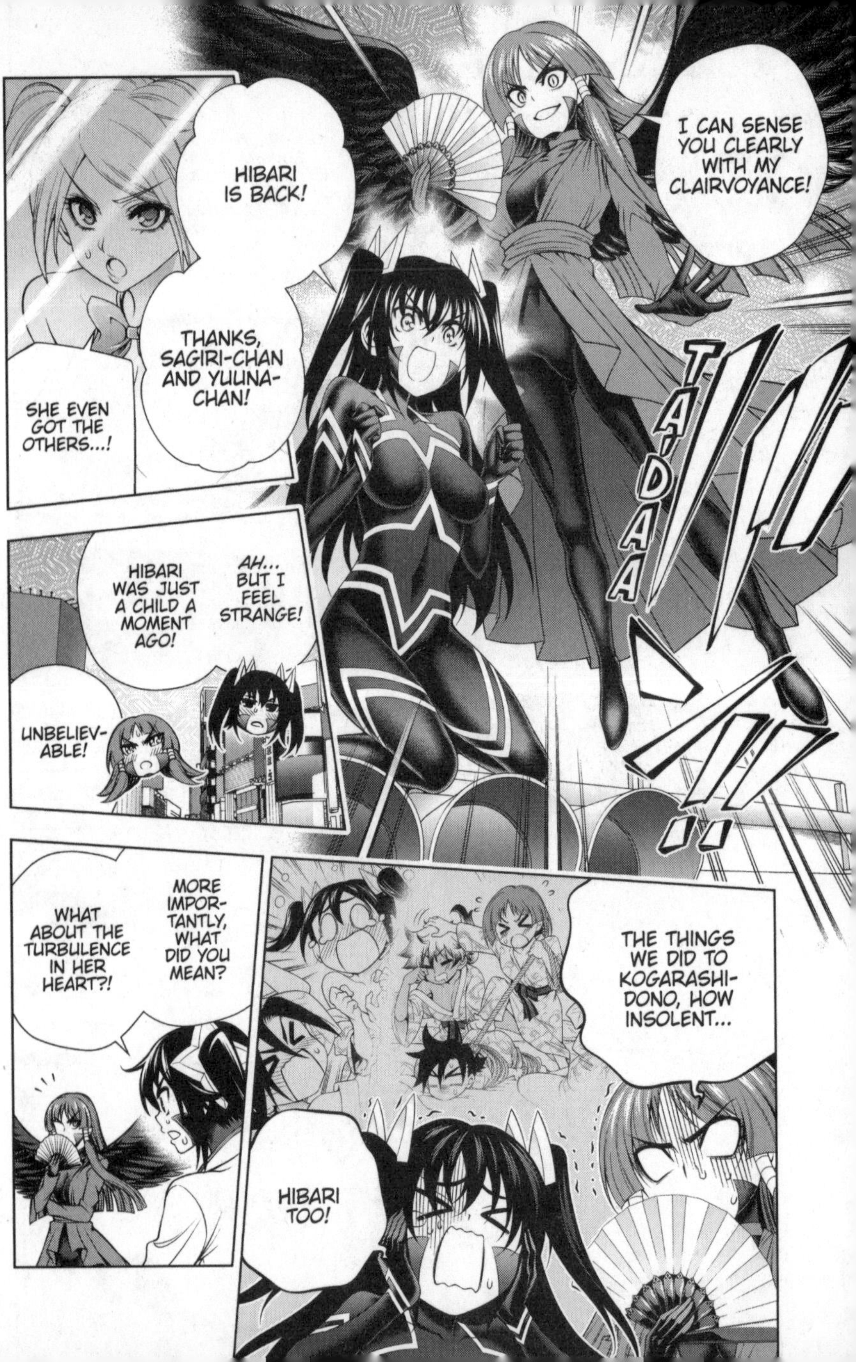
I CAN SENSE YOU CLEARLY WITH MY CLAIRVOYANCE!
TA-DAAA!!
THANKS, SAGIRI-CHAN AND YUUNA-CHAN!
HIBARI IS BACK!
SHE EVEN GOT THE OTHERS...!
AH... BUT I FEEL STRANGE!
HIBARI WAS JUST A CHILD A MOMENT AGO!
UNBELIEV-ABLE!
THE THINGS WE DID TO KOGARASHI-DONO, HOW INSOLENT...
HIBARI TOO!
MORE IMPOR-TANTLY, WHAT DID YOU MEAN?
WHAT ABOUT THE TURBULENCE IN HER HEART?!

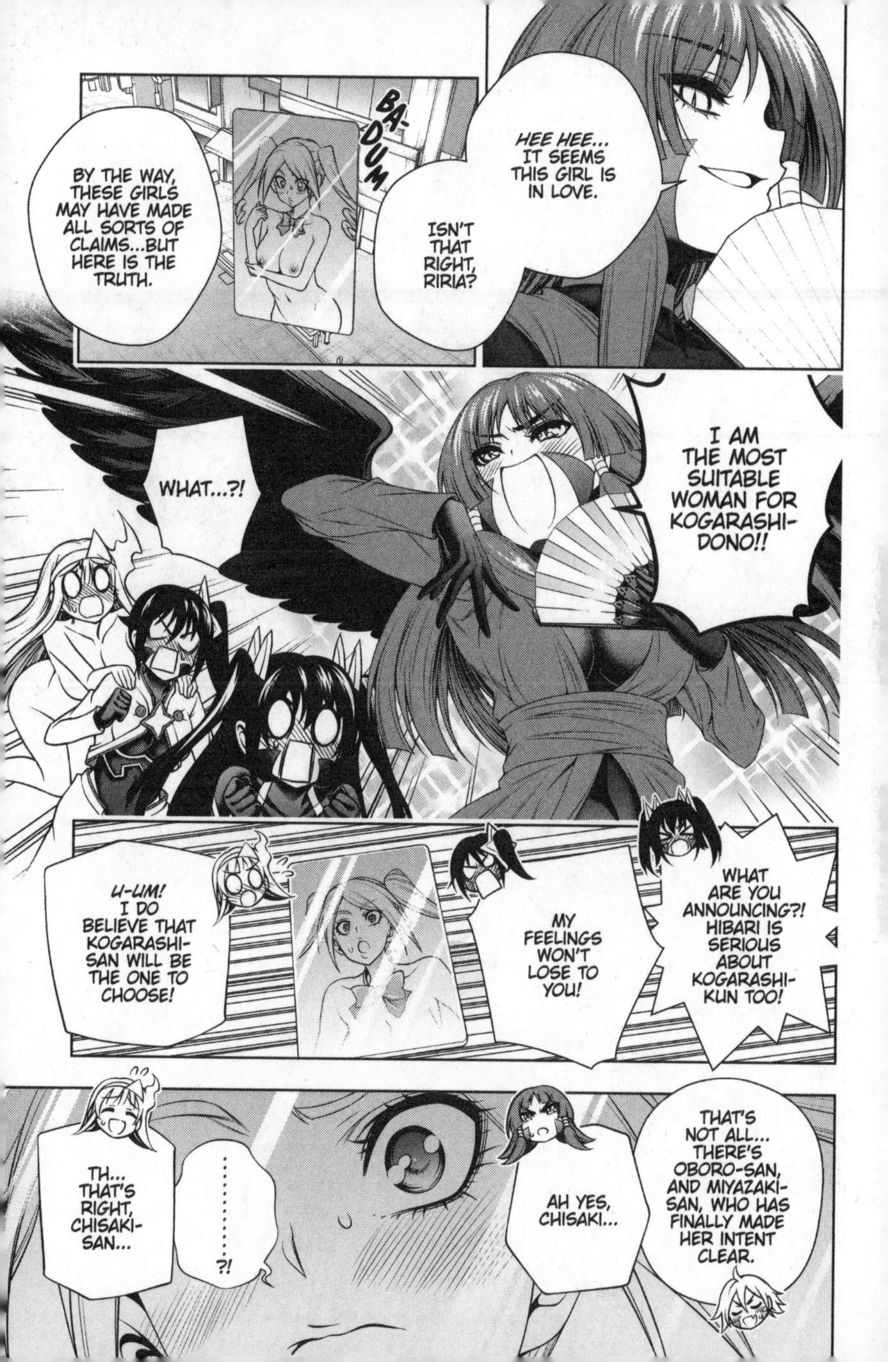
HEE HEE... IT SEEMS THIS GIRL IS IN LOVE.
ISN'T THAT RIGHT, RIRIA?
BA-DUM
BY THE WAY, THESE GIRLS MAY HAVE MADE ALL SORTS OF CLAIMS...BUT HERE IS THE TRUTH.
I AM THE MOST SUITABLE WOMAN FOR KOGARASHI-DONO!!
WHAT...?!
WHAT ARE YOU ANNOUNCING?! HIBARI IS SERIOUS ABOUT KOGARASHI-KUN TOO!
MY FEELINGS WON'T LOSE TO YOU!
U-UM! I DO BELIEVE THAT KOGARASHI-SAN WILL BE THE ONE TO CHOOSE!
THAT'S NOT ALL... THERE'S OBORO-SAN, AND MIYAZAKI-SAN, WHO HAS FINALLY MADE HER INTENT CLEAR.
AH YES, CHISAKI...
......
?!
TH... THAT'S RIGHT, CHISAKI-SAN...

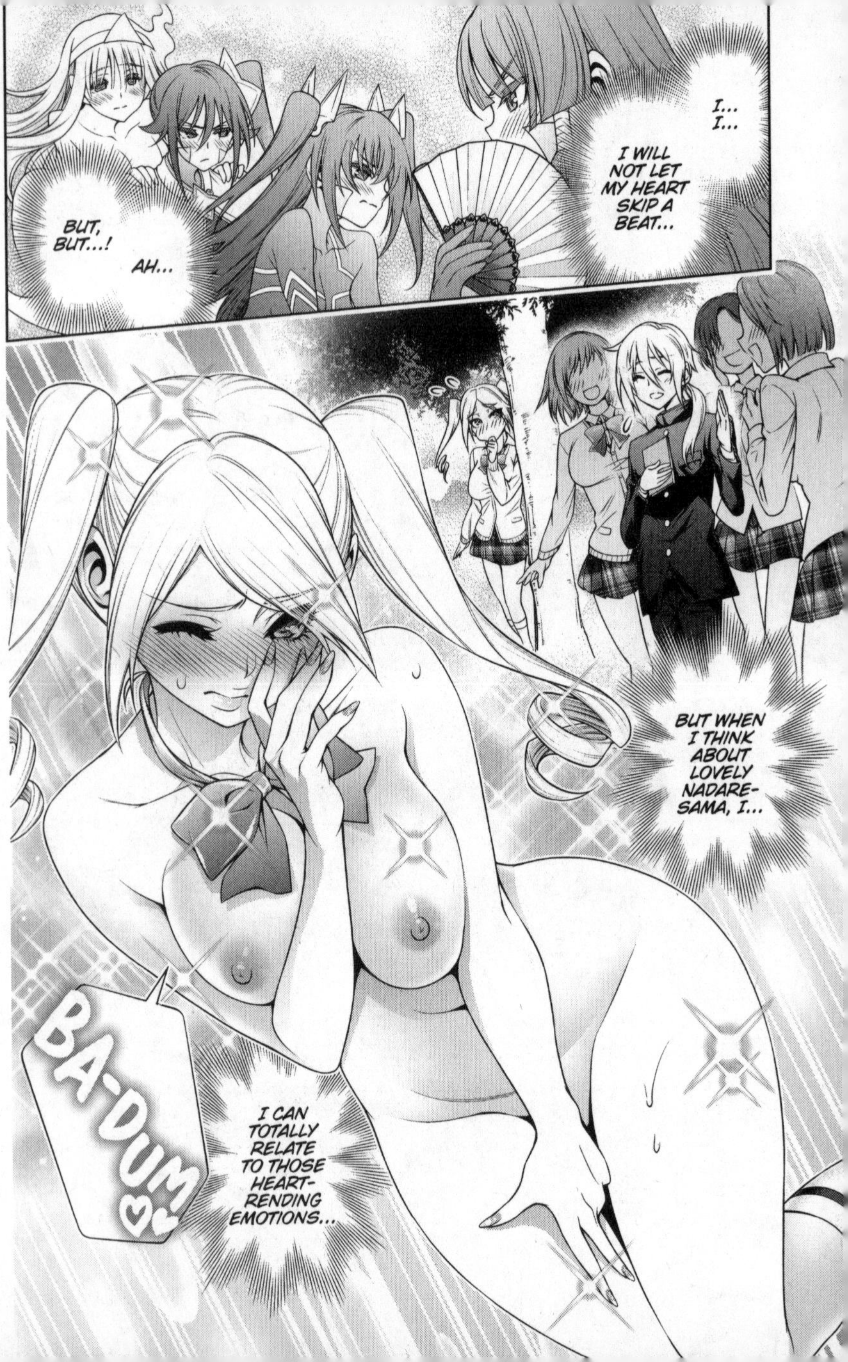
I...
I...
I WILL NOT LET MY HEART SKIP A BEAT...
BUT, BUT...!
AH...
BUT WHEN I THINK ABOUT LOVELY NADARE-SAMA, I...
I CAN TOTALLY RELATE TO THOSE HEART-RENDING EMOTIONS...
BA-DUM♡

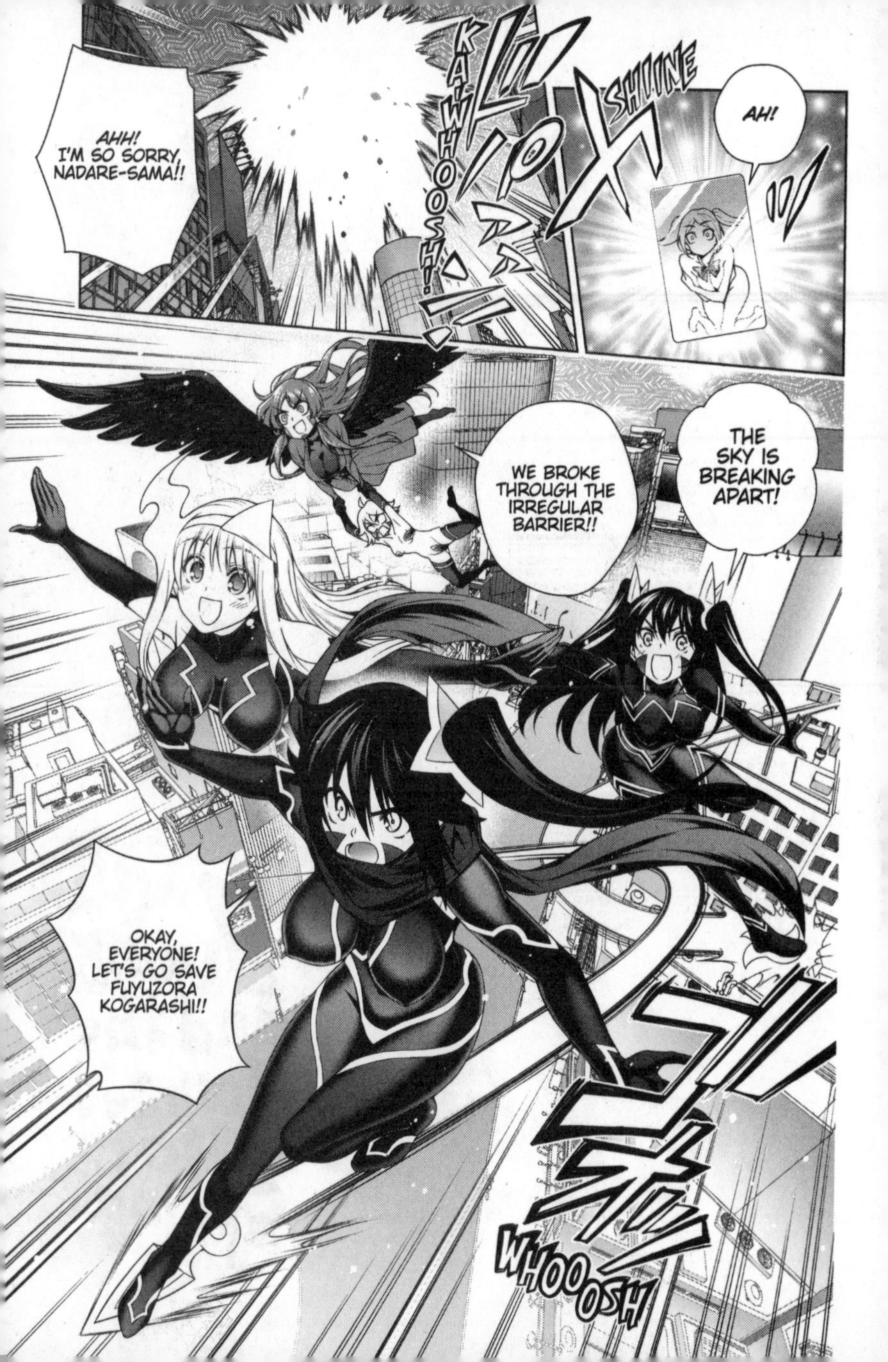

AH!
SHIINE
KAWHOOOSH!
AHH! I'M SO SORRY, NADARE-SAMA!!
THE SKY IS BREAKING APART!
WE BROKE THROUGH THE IRREGULAR BARRIER!!
OKAY, EVERYONE! LET'S GO SAVE FUYUZORA KOGARASHI!!
WHOOOOSH

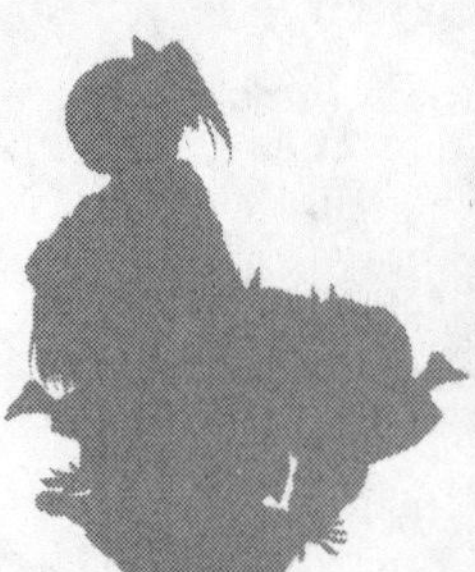

Yuuna and the Haunted Hot Springs

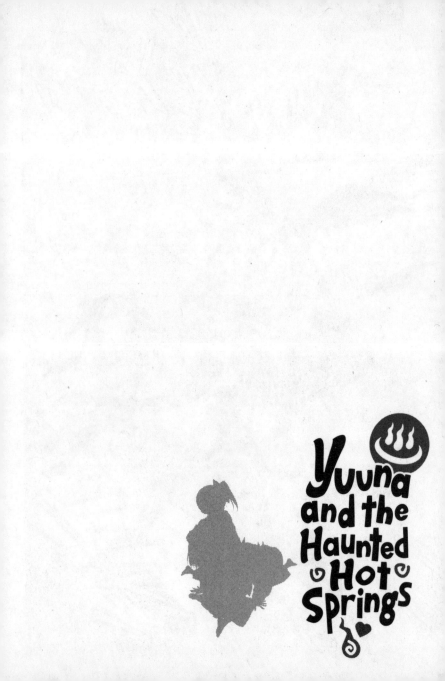

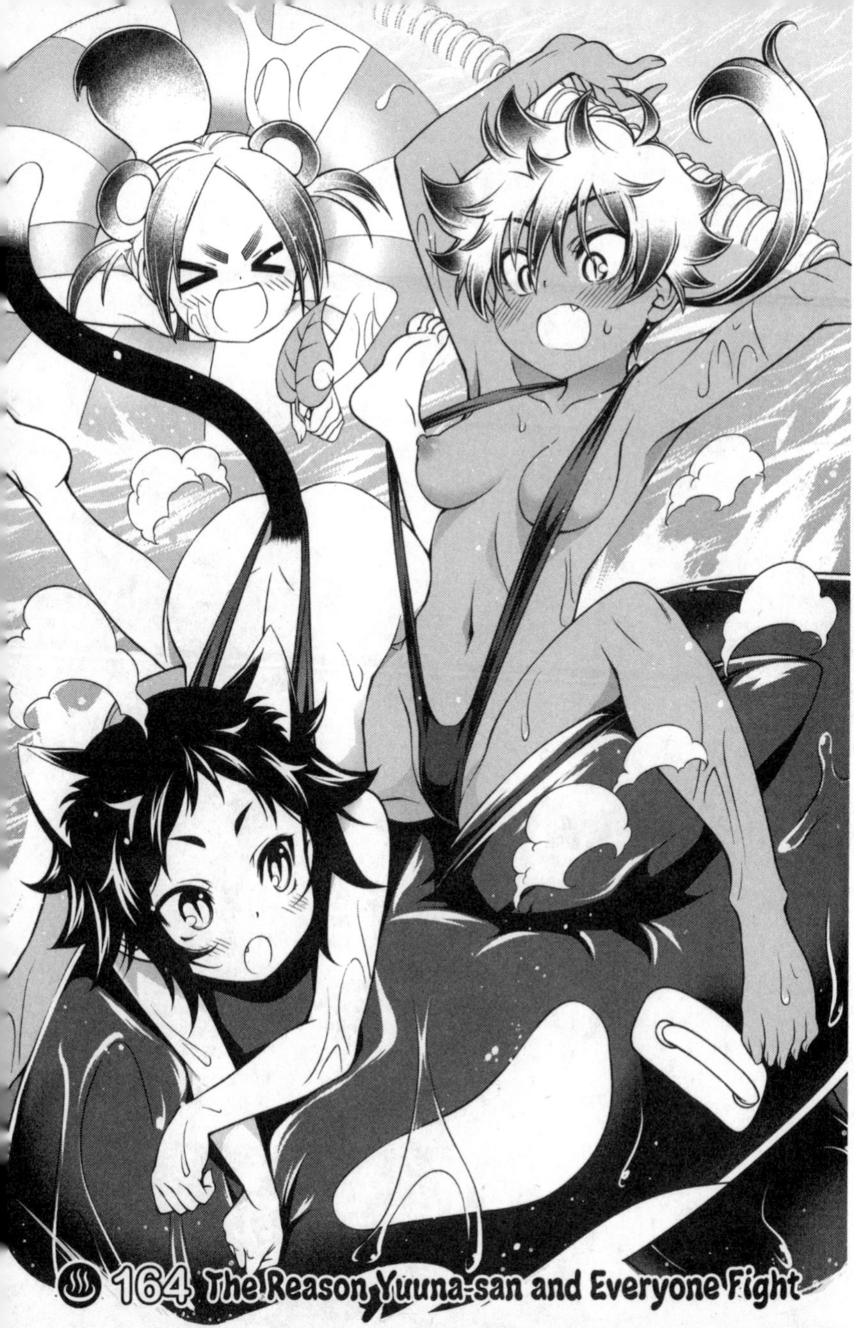
164 The Reason Yuuna-san and Everyone Fight

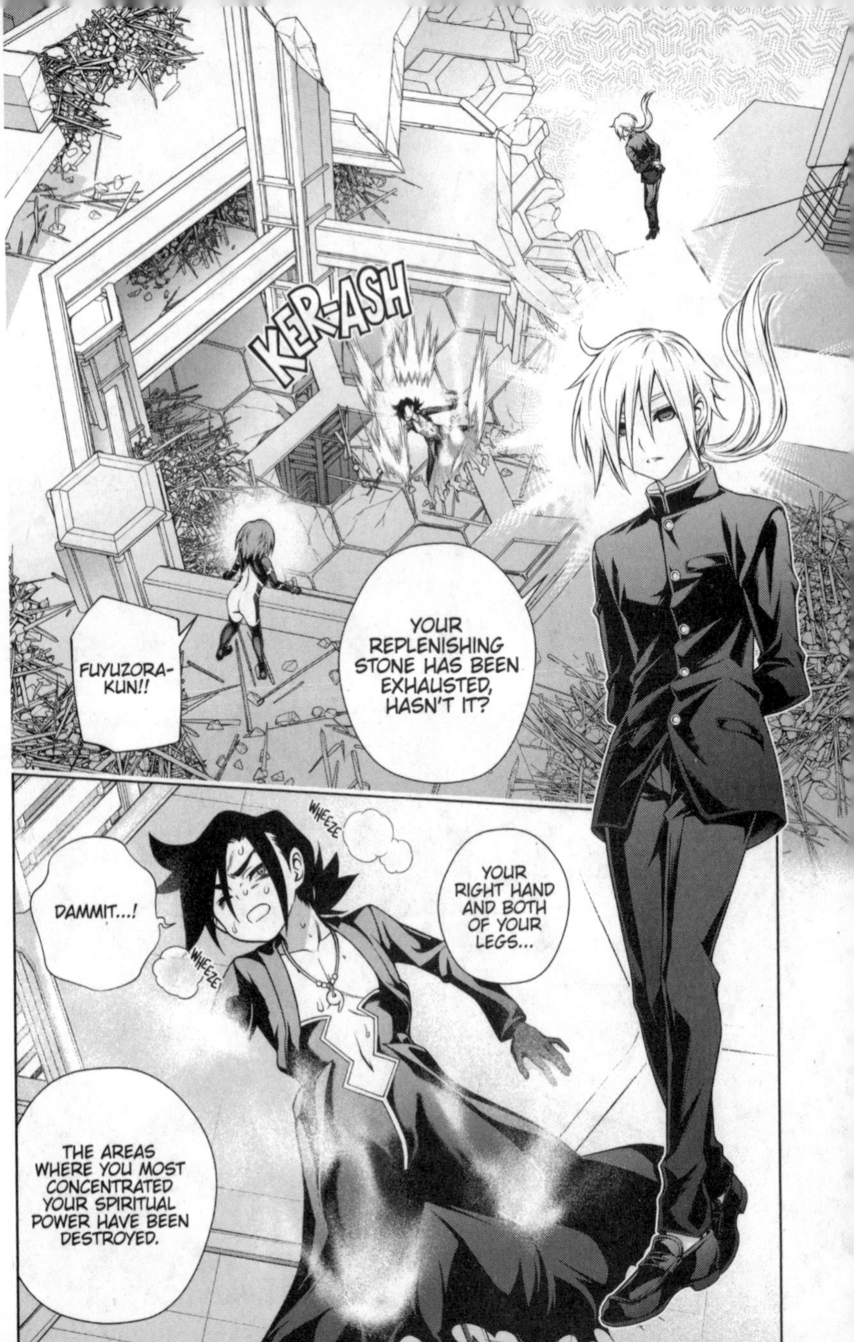
KER-ASH
YOUR REPLENISHING STONE HAS BEEN EXHAUSTED, HASN'T IT?
FUYUZORA-KUN!!
WHEEZE
YOUR RIGHT HAND AND BOTH OF YOUR LEGS...
DAMMIT...!
WHEEZE
THE AREAS WHERE YOU MOST CONCENTRATED YOUR SPIRITUAL POWER HAVE BEEN DESTROYED.

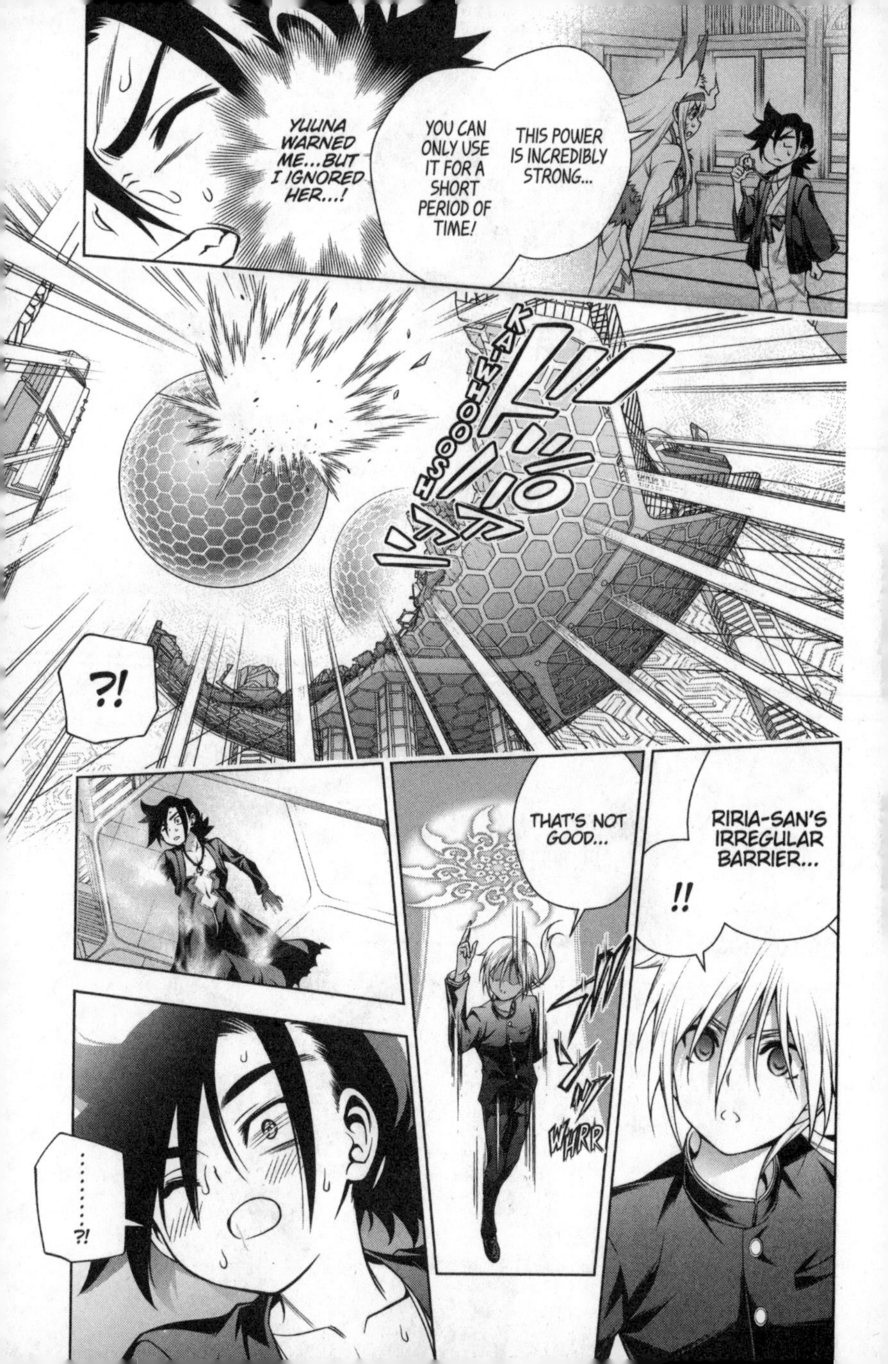
THIS POWER IS INCREDIBLY STRONG...
YOU CAN ONLY USE IT FOR A SHORT PERIOD OF TIME!
YUUNA WARNED ME...BUT I IGNORED HER...!
KA-WHOOOOSH
?!
RIRIA-SAN'S IRREGULAR BARRIER...
!!
THAT'S NOT GOOD...
WHRR
........?!

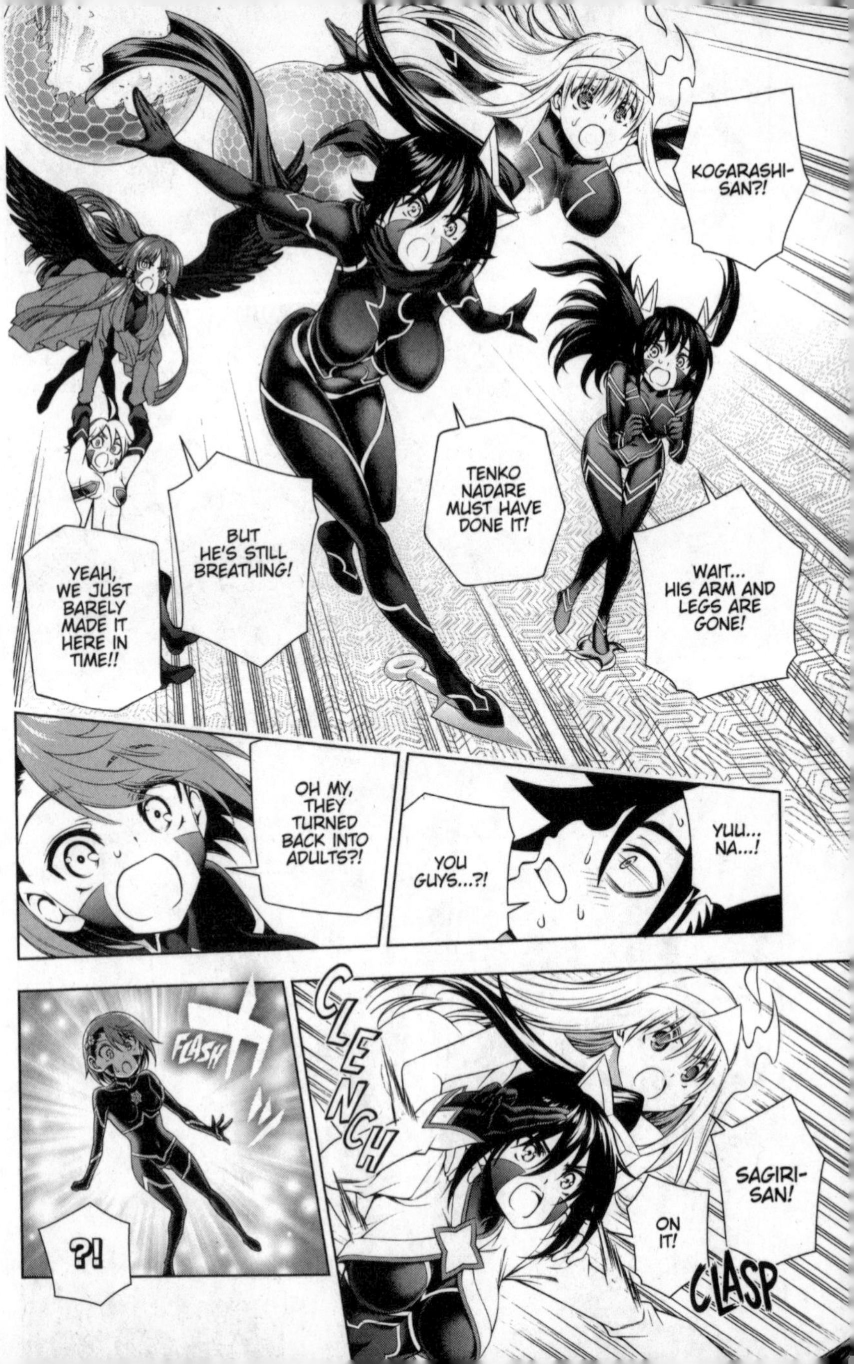
KOGARASHI-SAN?!
WAIT... HIS ARM AND LEGS ARE GONE!
TENKO NADARE MUST HAVE DONE IT!
BUT HE'S STILL BREATHING!
YEAH, WE JUST BARELY MADE IT HERE IN TIME!!
YUU... NA...!
YOU GUYS...?!
OH MY, THEY TURNED BACK INTO ADULTS?!
CLENCH
SAGIRI-SAN!
ON IT!
CLASP
FLASH
?!

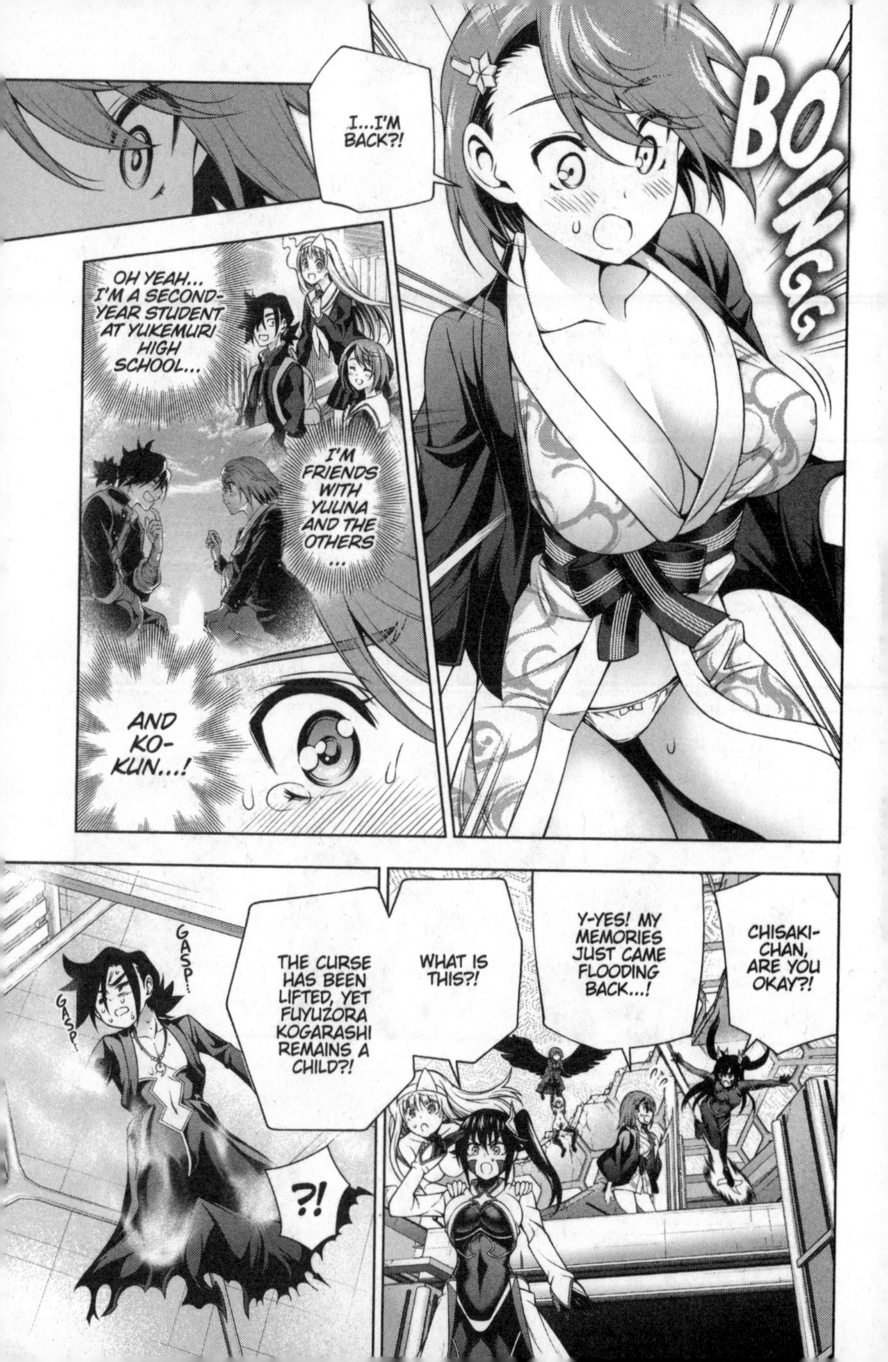

BOINGG
I...I'M BACK?!
OH YEAH... I'M A SECOND-YEAR STUDENT AT YUKEMURI HIGH SCHOOL...
I'M FRIENDS WITH YUUNA AND THE OTHERS...
AND KO-KUN...!
CHISAKI-CHAN, ARE YOU OKAY?!
Y-YES! MY MEMORIES JUST CAME FLOODING BACK...!
WHAT IS THIS?!
THE CURSE HAS BEEN LIFTED, YET FUYUZORA KOGARASHI REMAINS A CHILD?!
?!
GASP...
GASP...

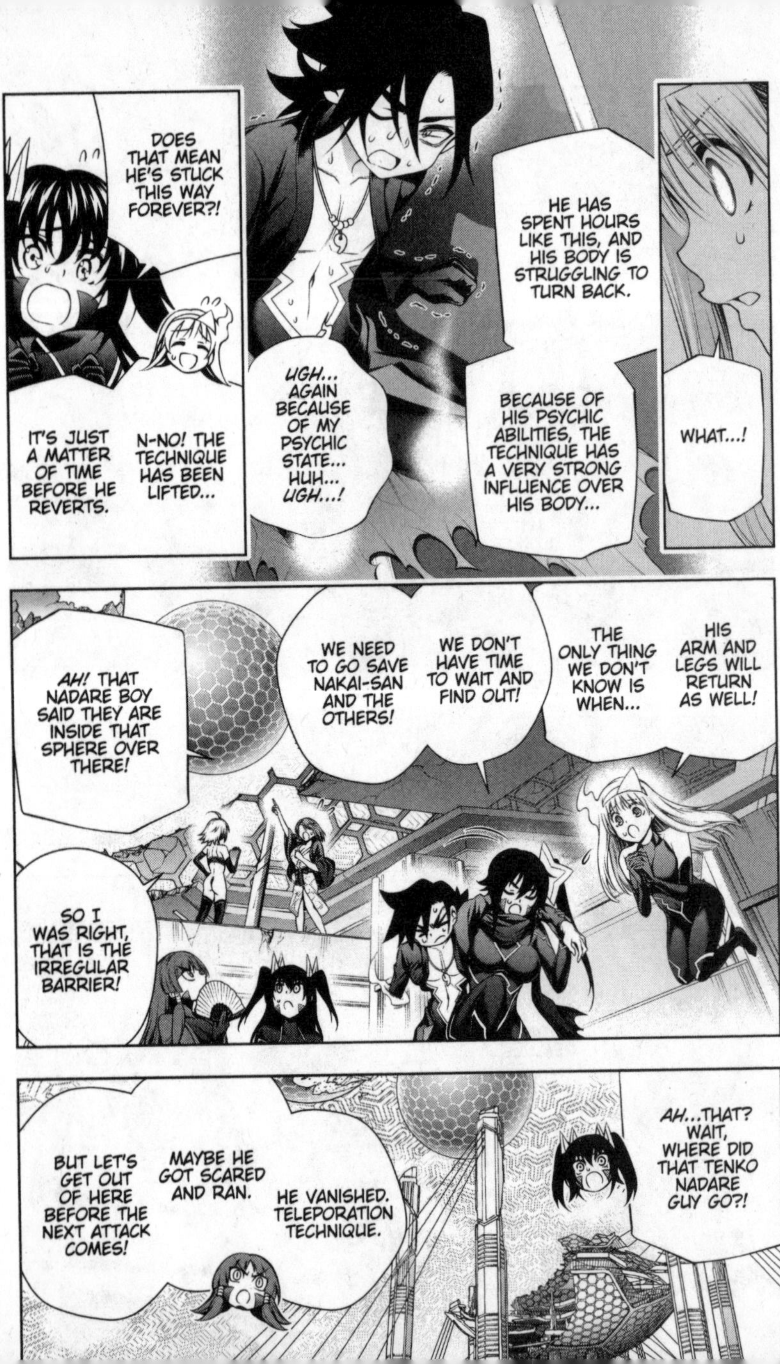

WHAT...!
HE HAS SPENT HOURS LIKE THIS, AND HIS BODY IS STRUGGLING TO TURN BACK.
BECAUSE OF HIS PSYCHIC ABILITIES, THE TECHNIQUE HAS A VERY STRONG INFLUENCE OVER HIS BODY...
UGH... AGAIN BECAUSE OF MY PSYCHIC STATE... HUH... *UGH...!*
DOES THAT MEAN HE'S STUCK THIS WAY FOREVER?!
N-NO! THE TECHNIQUE HAS BEEN LIFTED...
IT'S JUST A MATTER OF TIME BEFORE HE REVERTS.
HIS ARM AND LEGS WILL RETURN AS WELL!
THE ONLY THING WE DON'T KNOW IS WHEN...
WE DON'T HAVE TIME TO WAIT AND FIND OUT!
WE NEED TO GO SAVE NAKAI-SAN AND THE OTHERS!
AH! THAT NADARE BOY SAID THEY ARE INSIDE THAT SPHERE OVER THERE!
SO I WAS RIGHT, THAT IS THE IRREGULAR BARRIER!
*AH...*THAT? WAIT, WHERE DID THAT TENKO NADARE GUY GO?!
HE VANISHED. TELEPORATION TECHNIQUE.
MAYBE HE GOT SCARED AND RAN.
BUT LET'S GET OUT OF HERE BEFORE THE NEXT ATTACK COMES!

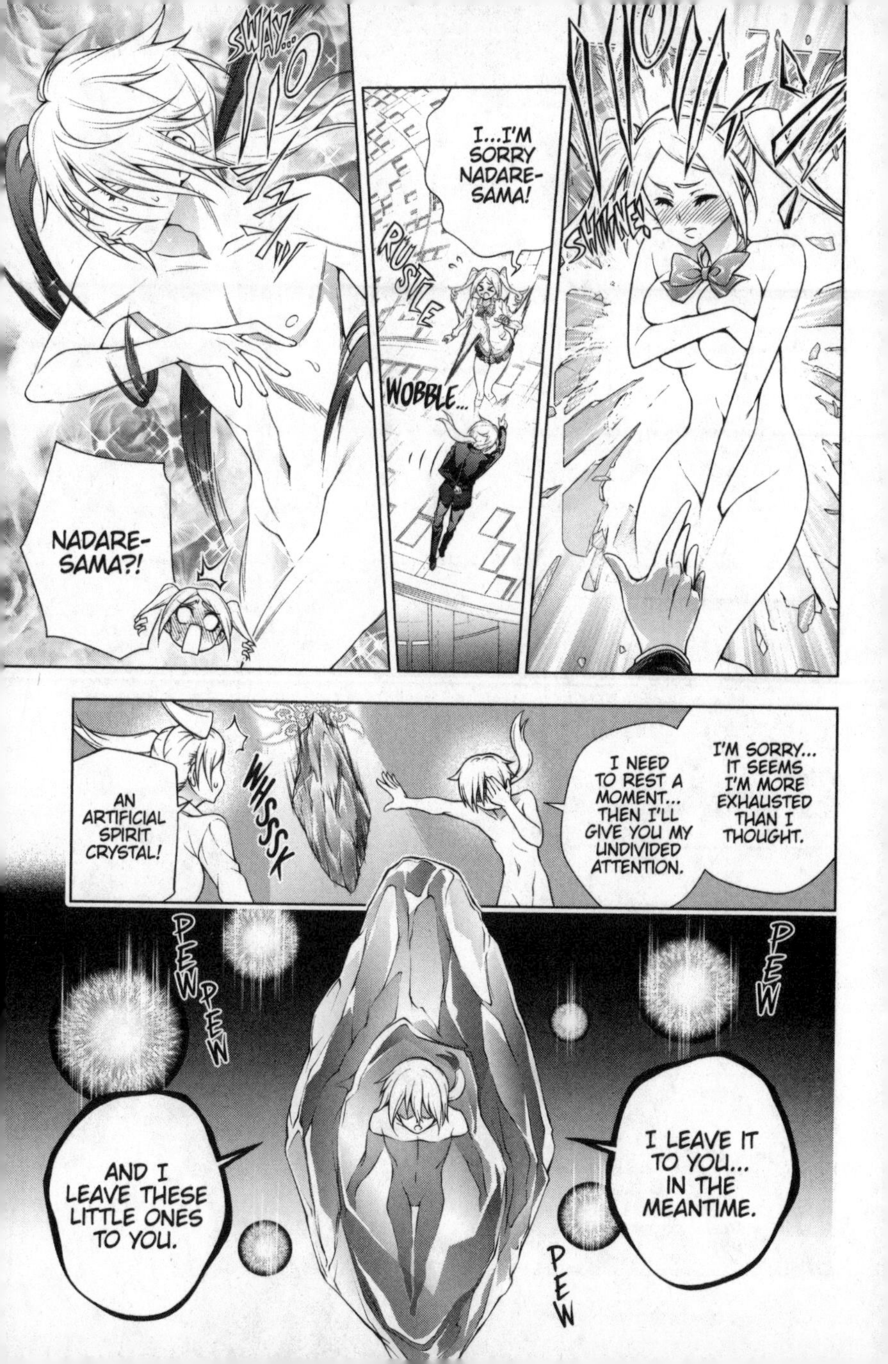
SHIIINE!
I...I'M SORRY NADARE-SAMA!
RUSTLE
WOBBLE...
SWAY...
NADARE-SAMA?!
I'M SORRY... IT SEEMS I'M MORE EXHAUSTED THAN I THOUGHT.
I NEED TO REST A MOMENT... THEN I'LL GIVE YOU MY UNDIVIDED ATTENTION.
WHSSSK
AN ARTIFICIAL SPIRIT CRYSTAL!
PEW
I LEAVE IT TO YOU... IN THE MEANTIME.
PEW
AND I LEAVE THESE LITTLE ONES TO YOU.
PEWPEWPEW

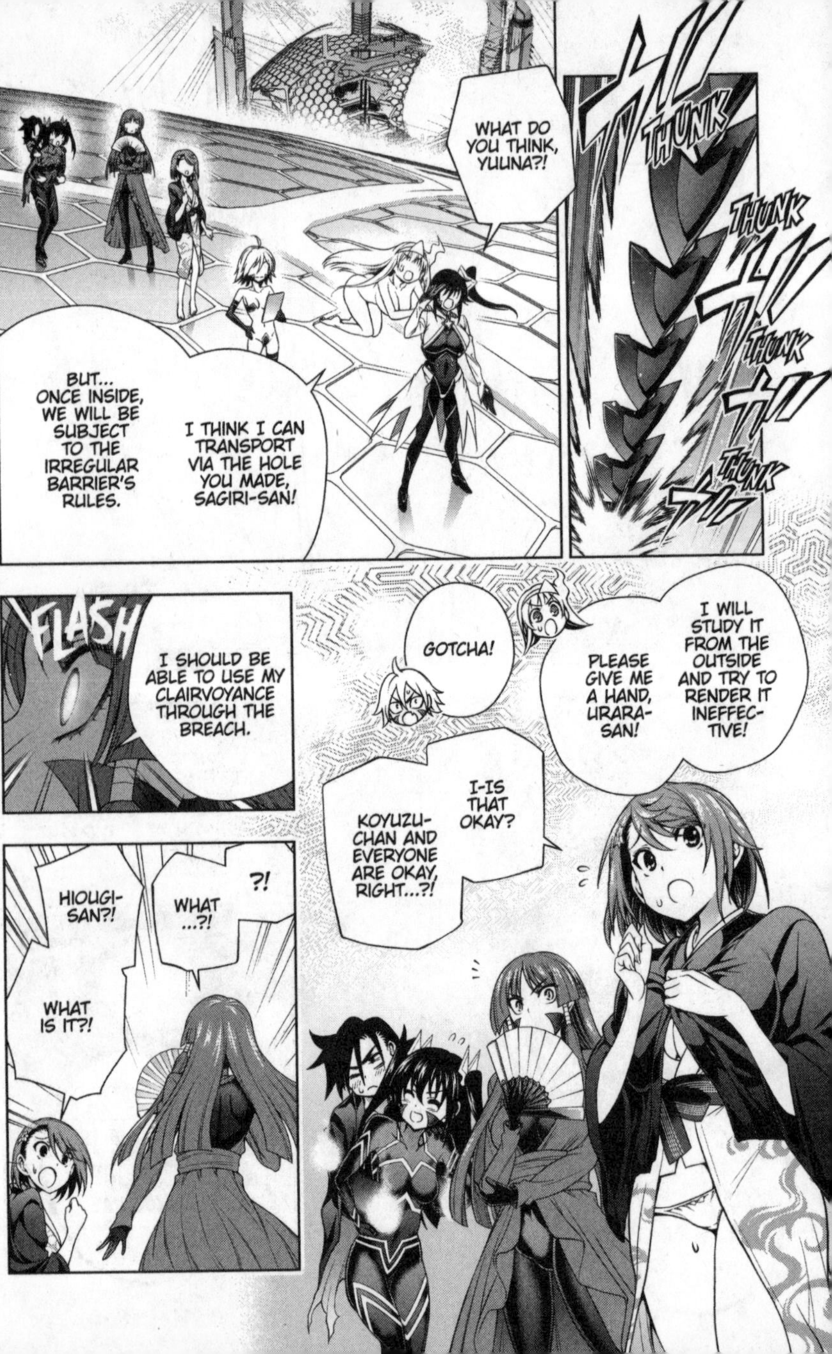
THUNK
THUNK
THUNK
THUNK
WHAT DO YOU THINK, YUUNA?!
I THINK I CAN TRANSPORT VIA THE HOLE YOU MADE, SAGIRI-SAN!
BUT... ONCE INSIDE, WE WILL BE SUBJECT TO THE IRREGULAR BARRIER'S RULES.
I WILL STUDY IT FROM THE OUTSIDE AND TRY TO RENDER IT INEFFECTIVE!
PLEASE GIVE ME A HAND, URARA-SAN!
GOTCHA!
I-IS THAT OKAY?
KOYUZU-CHAN AND EVERYONE ARE OKAY, RIGHT...?!
FLASH
I SHOULD BE ABLE TO USE MY CLAIRVOYANCE THROUGH THE BREACH.
?!
WHAT ...?!
HIOUGI-SAN?!
WHAT IS IT?!

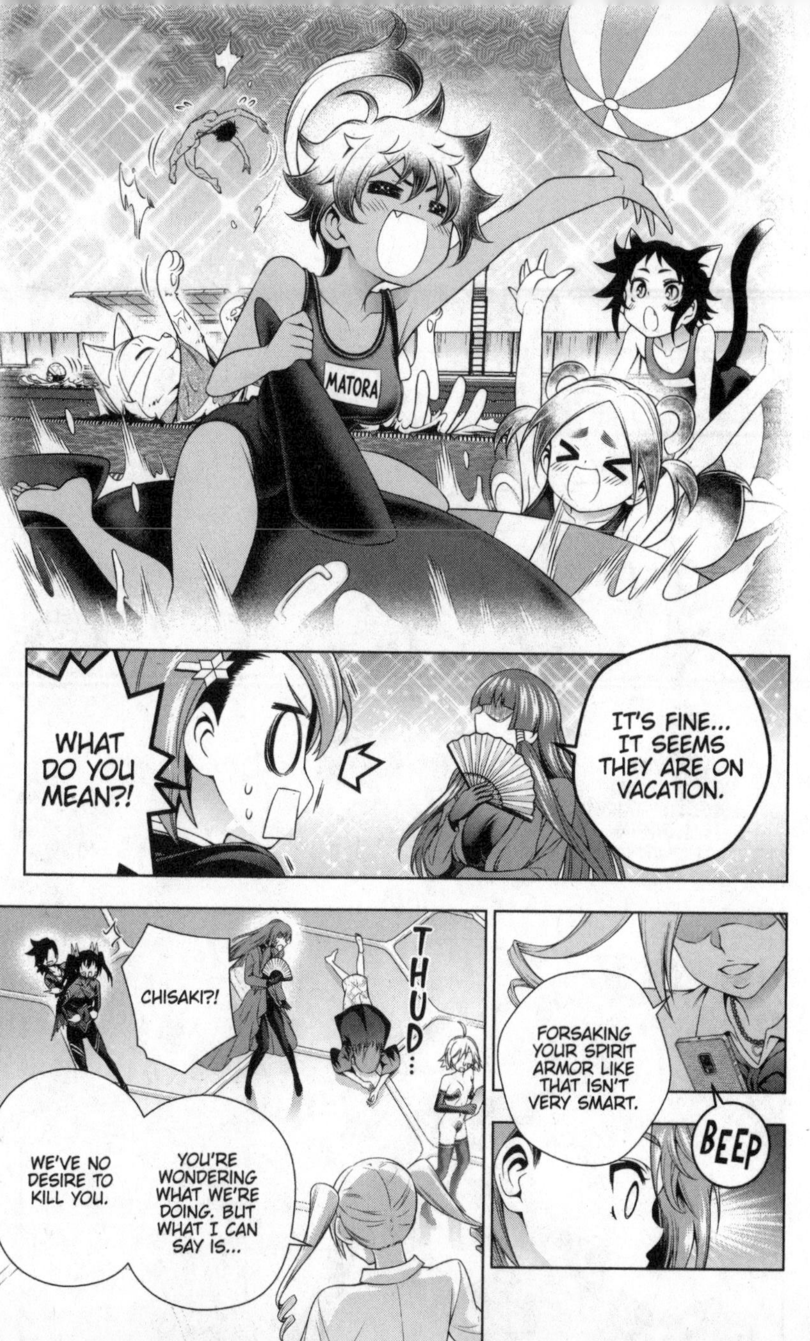
MATORA
IT'S FINE... IT SEEMS THEY ARE ON VACATION.
WHAT DO YOU MEAN?!
FORSAKING YOUR SPIRIT ARMOR LIKE THAT ISN'T VERY SMART.
BEEP
THUD...
CHISAKI?!
YOU'RE WONDERING WHAT WE'RE DOING. BUT WHAT I CAN SAY IS...
WE'VE NO DESIRE TO KILL YOU.

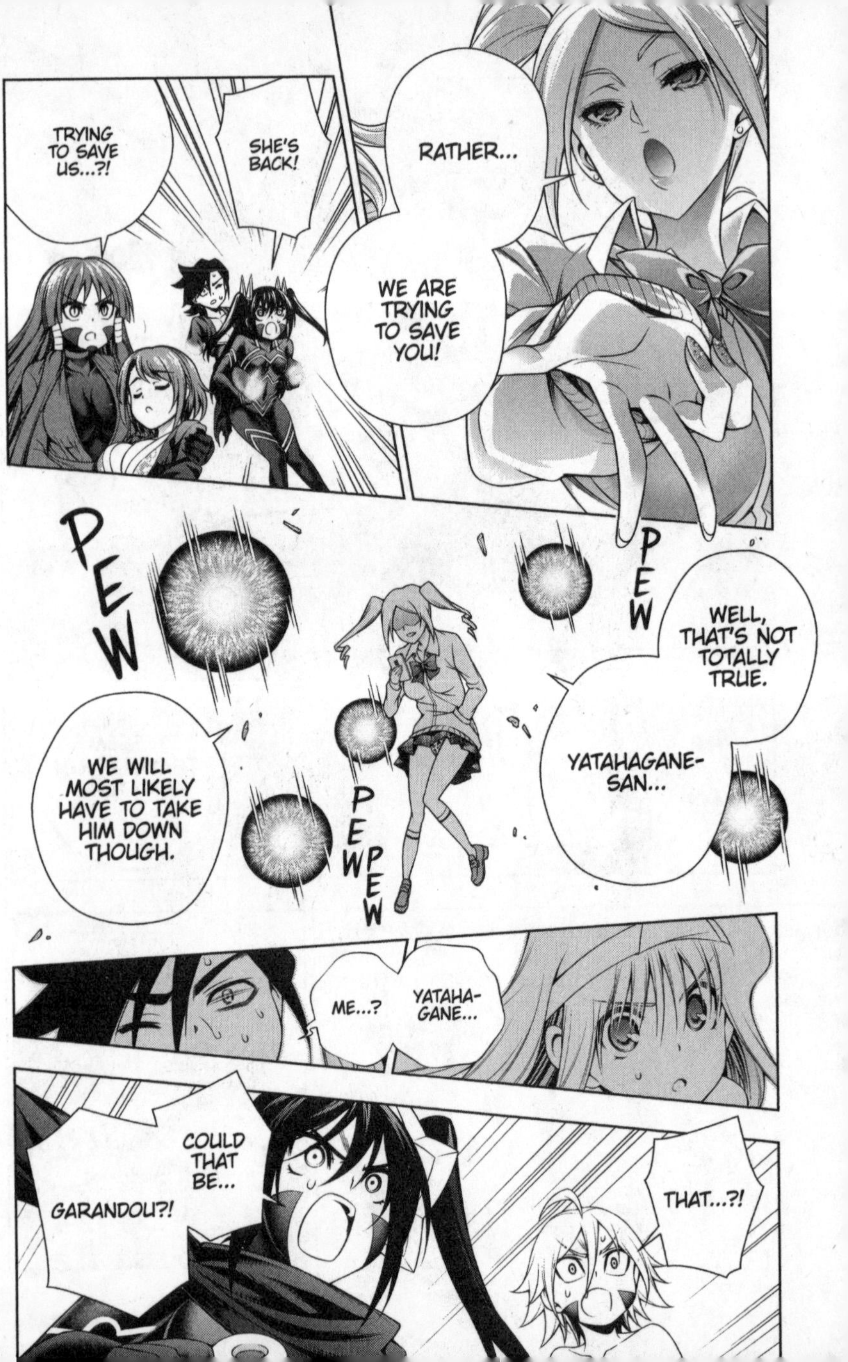
RATHER...
WE ARE TRYING TO SAVE YOU!
SHE'S BACK!
TRYING TO SAVE US...?!
PEW
WELL, THAT'S NOT TOTALLY TRUE.
YATAHAGANE-SAN...
PEW
PEW
PEW
WE WILL MOST LIKELY HAVE TO TAKE HIM DOWN THOUGH.
PEW
YATAHAGANE...
ME...?
THAT...?!
COULD THAT BE...
GARANDOU?!

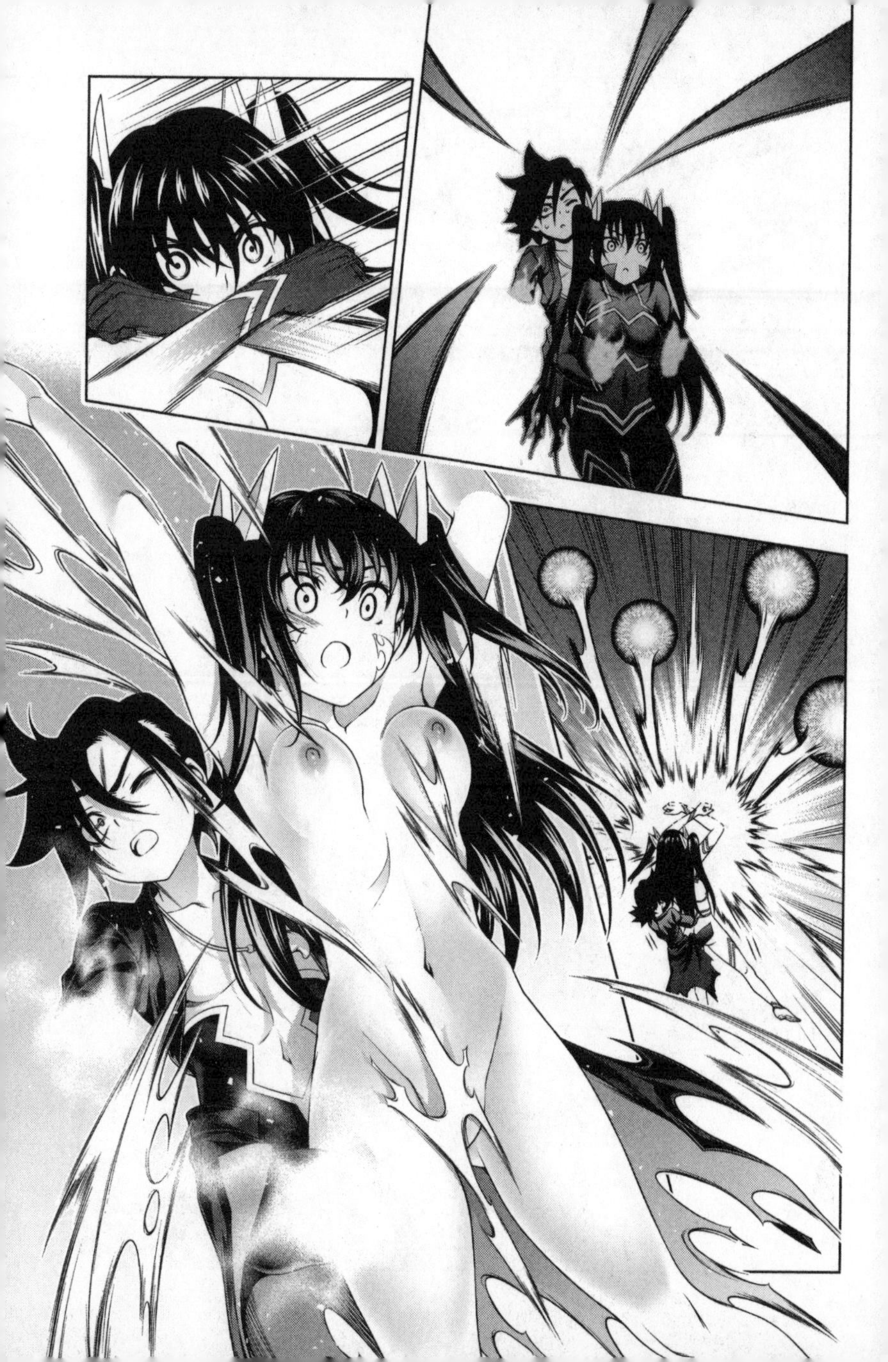

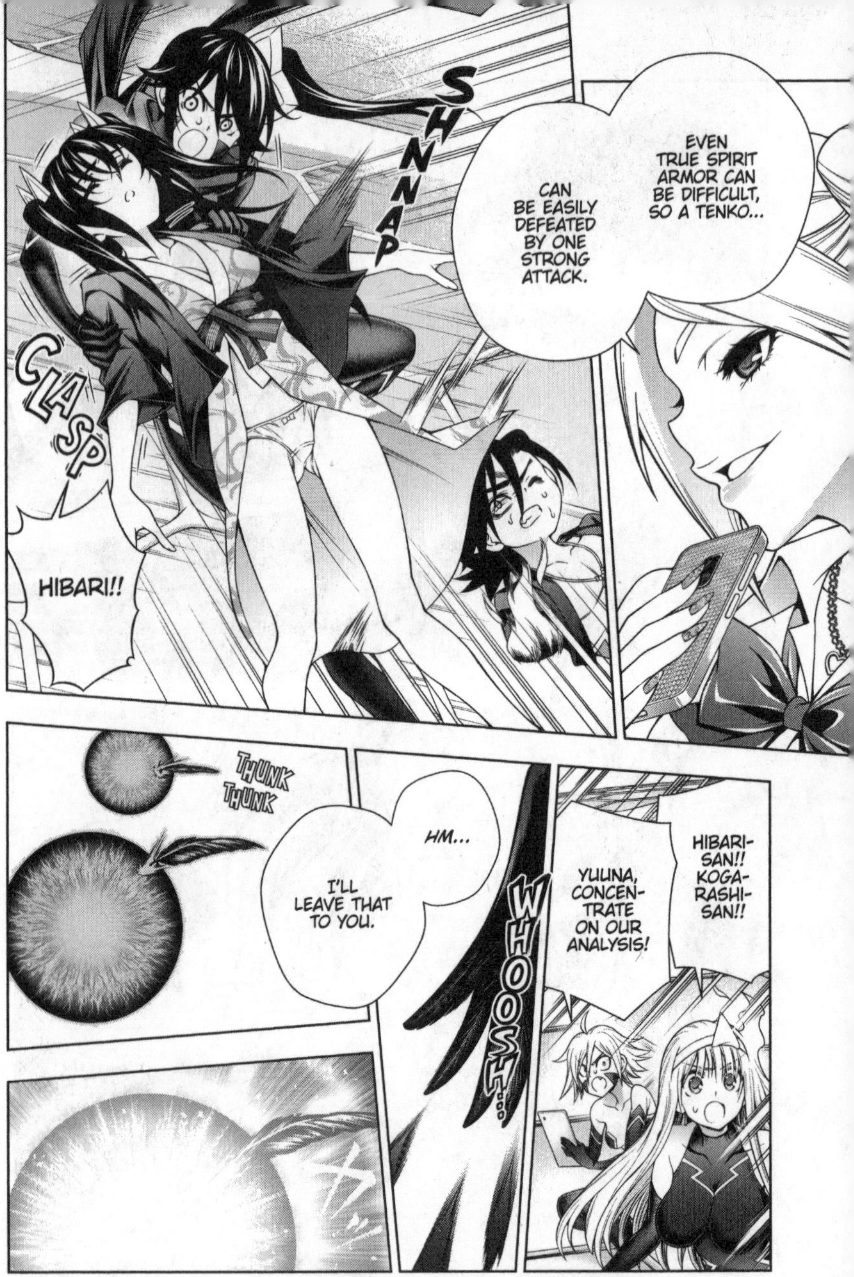
EVEN TRUE SPIRIT ARMOR CAN BE DIFFICULT, SO A TENKO...
CAN BE EASILY DEFEATED BY ONE STRONG ATTACK.
SHNNAP
CLASP
HIBARI!!
HIBARI-SAN!! KOGA-RASHI-SAN!!
YUUNA, CONCEN-TRATE ON OUR ANALYSIS!
HM...
I'LL LEAVE THAT TO YOU.
WHOOOSH...
THUNK
THUNK

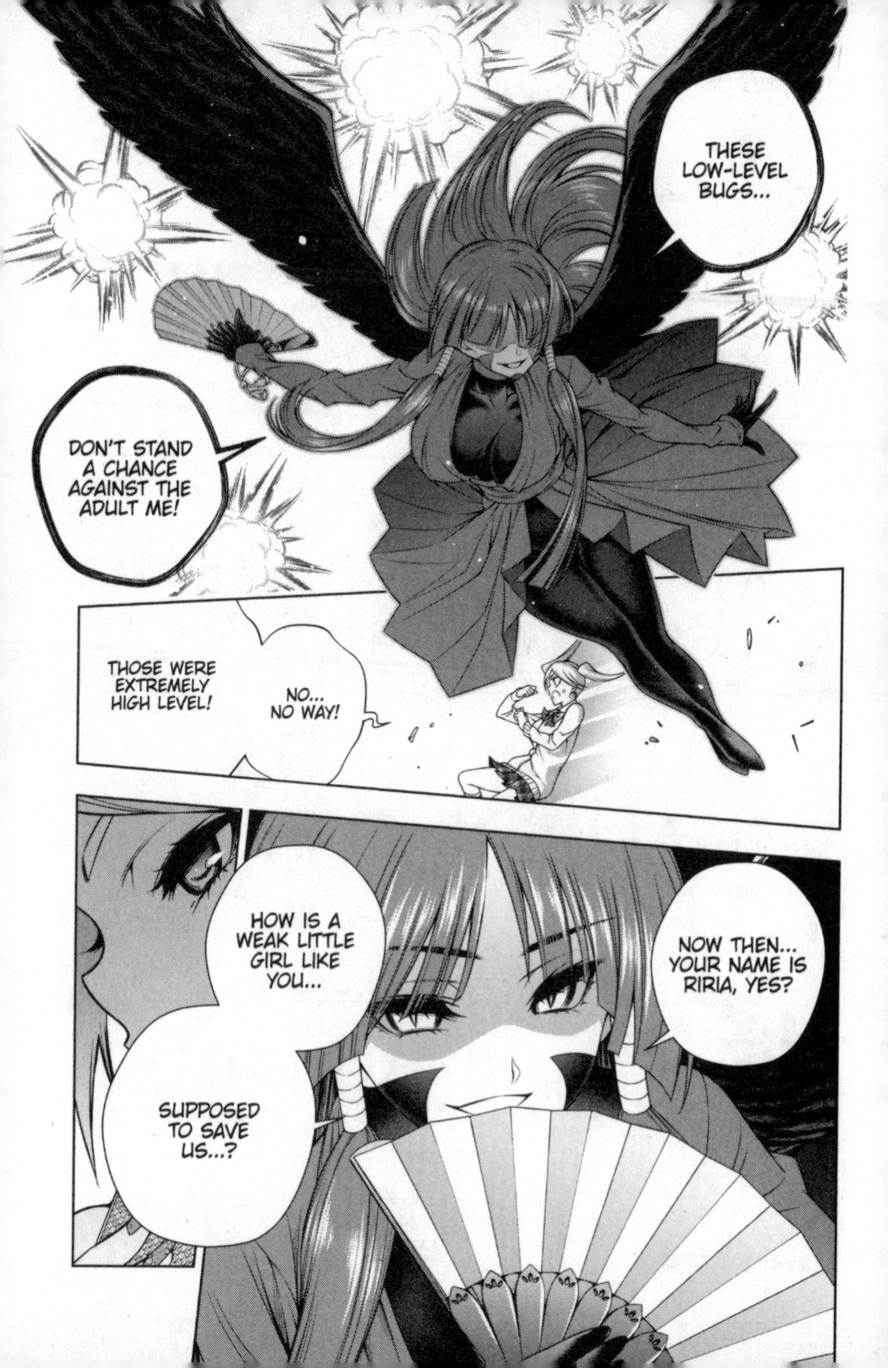
THESE LOW-LEVEL BUGS...
DON'T STAND A CHANCE AGAINST THE ADULT ME!
NO... NO WAY!
THOSE WERE EXTREMELY HIGH LEVEL!
NOW THEN... YOUR NAME IS RIRIA, YES?
HOW IS A WEAK LITTLE GIRL LIKE YOU...
SUPPOSED TO SAVE US...?

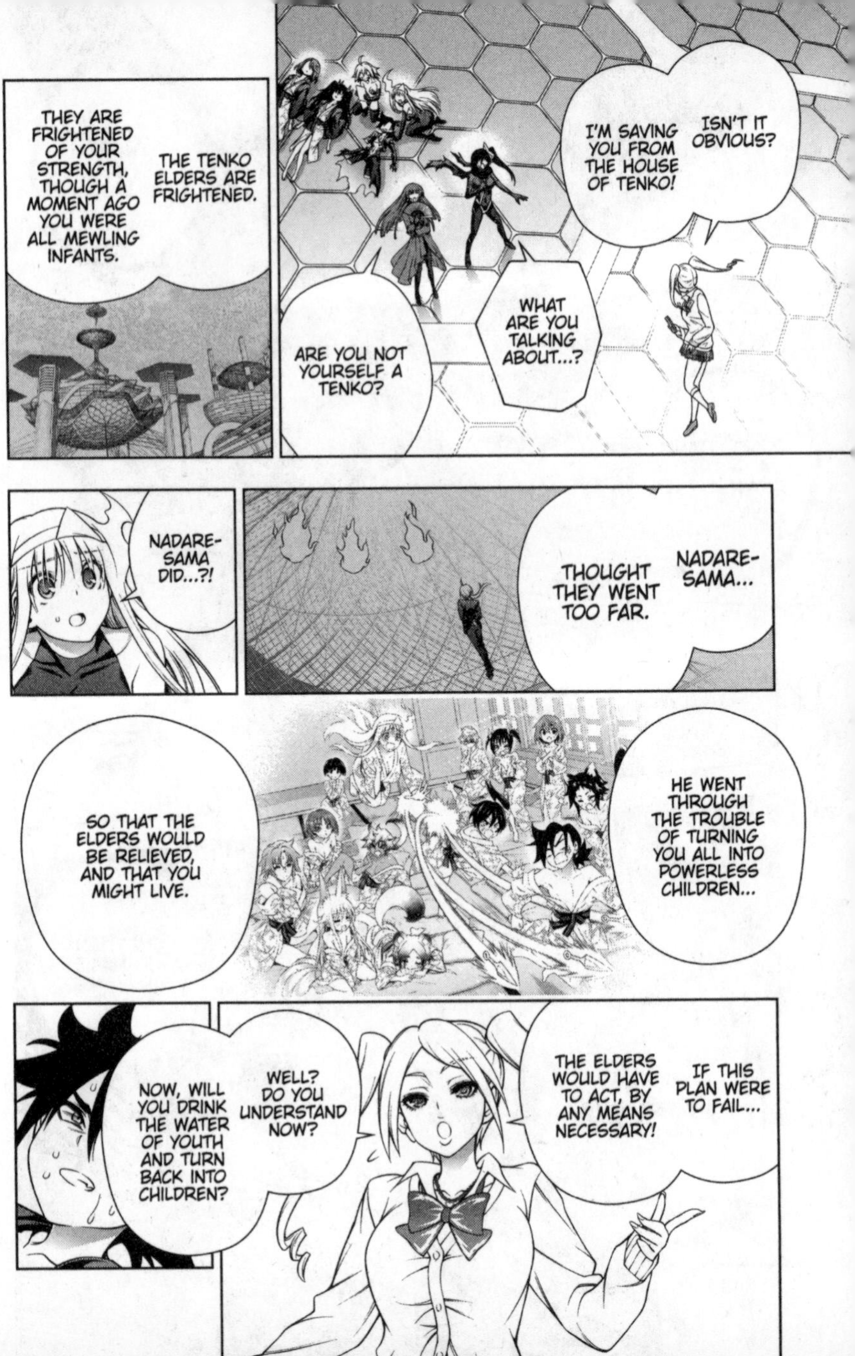
ISN'T IT OBVIOUS?
I'M SAVING YOU FROM THE HOUSE OF TENKO!
WHAT ARE YOU TALKING ABOUT...?
ARE YOU NOT YOURSELF A TENKO?
THE TENKO ELDERS ARE FRIGHTENED.
THEY ARE FRIGHTENED OF YOUR STRENGTH, THOUGH A MOMENT AGO YOU WERE ALL MEWLING INFANTS.
NADARE-SAMA...
THOUGHT THEY WENT TOO FAR.
NADARE-SAMA DID...?!
HE WENT THROUGH THE TROUBLE OF TURNING YOU ALL INTO POWERLESS CHILDREN...
SO THAT THE ELDERS WOULD BE RELIEVED, AND THAT YOU MIGHT LIVE.
IF THIS PLAN WERE TO FAIL...
THE ELDERS WOULD HAVE TO ACT, BY ANY MEANS NECESSARY!
WELL? DO YOU UNDERSTAND NOW?
NOW, WILL YOU DRINK THE WATER OF YOUTH AND TURN BACK INTO CHILDREN?

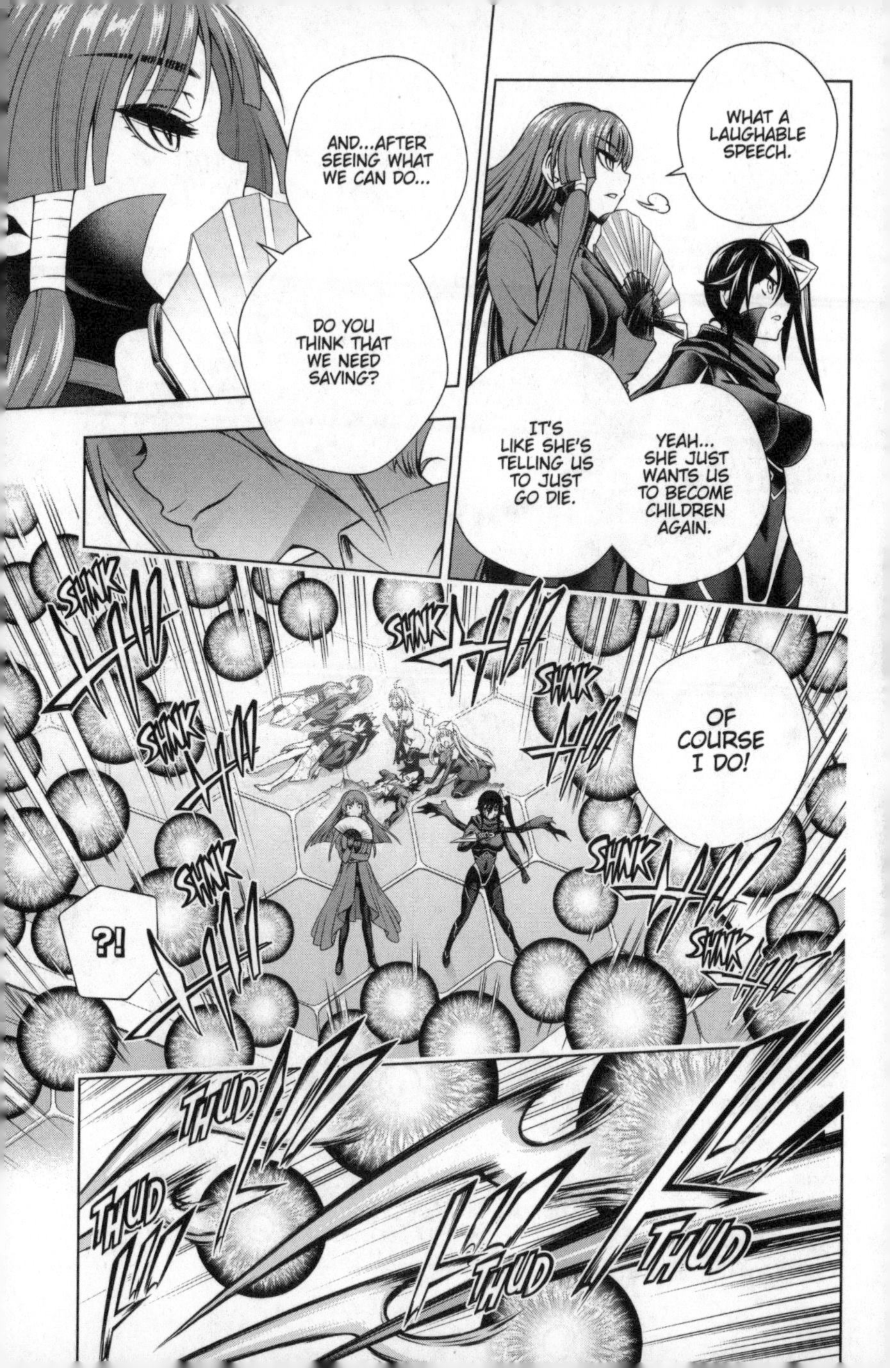
WHAT A LAUGHABLE SPEECH.
IT'S LIKE SHE'S TELLING US TO JUST GO DIE.
YEAH... SHE JUST WANTS US TO BECOME CHILDREN AGAIN.
AND...AFTER SEEING WHAT WE CAN DO...
DO YOU THINK THAT WE NEED SAVING?
OF COURSE I DO!
SHNK
SHNK
SHNK
SHNK
SHNK
SHNK
SHNK
?!
THUD
THUD
THUD
THUD

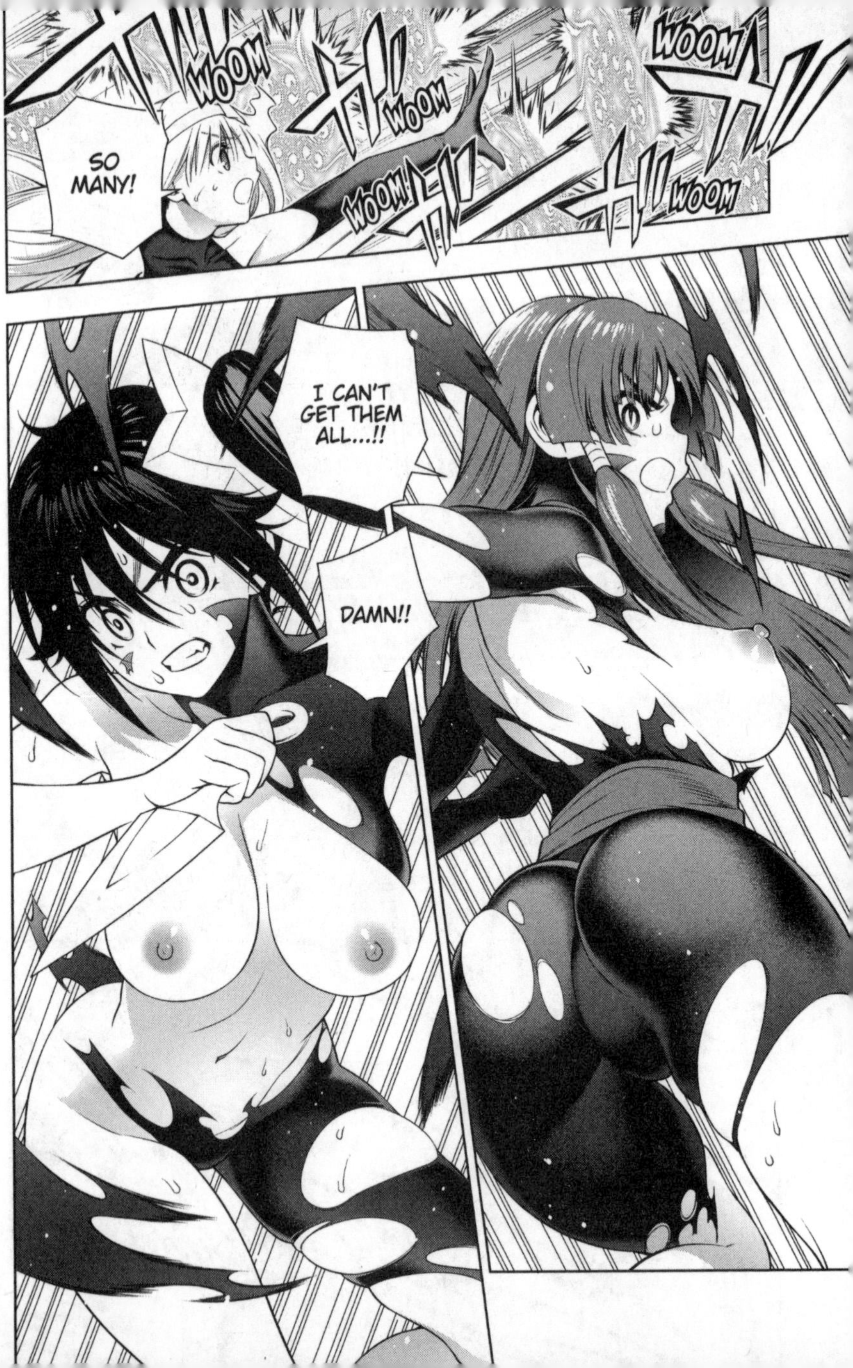
WOOM
WOOM
WOOM!
WOOM
WOOM
SO MANY!
I CAN'T GET THEM ALL...!!
DAMN!!

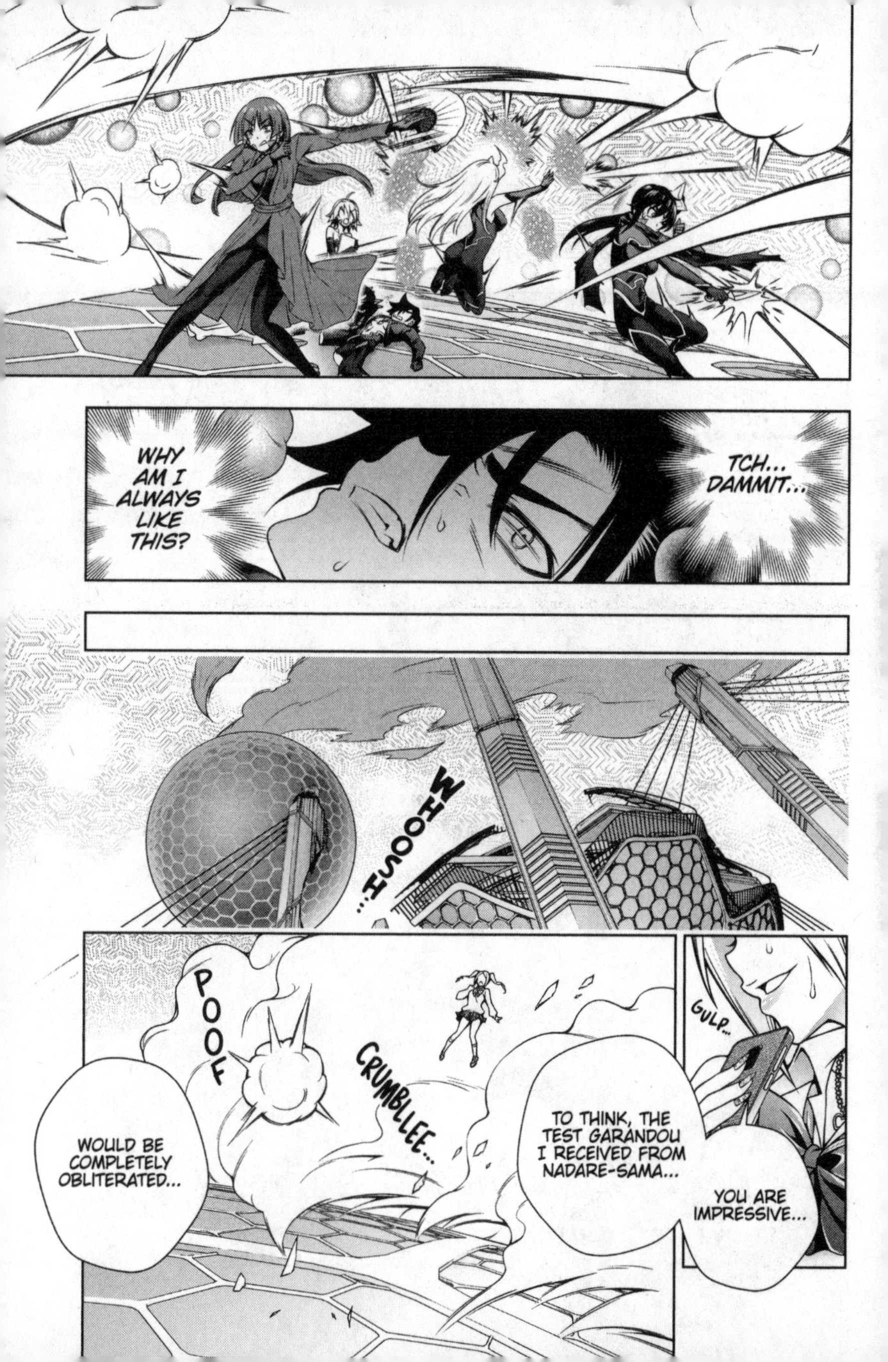
TCH... DAMMIT...
WHY AM I ALWAYS LIKE THIS?
WHOOSH...
GULP...
TO THINK, THE TEST GARANDOU I RECEIVED FROM NADARE-SAMA...
POOF
CRUMBLLEE...
WOULD BE COMPLETELY OBLITERATED...
YOU ARE IMPRESSIVE...

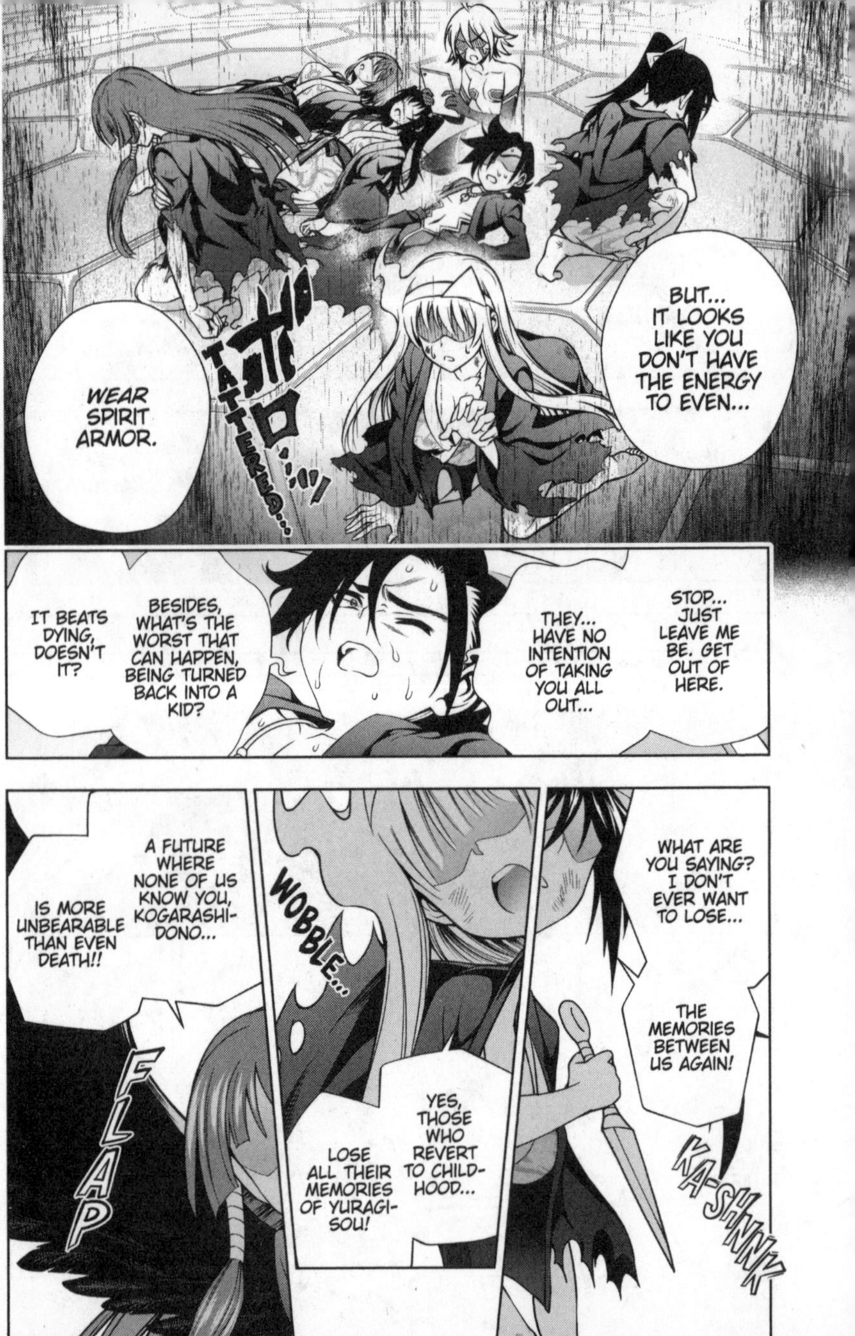
BUT... IT LOOKS LIKE YOU DON'T HAVE THE ENERGY TO EVEN...
TATTERED...
WEAR SPIRIT ARMOR.
STOP... JUST LEAVE ME BE. GET OUT OF HERE.
THEY... HAVE NO INTENTION OF TAKING YOU ALL OUT...
BESIDES, WHAT'S THE WORST THAT CAN HAPPEN, BEING TURNED BACK INTO A KID?
IT BEATS DYING, DOESN'T IT?
WHAT ARE YOU SAYING? I DON'T EVER WANT TO LOSE...
THE MEMORIES BETWEEN US AGAIN!
KA-SHNNK
YES, THOSE WHO REVERT TO CHILD-HOOD...
LOSE ALL THEIR MEMORIES OF YURAGI-SOU!
WOBBLE...
A FUTURE WHERE NONE OF US KNOW YOU, KOGARASHI-DONO...
IS MORE UNBEARABLE THAN EVEN DEATH!!
FLAP

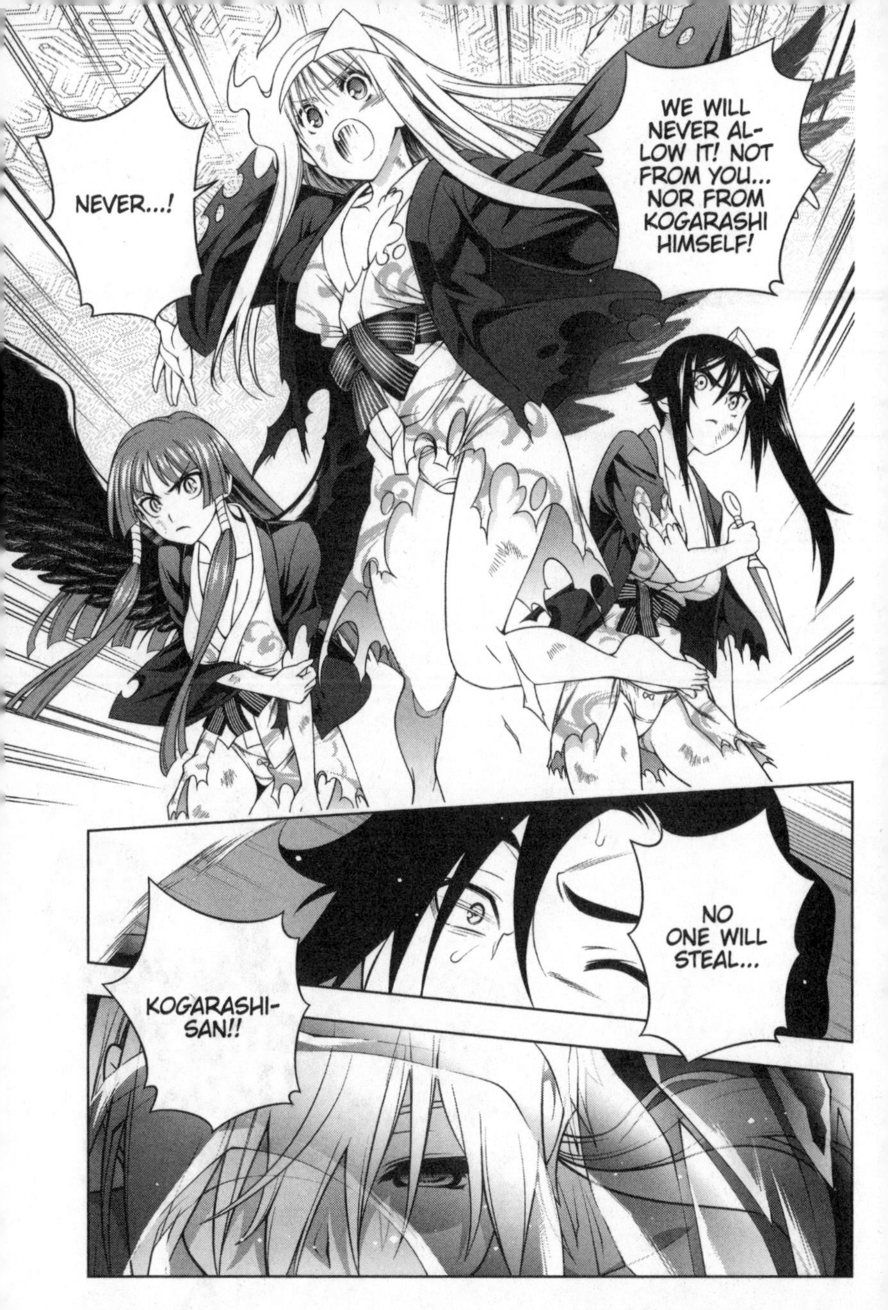
WE WILL NEVER AL-LOW IT! NOT FROM YOU... NOR FROM KOGARASHI HIMSELF!
NEVER...!
NO ONE WILL STEAL...
KOGARASHI-SAN!!

Yuuna
and the
Haunted
Hot
Springs

165 Kogarashi-kun the Medium

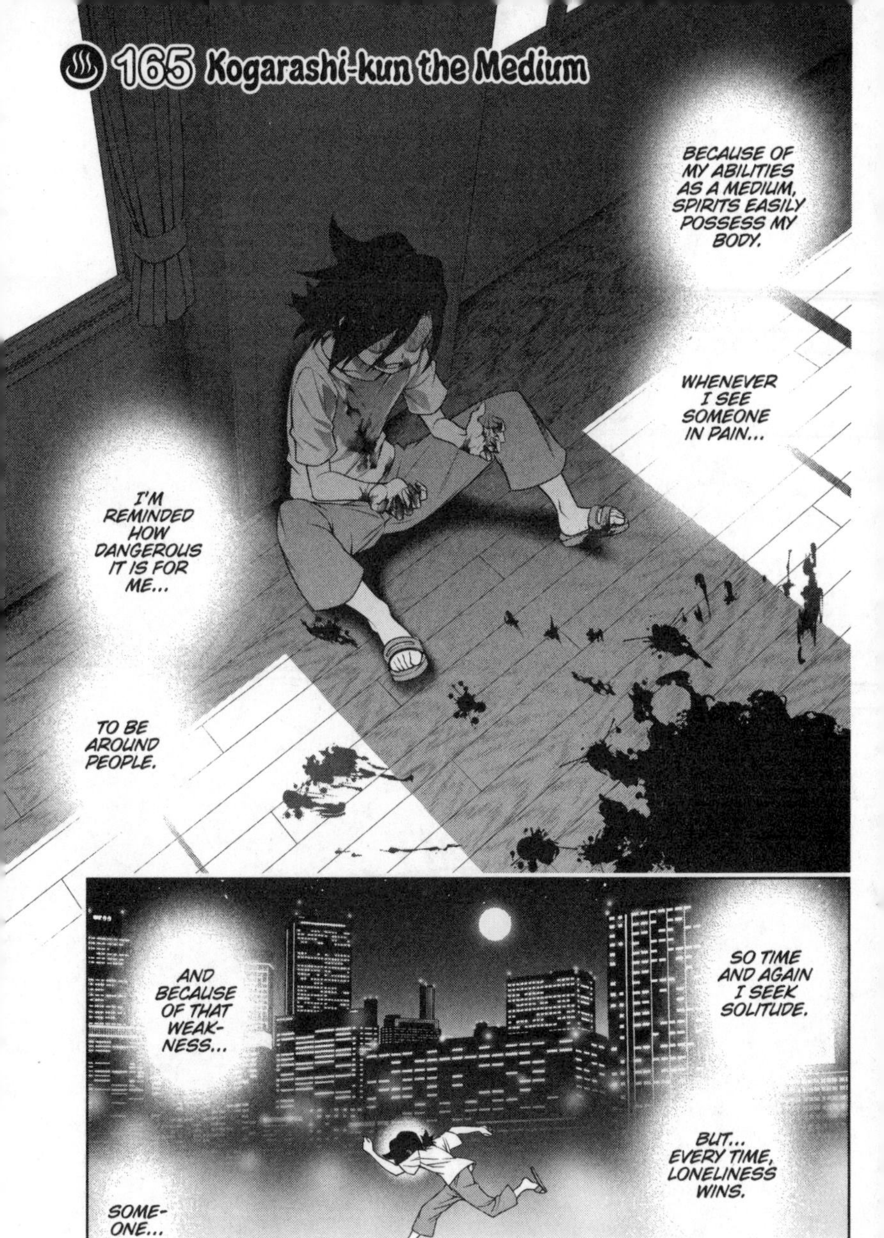
BECAUSE OF MY ABILITIES AS A MEDIUM, SPIRITS EASILY POSSESS MY BODY.
WHENEVER I SEE SOMEONE IN PAIN...
I'M REMINDED HOW DANGEROUS IT IS FOR ME...
TO BE AROUND PEOPLE.
SO TIME AND AGAIN I SEEK SOLITUDE.
AND BECAUSE OF THAT WEAK-NESS...
BUT... EVERY TIME, LONELINESS WINS.
SOME-ONE...

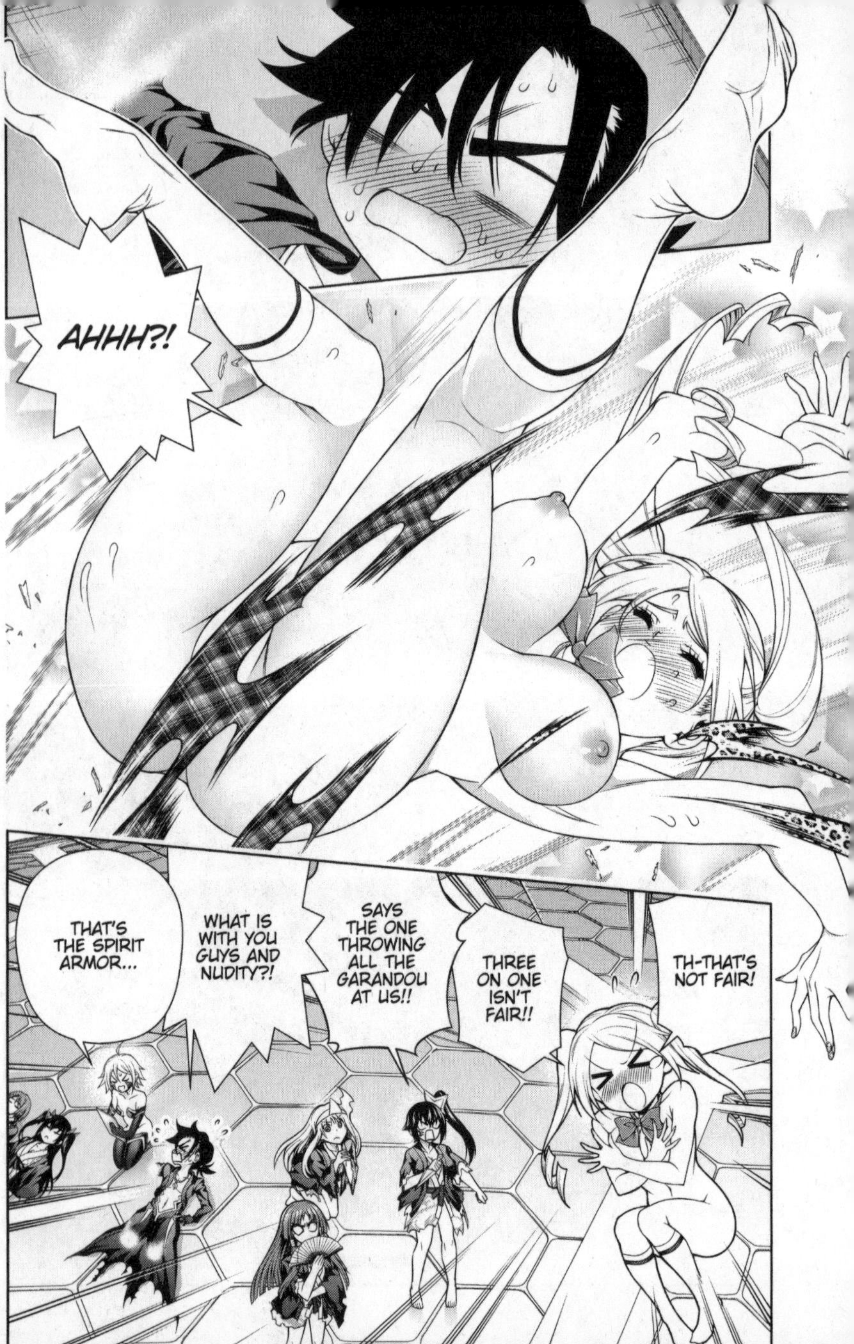
AHHH?!
TH-THAT'S NOT FAIR!
THREE ON ONE ISN'T FAIR!!
SAYS THE ONE THROWING ALL THE GARANDOU AT US!!
WHAT IS WITH YOU GUYS AND NUDITY?!
THAT'S THE SPIRIT ARMOR...

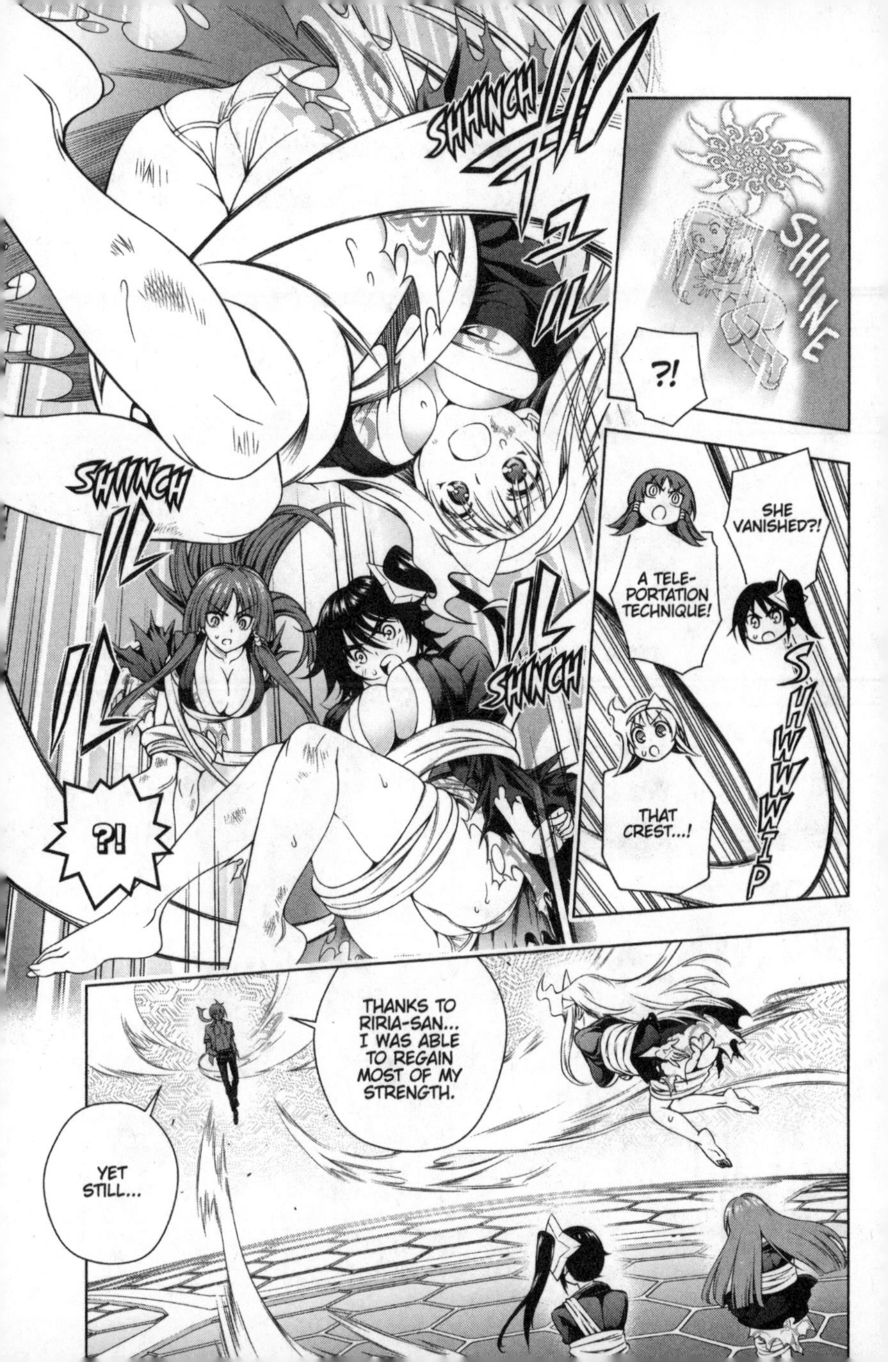
SHINE
?!
SHE VANISHED?!
A TELE-PORTATION TECHNIQUE!
SHWWWWIP
THAT CREST...!
SHHINCH
SHINCH
SHHINCH
?!
THANKS TO RIRIA-SAN... I WAS ABLE TO REGAIN MOST OF MY STRENGTH.
YET STILL...

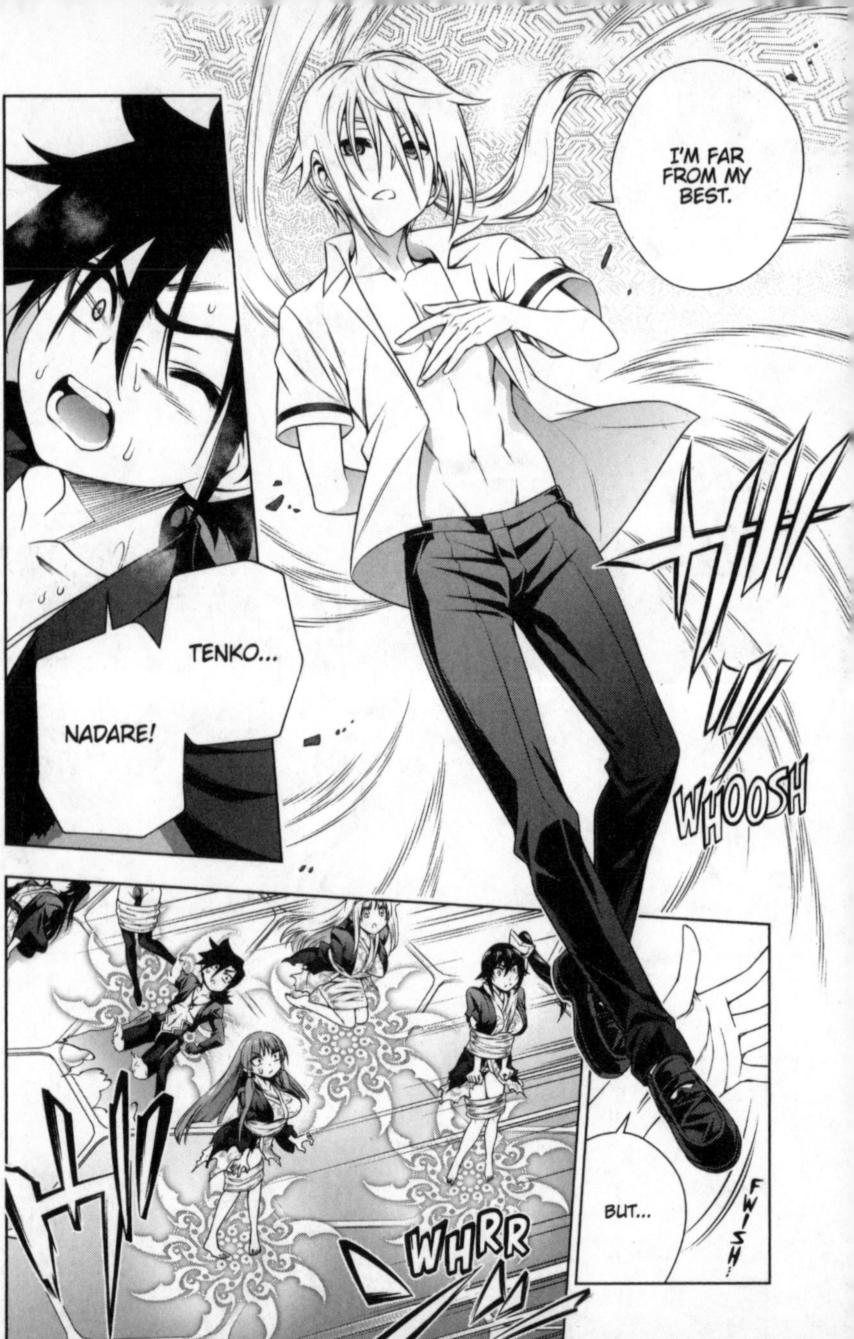

I'M FAR FROM MY BEST.
WHOOSH
TENKO...
NADARE!
BUT...
FWISH!
WHRR

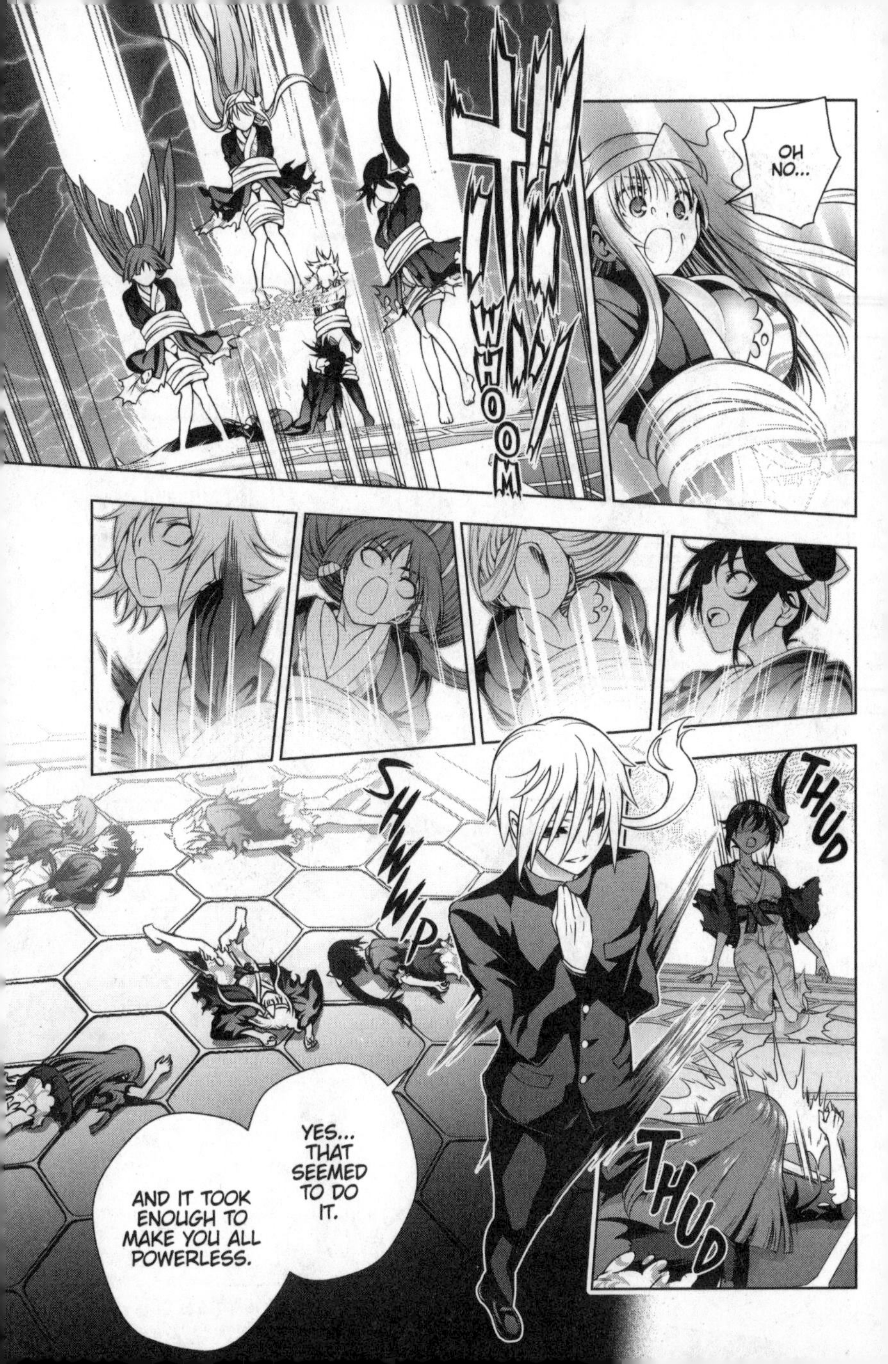
OH NO...
WHOOOOM
THUD
SHWWIP
YES... THAT SEEMED TO DO IT.
AND IT TOOK ENOUGH TO MAKE YOU ALL POWERLESS.
THUD

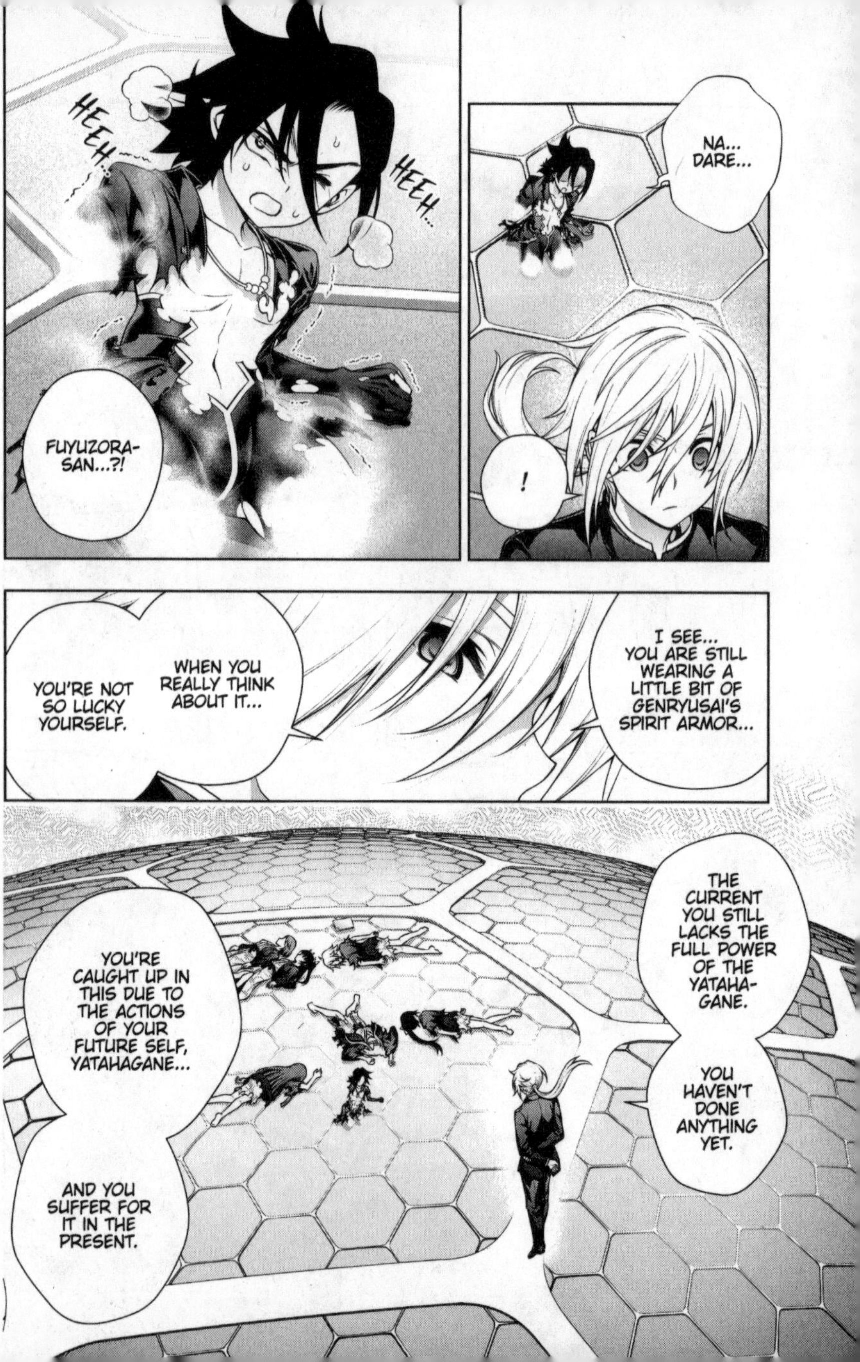
NA... DARE...
!
HEEH...
HEEH...
FUYUZORA-SAN...?!
I SEE... YOU ARE STILL WEARING A LITTLE BIT OF GENRYUSAI'S SPIRIT ARMOR...
WHEN YOU REALLY THINK ABOUT IT...
YOU'RE NOT SO LUCKY YOURSELF.
THE CURRENT YOU STILL LACKS THE FULL POWER OF THE YATAHA-GANE.
YOU HAVEN'T DONE ANYTHING YET.
YOU'RE CAUGHT UP IN THIS DUE TO THE ACTIONS OF YOUR FUTURE SELF, YATAHAGANE...
AND YOU SUFFER FOR IT IN THE PRESENT.

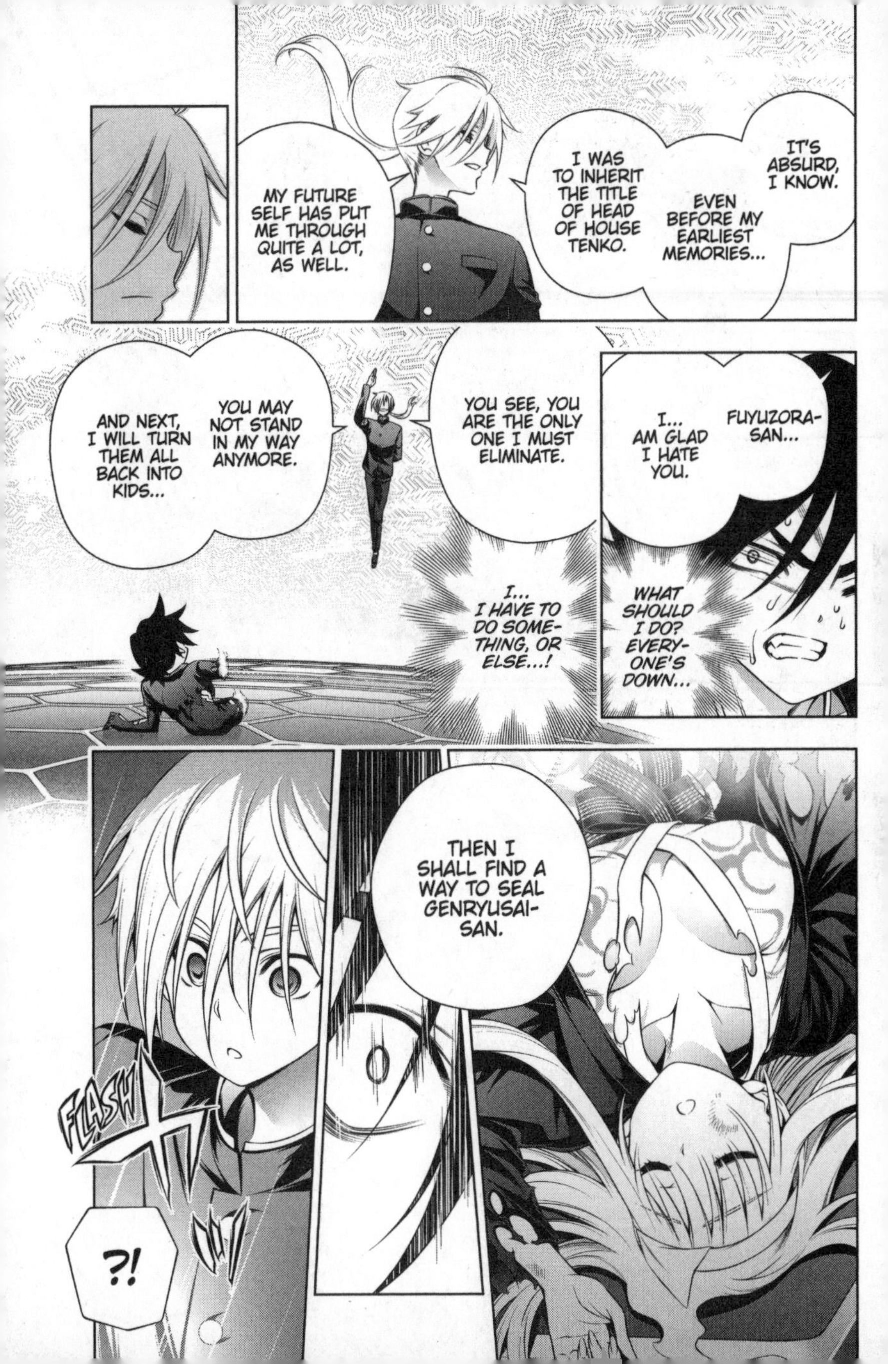
IT'S ABSURD, I KNOW.
EVEN BEFORE MY EARLIEST MEMORIES...
I WAS TO INHERIT THE TITLE OF HEAD OF HOUSE TENKO.
MY FUTURE SELF HAS PUT ME THROUGH QUITE A LOT, AS WELL.
FUYUZORA-SAN...
I... AM GLAD I HATE YOU.
WHAT SHOULD I DO? EVERYONE'S DOWN...
I... I HAVE TO DO SOMETHING, OR ELSE...!
YOU SEE, YOU ARE THE ONLY ONE I MUST ELIMINATE.
YOU MAY NOT STAND IN MY WAY ANYMORE.
AND NEXT, I WILL TURN THEM ALL BACK INTO KIDS...
THEN I SHALL FIND A WAY TO SEAL GENRYUSAI-SAN.
FLASH
?!

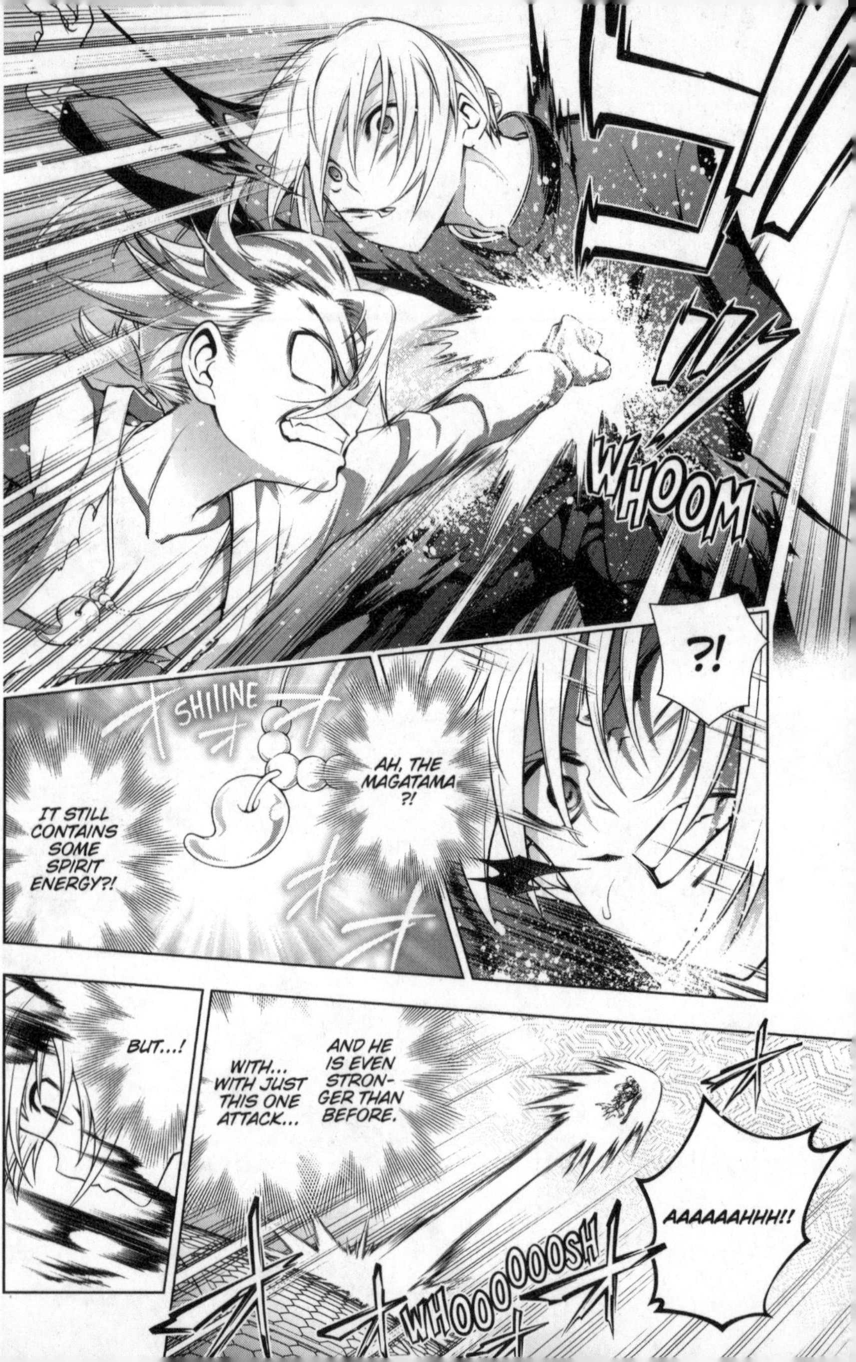
WHOOM
?!
SHIIINE
AH, THE MAGATAMA?!
IT STILL CONTAINS SOME SPIRIT ENERGY?!
AND HE IS EVEN STRONGER THAN BEFORE.
WITH... WITH JUST THIS ONE ATTACK...
AAAAAAHHH!!
WHOOOOOOSH
BUT...!

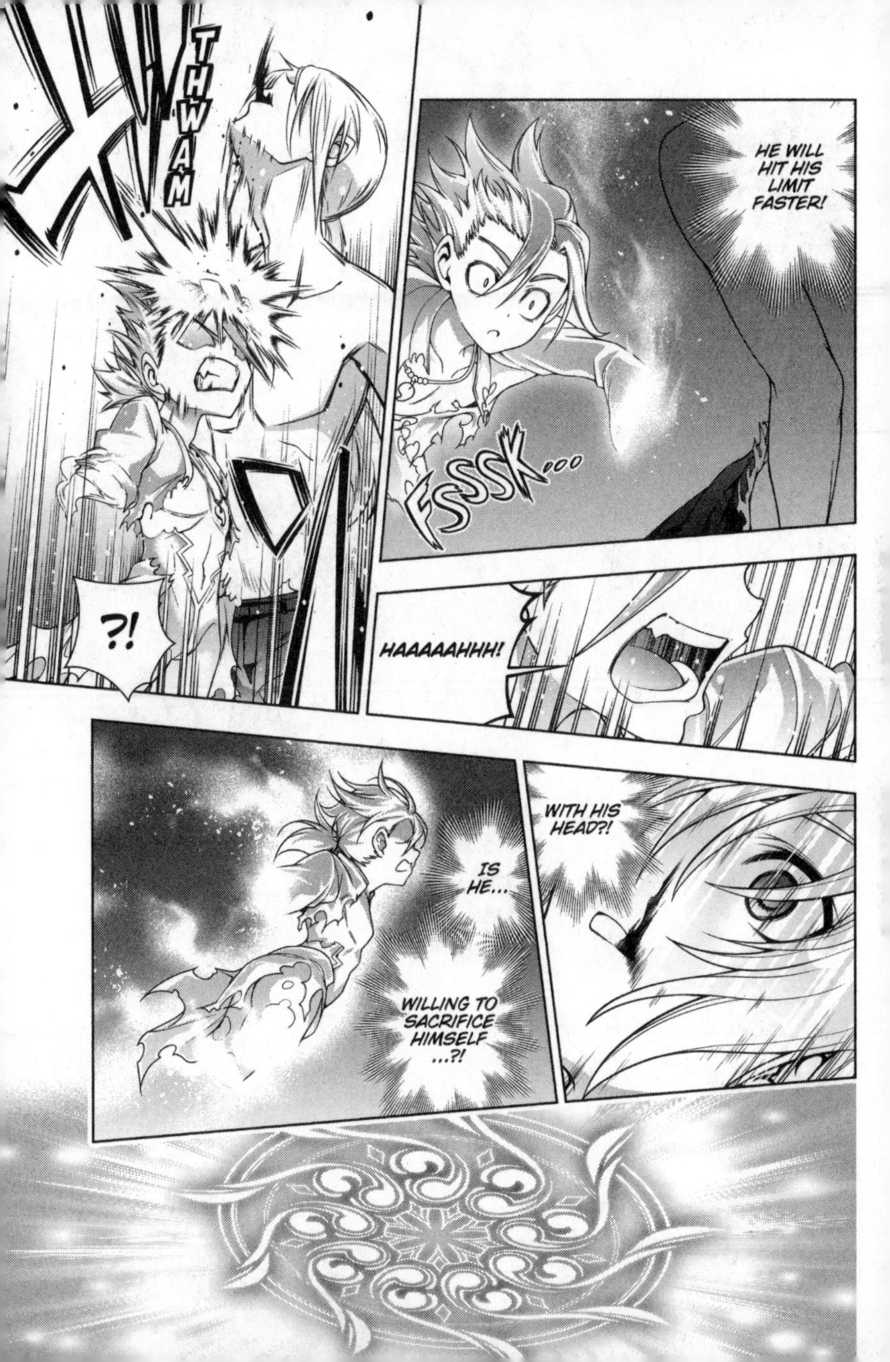
HE WILL HIT HIS LIMIT FASTER!
FSSSK...
HAAAAAHHH!
THWAM
?!
WITH HIS HEAD?!
IS HE...
WILLING TO SACRIFICE HIMSELF ...?!

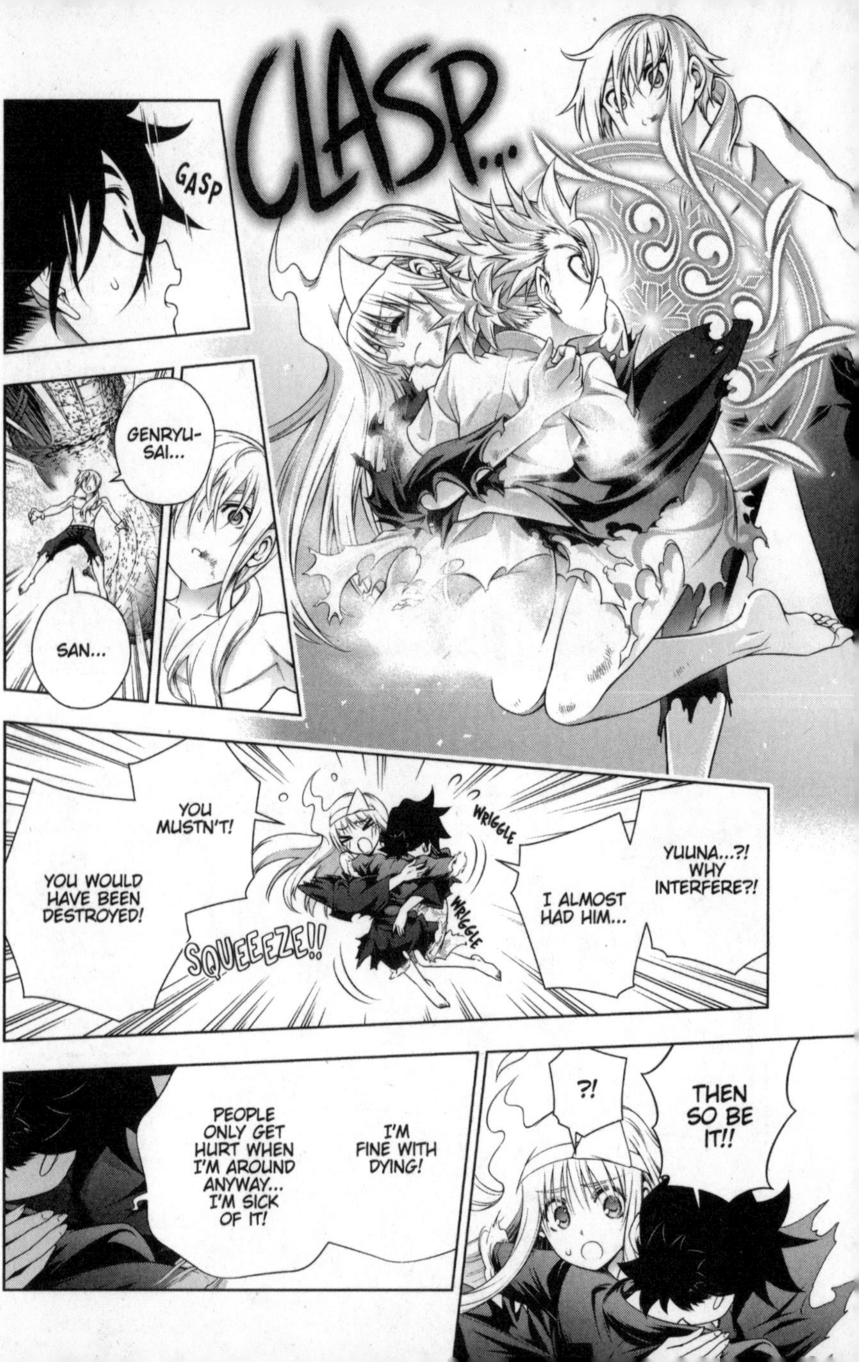
CLASP...
GASP
GENRYU-SAI...
SAN...
YUUNA...?! WHY INTERFERE?!
I ALMOST HAD HIM...
WRIGGLE
WRIGGLE
YOU MUSTN'T!
YOU WOULD HAVE BEEN DESTROYED!
SQUEEEEZE!!
THEN SO BE IT!!
?!
I'M FINE WITH DYING!
PEOPLE ONLY GET HURT WHEN I'M AROUND ANYWAY... I'M SICK OF IT!

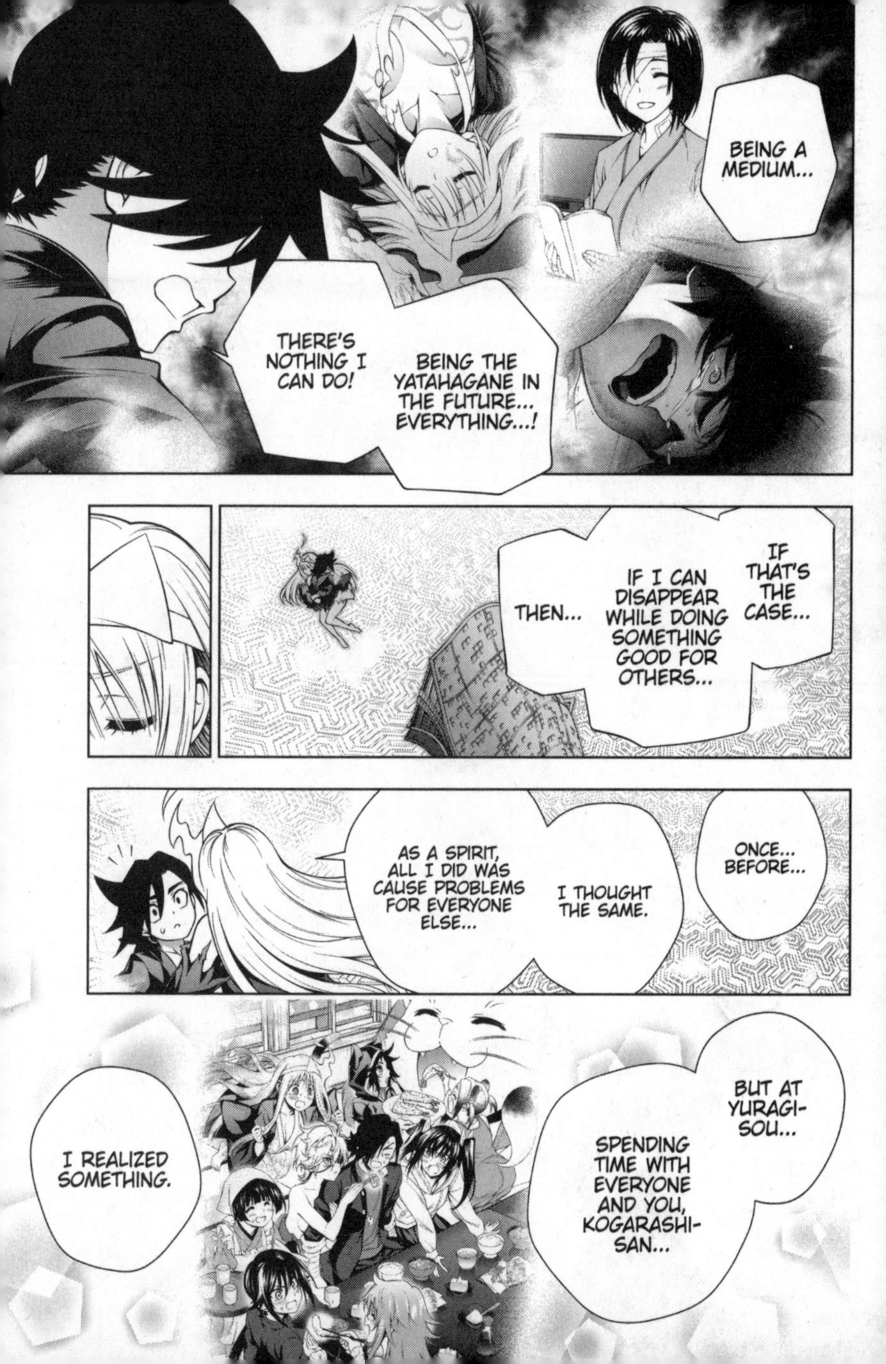
BEING A MEDIUM...
BEING THE YATAHAGANE IN THE FUTURE... EVERYTHING...!
THERE'S NOTHING I CAN DO!
IF THAT'S THE CASE...
IF I CAN DISAPPEAR WHILE DOING SOMETHING GOOD FOR OTHERS...
THEN...
ONCE... BEFORE...
I THOUGHT THE SAME.
AS A SPIRIT, ALL I DID WAS CAUSE PROBLEMS FOR EVERYONE ELSE...
BUT AT YURAGI-SOU...
SPENDING TIME WITH EVERYONE AND YOU, KOGARASHI-SAN...
I REALIZED SOMETHING.

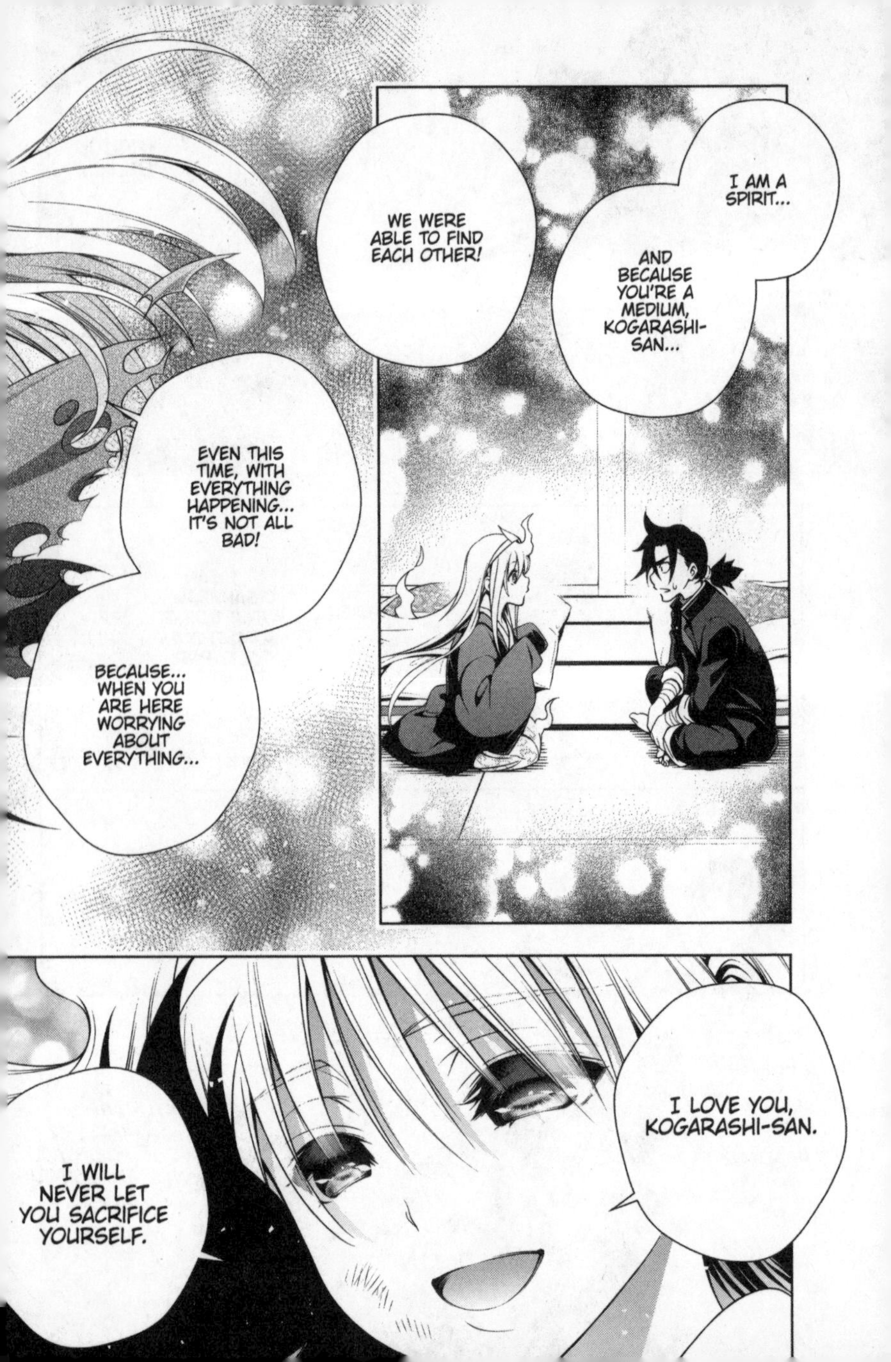
I AM A SPIRIT...
AND BECAUSE YOU'RE A MEDIUM, KOGARASHI-SAN...
WE WERE ABLE TO FIND EACH OTHER!
EVEN THIS TIME, WITH EVERYTHING HAPPENING... IT'S NOT ALL BAD!
BECAUSE... WHEN YOU ARE HERE WORRYING ABOUT EVERYTHING...
I LOVE YOU, KOGARASHI-SAN.
I WILL NEVER LET YOU SACRIFICE YOURSELF.

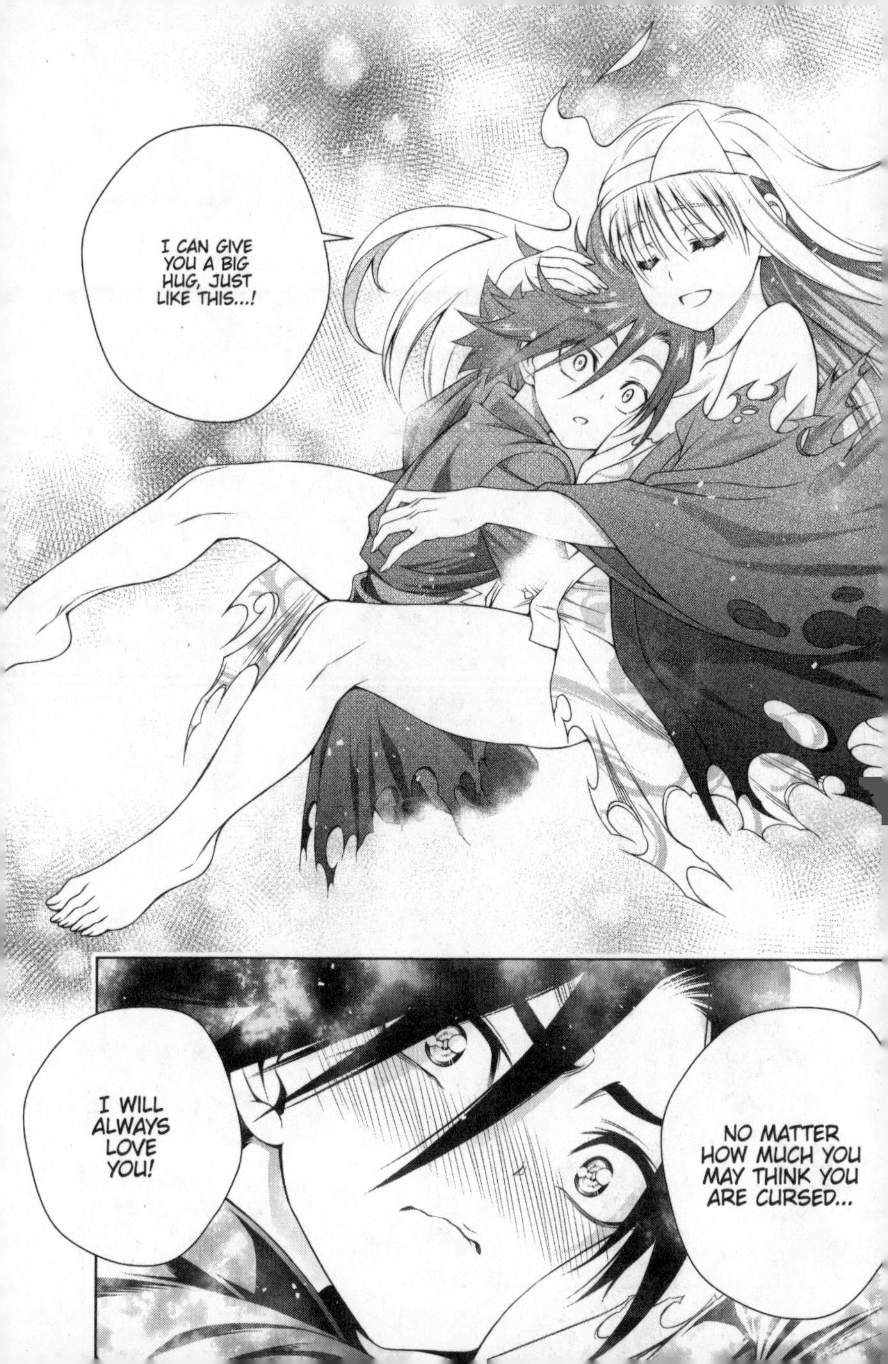
I CAN GIVE YOU A BIG HUG, JUST LIKE THIS...!
NO MATTER HOW MUCH YOU MAY THINK YOU ARE CURSED...
I WILL ALWAYS LOVE YOU!

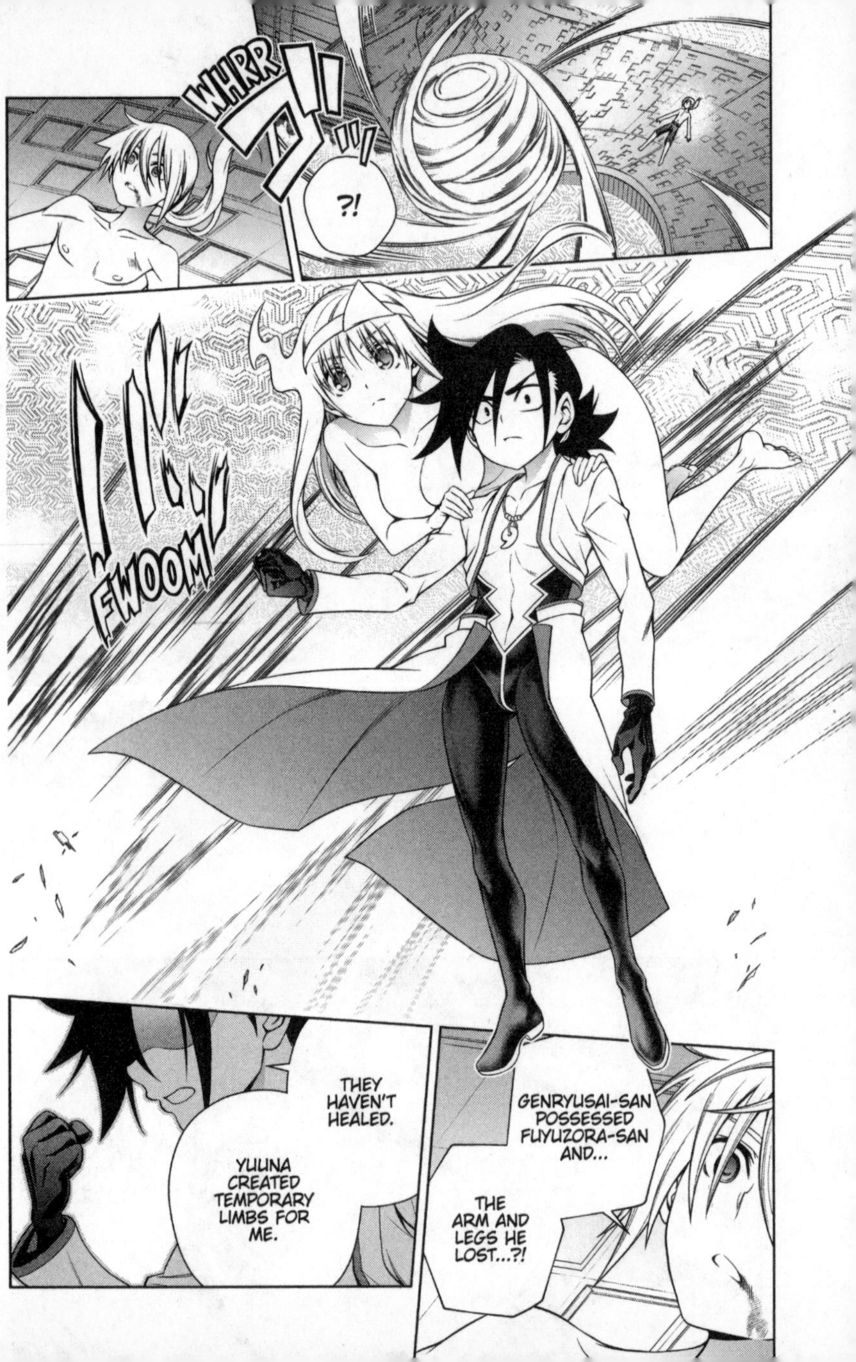
WHRR
?!
FWOOM
GENRYUSAI-SAN POSSESSED FUYUZORA-SAN AND...
THE ARM AND LEGS HE LOST...?!
THEY HAVEN'T HEALED.
YUUNA CREATED TEMPORARY LIMBS FOR ME.

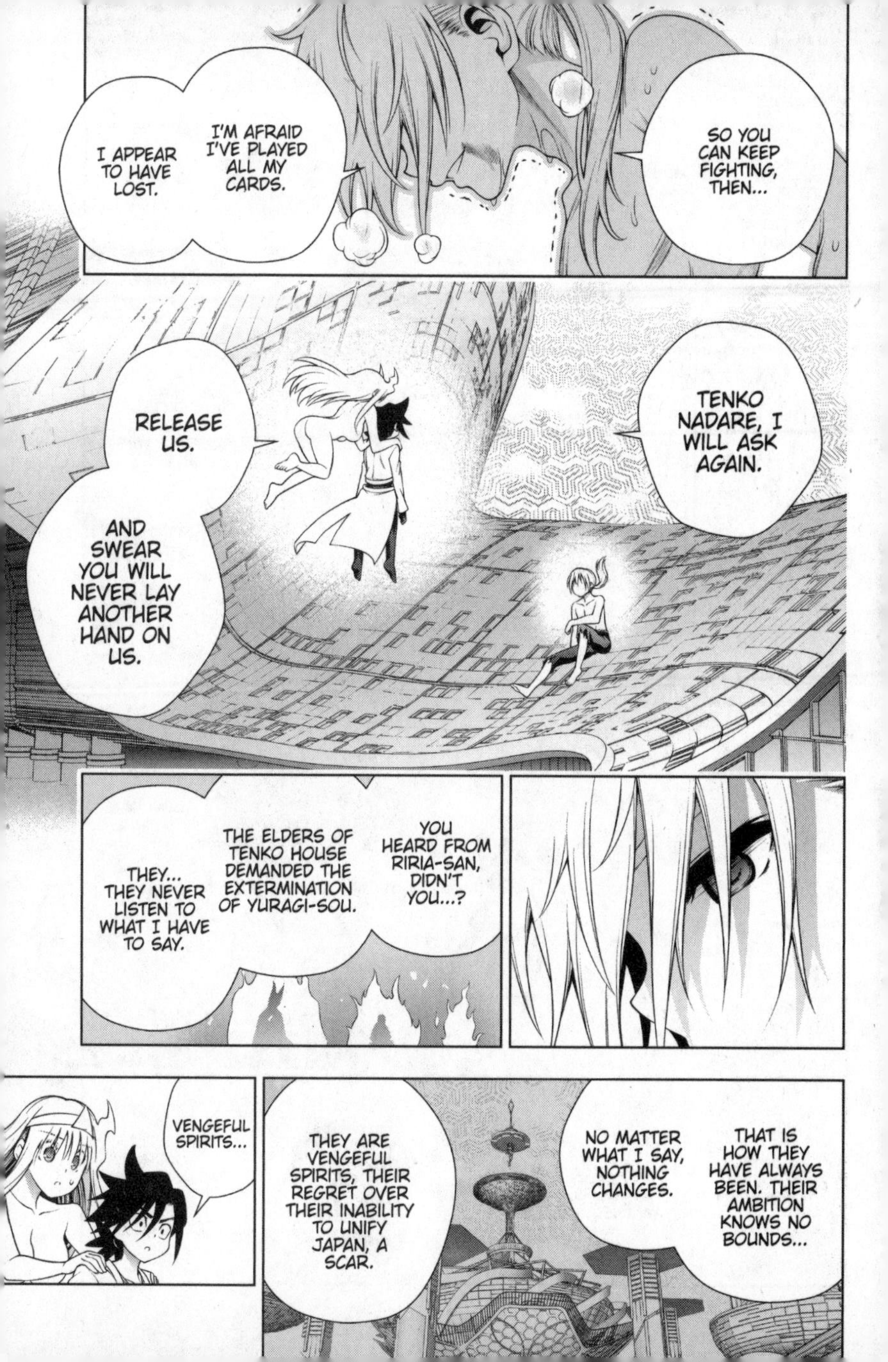
SO YOU CAN KEEP FIGHTING, THEN...
I'M AFRAID I'VE PLAYED ALL MY CARDS.
I APPEAR TO HAVE LOST.
TENKO NADARE, I WILL ASK AGAIN.
RELEASE US.
AND SWEAR YOU WILL NEVER LAY ANOTHER HAND ON US.
YOU HEARD FROM RIRIA-SAN, DIDN'T YOU...?
THE ELDERS OF TENKO HOUSE DEMANDED THE EXTERMINATION OF YURAGI-SOU.
THEY... THEY NEVER LISTEN TO WHAT I HAVE TO SAY.
THAT IS HOW THEY HAVE ALWAYS BEEN. THEIR AMBITION KNOWS NO BOUNDS...
NO MATTER WHAT I SAY, NOTHING CHANGES.
THEY ARE VENGEFUL SPIRITS, THEIR REGRET OVER THEIR INABILITY TO UNIFY JAPAN, A SCAR.
VENGEFUL SPIRITS...

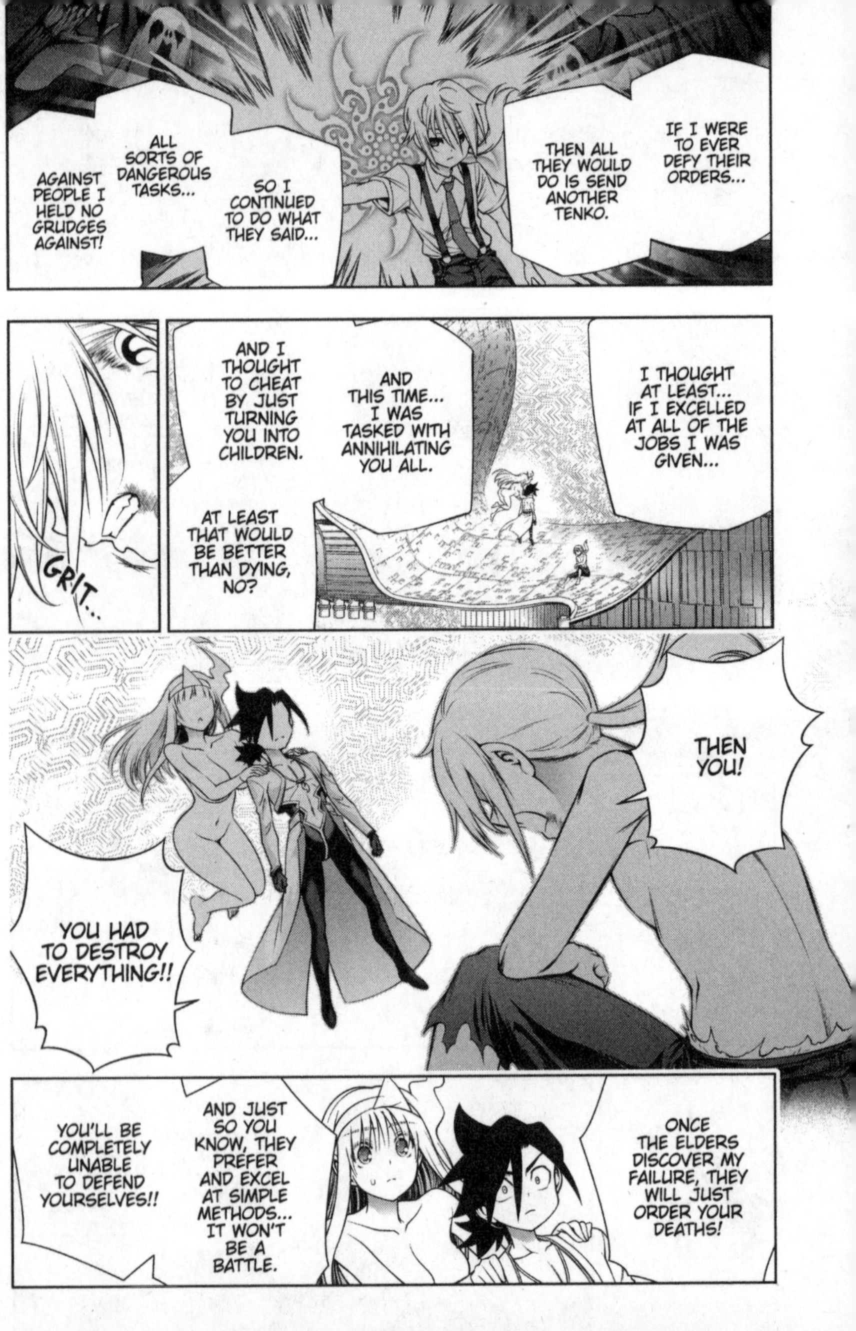

IF I WERE TO EVER DEFY THEIR ORDERS...
THEN ALL THEY WOULD DO IS SEND ANOTHER TENKO.
SO I CONTINUED TO DO WHAT THEY SAID...
ALL SORTS OF DANGEROUS TASKS...
AGAINST PEOPLE I HELD NO GRUDGES AGAINST!
I THOUGHT AT LEAST... IF I EXCELLED AT ALL OF THE JOBS I WAS GIVEN...
AND THIS TIME... I WAS TASKED WITH ANNIHILATING YOU ALL.
AND I THOUGHT TO CHEAT BY JUST TURNING YOU INTO CHILDREN.
AT LEAST THAT WOULD BE BETTER THAN DYING, NO?
GRIT...
THEN YOU!
YOU HAD TO DESTROY EVERYTHING!!
ONCE THE ELDERS DISCOVER MY FAILURE, THEY WILL JUST ORDER YOUR DEATHS!
AND JUST SO YOU KNOW, THEY PREFER AND EXCEL AT SIMPLE METHODS... IT WON'T BE A BATTLE.
YOU'LL BE COMPLETELY UNABLE TO DEFEND YOURSELVES!!

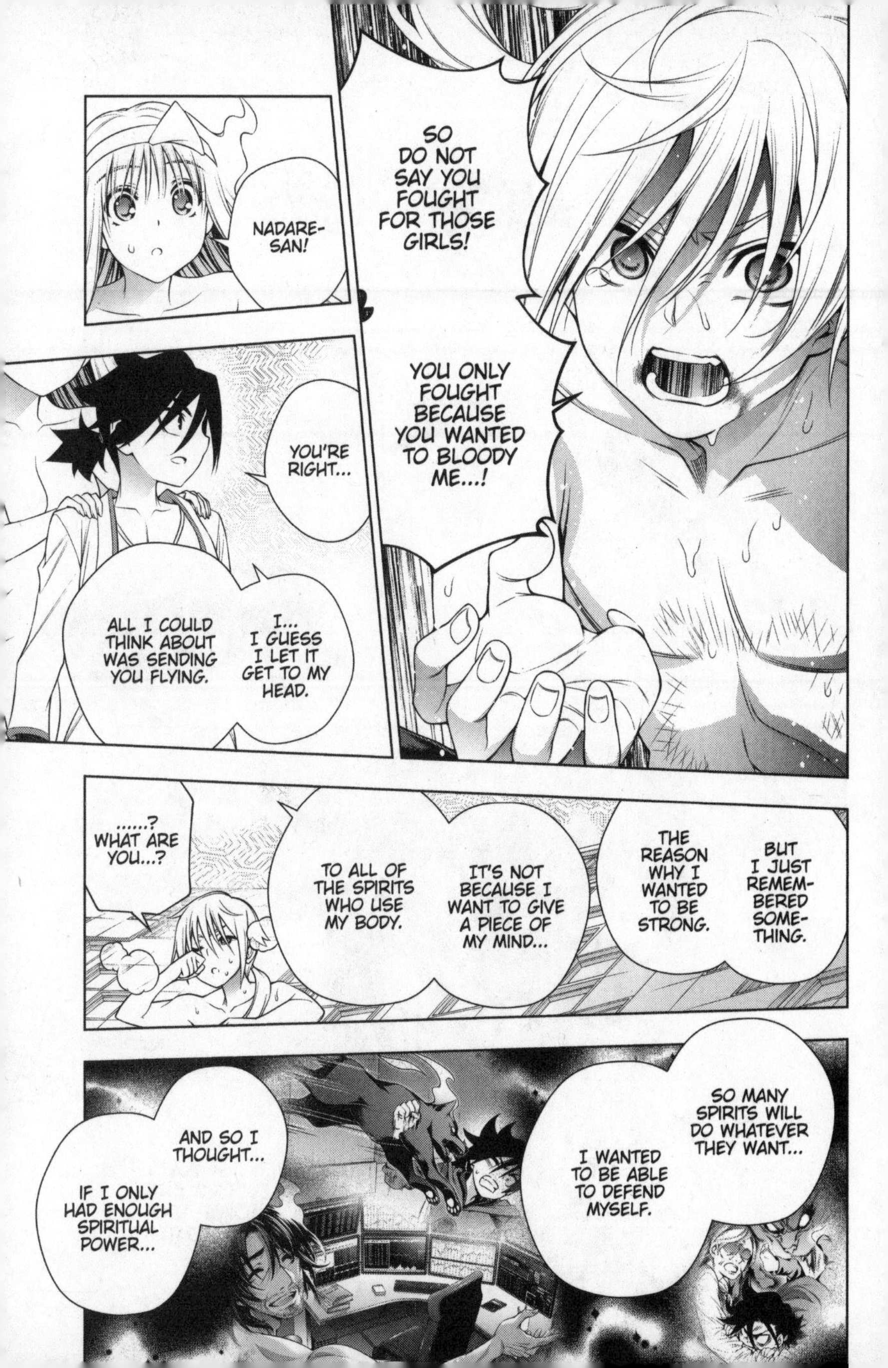
SO DO NOT SAY YOU FOUGHT FOR THOSE GIRLS!
YOU ONLY FOUGHT BECAUSE YOU WANTED TO BLOODY ME...!
NADARE-SAN!
YOU'RE RIGHT...
I... I GUESS I LET IT GET TO MY HEAD.
ALL I COULD THINK ABOUT WAS SENDING YOU FLYING.
BUT I JUST REMEMBERED SOMETHING.
THE REASON WHY I WANTED TO BE STRONG.
IT'S NOT BECAUSE I WANT TO GIVE A PIECE OF MY MIND...
TO ALL OF THE SPIRITS WHO USE MY BODY.
.....? WHAT ARE YOU...?
SO MANY SPIRITS WILL DO WHATEVER THEY WANT...
I WANTED TO BE ABLE TO DEFEND MYSELF.
AND SO I THOUGHT...
IF I ONLY HAD ENOUGH SPIRITUAL POWER...

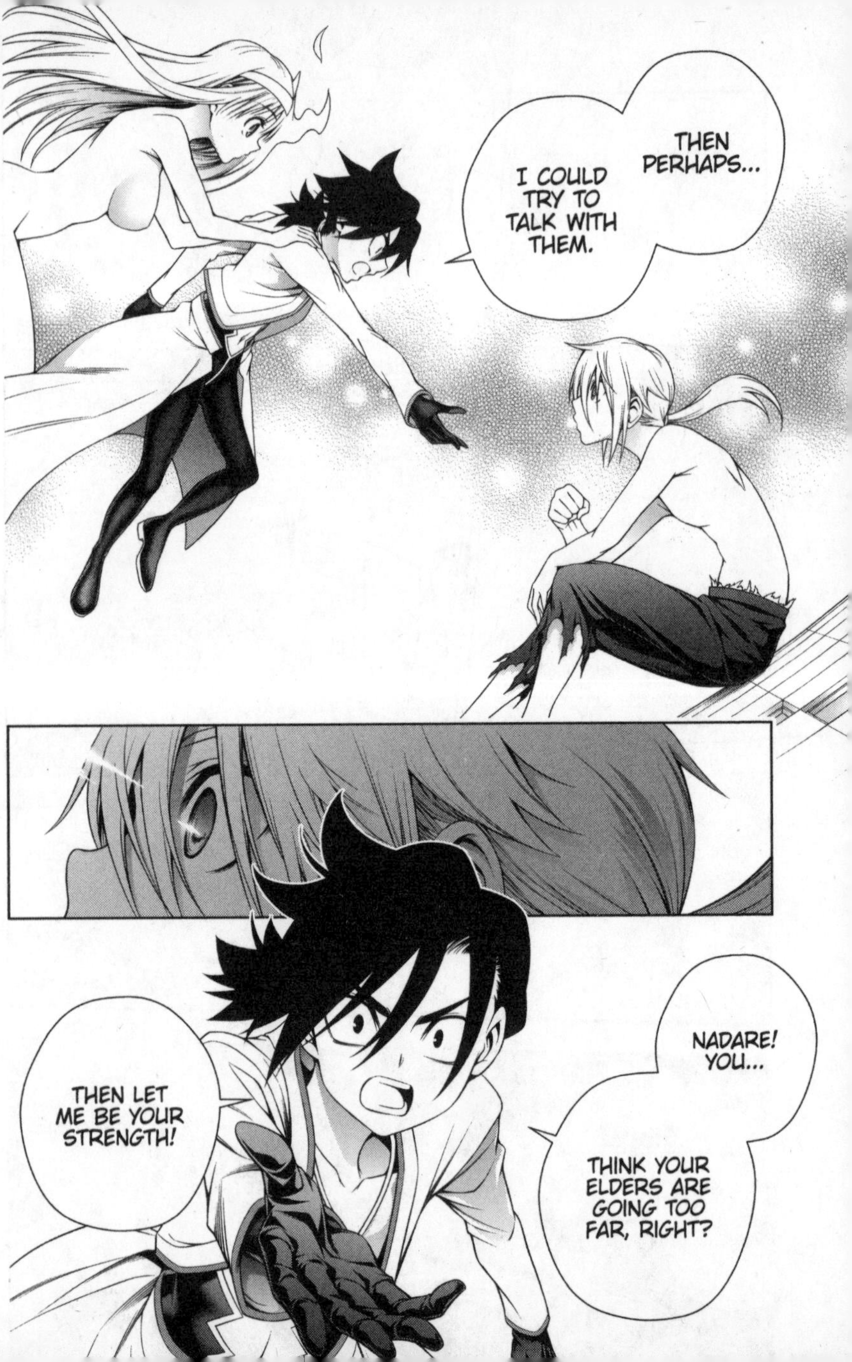
THEN PERHAPS... I COULD TRY TO TALK WITH THEM.
NADARE! YOU... THINK YOUR ELDERS ARE GOING TOO FAR, RIGHT?
THEN LET ME BE YOUR STRENGTH!

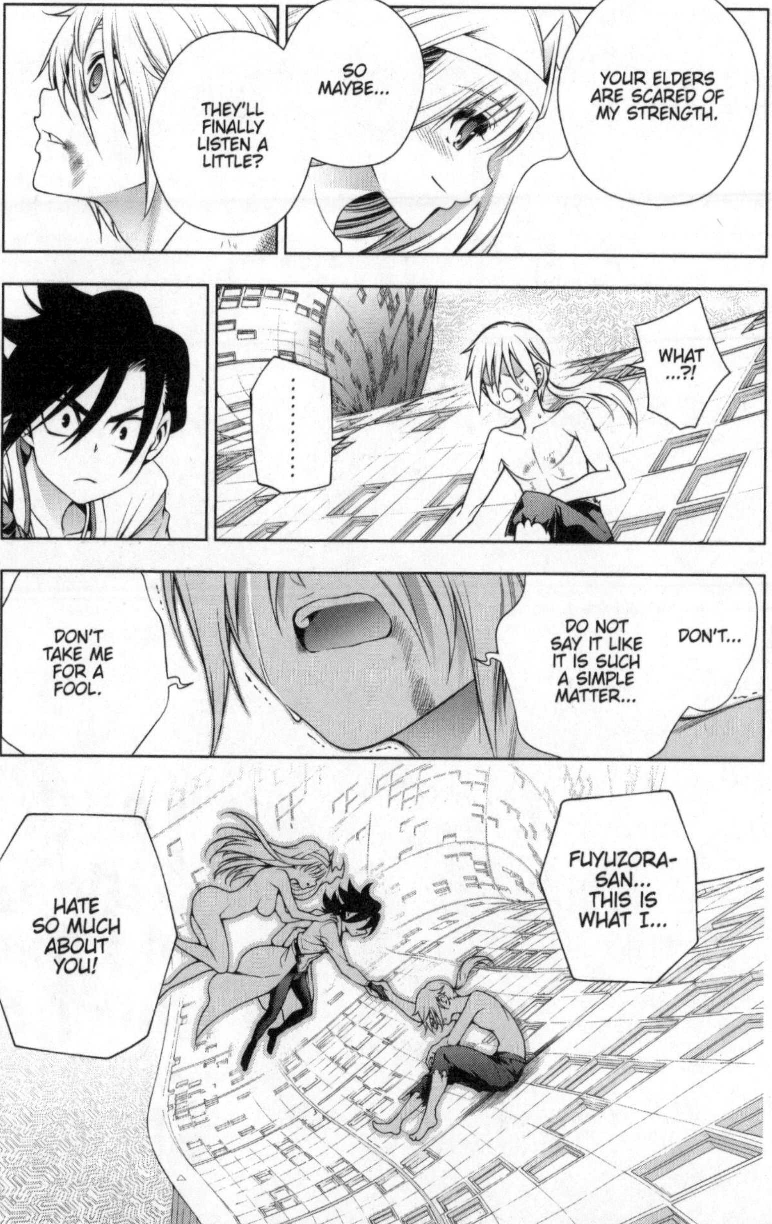
YOUR ELDERS ARE SCARED OF MY STRENGTH.
SO MAYBE...
THEY'LL FINALLY LISTEN A LITTLE?
WHAT ...?!
......
DON'T...
DO NOT SAY IT LIKE IT IS SUCH A SIMPLE MATTER...
DON'T TAKE ME FOR A FOOL.
FUYUZORA-SAN... THIS IS WHAT I...
HATE SO MUCH ABOUT YOU!

Yuuna
and the
Haunted
Hot
Springs

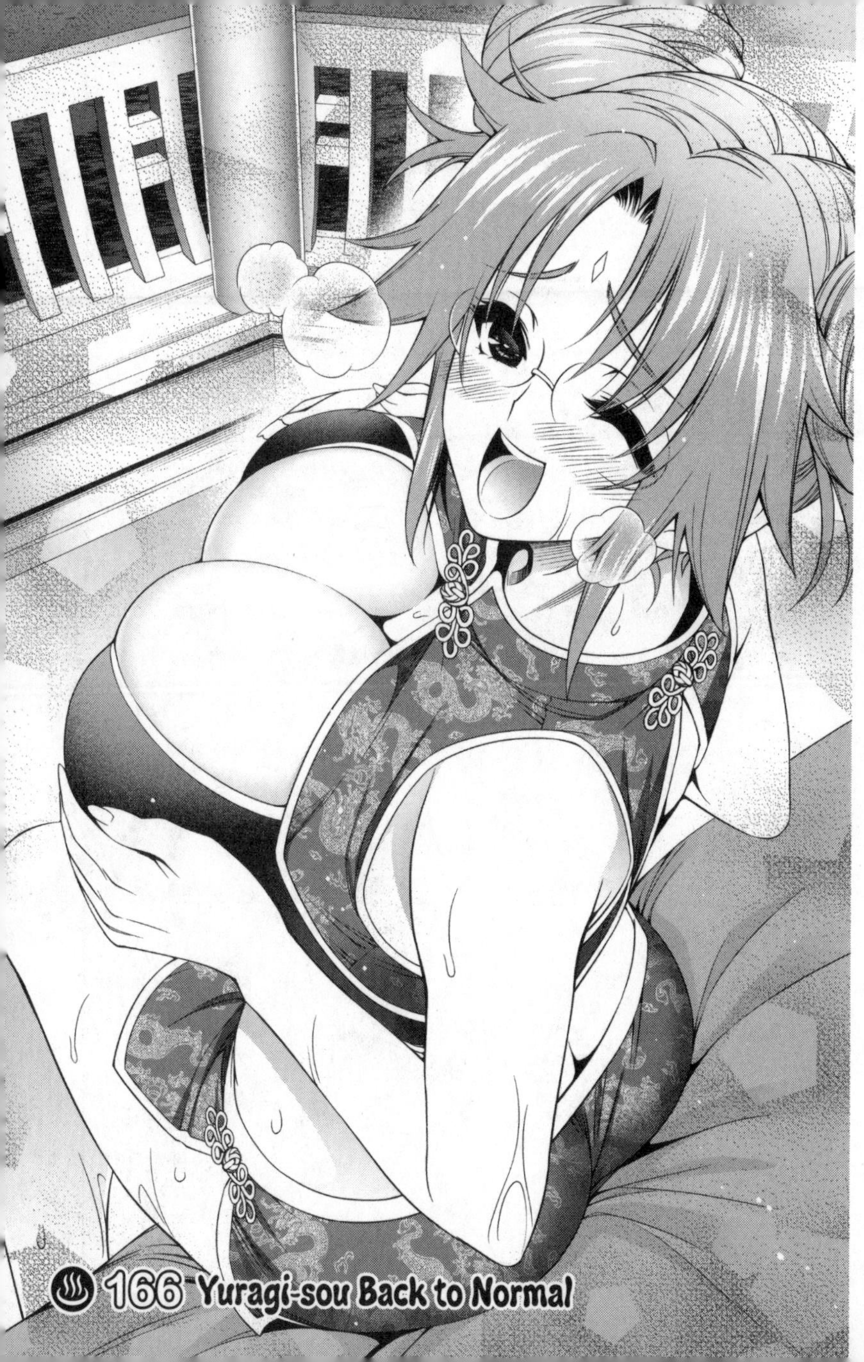
166 Yuragi-sou Back to Normal

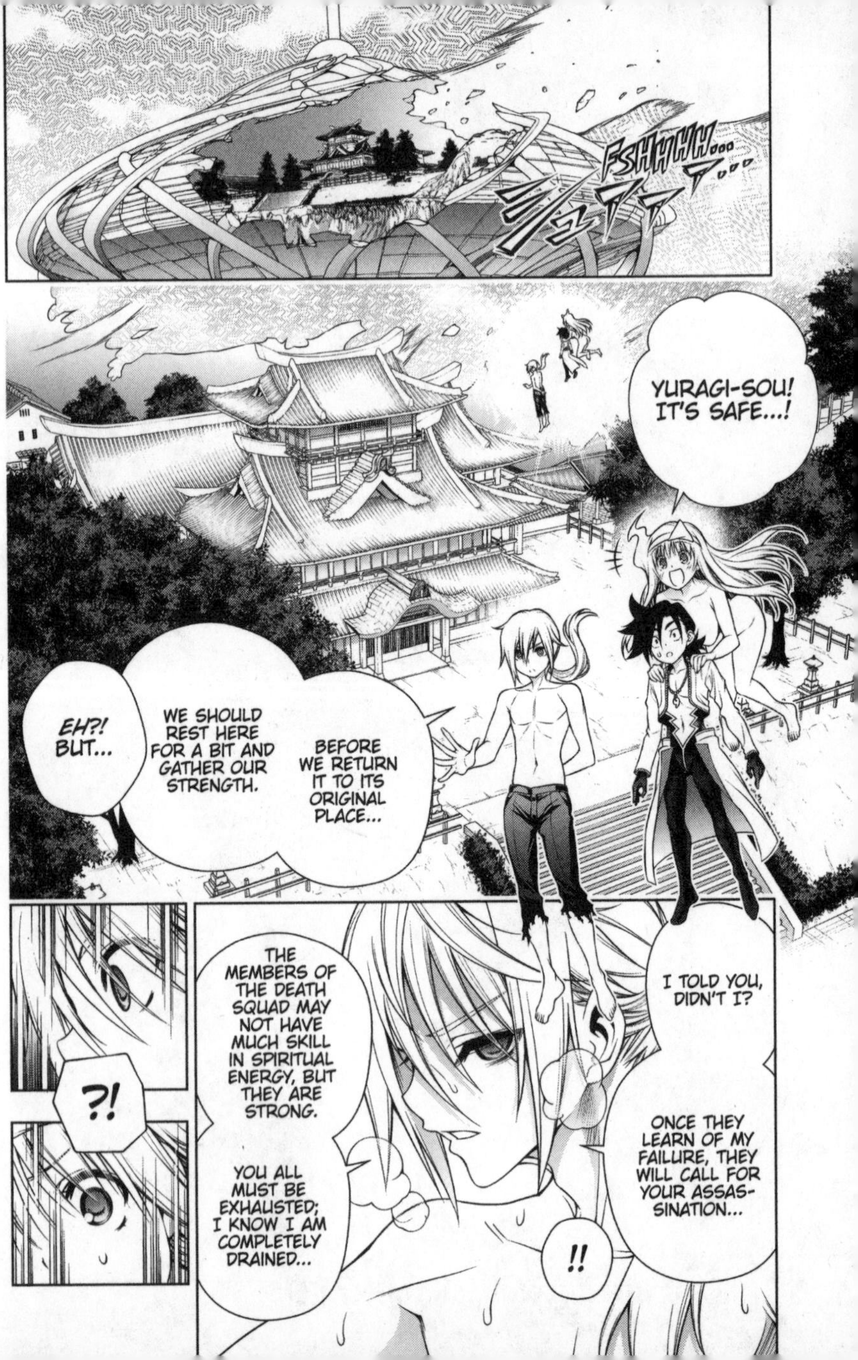
FSHHHH...
YURAGI-SOU! IT'S SAFE...!
BEFORE WE RETURN IT TO ITS ORIGINAL PLACE...
WE SHOULD REST HERE FOR A BIT AND GATHER OUR STRENGTH.
EH?! BUT...
I TOLD YOU, DIDN'T I?
THE MEMBERS OF THE DEATH SQUAD MAY NOT HAVE MUCH SKILL IN SPIRITUAL ENERGY, BUT THEY ARE STRONG.
ONCE THEY LEARN OF MY FAILURE, THEY WILL CALL FOR YOUR ASSAS-SINATION...
YOU ALL MUST BE EXHAUSTED; I KNOW I AM COMPLETELY DRAINED...
!!
?!

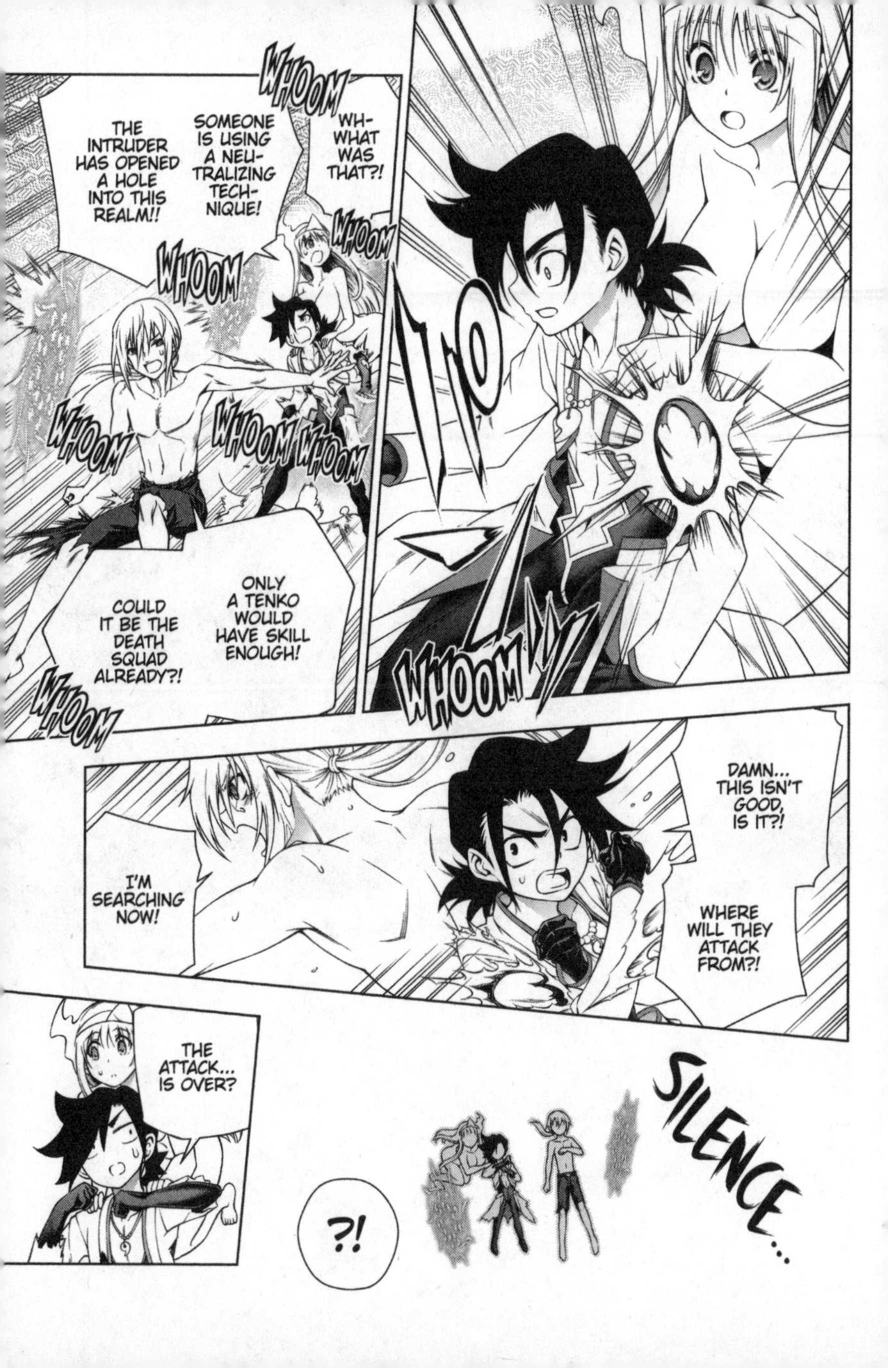
WHOOM
WH-WHAT WAS THAT?!
SOMEONE IS USING A NEUTRALIZING TECHNIQUE!
THE INTRUDER HAS OPENED A HOLE INTO THIS REALM!!
WHOOM
WHOOM
WHOOM
WHOOM WHOOM
WHOOM
ONLY A TENKO WOULD HAVE SKILL ENOUGH!
COULD IT BE THE DEATH SQUAD ALREADY?!
WHOOM
DAMN... THIS ISN'T GOOD, IS IT?!
WHERE WILL THEY ATTACK FROM?!
I'M SEARCHING NOW!
SILENCE...
?!
THE ATTACK... IS OVER?

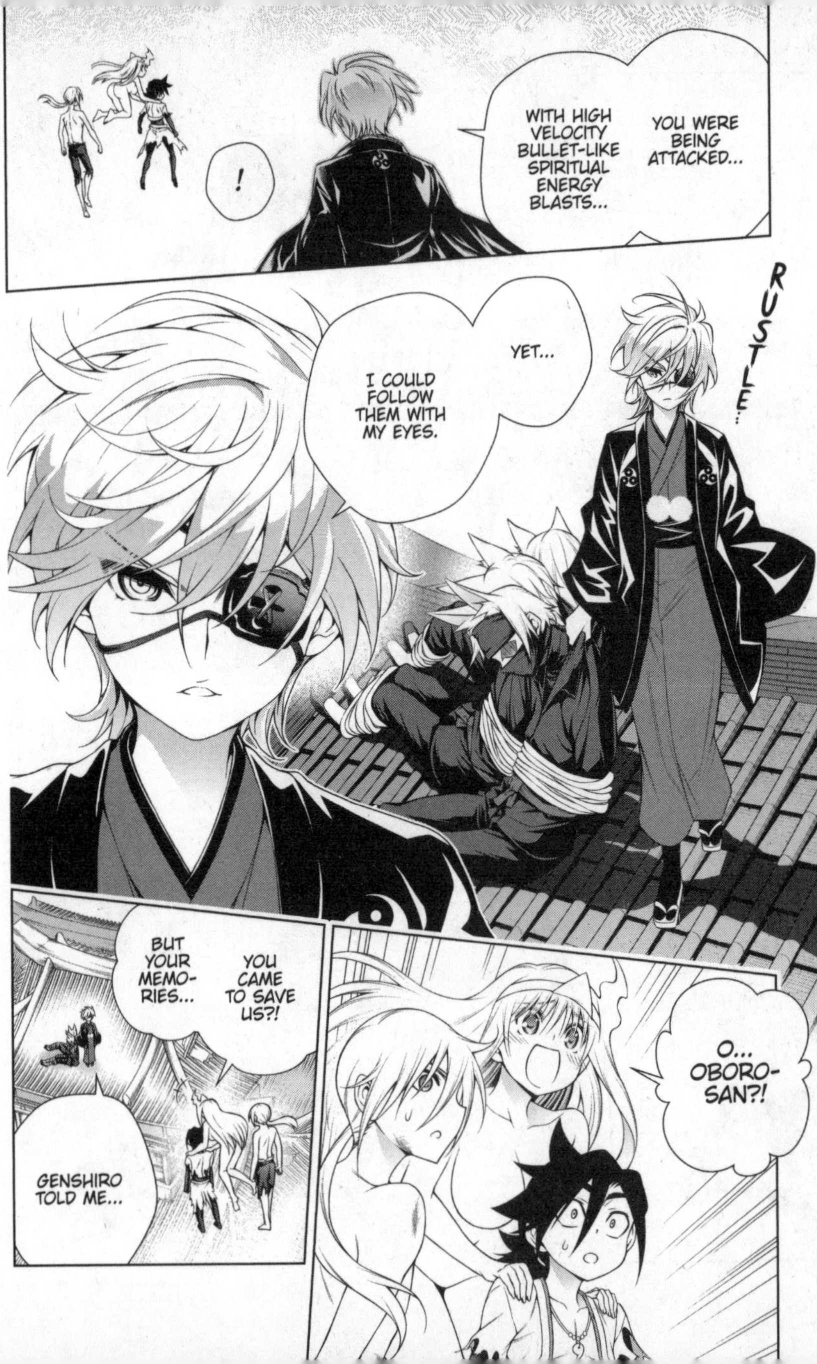
YOU WERE BEING ATTACKED...
WITH HIGH VELOCITY BULLET-LIKE SPIRITUAL ENERGY BLASTS...
!
RUSTLE...
YET...
I COULD FOLLOW THEM WITH MY EYES.
O... OBORO-SAN?!
YOU CAME TO SAVE US?!
BUT YOUR MEMO-RIES...
GENSHIRO TOLD ME...

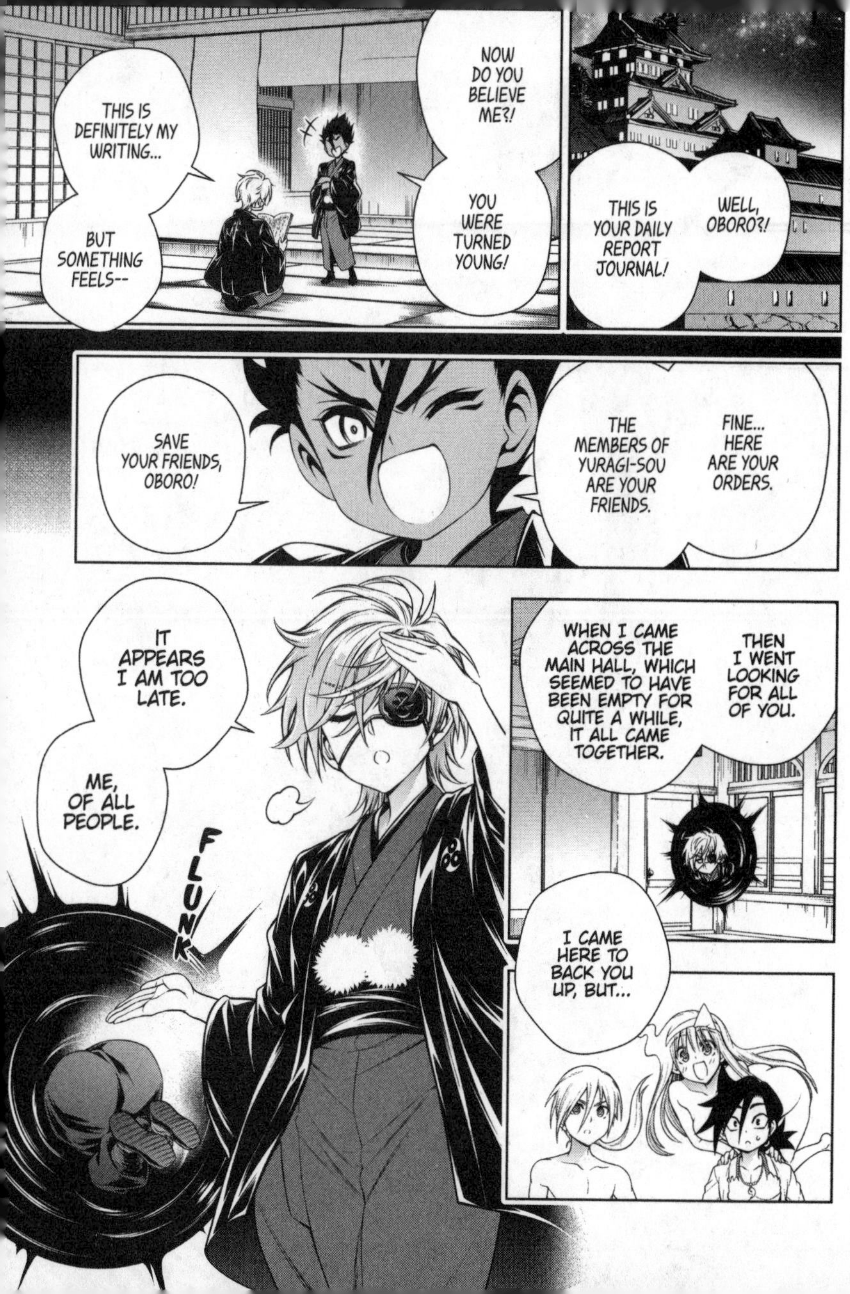
WELL, OBORO?!
THIS IS YOUR DAILY REPORT JOURNAL!
NOW DO YOU BELIEVE ME?!
YOU WERE TURNED YOUNG!
THIS IS DEFINITELY MY WRITING...
BUT SOMETHING FEELS--
FINE... HERE ARE YOUR ORDERS.
THE MEMBERS OF YURAGI-SOU ARE YOUR FRIENDS.
SAVE YOUR FRIENDS, OBORO!
THEN I WENT LOOKING FOR ALL OF YOU.
WHEN I CAME ACROSS THE MAIN HALL, WHICH SEEMED TO HAVE BEEN EMPTY FOR QUITE A WHILE, IT ALL CAME TOGETHER.
I CAME HERE TO BACK YOU UP, BUT...
IT APPEARS I AM TOO LATE.
ME, OF ALL PEOPLE.
FLUNK

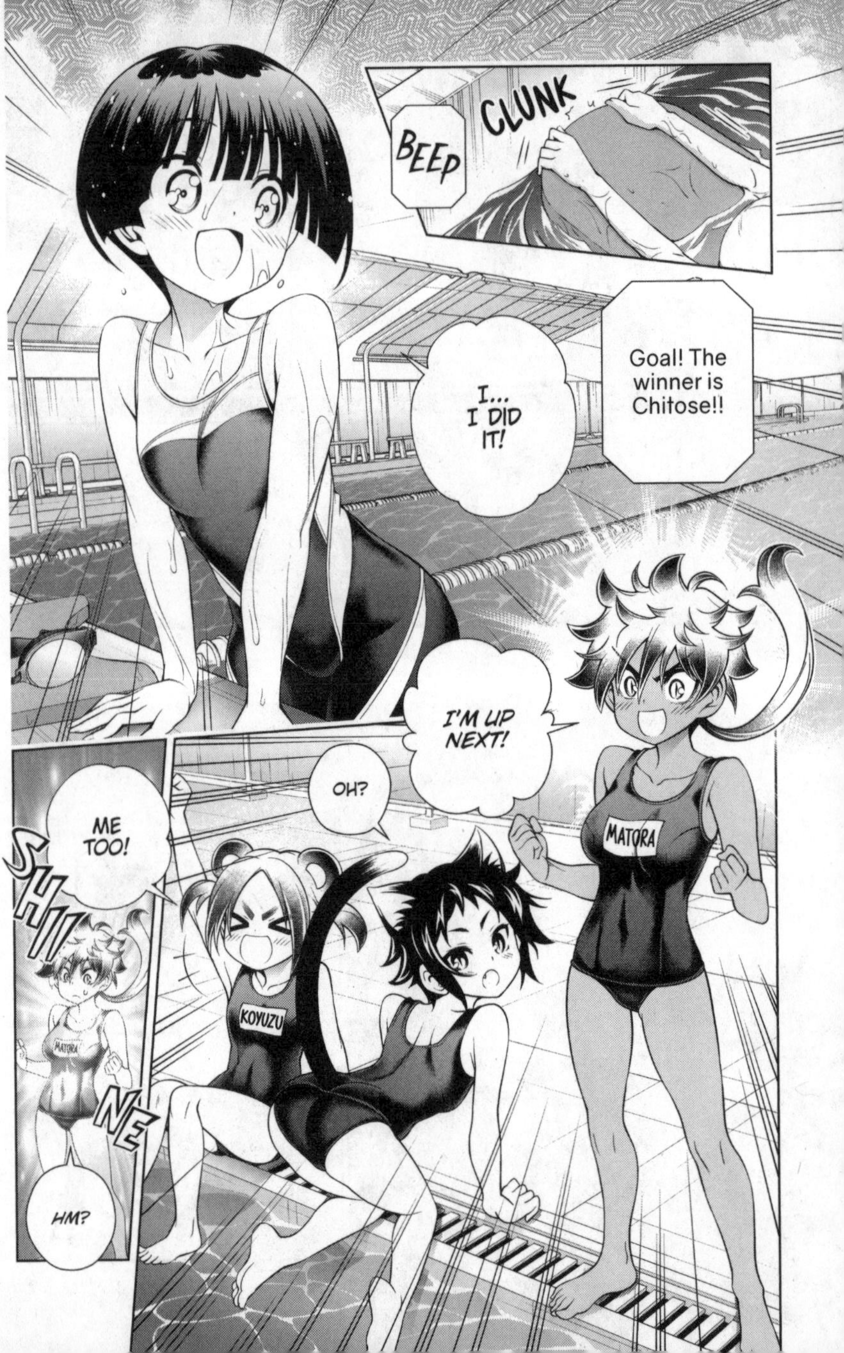
CLUNK
BEEP
Goal! The winner is Chitose!!
I... I DID IT!
I'M UP NEXT!
OH?
ME TOO!
SHIINE
HM?

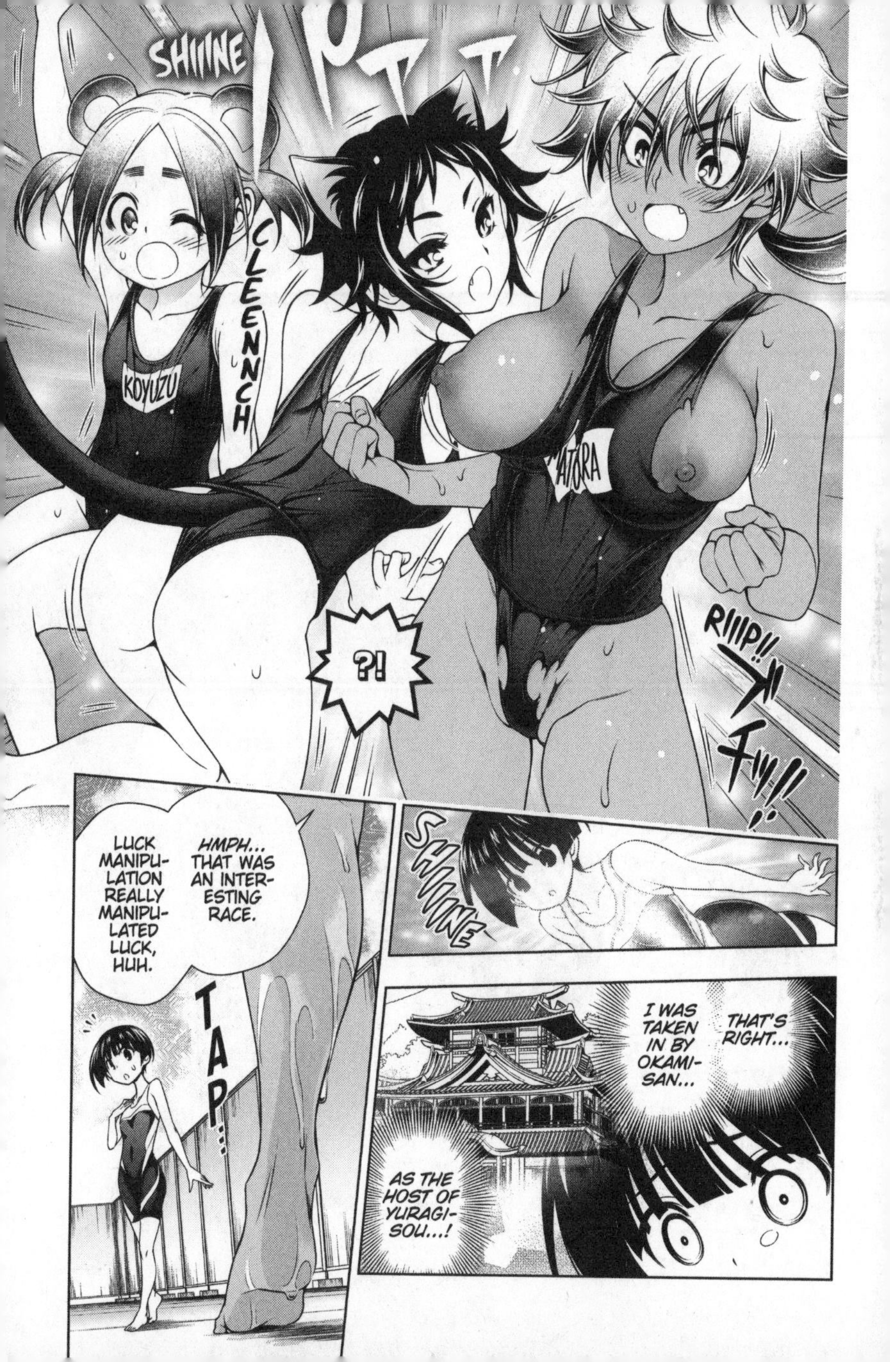
SHIIINE
CLEENNCH
KOYUZU
MATORA
?!
RIIIP!!
SHIIINE
THAT'S RIGHT...
I WAS TAKEN IN BY OKAMI-SAN...
AS THE HOST OF YURAGI-SOU...!
HMPH... THAT WAS AN INTERESTING RACE.
LUCK MANIPULATION REALLY MANIPULATED LUCK, HUH.
TAP...

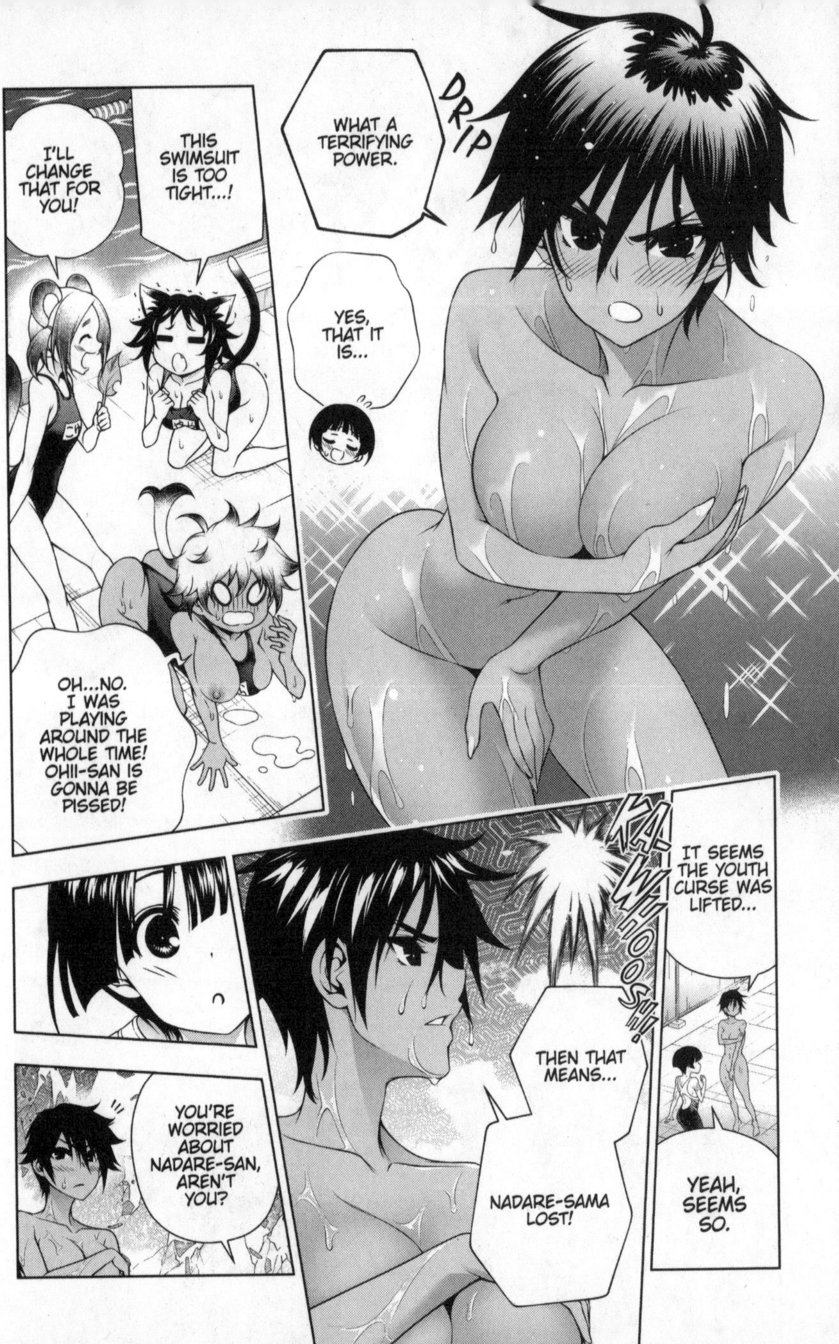
DRIP
WHAT A TERRIFYING POWER.
YES, THAT IT IS...
THIS SWIMSUIT IS TOO TIGHT...!
I'LL CHANGE THAT FOR YOU!
OH...NO. I WAS PLAYING AROUND THE WHOLE TIME! OHII-SAN IS GONNA BE PISSED!
IT SEEMS THE YOUTH CURSE WAS LIFTED...
YEAH, SEEMS SO.
KA-WHOOSH!!
THEN THAT MEANS...
NADARE-SAMA LOST!
YOU'RE WORRIED ABOUT NADARE-SAN, AREN'T YOU?

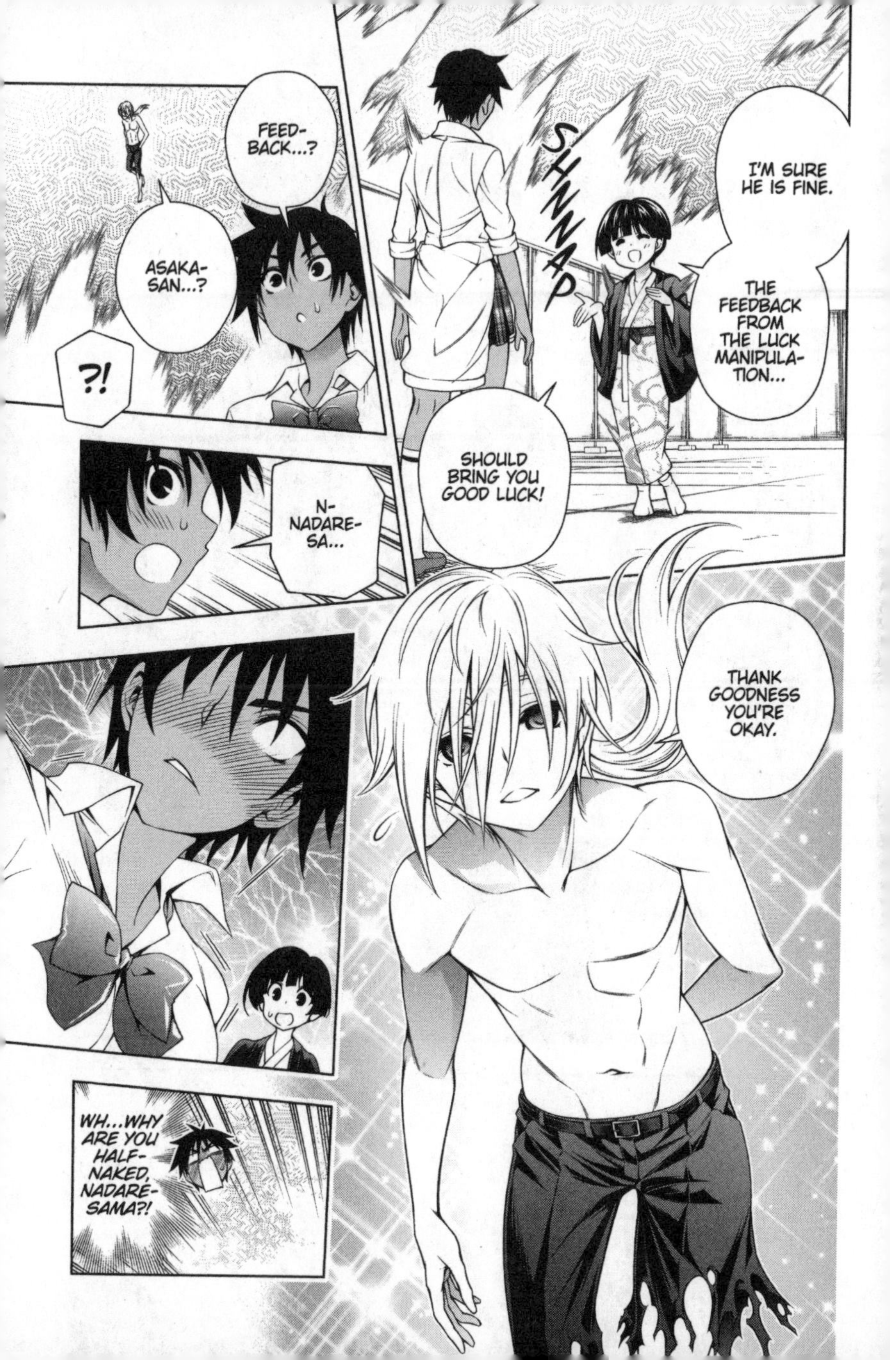
I'M SURE HE IS FINE.
THE FEEDBACK FROM THE LUCK MANIPULATION...
SHNNAP
SHOULD BRING YOU GOOD LUCK!
FEED-BACK...?
ASAKA-SAN...?
?!
N-NADARE-SA...
THANK GOODNESS YOU'RE OKAY.
WH...WHY ARE YOU HALF-NAKED, NADARE-SAMA?!

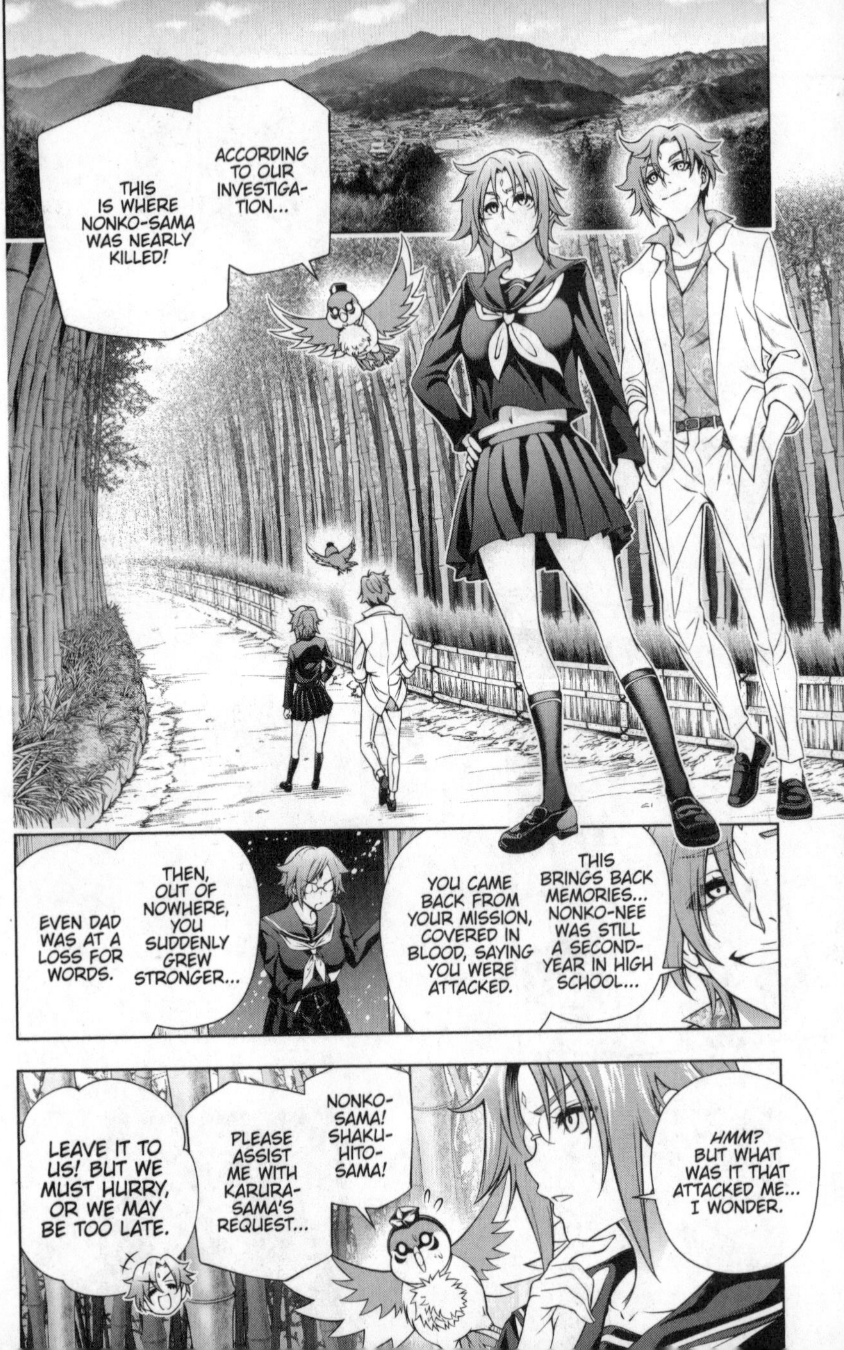
ACCORDING TO OUR INVESTIGATION...
THIS IS WHERE NONKO-SAMA WAS NEARLY KILLED!
THIS BRINGS BACK MEMORIES... NONKO-NEE WAS STILL A SECOND-YEAR IN HIGH SCHOOL...
YOU CAME BACK FROM YOUR MISSION, COVERED IN BLOOD, SAYING YOU WERE ATTACKED.
THEN, OUT OF NOWHERE, YOU SUDDENLY GREW STRONGER...
EVEN DAD WAS AT A LOSS FOR WORDS.
HMM? BUT WHAT WAS IT THAT ATTACKED ME... I WONDER.
NONKO-SAMA! SHAKUHITO-SAMA!
PLEASE ASSIST ME WITH KARURA-SAMA'S REQUEST...
LEAVE IT TO US! BUT WE MUST HURRY, OR WE MAY BE TOO LATE.

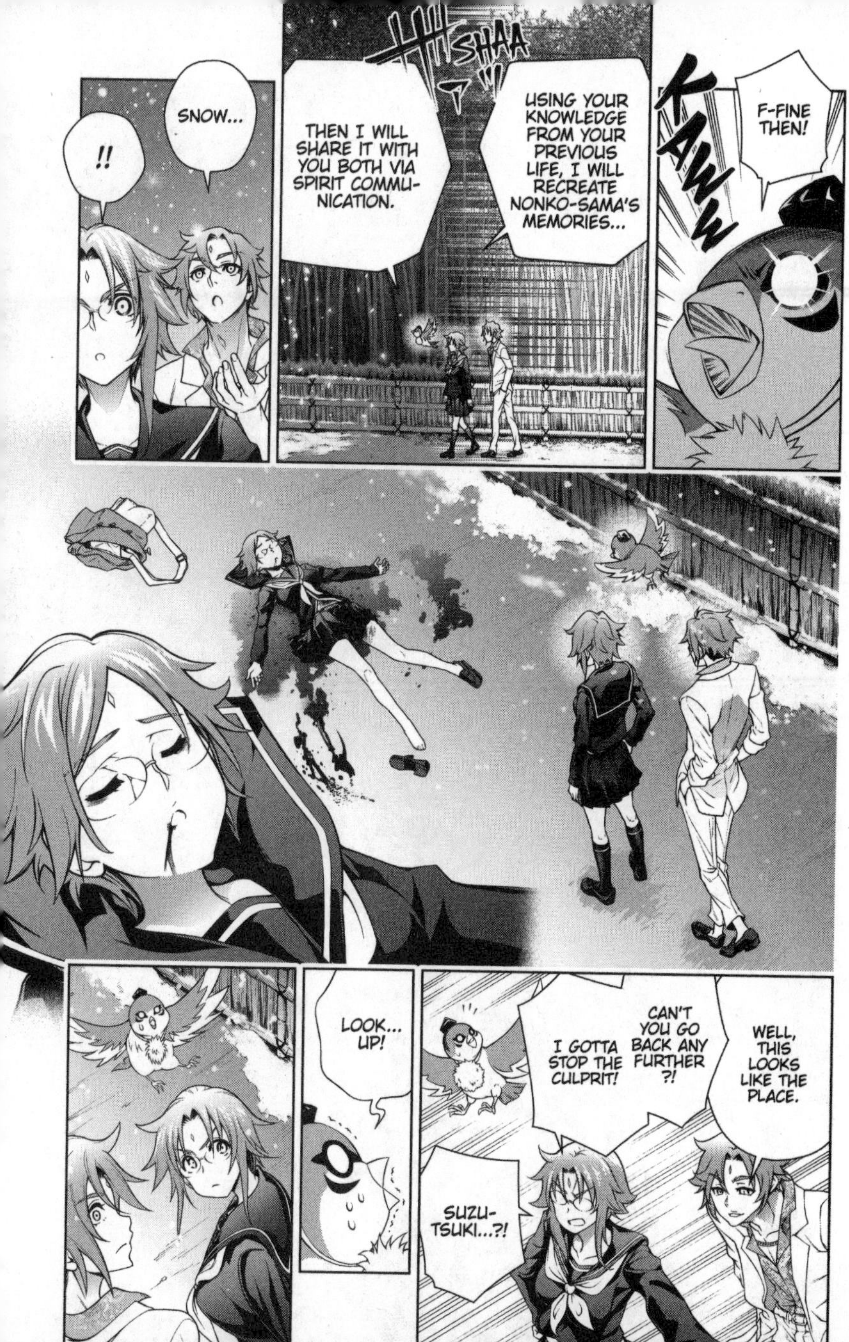
KAWW
F-FINE THEN!
SHAA
USING YOUR KNOWLEDGE FROM YOUR PREVIOUS LIFE, I WILL RECREATE NONKO-SAMA'S MEMORIES...
THEN I WILL SHARE IT WITH YOU BOTH VIA SPIRIT COMMUNICATION.
SNOW...
!!
WELL, THIS LOOKS LIKE THE PLACE.
CAN'T YOU GO BACK ANY FURTHER ?!
I GOTTA STOP THE CULPRIT!
SUZU-TSUKI...?!
LOOK... UP!

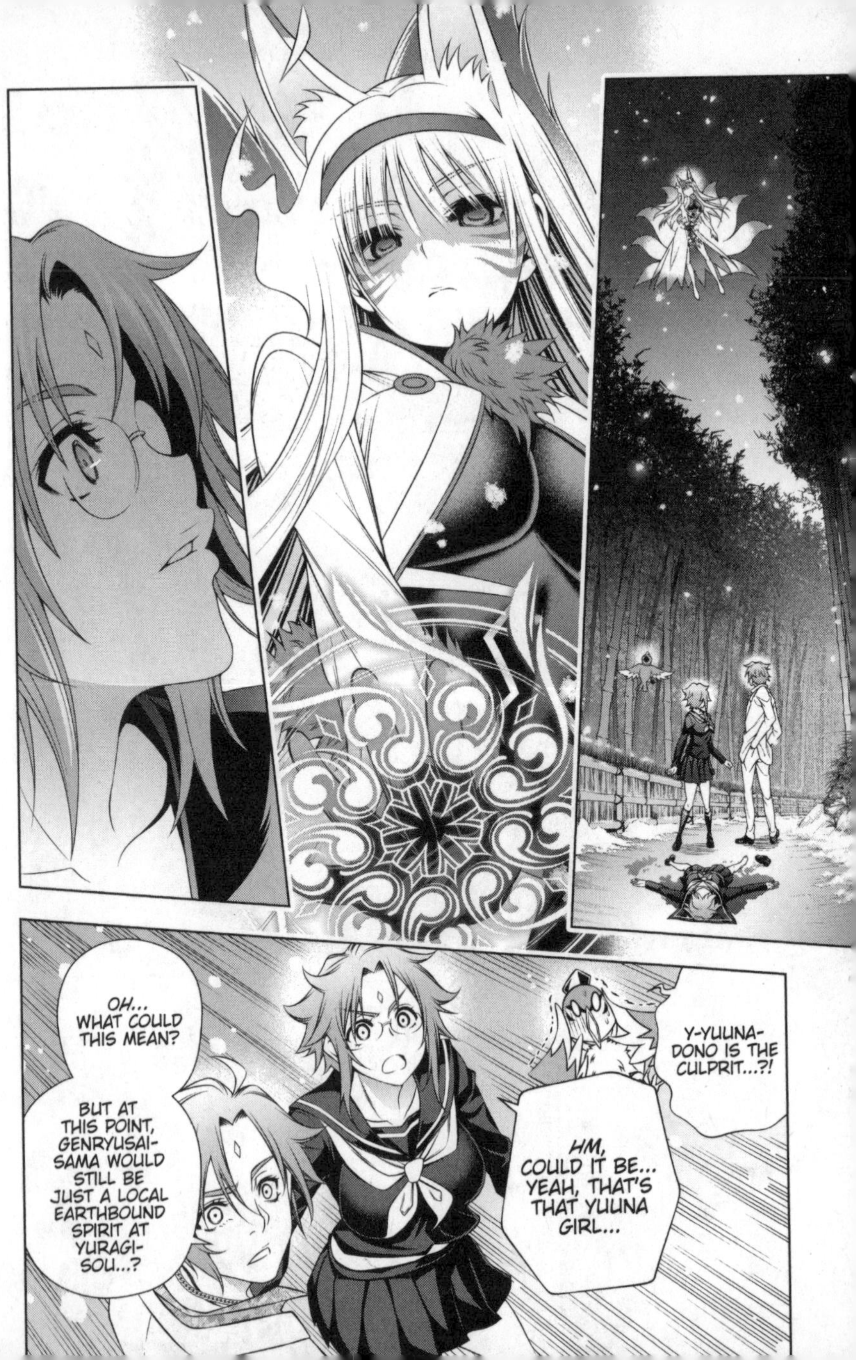
Y-YUUNA-DONO IS THE CULPRIT...?!
HM, COULD IT BE... YEAH, THAT'S THAT YUUNA GIRL...
OH... WHAT COULD THIS MEAN?
BUT AT THIS POINT, GENRYUSAI-SAMA WOULD STILL BE JUST A LOCAL EARTHBOUND SPIRIT AT YURAGI-SOU...?

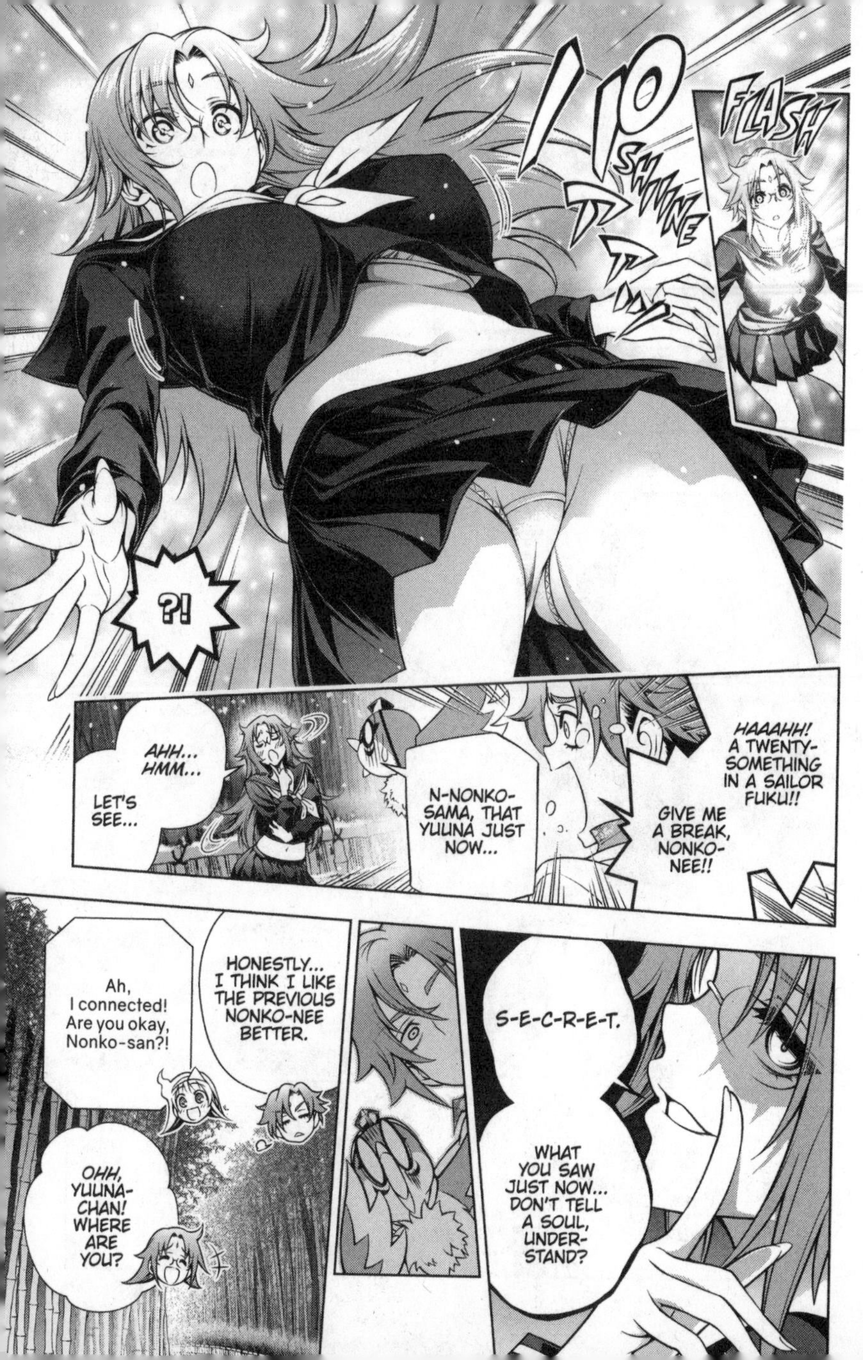
FLASH
SHINE
?!
HAAAHH! A TWENTY-SOMETHING IN A SAILOR FUKU!!
GIVE ME A BREAK, NONKO-NEE!!
N-NONKO-SAMA, THAT YUUNA JUST NOW...
AHH... HMM...
LET'S SEE...
S-E-C-R-E-T.
WHAT YOU SAW JUST NOW... DON'T TELL A SOUL, UNDERSTAND?
HONESTLY... I THINK I LIKE THE PREVIOUS NONKO-NEE BETTER.
Ah, I connected! Are you okay, Nonko-san?!
OHH, YUUNA-CHAN! WHERE ARE YOU?

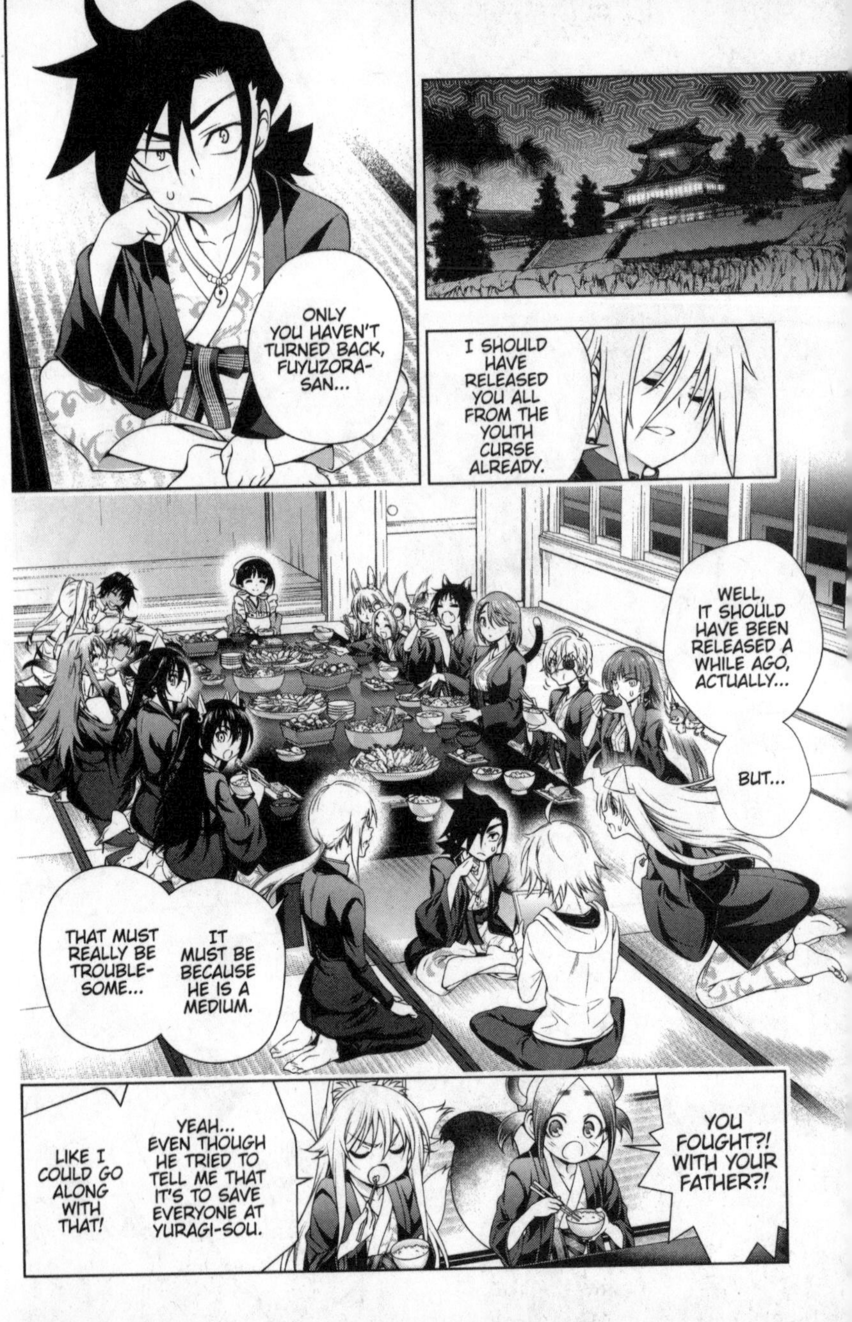
I SHOULD HAVE RELEASED YOU ALL FROM THE YOUTH CURSE ALREADY.
ONLY YOU HAVEN'T TURNED BACK, FUYUZORA-SAN...
WELL, IT SHOULD HAVE BEEN RELEASED A WHILE AGO, ACTUALLY...
BUT...
IT MUST BE BECAUSE HE IS A MEDIUM.
THAT MUST REALLY BE TROUBLE-SOME...
YOU FOUGHT?! WITH YOUR FATHER?!
YEAH... EVEN THOUGH HE TRIED TO TELL ME THAT IT'S TO SAVE EVERYONE AT YURAGI-SOU.
LIKE I COULD GO ALONG WITH THAT!

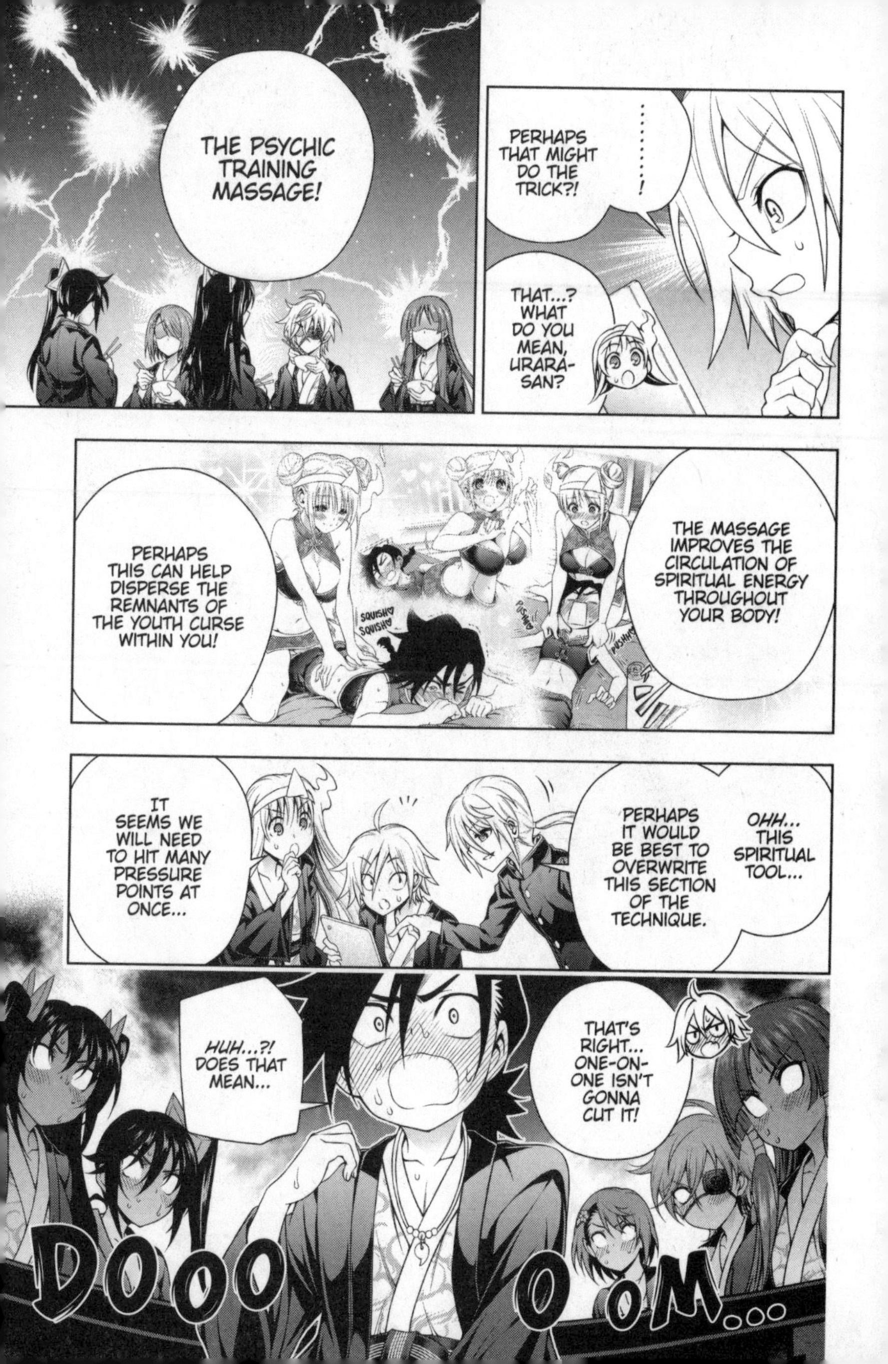
......!
PERHAPS THAT MIGHT DO THE TRICK?!
THAT...? WHAT DO YOU MEAN, URARA-SAN?
THE PSYCHIC TRAINING MASSAGE!
THE MASSAGE IMPROVES THE CIRCULATION OF SPIRITUAL ENERGY THROUGHOUT YOUR BODY!
PUSHH
SQUISH♥ SQUISH♥
PERHAPS THIS CAN HELP DISPERSE THE REMNANTS OF THE YOUTH CURSE WITHIN YOU!
OHH... THIS SPIRITUAL TOOL...
PERHAPS IT WOULD BE BEST TO OVERWRITE THIS SECTION OF THE TECHNIQUE.
IT SEEMS WE WILL NEED TO HIT MANY PRESSURE POINTS AT ONCE...
THAT'S RIGHT... ONE-ON-ONE ISN'T GONNA CUT IT!
HUH...?! DOES THAT MEAN...
DOOOO O OM...

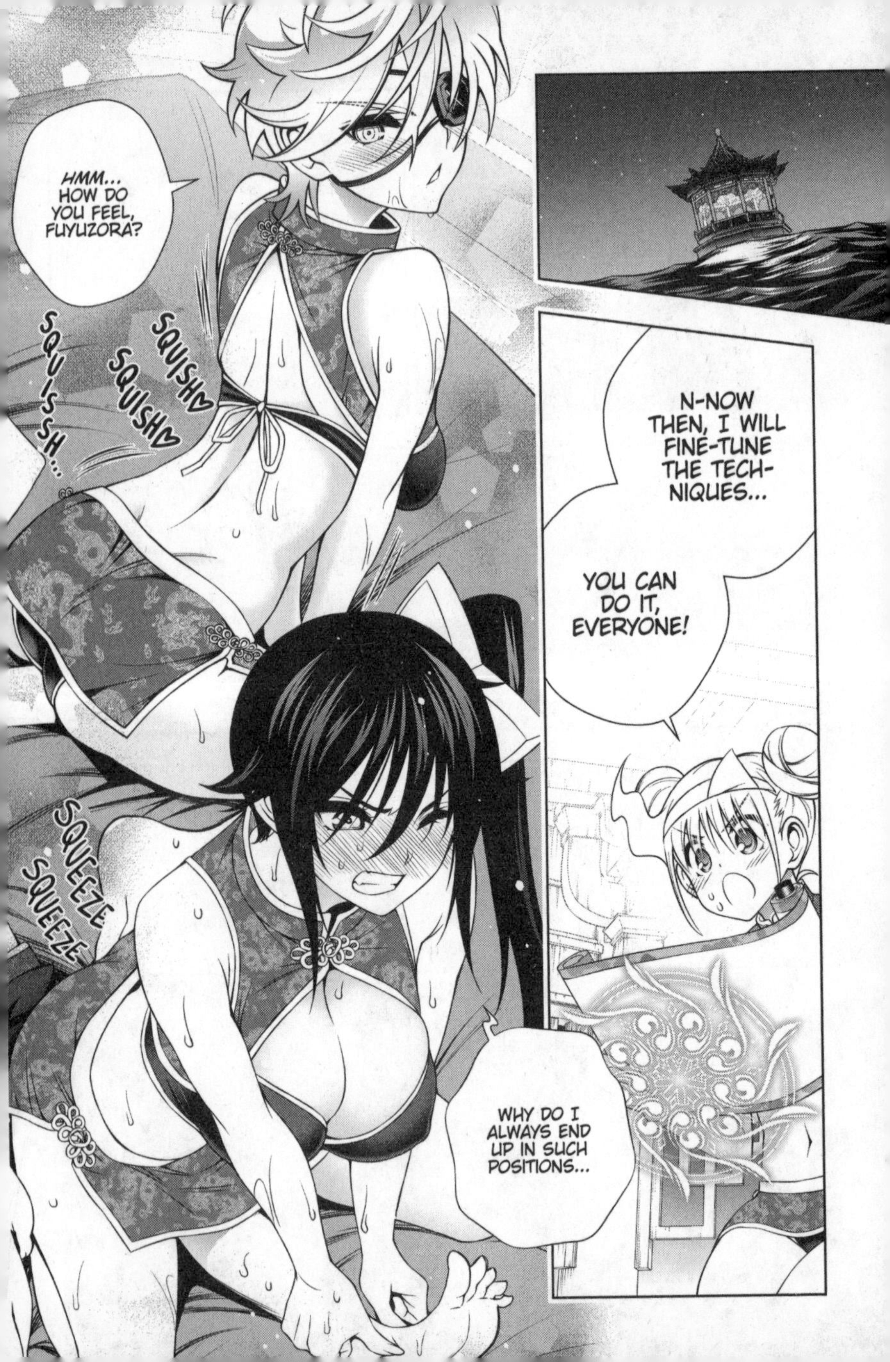
N-NOW THEN, I WILL FINE-TUNE THE TECH-NIQUES...
YOU CAN DO IT, EVERYONE!
HMM... HOW DO YOU FEEL, FUYUZORA?
SQUISH♥ SQUISH♥ SQUISSH...
WHY DO I ALWAYS END UP IN SUCH POSITIONS...
SQUEEZE SQUEEZE

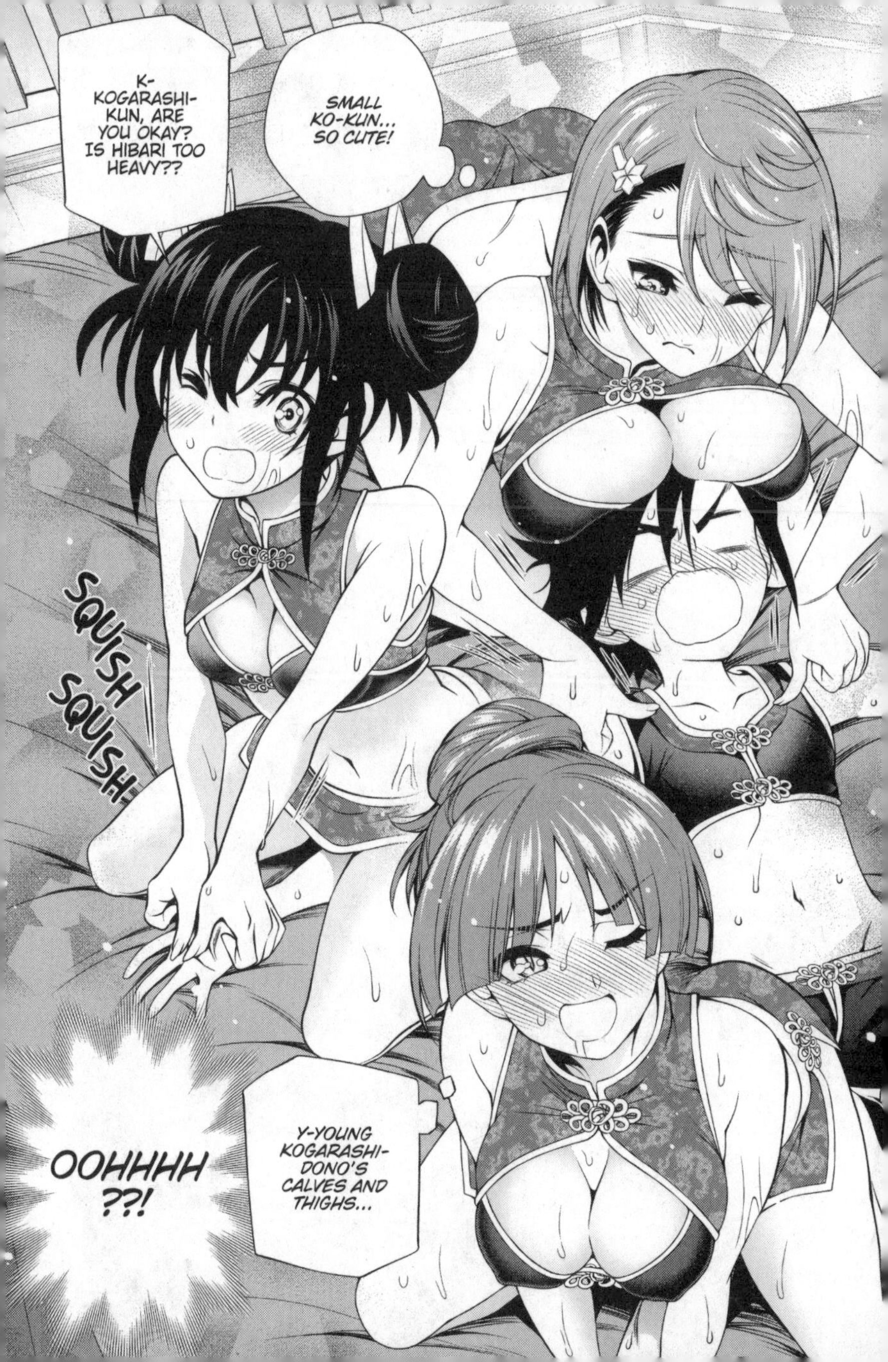
SMALL KO-KUN... SO CUTE!
K-KOGARASHI-KUN, ARE YOU OKAY? IS HIBARI TOO HEAVY??
SQUISH SQUISH
Y-YOUNG KOGARASHI-DONO'S CALVES AND THIGHS...
OOHHHH ??!

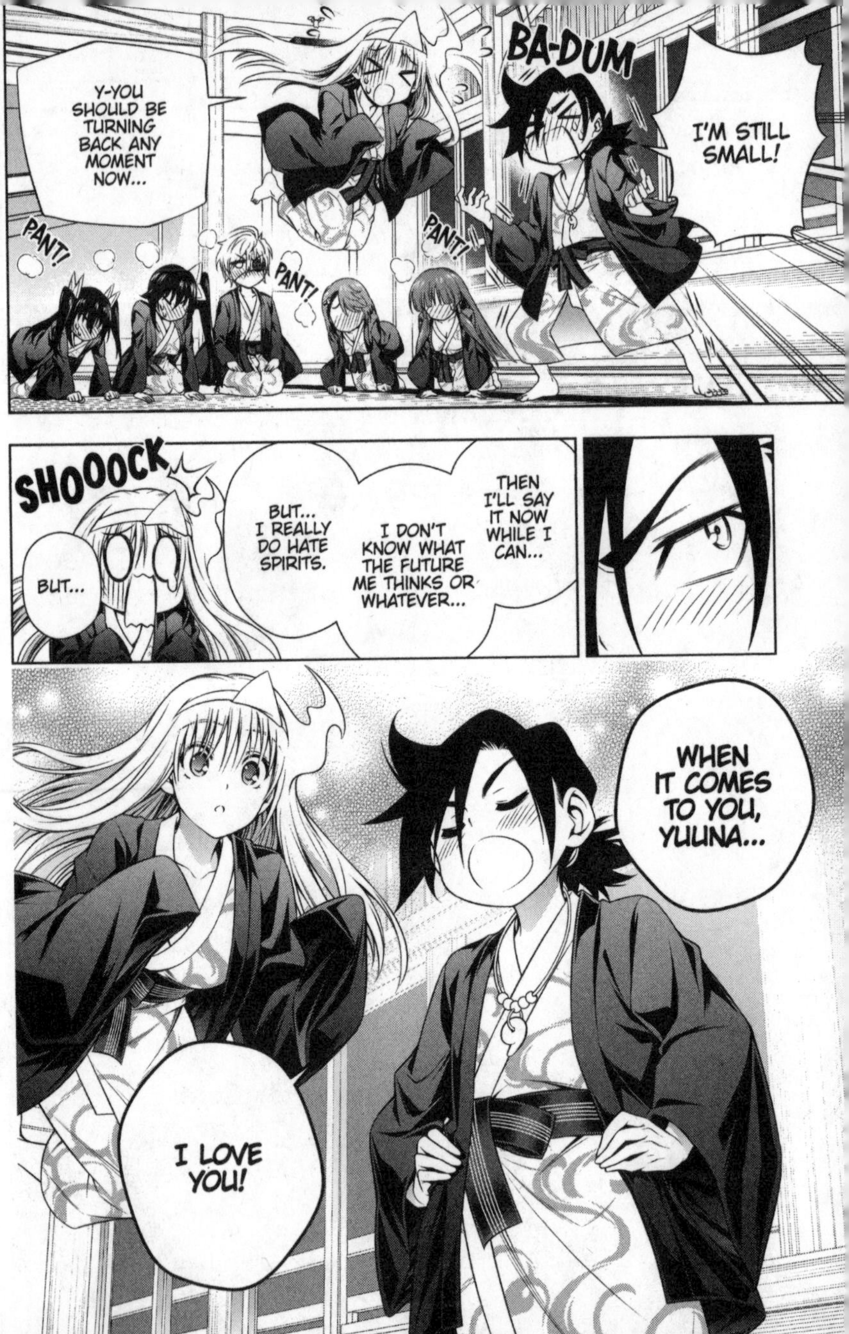
BA-DUM
I'M STILL SMALL!
PANT!
PANT!
Y-YOU SHOULD BE TURNING BACK ANY MOMENT NOW...
PANT!
THEN I'LL SAY IT NOW WHILE I CAN...
I DON'T KNOW WHAT THE FUTURE ME THINKS OR WHATEVER...
BUT... I REALLY DO HATE SPIRITS.
SHOOOCK
BUT...
WHEN IT COMES TO YOU, YUUNA...
I LOVE YOU!

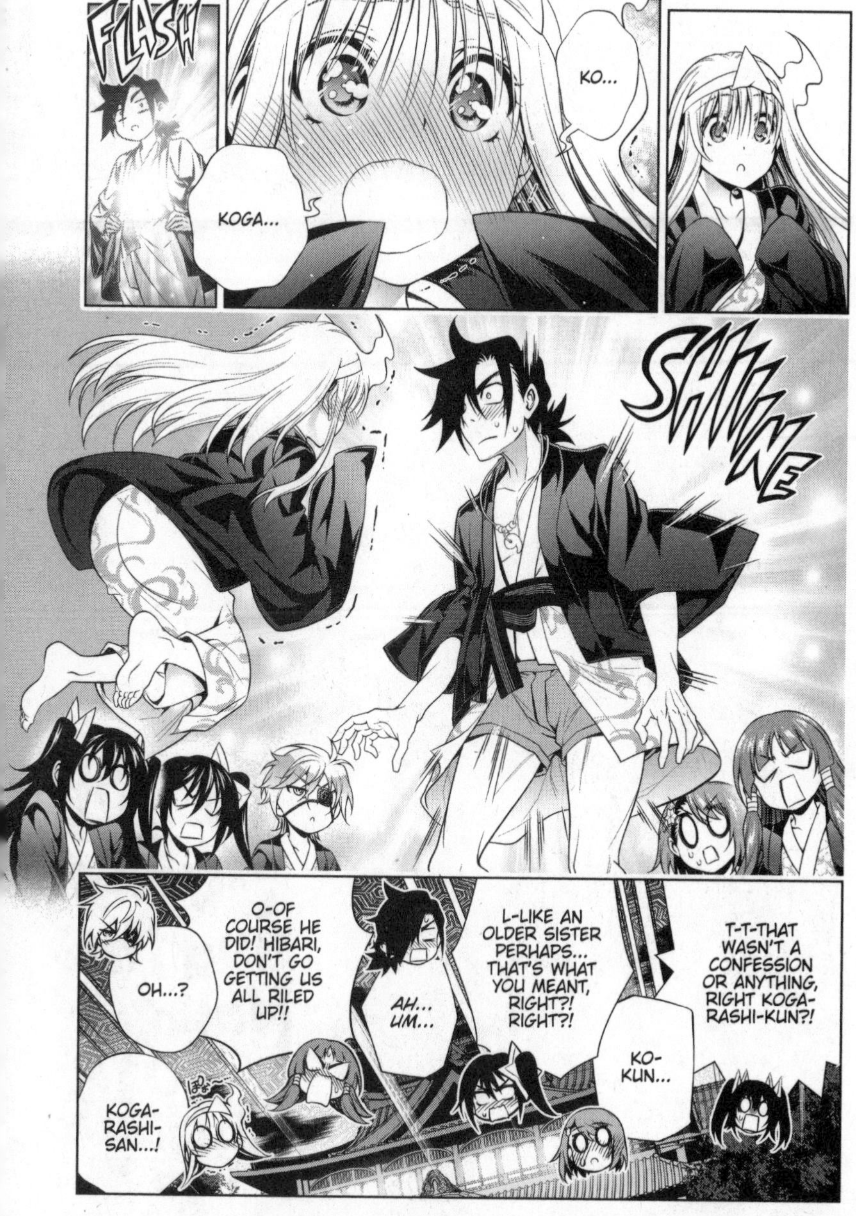
KO...
KOGA...
FLASH
SHINE
T-T-THAT WASN'T A CONFESSION OR ANYTHING, RIGHT KOGA-RASHI-KUN?!
KO-KUN...
L-LIKE AN OLDER SISTER PERHAPS... THAT'S WHAT YOU MEANT, RIGHT?! RIGHT?!
AH... UM...
O-OF COURSE HE DID! HIBARI, DON'T GO GETTING US ALL RILED UP!!
OH...?
KOGA-RASHI-SAN...!

Yuuna
and the
Haunted
Hot
Springs

167 Kogarashi-kun and the Great Danger

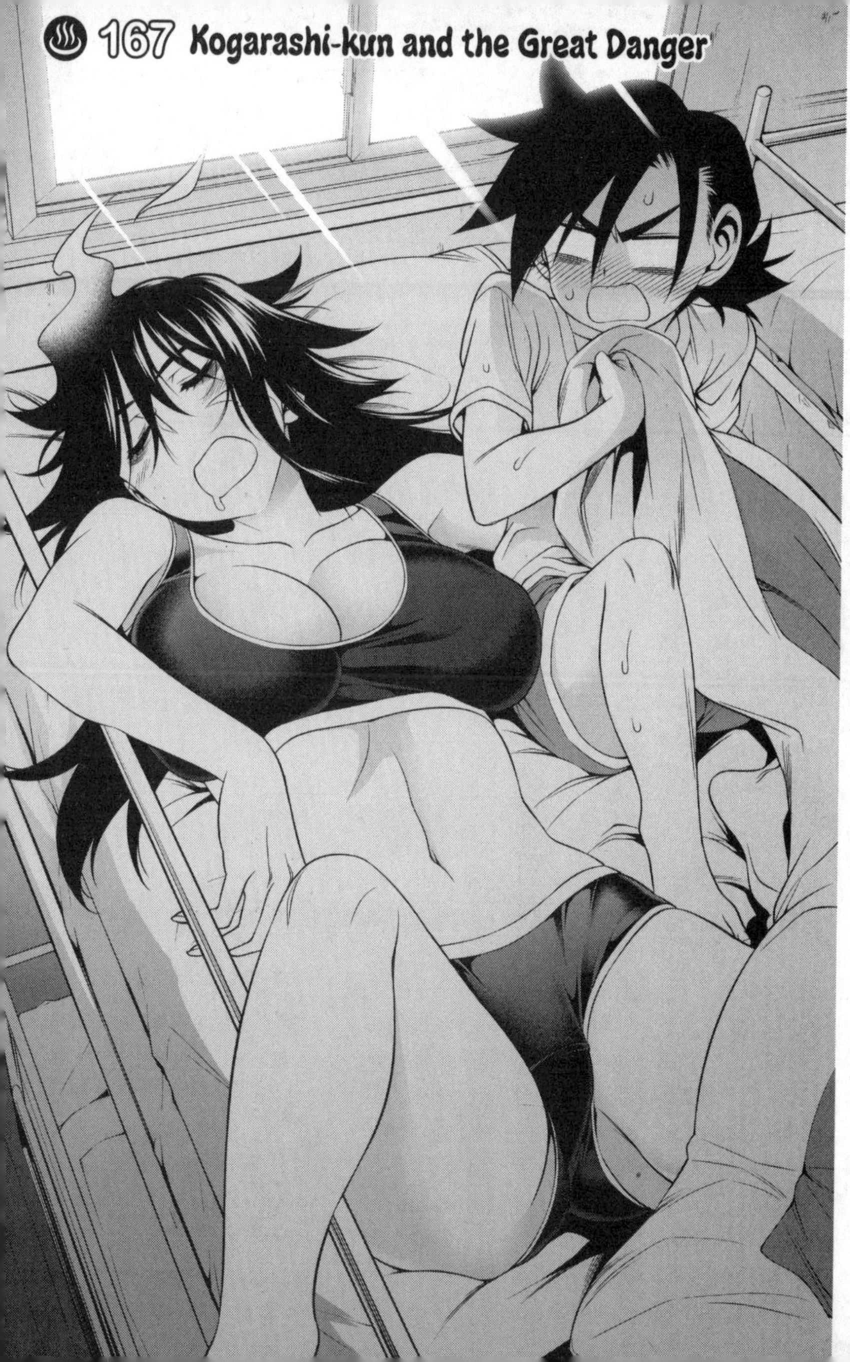

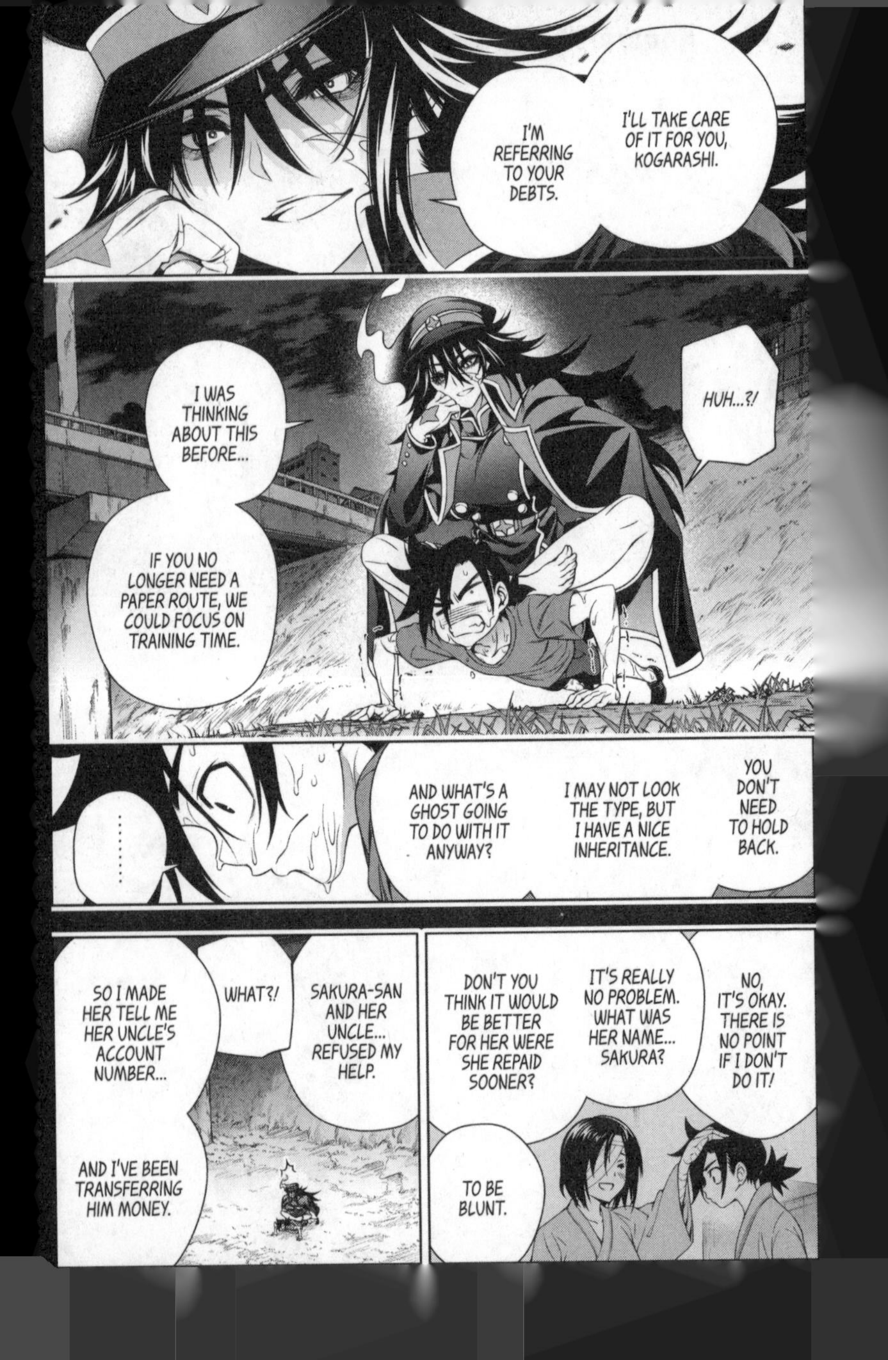

I'LL TAKE CARE OF IT FOR YOU, KOGARASHI.
I'M REFERRING TO YOUR DEBTS.
HUH...?!
I WAS THINKING ABOUT THIS BEFORE...
IF YOU NO LONGER NEED A PAPER ROUTE, WE COULD FOCUS ON TRAINING TIME.
YOU DON'T NEED TO HOLD BACK.
I MAY NOT LOOK THE TYPE, BUT I HAVE A NICE INHERITANCE.
AND WHAT'S A GHOST GOING TO DO WITH IT ANYWAY?
......
NO, IT'S OKAY. THERE IS NO POINT IF I DON'T DO IT!
IT'S REALLY NO PROBLEM. WHAT WAS HER NAME... SAKURA?
DON'T YOU THINK IT WOULD BE BETTER FOR HER WERE SHE REPAID SOONER?
TO BE BLUNT.
SAKURA-SAN AND HER UNCLE... REFUSED MY HELP.
WHAT?!
SO I MADE HER TELL ME HER UNCLE'S ACCOUNT NUMBER...
AND I'VE BEEN TRANSFERRING HIM MONEY.

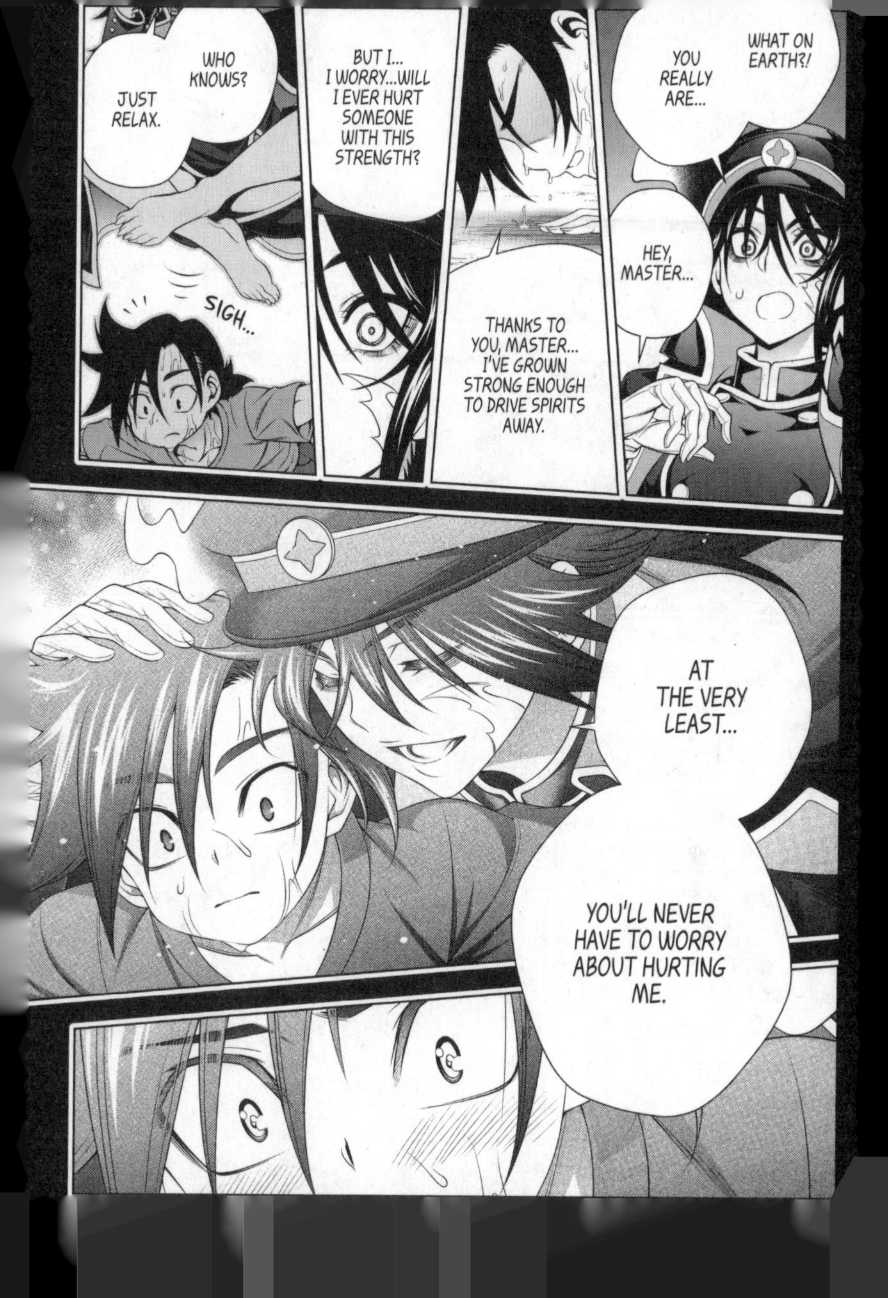
WHAT ON EARTH?!
YOU REALLY ARE...
HEY, MASTER...
THANKS TO YOU, MASTER... I'VE GROWN STRONG ENOUGH TO DRIVE SPIRITS AWAY.
BUT I... I WORRY...WILL I EVER HURT SOMEONE WITH THIS STRENGTH?
WHO KNOWS?
JUST RELAX.
SIGH...
AT THE VERY LEAST...
YOU'LL NEVER HAVE TO WORRY ABOUT HURTING ME.

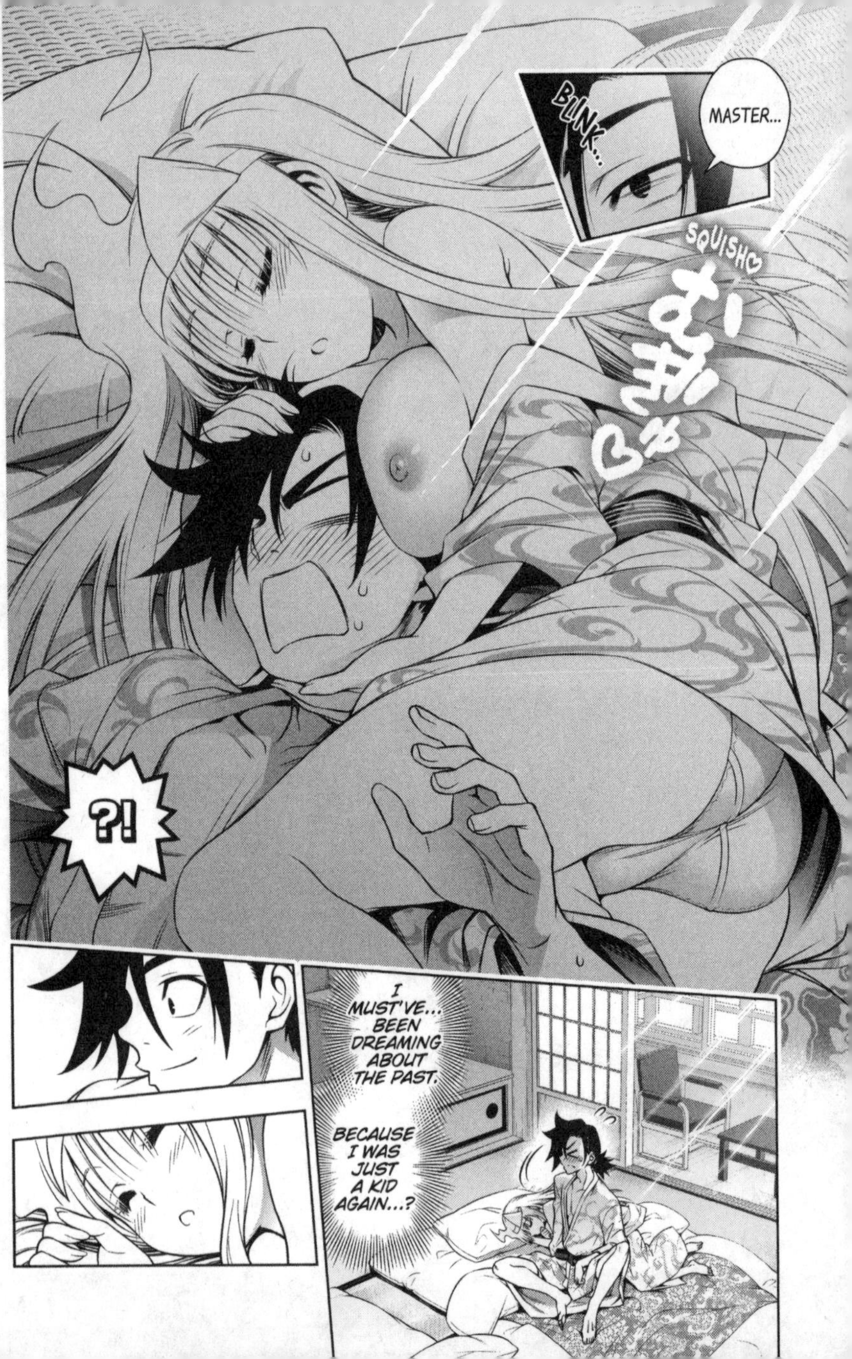
BLINK...
MASTER...
SQUISH♡
?!
I MUST'VE... BEEN DREAMING ABOUT THE PAST.
BECAUSE I WAS JUST A KID AGAIN...?

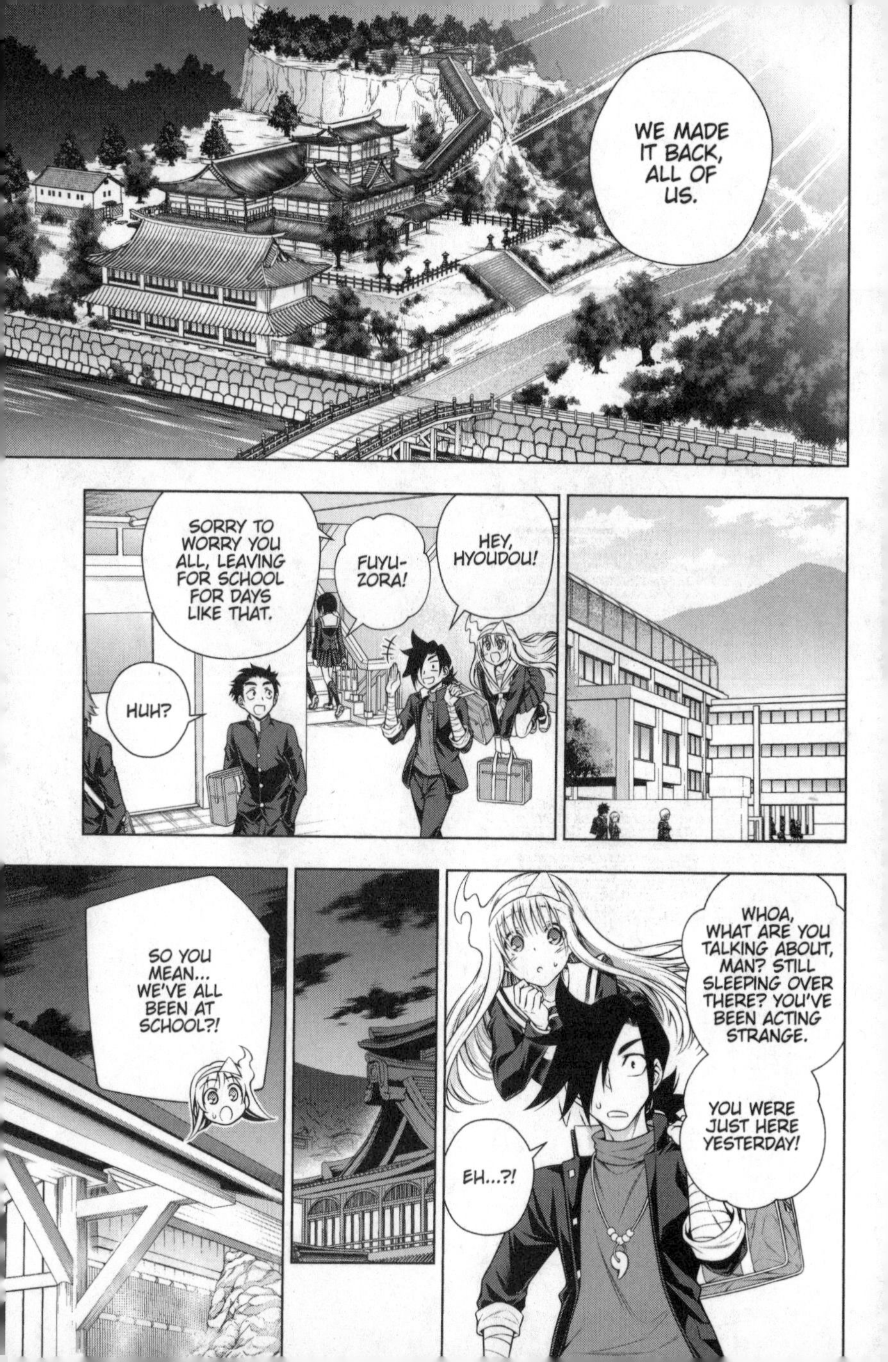
WE MADE IT BACK, ALL OF US.
HEY, HYOUDOU!
FUYU-ZORA!
SORRY TO WORRY YOU ALL, LEAVING FOR SCHOOL FOR DAYS LIKE THAT.
HUH?
WHOA, WHAT ARE YOU TALKING ABOUT, MAN? STILL SLEEPING OVER THERE? YOU'VE BEEN ACTING STRANGE.
YOU WERE JUST HERE YESTERDAY!
EH...?!
SO YOU MEAN... WE'VE ALL BEEN AT SCHOOL?!

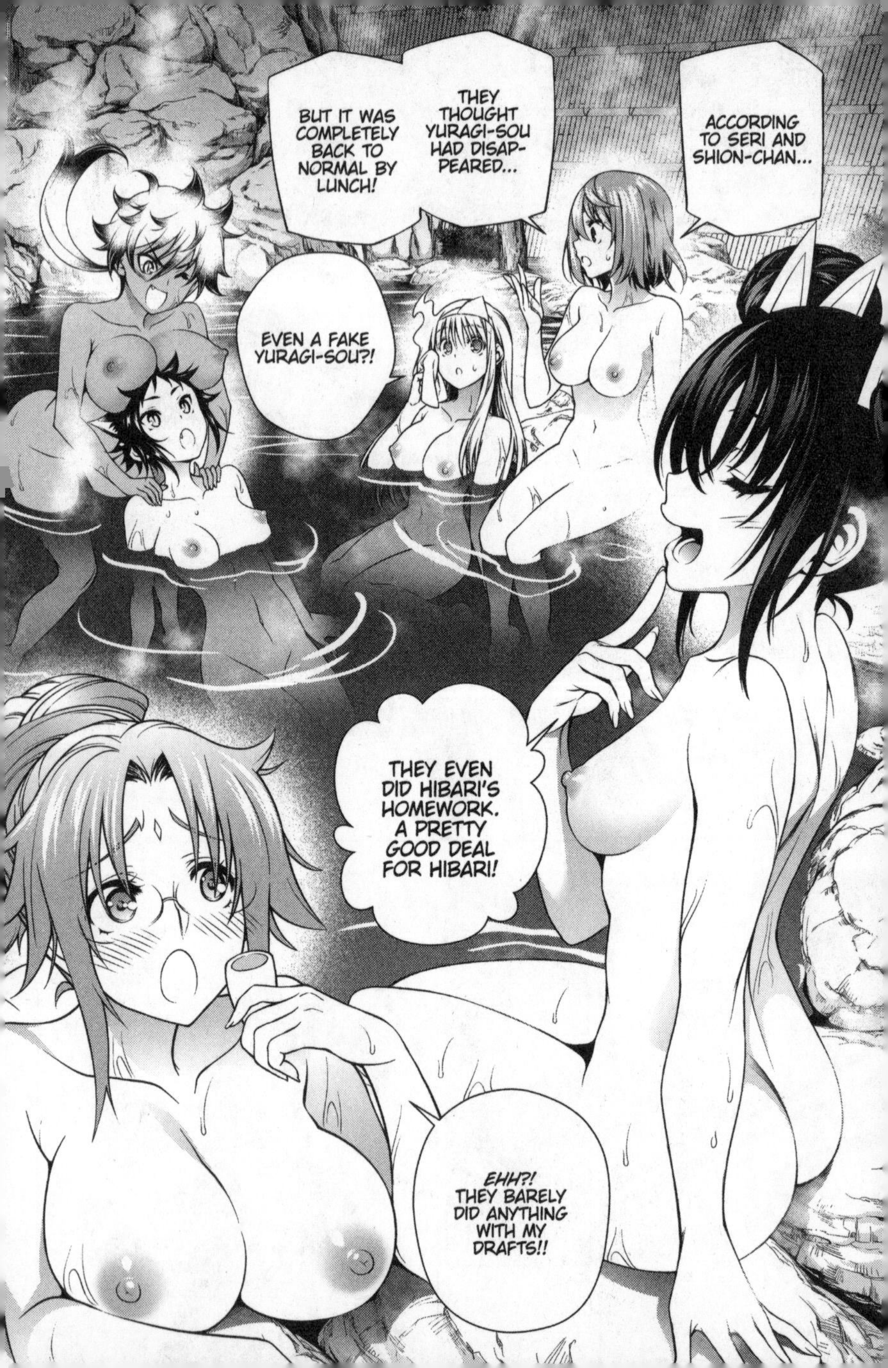
ACCORDING TO SERI AND SHION-CHAN...
THEY THOUGHT YURAGI-SOU HAD DISAPPEARED...
BUT IT WAS COMPLETELY BACK TO NORMAL BY LUNCH!
EVEN A FAKE YURAGI-SOU?!
THEY EVEN DID HIBARI'S HOMEWORK. A PRETTY GOOD DEAL FOR HIBARI!
EHH?! THEY BARELY DID ANYTHING WITH MY DRAFTS!!

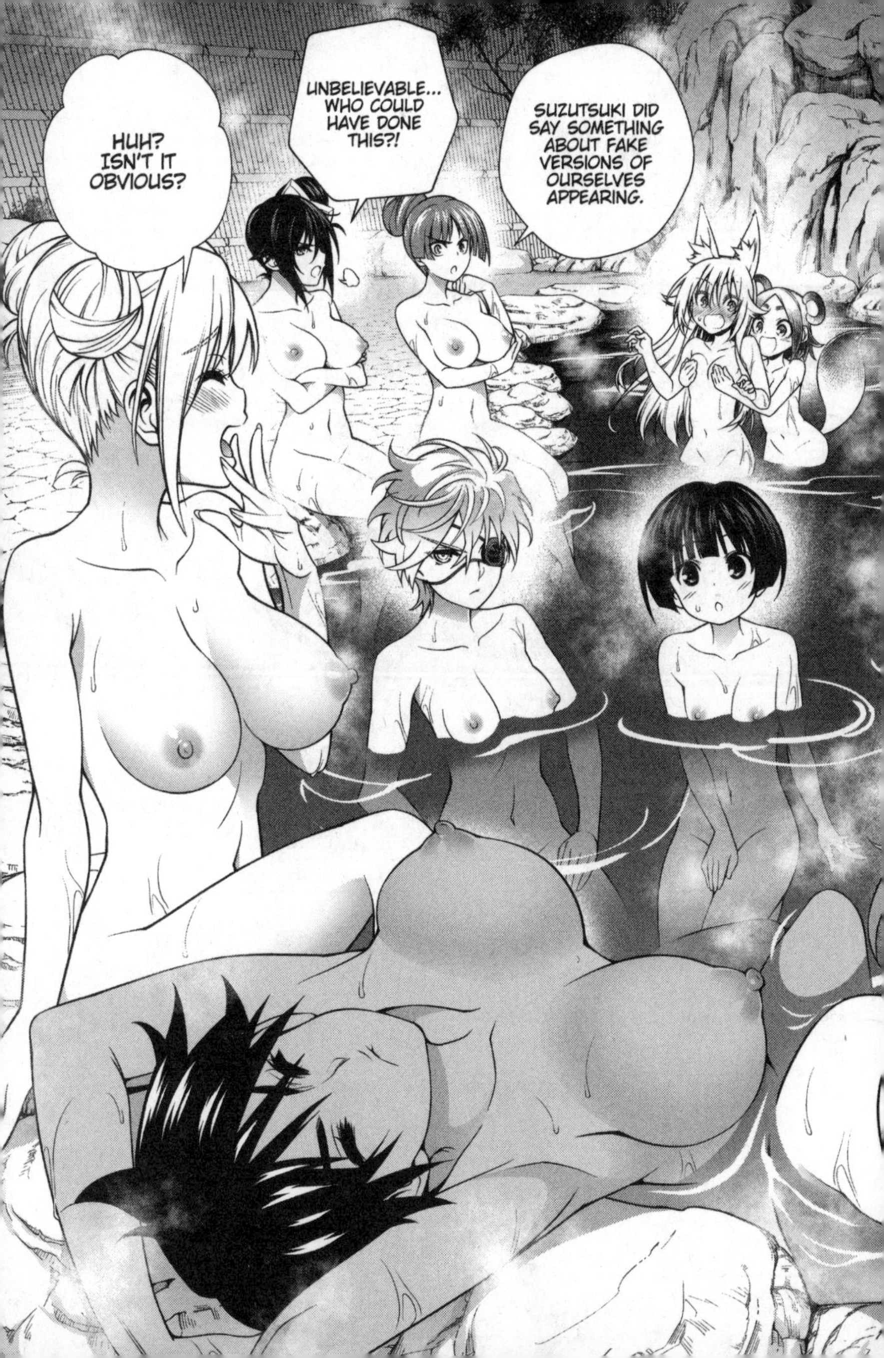
SUZUTSUKI DID SAY SOMETHING ABOUT FAKE VERSIONS OF OURSELVES APPEARING.
UNBELIEVABLE... WHO COULD HAVE DONE THIS?!
HUH? ISN'T IT OBVIOUS?

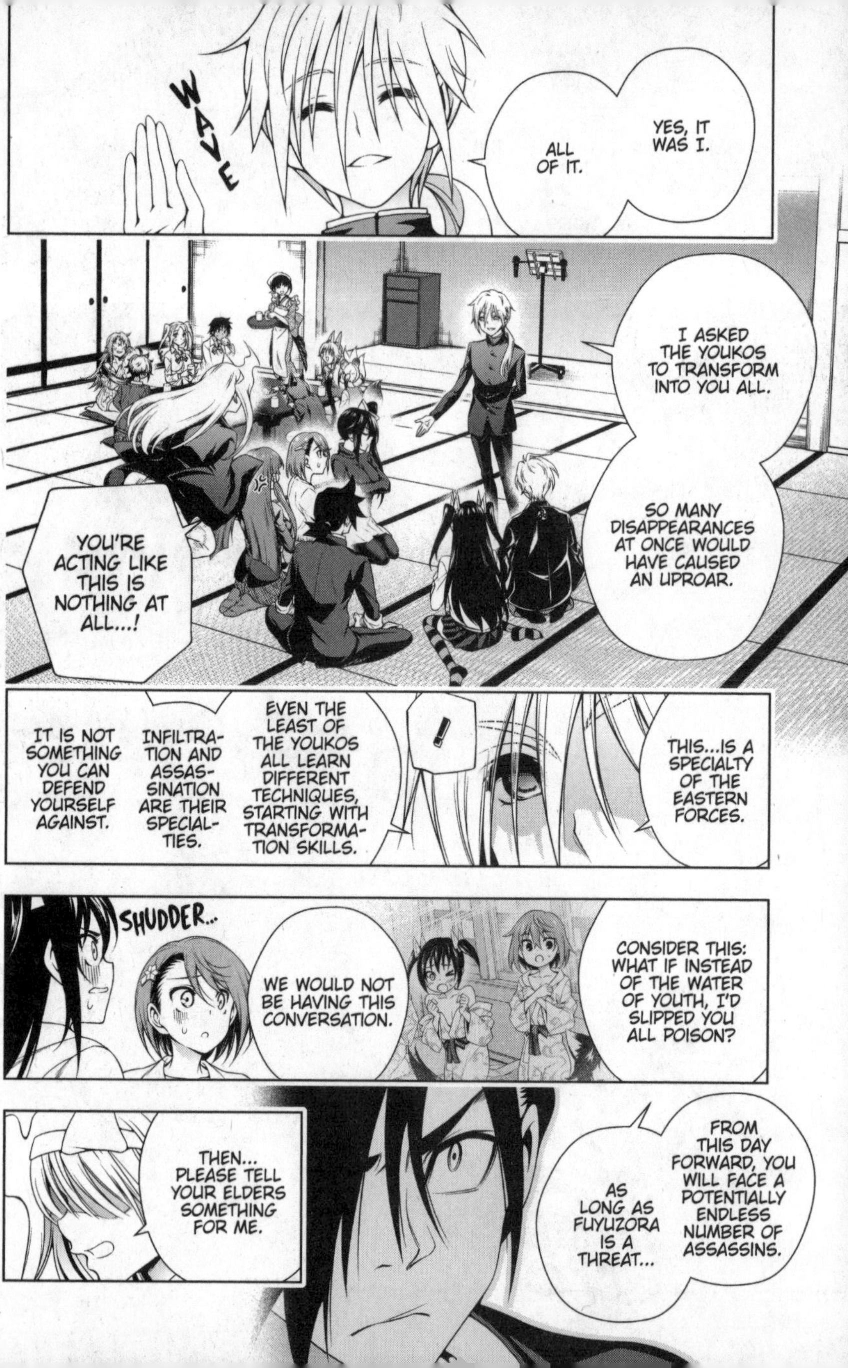
YES, IT WAS I.
ALL OF IT.
WAVE
I ASKED THE YOUKOS TO TRANSFORM INTO YOU ALL.
SO MANY DISAPPEARANCES AT ONCE WOULD HAVE CAUSED AN UPROAR.
YOU'RE ACTING LIKE THIS IS NOTHING AT ALL...!
THIS...IS A SPECIALTY OF THE EASTERN FORCES.
!
EVEN THE LEAST OF THE YOUKOS ALL LEARN DIFFERENT TECHNIQUES, STARTING WITH TRANSFORMATION SKILLS.
INFILTRATION AND ASSASSINATION ARE THEIR SPECIALTIES.
IT IS NOT SOMETHING YOU CAN DEFEND YOURSELF AGAINST.
CONSIDER THIS: WHAT IF INSTEAD OF THE WATER OF YOUTH, I'D SLIPPED YOU ALL POISON?
WE WOULD NOT BE HAVING THIS CONVERSATION.
SHUDDER...
FROM THIS DAY FORWARD, YOU WILL FACE A POTENTIALLY ENDLESS NUMBER OF ASSASSINS.
AS LONG AS FUYUZORA IS A THREAT...
THEN... PLEASE TELL YOUR ELDERS SOMETHING FOR ME.

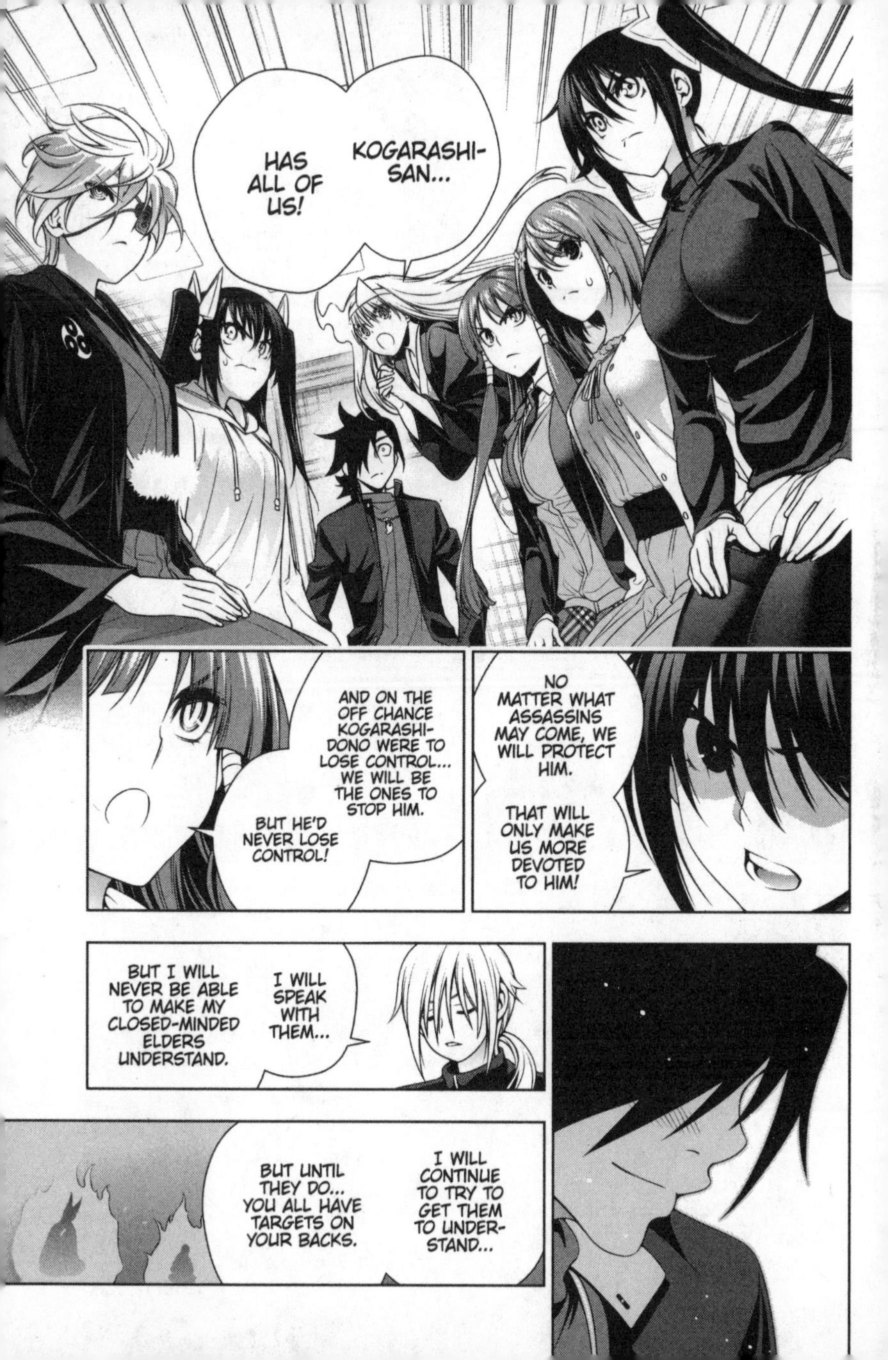
KOGARASHI-SAN...
HAS ALL OF US!
NO MATTER WHAT ASSASSINS MAY COME, WE WILL PROTECT HIM.
THAT WILL ONLY MAKE US MORE DEVOTED TO HIM!
AND ON THE OFF CHANCE KOGARASHI-DONO WERE TO LOSE CONTROL... WE WILL BE THE ONES TO STOP HIM.
BUT HE'D NEVER LOSE CONTROL!
I WILL SPEAK WITH THEM...
BUT I WILL NEVER BE ABLE TO MAKE MY CLOSED-MINDED ELDERS UNDERSTAND.
I WILL CONTINUE TO TRY TO GET THEM TO UNDERSTAND...
BUT UNTIL THEY DO... YOU ALL HAVE TARGETS ON YOUR BACKS.

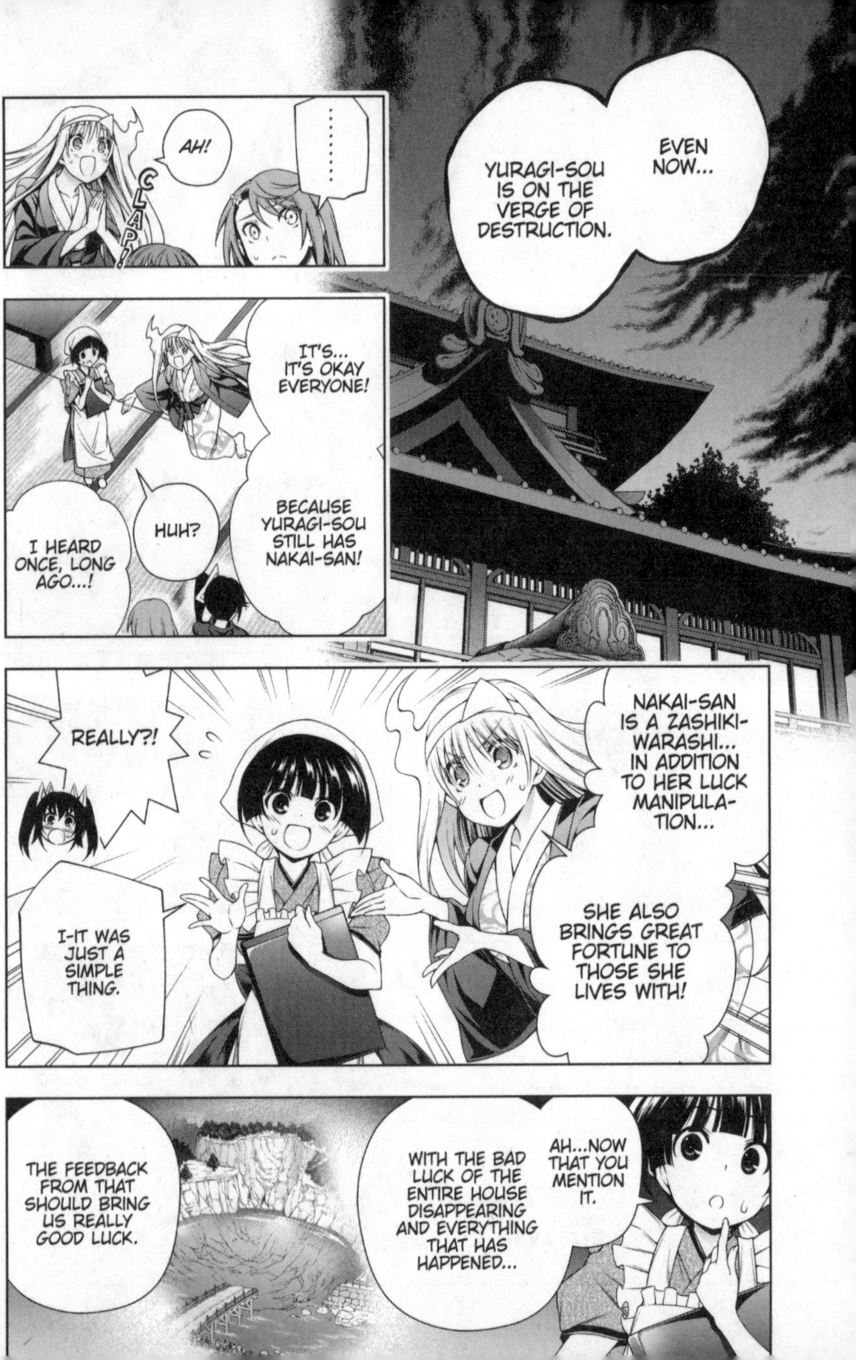
EVEN NOW...
YURAGI-SOU IS ON THE VERGE OF DESTRUCTION.
......
AH!
CLAP!
IT'S... IT'S OKAY EVERYONE!
BECAUSE YURAGI-SOU STILL HAS NAKAI-SAN!
HUH?
I HEARD ONCE, LONG AGO...!
NAKAI-SAN IS A ZASHIKI-WARASHI... IN ADDITION TO HER LUCK MANIPULATION...
SHE ALSO BRINGS GREAT FORTUNE TO THOSE SHE LIVES WITH!
REALLY?!
I-IT WAS JUST A SIMPLE THING.
AH...NOW THAT YOU MENTION IT.
WITH THE BAD LUCK OF THE ENTIRE HOUSE DISAPPEARING AND EVERYTHING THAT HAS HAPPENED...
THE FEEDBACK FROM THAT SHOULD BRING US REALLY GOOD LUCK.

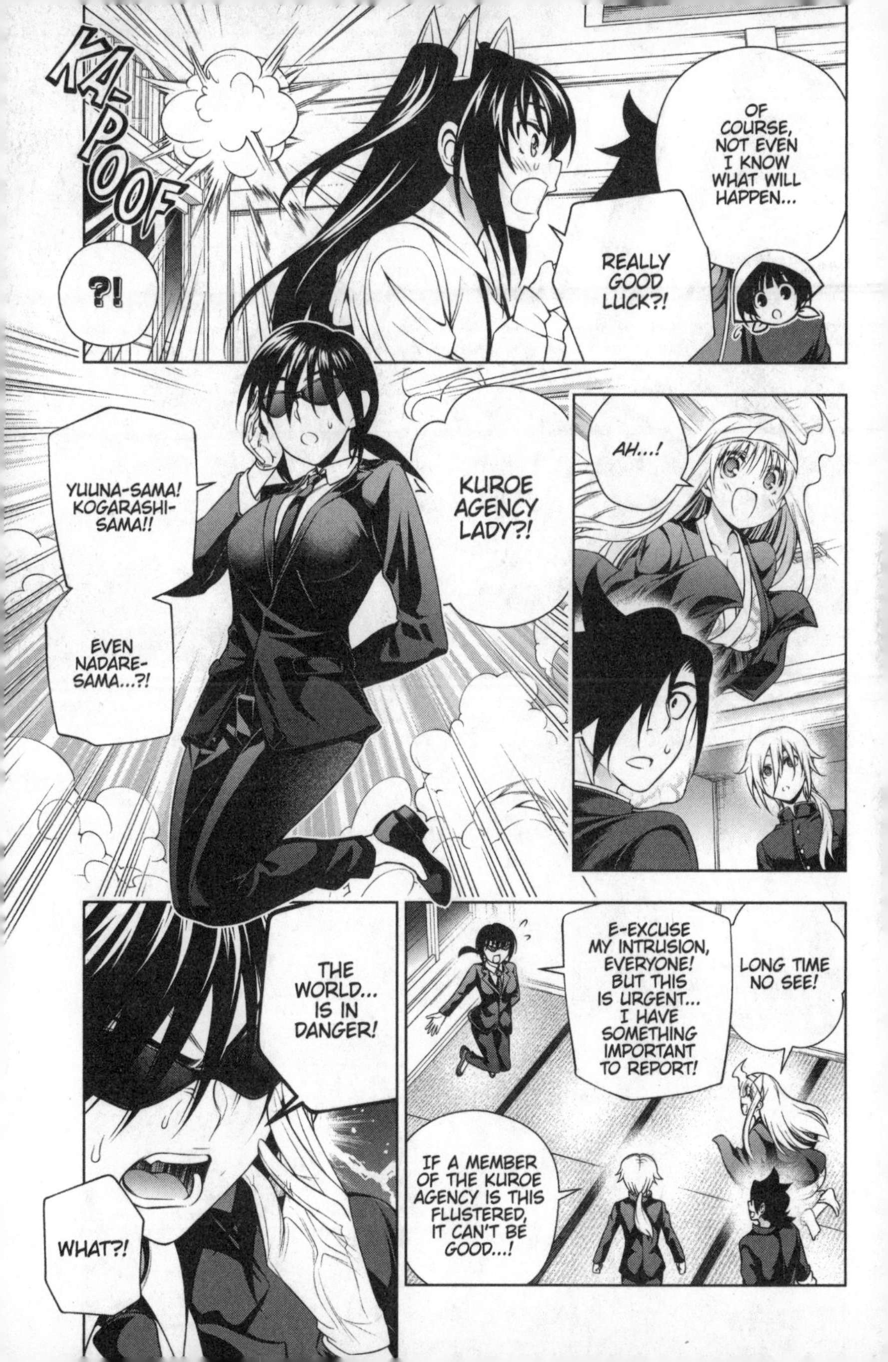
OF COURSE, NOT EVEN I KNOW WHAT WILL HAPPEN...
REALLY GOOD LUCK?!
KA-POOF
?!
AH...!
KUROE AGENCY LADY?!
YUUNA-SAMA! KOGARASHI-SAMA!!
EVEN NADARE-SAMA...?!
LONG TIME NO SEE!
E-EXCUSE MY INTRUSION, EVERYONE! BUT THIS IS URGENT... I HAVE SOMETHING IMPORTANT TO REPORT!
IF A MEMBER OF THE KUROE AGENCY IS THIS FLUSTERED, IT CAN'T BE GOOD...!
THE WORLD... IS IN DANGER!
WHAT?!

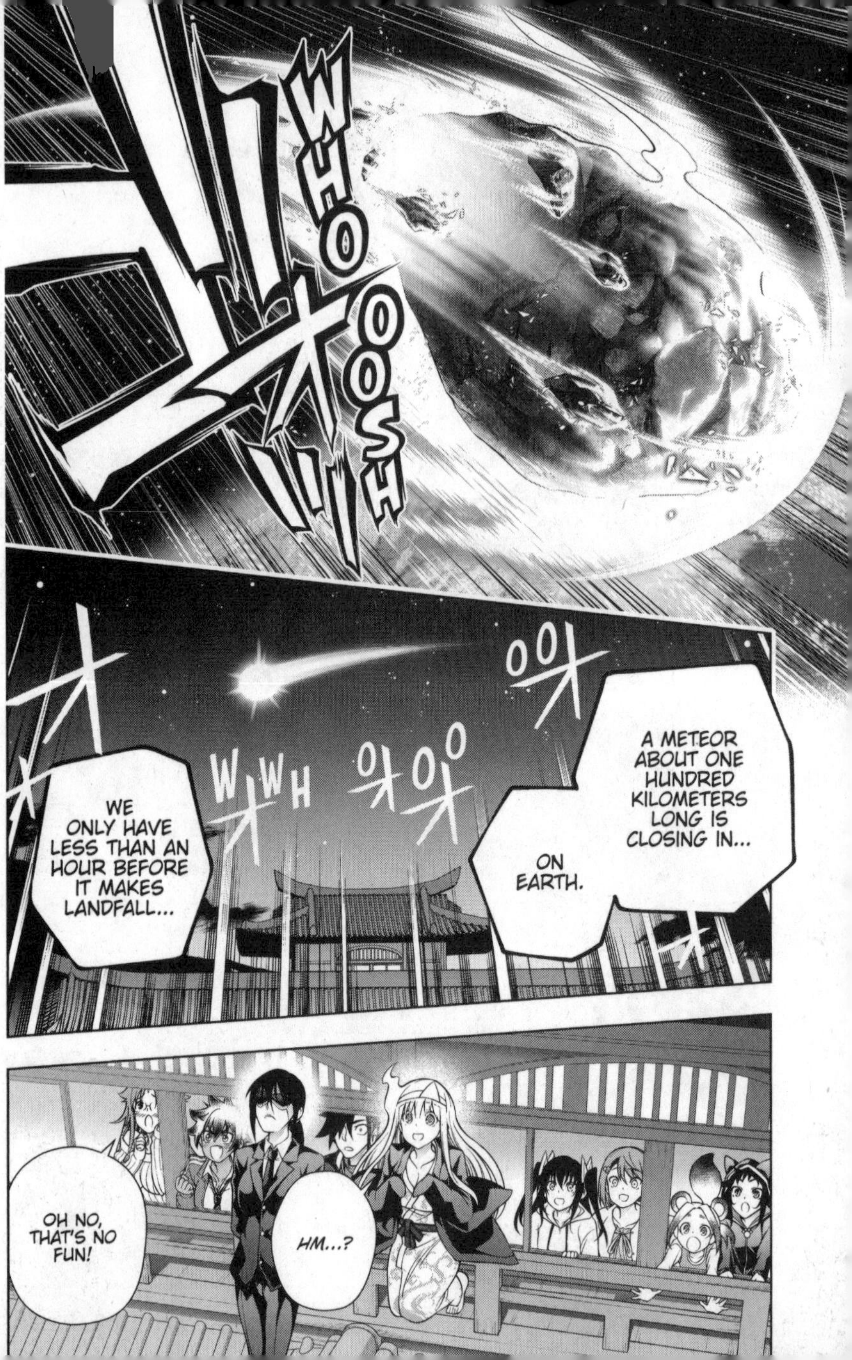
WHOOOSH
A METEOR ABOUT ONE HUNDRED KILOMETERS LONG IS CLOSING IN...
ON EARTH.
WE ONLY HAVE LESS THAN AN HOUR BEFORE IT MAKES LANDFALL...
HM...?
OH NO, THAT'S NO FUN!

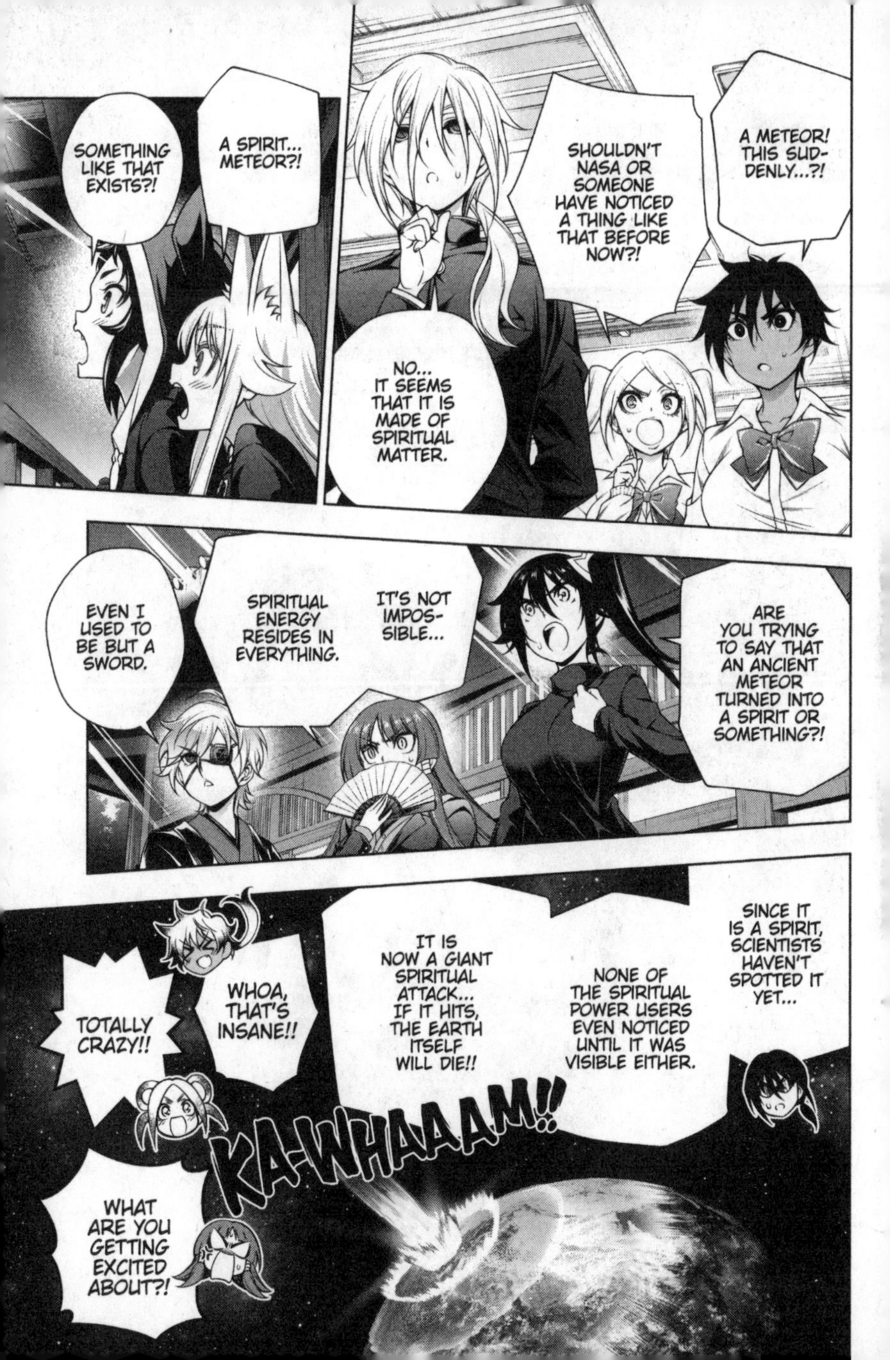
A METEOR! THIS SUDDENLY...?!
SHOULDN'T NASA OR SOMEONE HAVE NOTICED A THING LIKE THAT BEFORE NOW?!
NO... IT SEEMS THAT IT IS MADE OF SPIRITUAL MATTER.
A SPIRIT... METEOR?!
SOMETHING LIKE THAT EXISTS?!
ARE YOU TRYING TO SAY THAT AN ANCIENT METEOR TURNED INTO A SPIRIT OR SOMETHING?!
IT'S NOT IMPOSSIBLE...
SPIRITUAL ENERGY RESIDES IN EVERYTHING.
EVEN I USED TO BE BUT A SWORD.
SINCE IT IS A SPIRIT, SCIENTISTS HAVEN'T SPOTTED IT YET...
NONE OF THE SPIRITUAL POWER USERS EVEN NOTICED UNTIL IT WAS VISIBLE EITHER.
IT IS NOW A GIANT SPIRITUAL ATTACK... IF IT HITS, THE EARTH ITSELF WILL DIE!!
WHOA, THAT'S INSANE!!
TOTALLY CRAZY!!
KA-WHAAAAM!!
WHAT ARE YOU GETTING EXCITED ABOUT?!

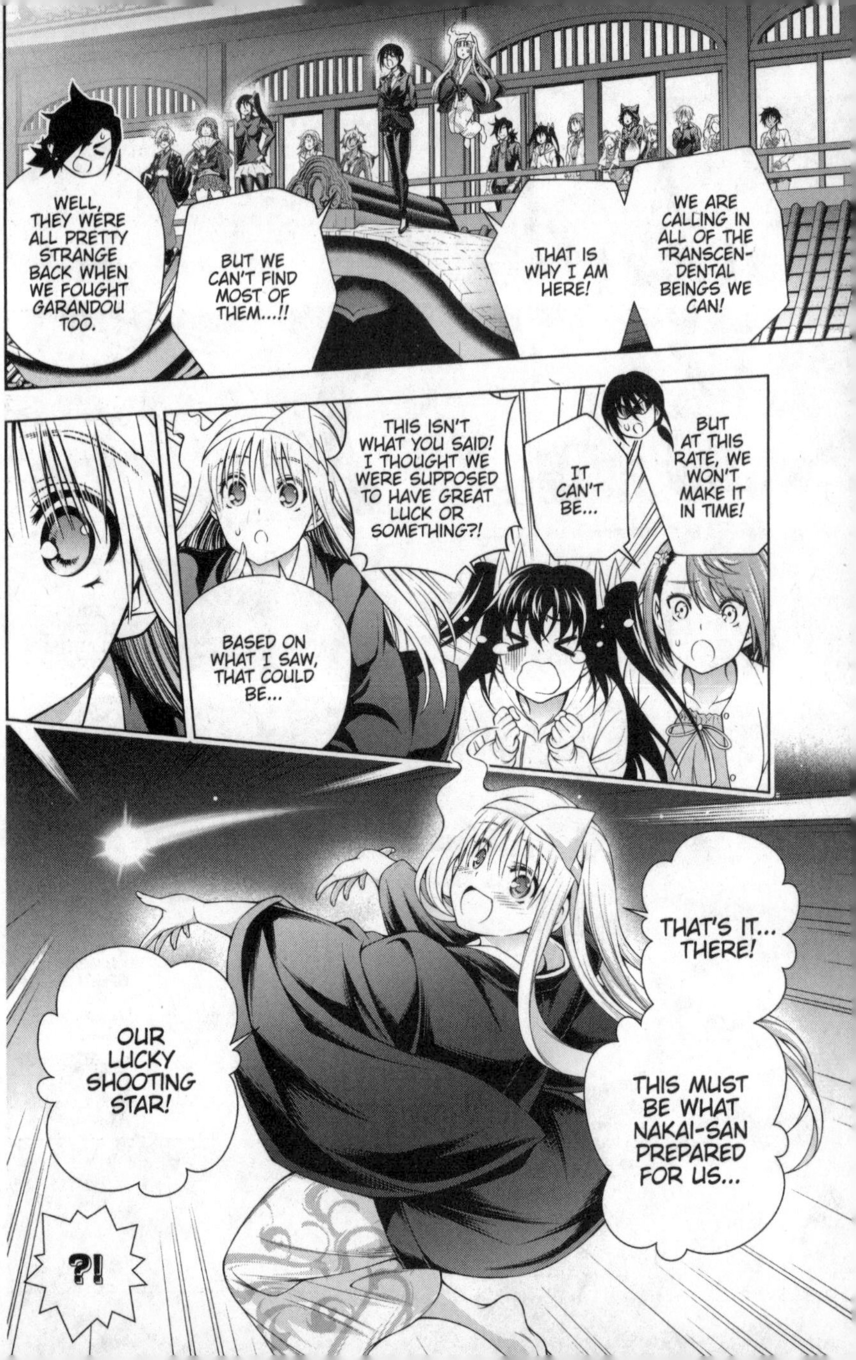
WE ARE CALLING IN ALL OF THE TRANSCENDENTAL BEINGS WE CAN!
THAT IS WHY I AM HERE!
BUT WE CAN'T FIND MOST OF THEM...!!
WELL, THEY WERE ALL PRETTY STRANGE BACK WHEN WE FOUGHT GARANDOU TOO.
BUT AT THIS RATE, WE WON'T MAKE IT IN TIME!
IT CAN'T BE...
THIS ISN'T WHAT YOU SAID! I THOUGHT WE WERE SUPPOSED TO HAVE GREAT LUCK OR SOMETHING?!
BASED ON WHAT I SAW, THAT COULD BE...
THAT'S IT... THERE!
THIS MUST BE WHAT NAKAI-SAN PREPARED FOR US...
OUR LUCKY SHOOTING STAR!
?!

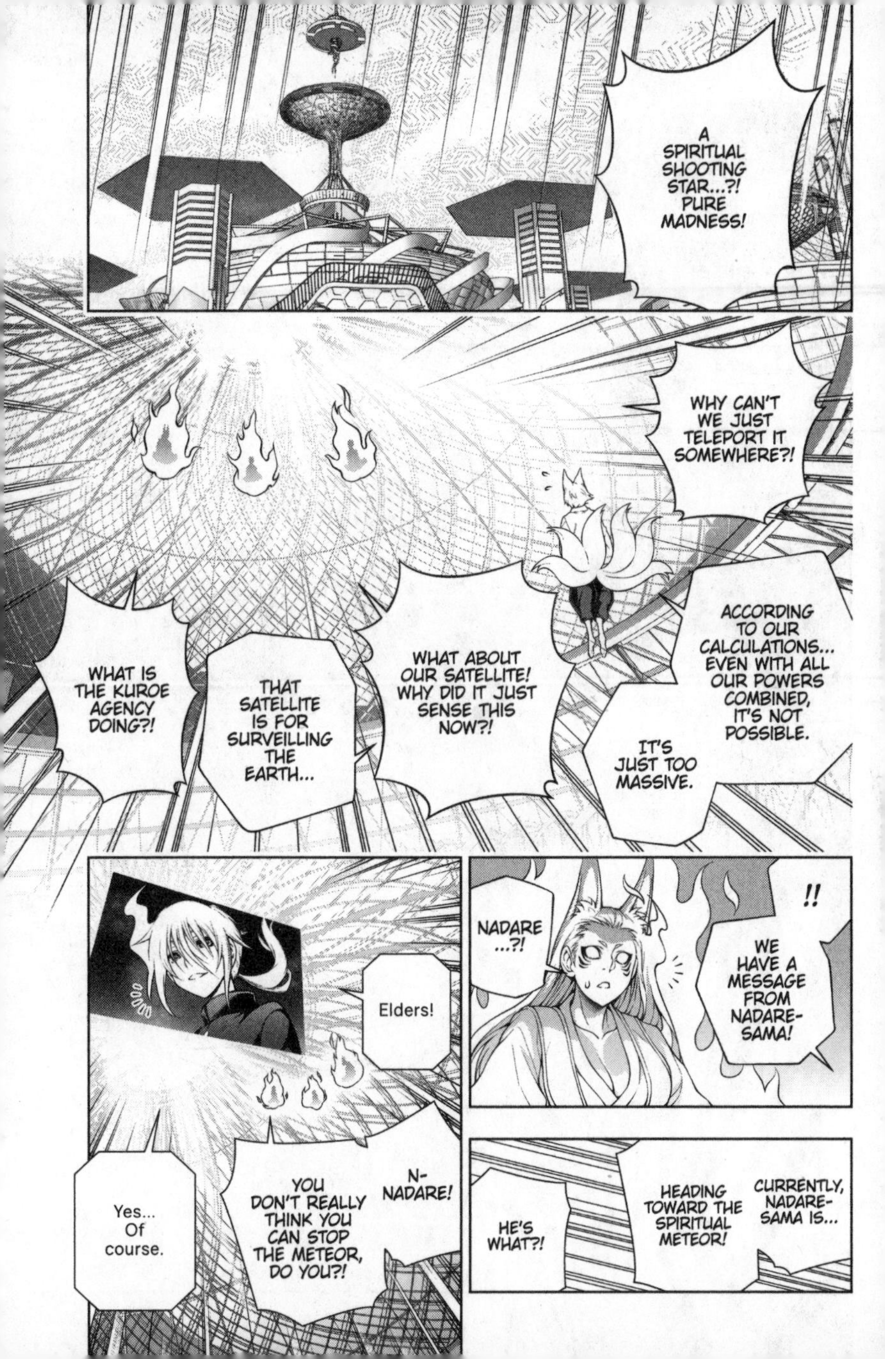
A SPIRITUAL SHOOTING STAR...?! PURE MADNESS!
WHY CAN'T WE JUST TELEPORT IT SOMEWHERE?!
ACCORDING TO OUR CALCULATIONS... EVEN WITH ALL OUR POWERS COMBINED, IT'S NOT POSSIBLE.
IT'S JUST TOO MASSIVE.
WHAT ABOUT OUR SATELLITE! WHY DID IT JUST SENSE THIS NOW?!
THAT SATELLITE IS FOR SURVEILLING THE EARTH...
WHAT IS THE KUROE AGENCY DOING?!
!!
WE HAVE A MESSAGE FROM NADARE-SAMA!
NADARE ...?!
CURRENTLY, NADARE-SAMA IS...
HEADING TOWARD THE SPIRITUAL METEOR!
HE'S WHAT?!
Elders!
N-NADARE!
YOU DON'T REALLY THINK YOU CAN STOP THE METEOR, DO YOU?!
Yes... Of course.

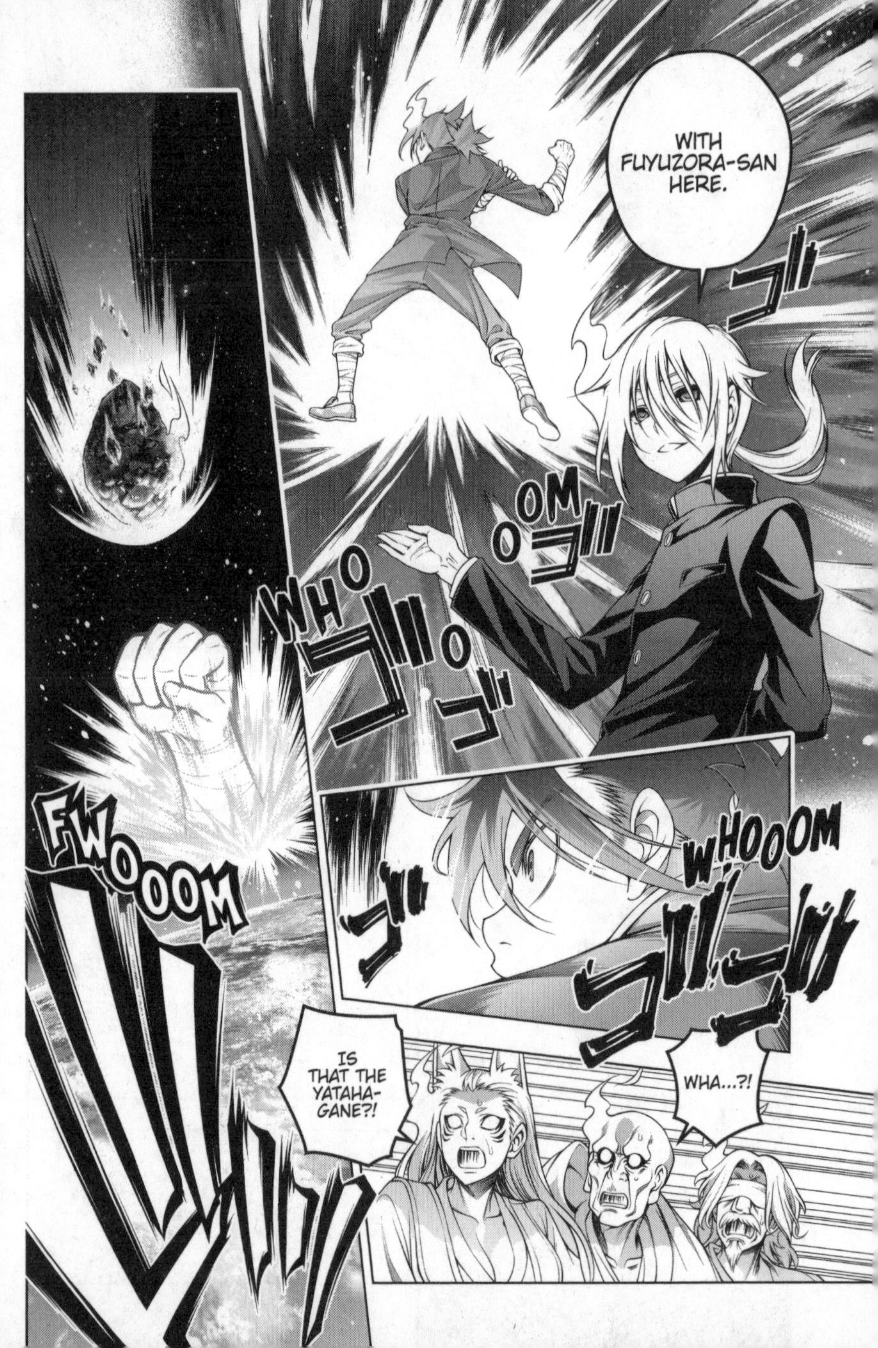
WITH FUYUZORA-SAN HERE.
WHOOOM
WHOOOM
WHA...?!
IS THAT THE YATAHA-GANE?!
FWOOOM

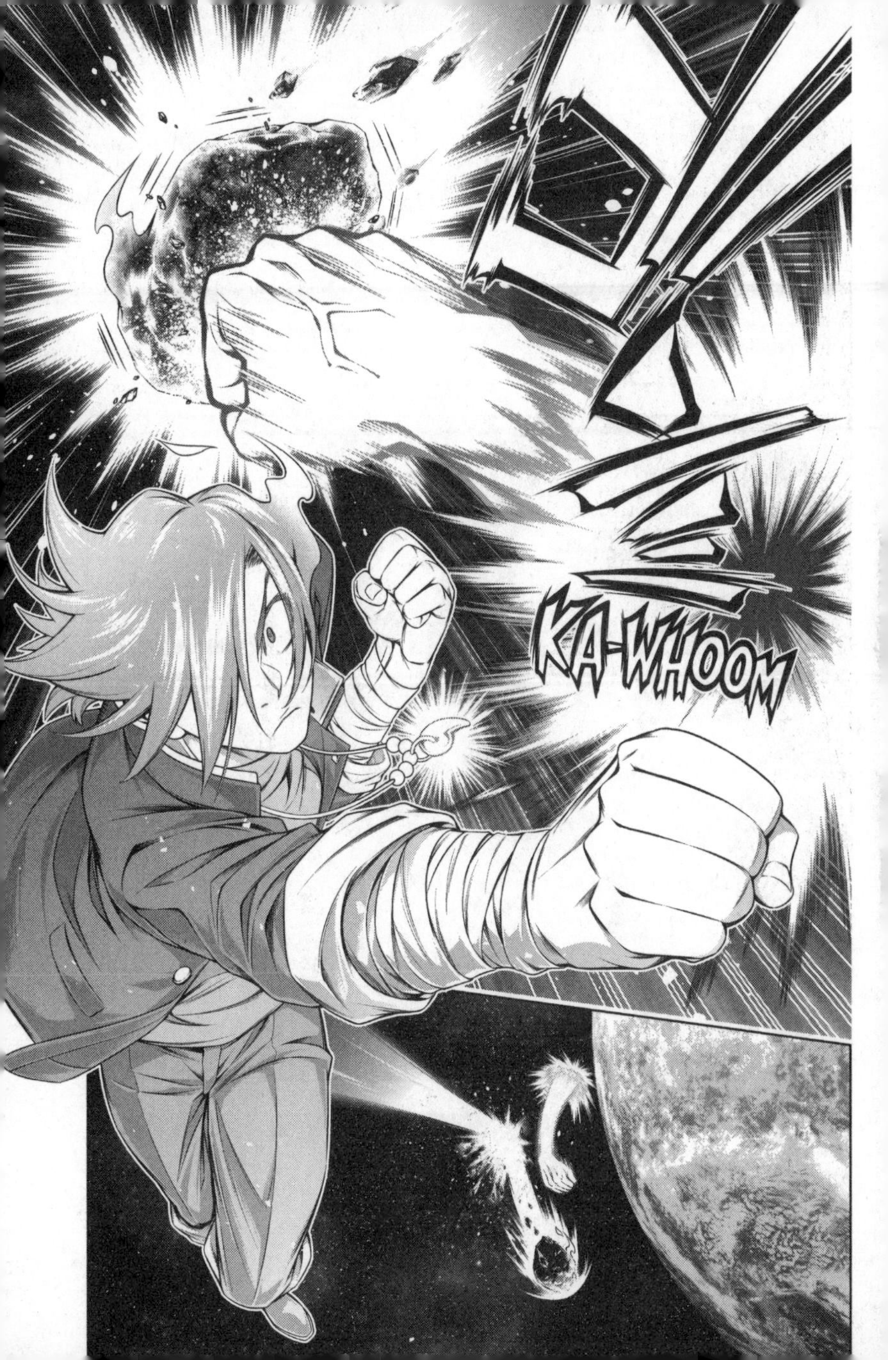
KA-WHOOM

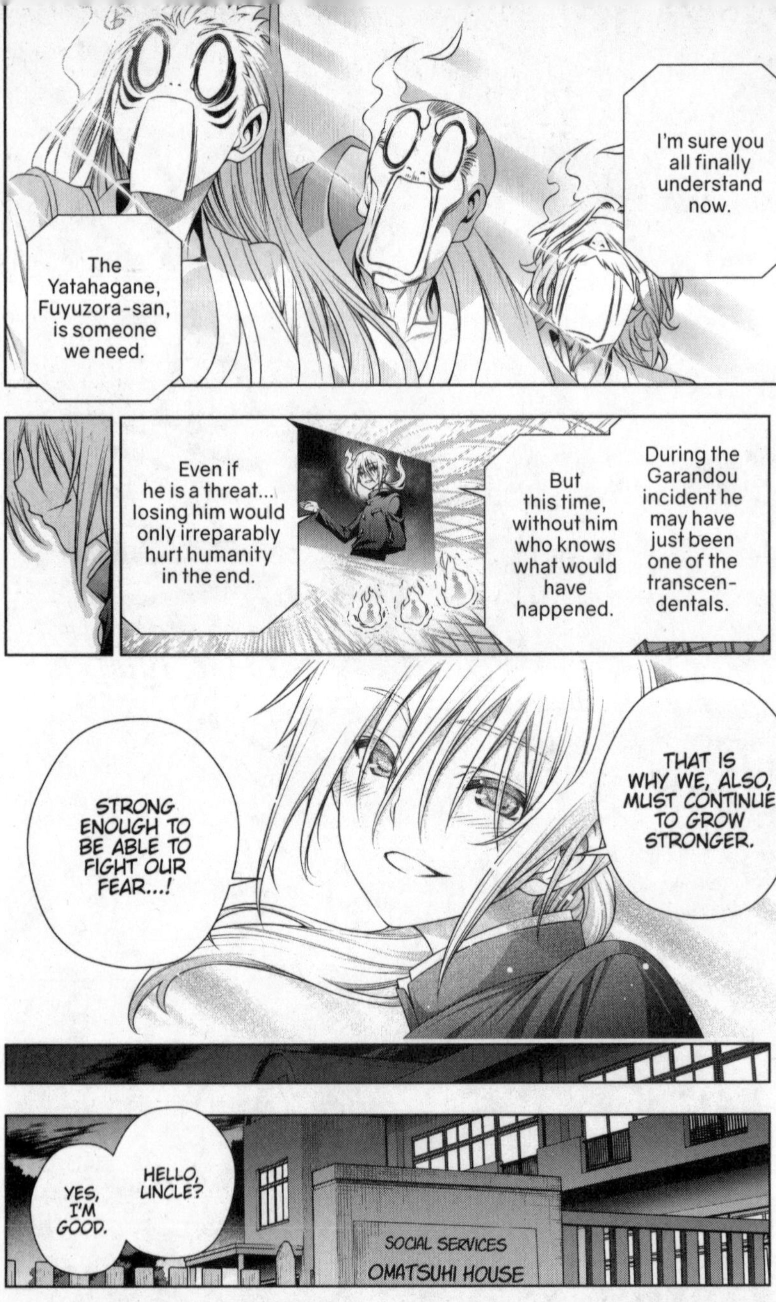
I'm sure you all finally understand now.
The Yatahagane, Fuyuzora-san, is someone we need.
During the Garandou incident he may have just been one of the transcendentals.
But this time, without him who knows what would have happened.
Even if he is a threat... losing him would only irreparably hurt humanity in the end.
THAT IS WHY WE, ALSO, MUST CONTINUE TO GROW STRONGER.
STRONG ENOUGH TO BE ABLE TO FIGHT OUR FEAR...!
HELLO, UNCLE?
YES, I'M GOOD.
SOCIAL SERVICES
OMATSUHI HOUSE

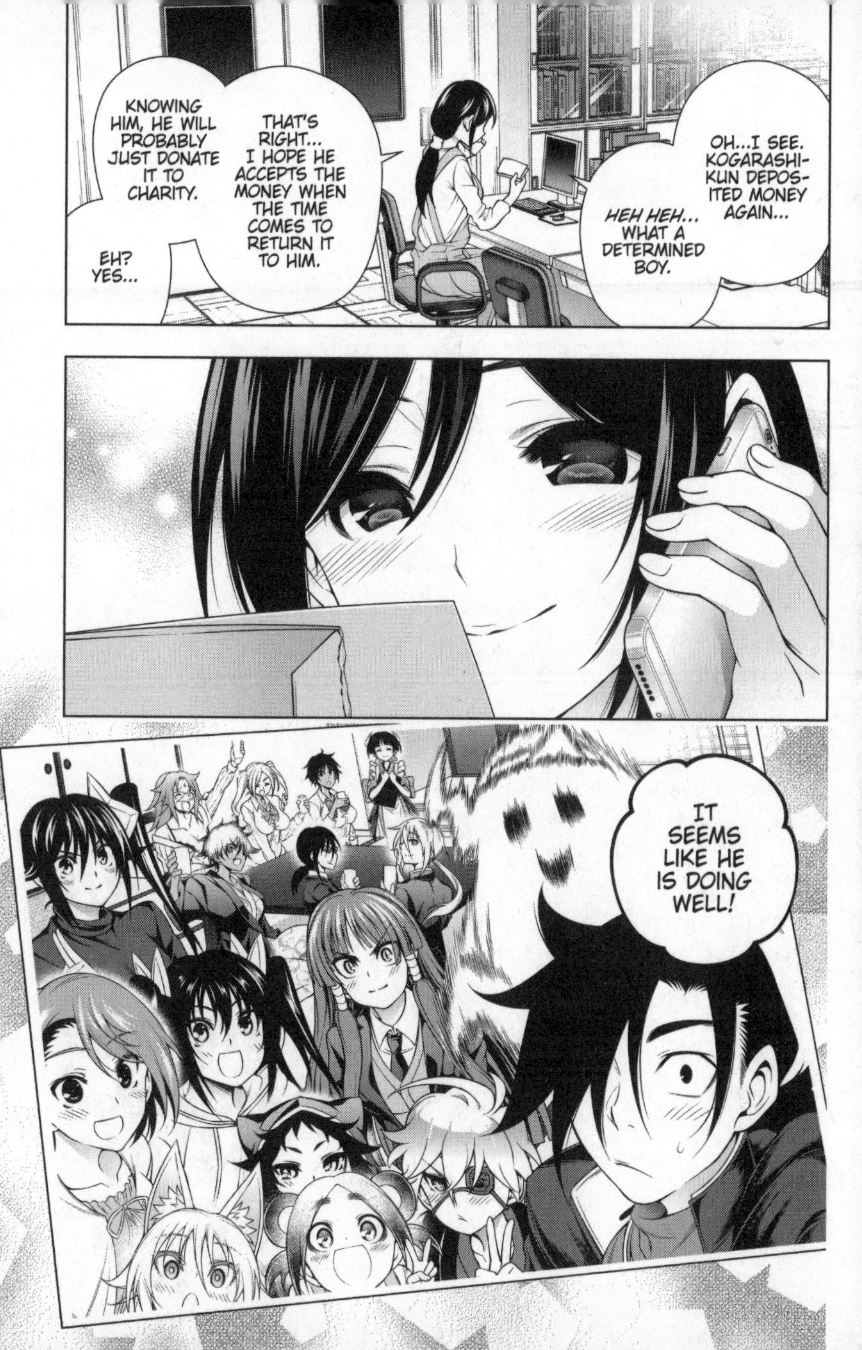
OH...I SEE. KOGARASHI-KUN DEPOSITED MONEY AGAIN...
HEH HEH... WHAT A DETERMINED BOY.
THAT'S RIGHT... I HOPE HE ACCEPTS THE MONEY WHEN THE TIME COMES TO RETURN IT TO HIM.
KNOWING HIM, HE WILL PROBABLY JUST DONATE IT TO CHARITY.
EH? YES...
IT SEEMS LIKE HE IS DOING WELL!

Yuuna and the Haunted Hot Springs

168 The Seven Wonders of Yukemuri High School: Report ③

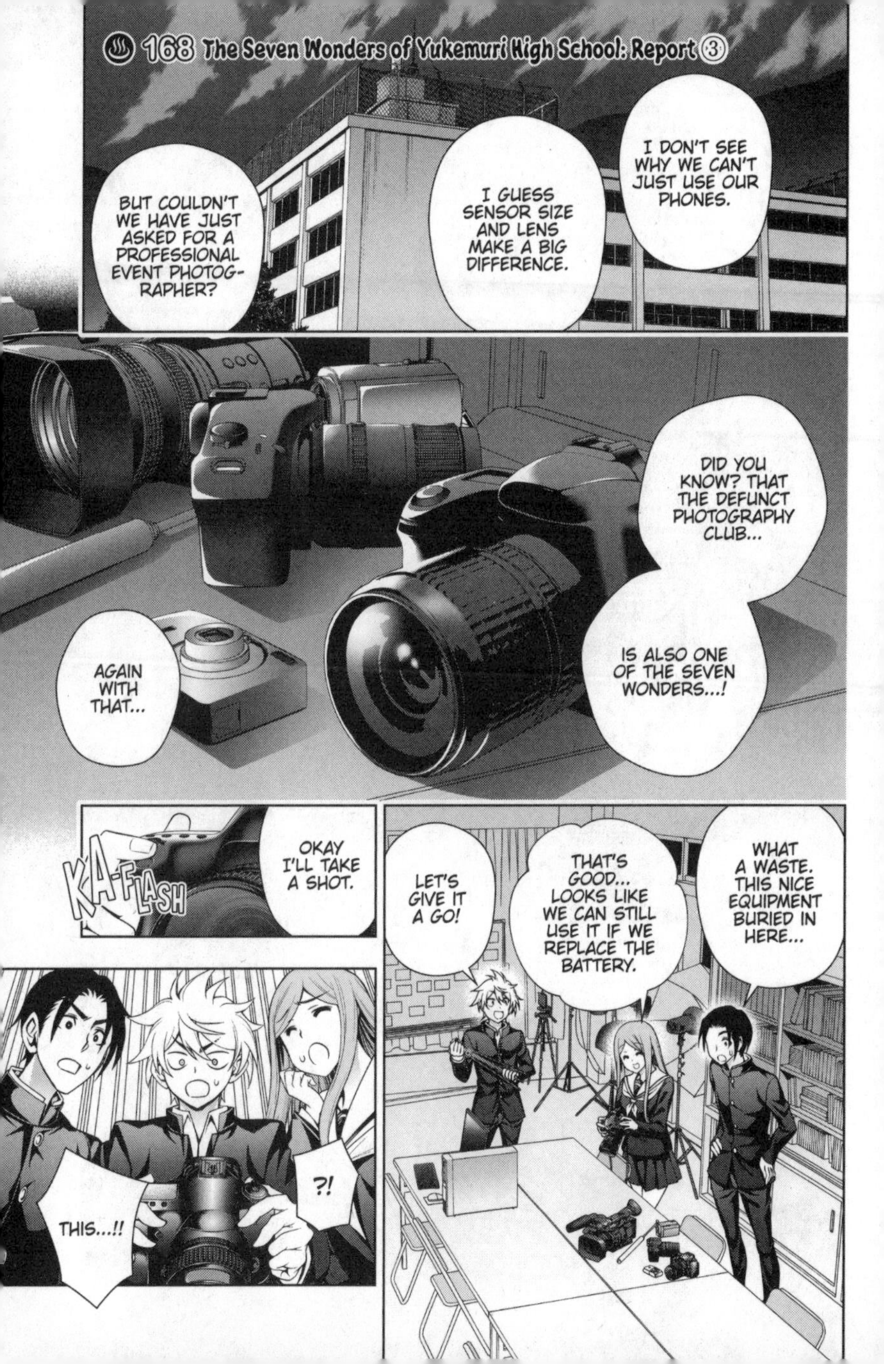
I DON'T SEE WHY WE CAN'T JUST USE OUR PHONES.
I GUESS SENSOR SIZE AND LENS MAKE A BIG DIFFERENCE.
BUT COULDN'T WE HAVE JUST ASKED FOR A PROFESSIONAL EVENT PHOTOG-RAPHER?
DID YOU KNOW? THAT THE DEFUNCT PHOTOGRAPHY CLUB...
IS ALSO ONE OF THE SEVEN WONDERS...!
AGAIN WITH THAT...
WHAT A WASTE. THIS NICE EQUIPMENT BURIED IN HERE...
THAT'S GOOD... LOOKS LIKE WE CAN STILL USE IT IF WE REPLACE THE BATTERY.
LET'S GIVE IT A GO!
OKAY I'LL TAKE A SHOT.
KA-FLASH
?!
THIS...!!

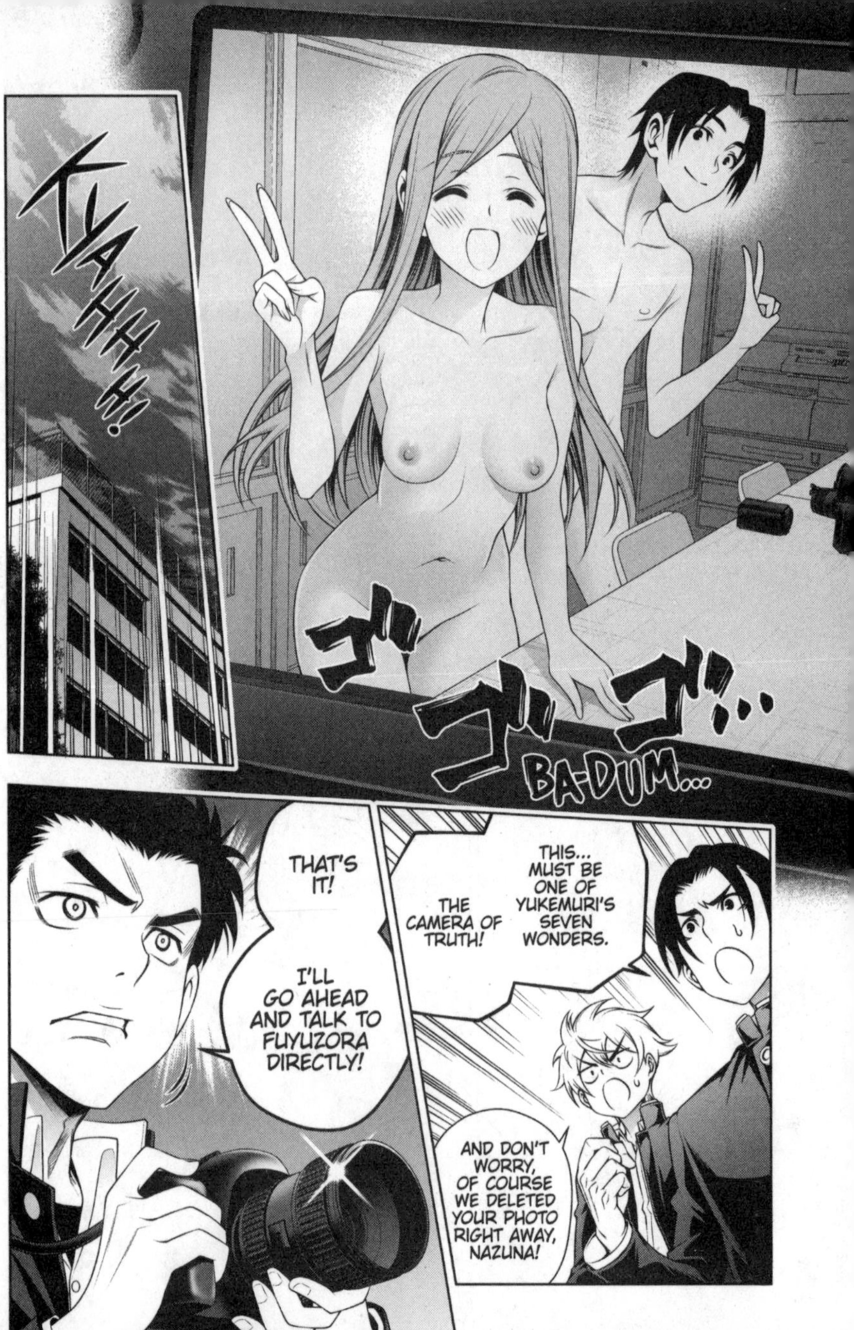
BA-DUM...
KYAHHHH!
THIS... MUST BE ONE OF YUKEMURI'S SEVEN WONDERS.
THE CAMERA OF TRUTH!
AND DON'T WORRY, OF COURSE WE DELETED YOUR PHOTO RIGHT AWAY, NAZUNA!
THAT'S IT!
I'LL GO AHEAD AND TALK TO FUYUZORA DIRECTLY!

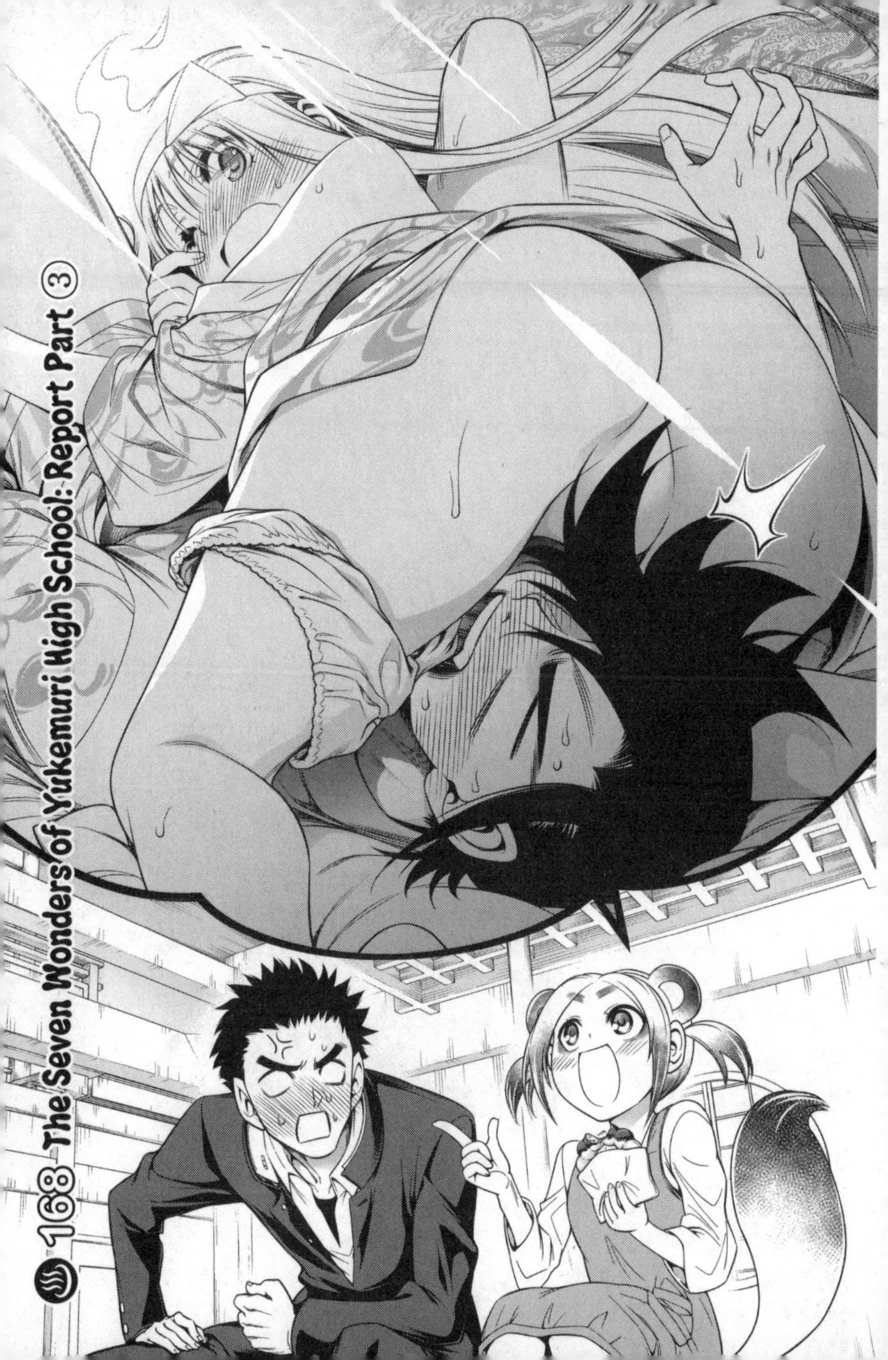

♨168 The Seven Wonders of Yukemuri High School: Report Part ③

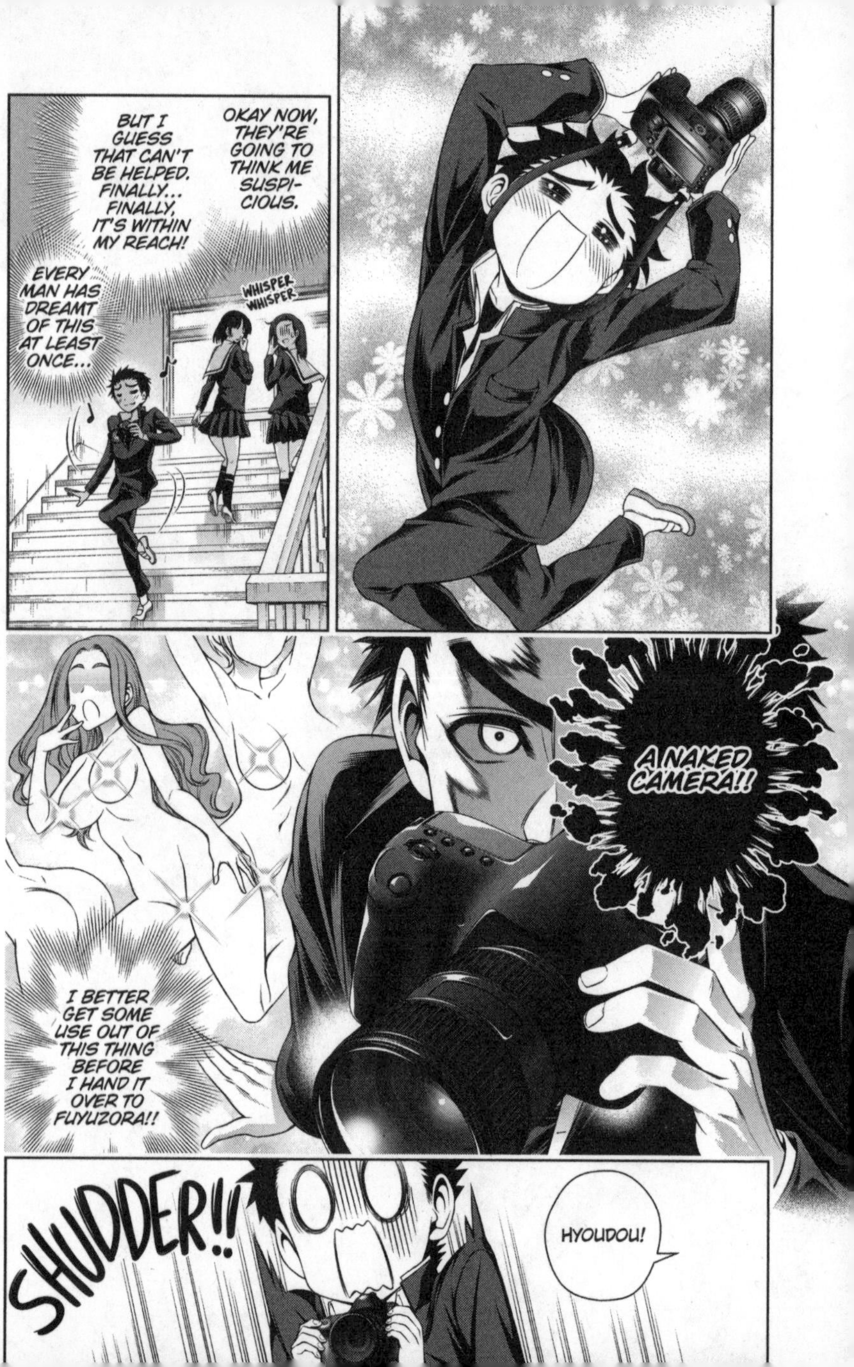
OKAY NOW, THEY'RE GOING TO THINK ME SUSPICIOUS.
BUT I GUESS THAT CAN'T BE HELPED. FINALLY... FINALLY, IT'S WITHIN MY REACH!
WHISPER WHISPER
EVERY MAN HAS DREAMT OF THIS AT LEAST ONCE...
A NAKED CAMERA!!
I BETTER GET SOME USE OUT OF THIS THING BEFORE I HAND IT OVER TO FUYUZORA!!
HYOUDOU!
SHUDDER!!

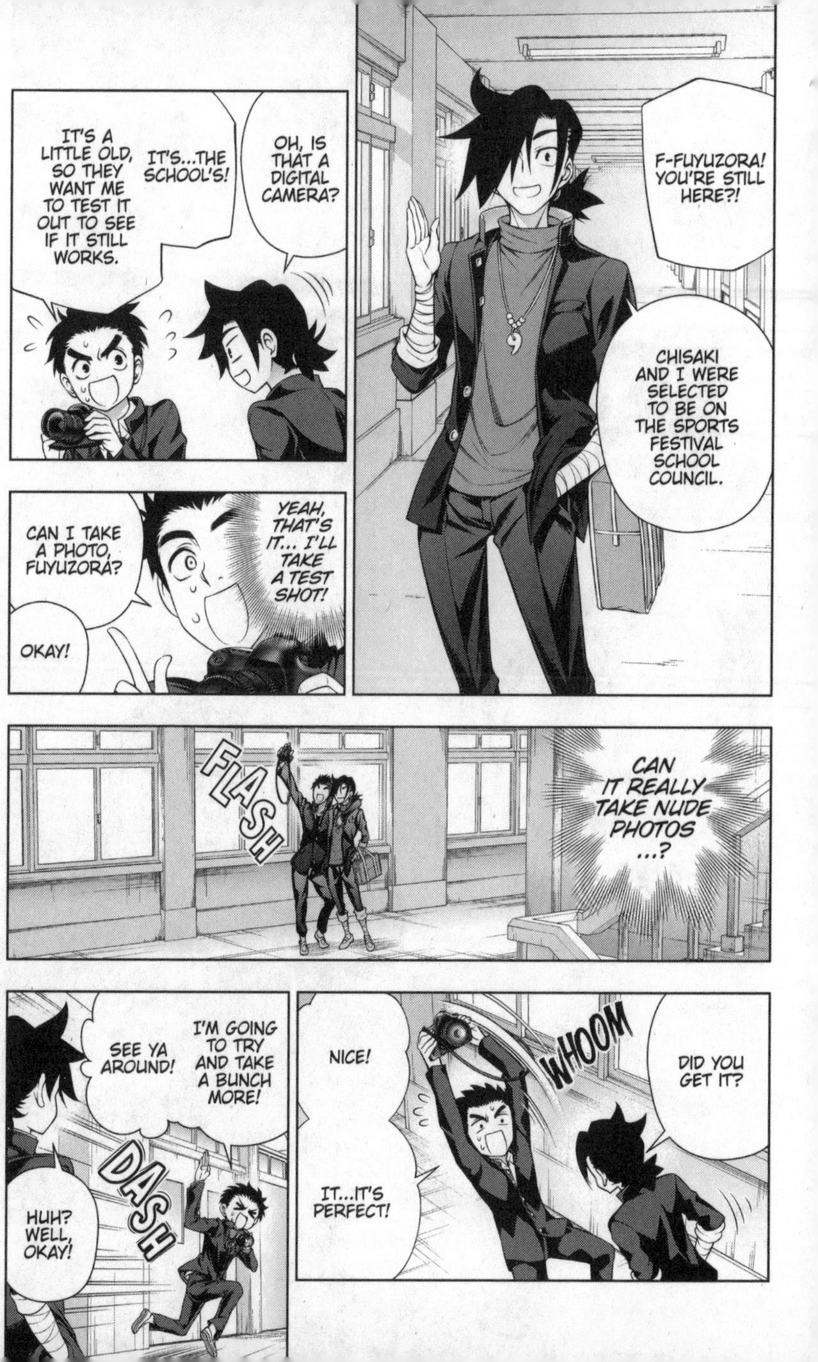
F-FUYUZORA! YOU'RE STILL HERE?!
CHISAKI AND I WERE SELECTED TO BE ON THE SPORTS FESTIVAL SCHOOL COUNCIL.
OH, IS THAT A DIGITAL CAMERA?
IT'S...THE SCHOOL'S!
IT'S A LITTLE OLD, SO THEY WANT ME TO TEST IT OUT TO SEE IF IT STILL WORKS.
YEAH, THAT'S IT... I'LL TAKE A TEST SHOT!
CAN I TAKE A PHOTO, FUYUZORA?
OKAY!
CAN IT REALLY TAKE NUDE PHOTOS ...?
FLASH
DID YOU GET IT?
WHOOM
NICE!
IT...IT'S PERFECT!
I'M GOING TO TRY AND TAKE A BUNCH MORE!
SEE YA AROUND!
DASH
HUH? WELL, OKAY!

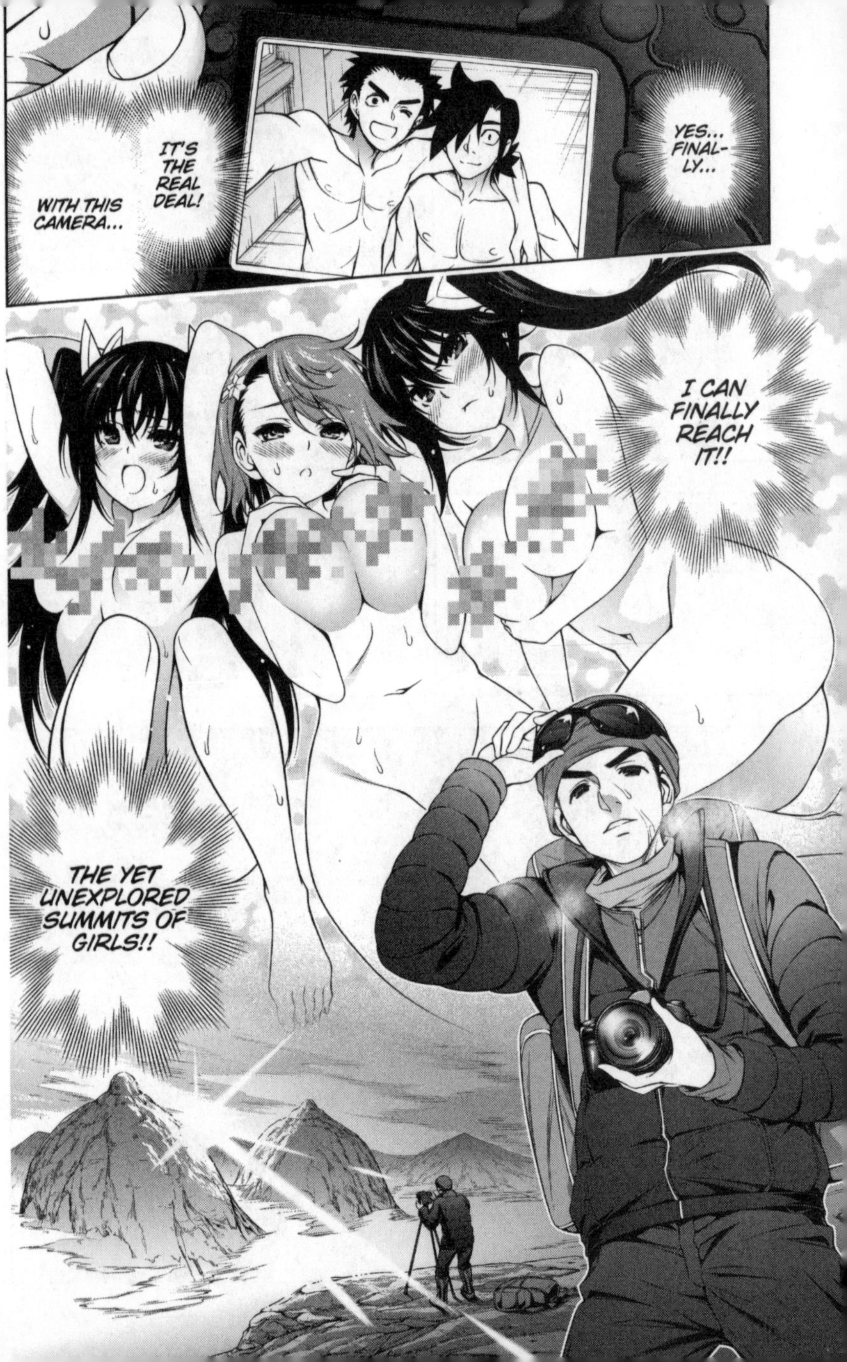
YES... FINALLY...
IT'S THE REAL DEAL!
WITH THIS CAMERA...
I CAN FINALLY REACH IT!!
THE YET UNEXPLORED SUMMITS OF GIRLS!!

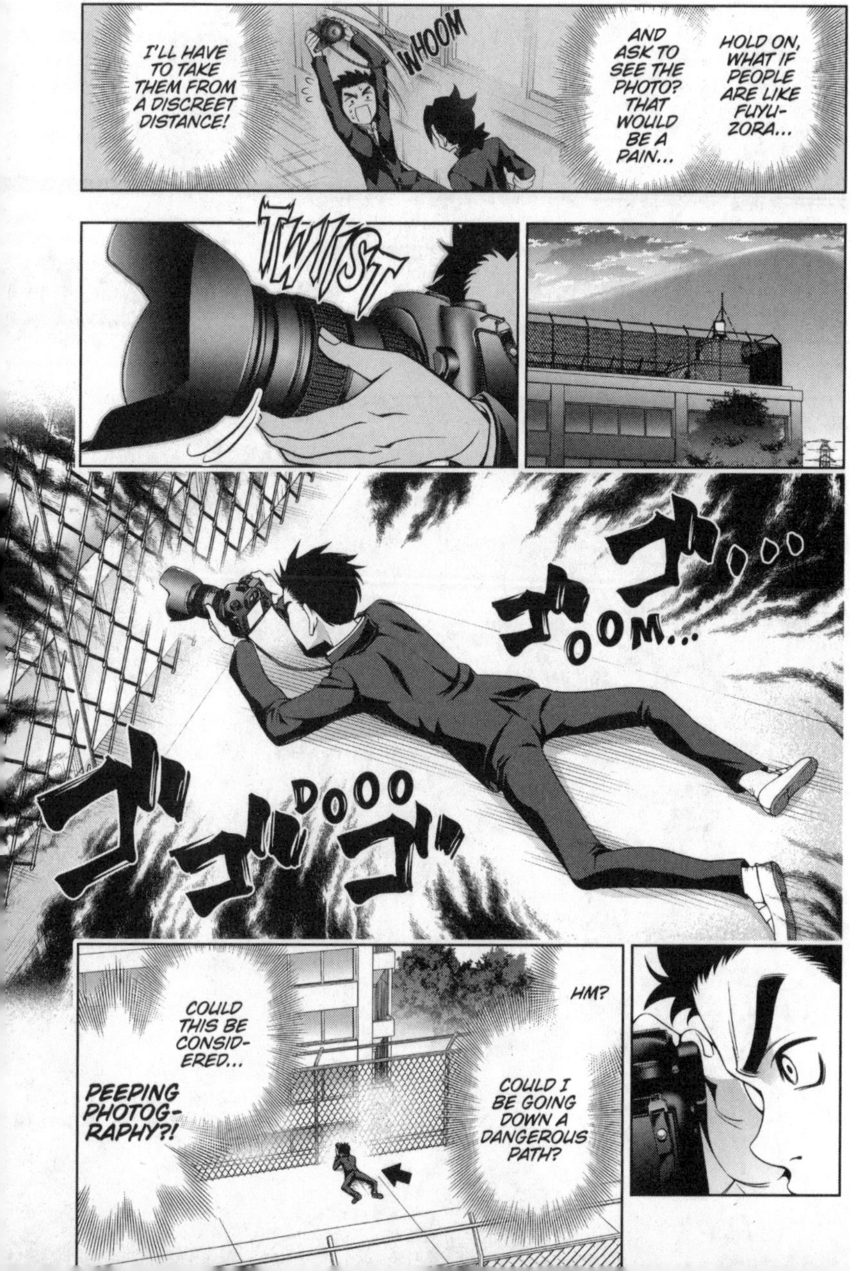
HOLD ON, WHAT IF PEOPLE ARE LIKE FUYU-ZORA...
AND ASK TO SEE THE PHOTO? THAT WOULD BE A PAIN...
WHOOM
I'LL HAVE TO TAKE THEM FROM A DISCREET DISTANCE!
TWIST
OOM...
DOOO
HM?
COULD I BE GOING DOWN A DANGEROUS PATH?
COULD THIS BE CONSIDERED...
PEEPING PHOTOGRAPHY?!

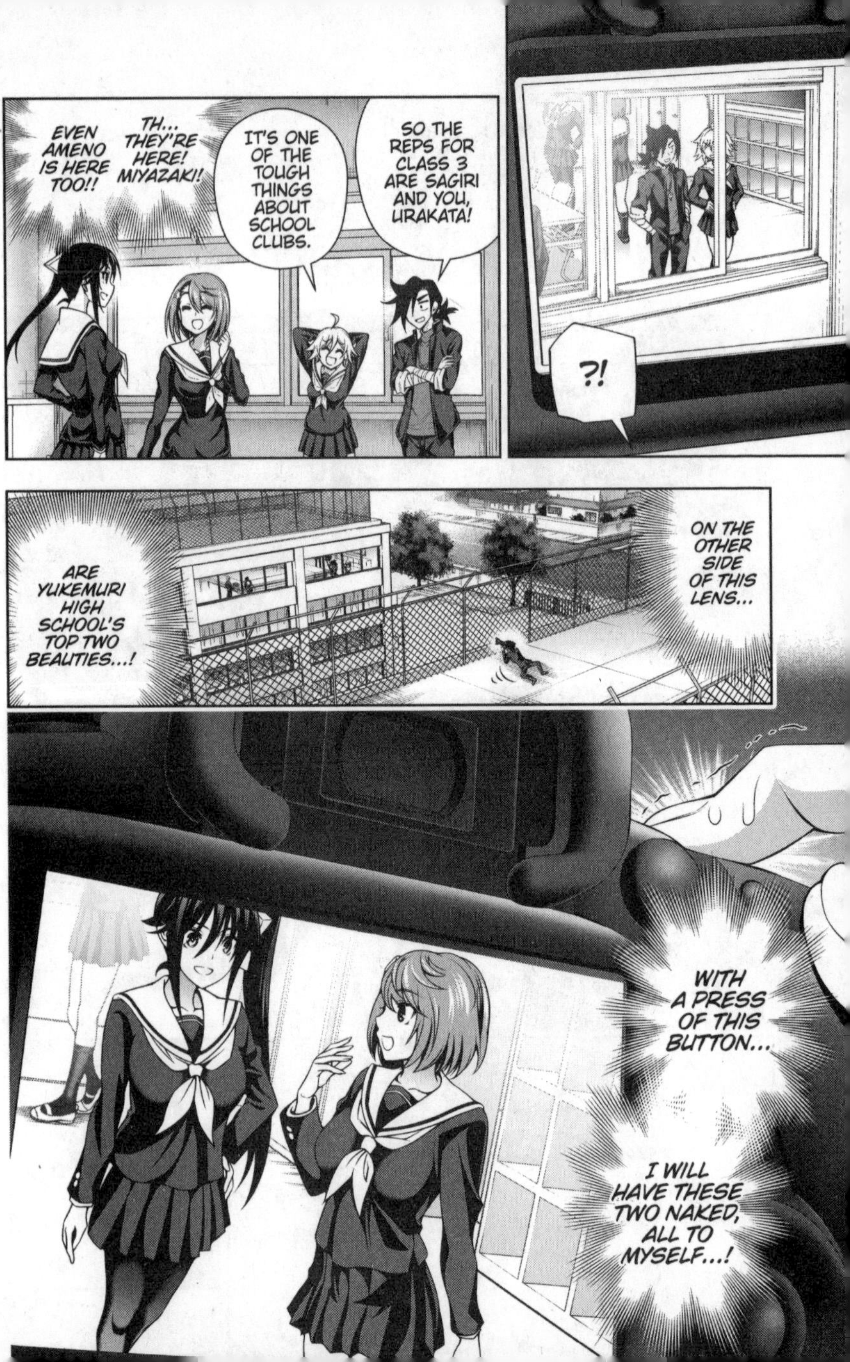
?!
SO THE REPS FOR CLASS 3 ARE SAGIRI AND YOU, URAKATA!
IT'S ONE OF THE TOUGH THINGS ABOUT SCHOOL CLUBS.
TH... THEY'RE HERE! MIYAZAKI!
EVEN AMENO IS HERE TOO!!
ON THE OTHER SIDE OF THIS LENS...
ARE YUKEMURI HIGH SCHOOL'S TOP TWO BEAUTIES...!
WITH A PRESS OF THIS BUTTON...
I WILL HAVE THESE TWO NAKED, ALL TO MYSELF...!

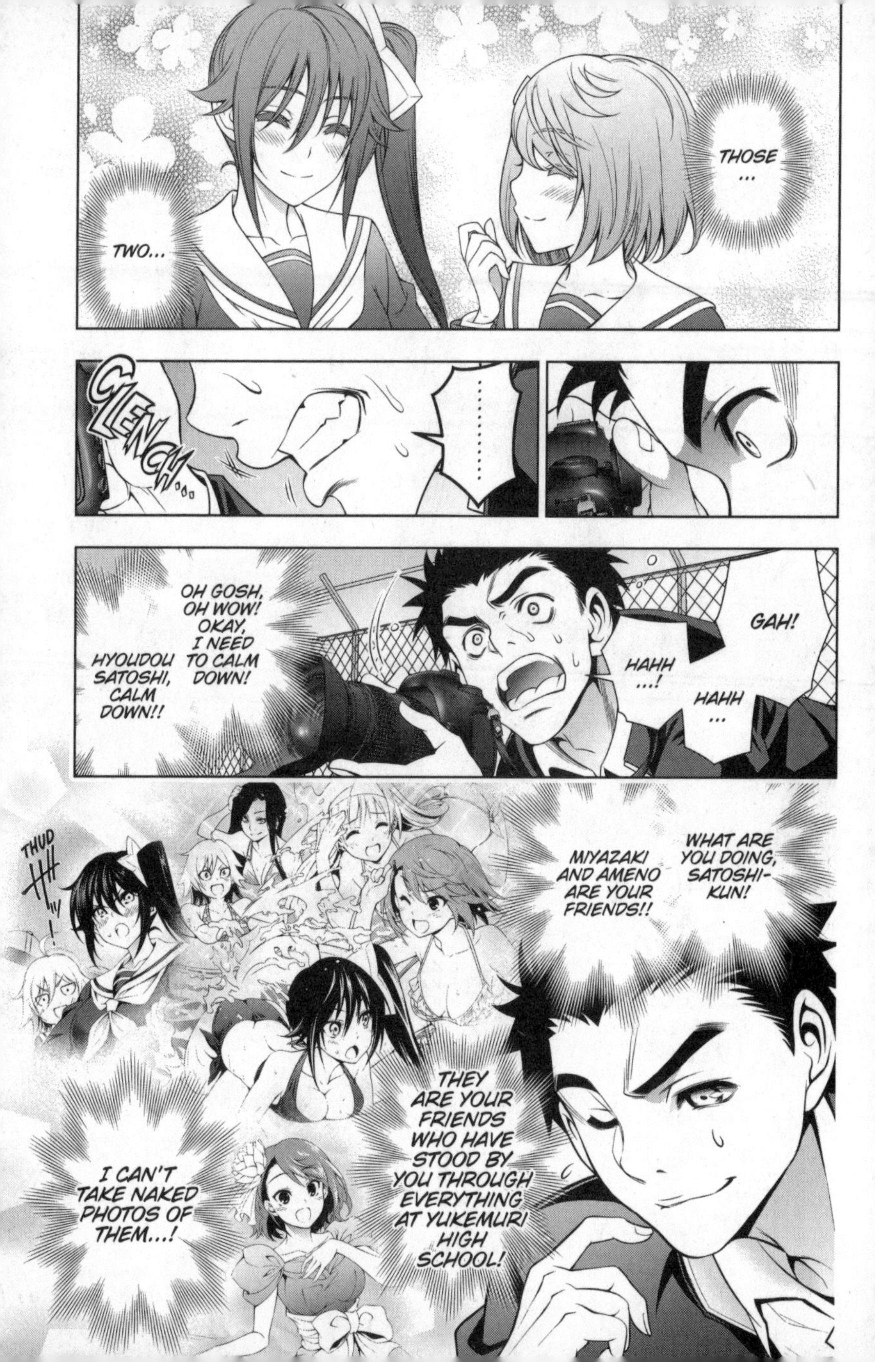
THOSE...
TWO...
......
CLENCH...
GAH!
HAHH...!
HAHH...
OH GOSH, OH WOW! OKAY, I NEED TO CALM DOWN!
HYOUDOU SATOSHI, CALM DOWN!!
WHAT ARE YOU DOING, SATOSHI-KUN!
MIYAZAKI AND AMENO ARE YOUR FRIENDS!!
THUD
THEY ARE YOUR FRIENDS WHO HAVE STOOD BY YOU THROUGH EVERYTHING AT YUKEMURI HIGH SCHOOL!
I CAN'T TAKE NAKED PHOTOS OF THEM...!

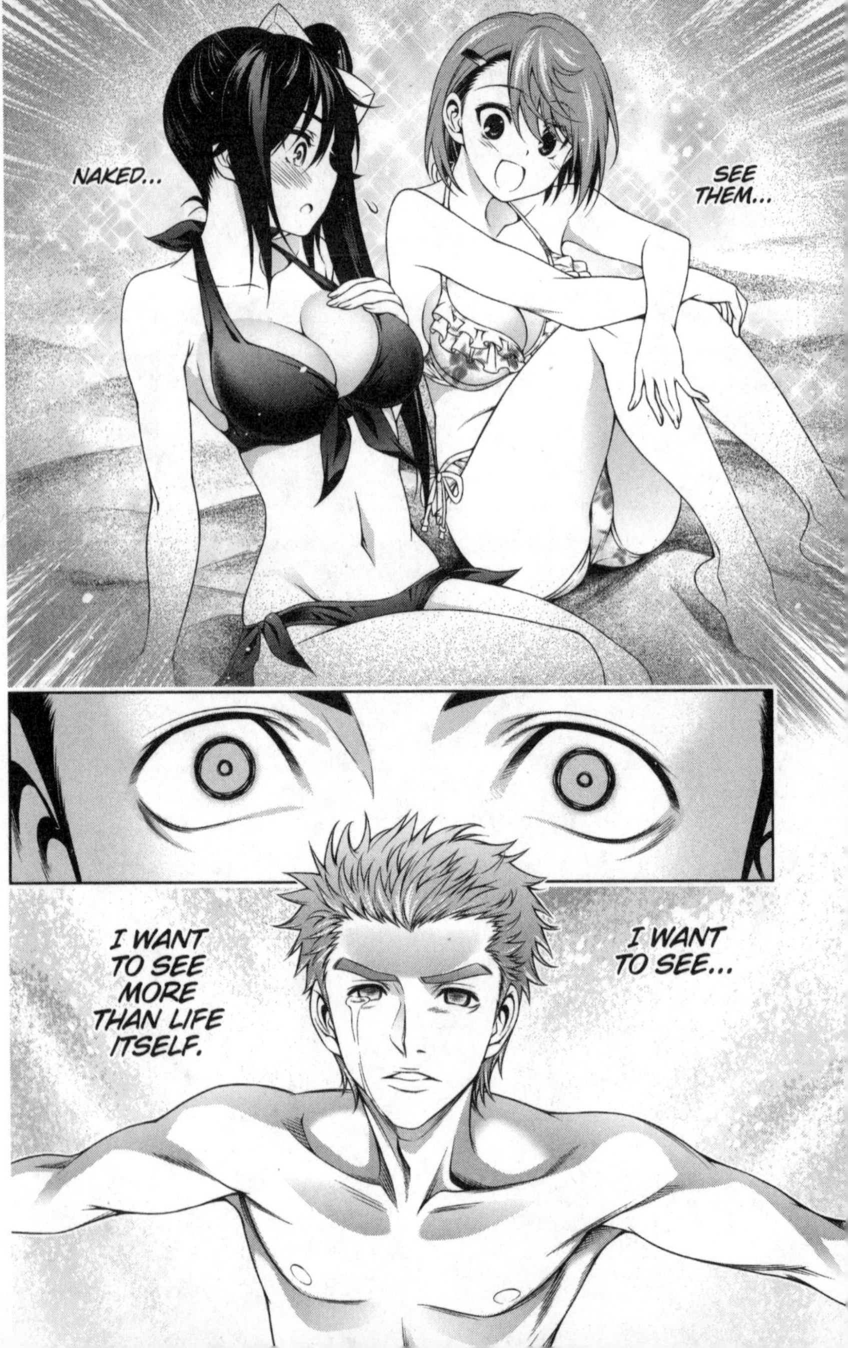
SEE THEM...
NAKED...
I WANT TO SEE...
I WANT TO SEE MORE THAN LIFE ITSELF.

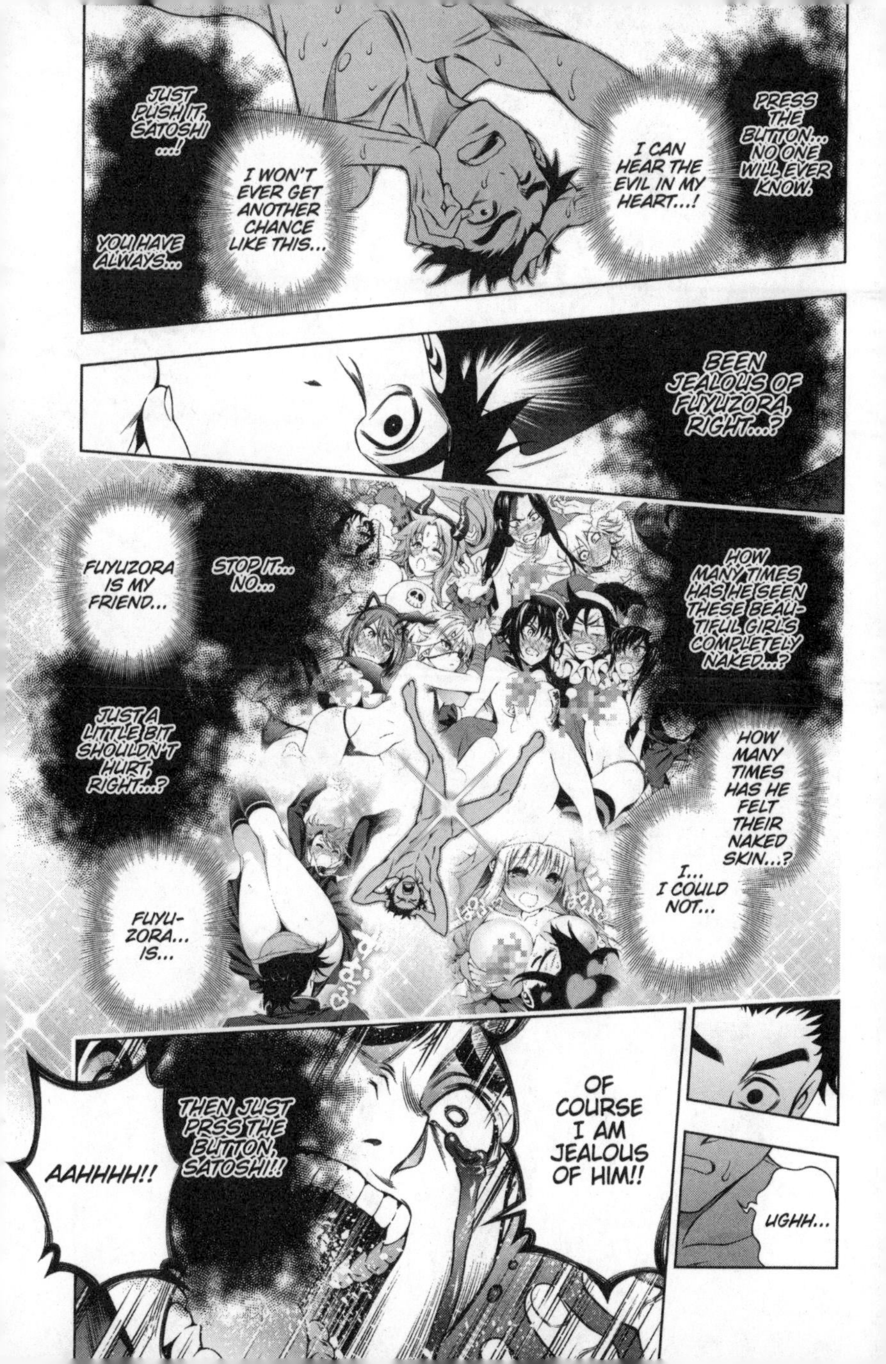
PRESS THE BUTTON... NO ONE WILL EVER KNOW.
I CAN HEAR THE EVIL IN MY HEART...!
I WON'T EVER GET ANOTHER CHANCE LIKE THIS...
JUST PUSH IT, SATOSHI ....!
YOU HAVE ALWAYS...
BEEN JEALOUS OF FUYUZORA, RIGHT...?
HOW MANY TIMES HAS HE SEEN THESE BEAU-TIFUL GIRLS COMPLETELY NAKED...?
STOP IT... NO...
FUYUZORA IS MY FRIEND...
HOW MANY TIMES HAS HE FELT THEIR NAKED SKIN...?
JUST A LITTLE BIT SHOULDN'T HURT, RIGHT...?
I... I COULD NOT...
FUYU-ZORA... IS...
UGHH...
OF COURSE I AM JEALOUS OF HIM!!
THEN JUST PRSS THE BUTTON, SATOSHI!!
AAHHHH!!

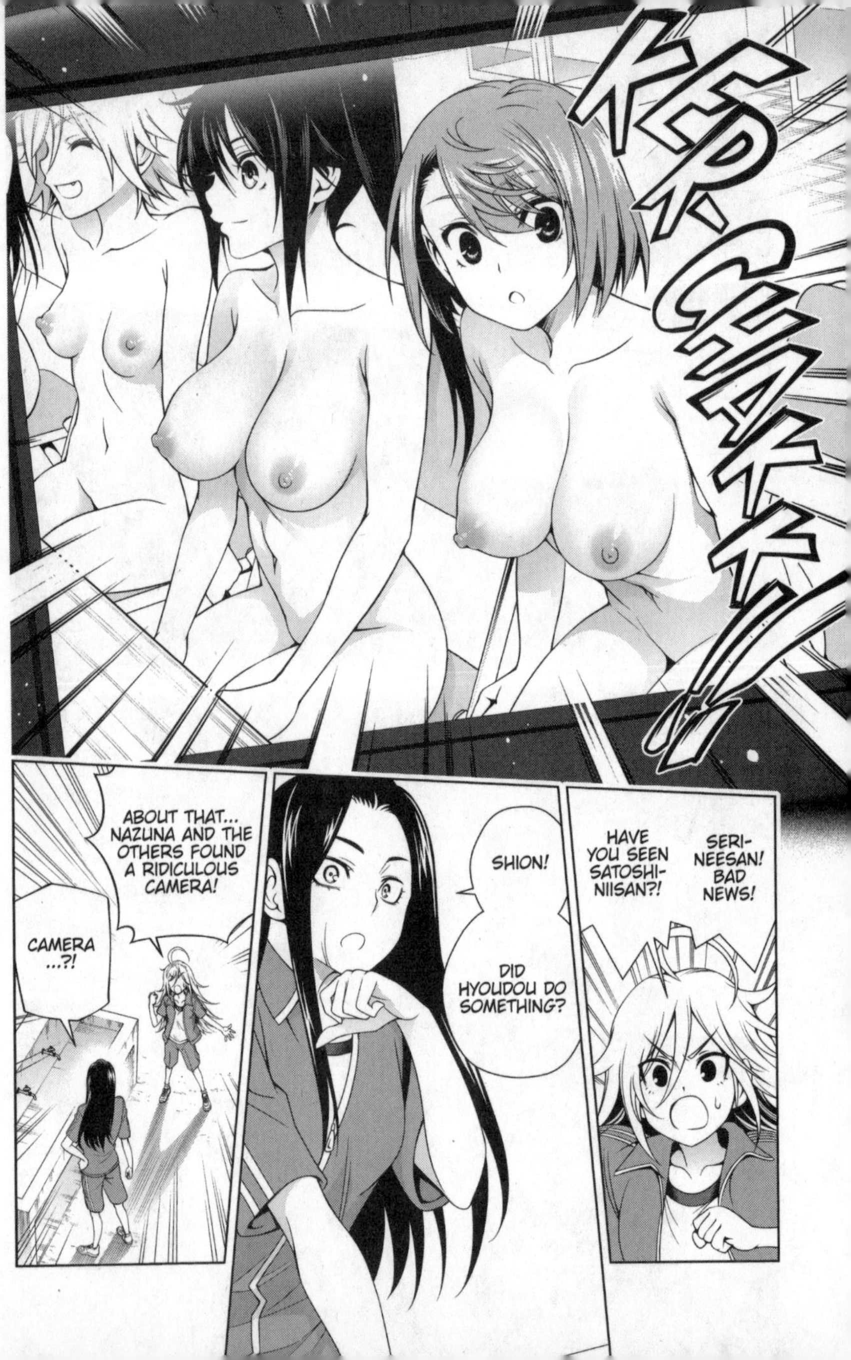
KER-CHAK!!
SERI-NEESAN! BAD NEWS!
HAVE YOU SEEN SATOSHI-NIISAN?!
SHION!
DID HYOUDOU DO SOMETHING?
ABOUT THAT... NAZUNA AND THE OTHERS FOUND A RIDICULOUS CAMERA!
CAMERA ...?!

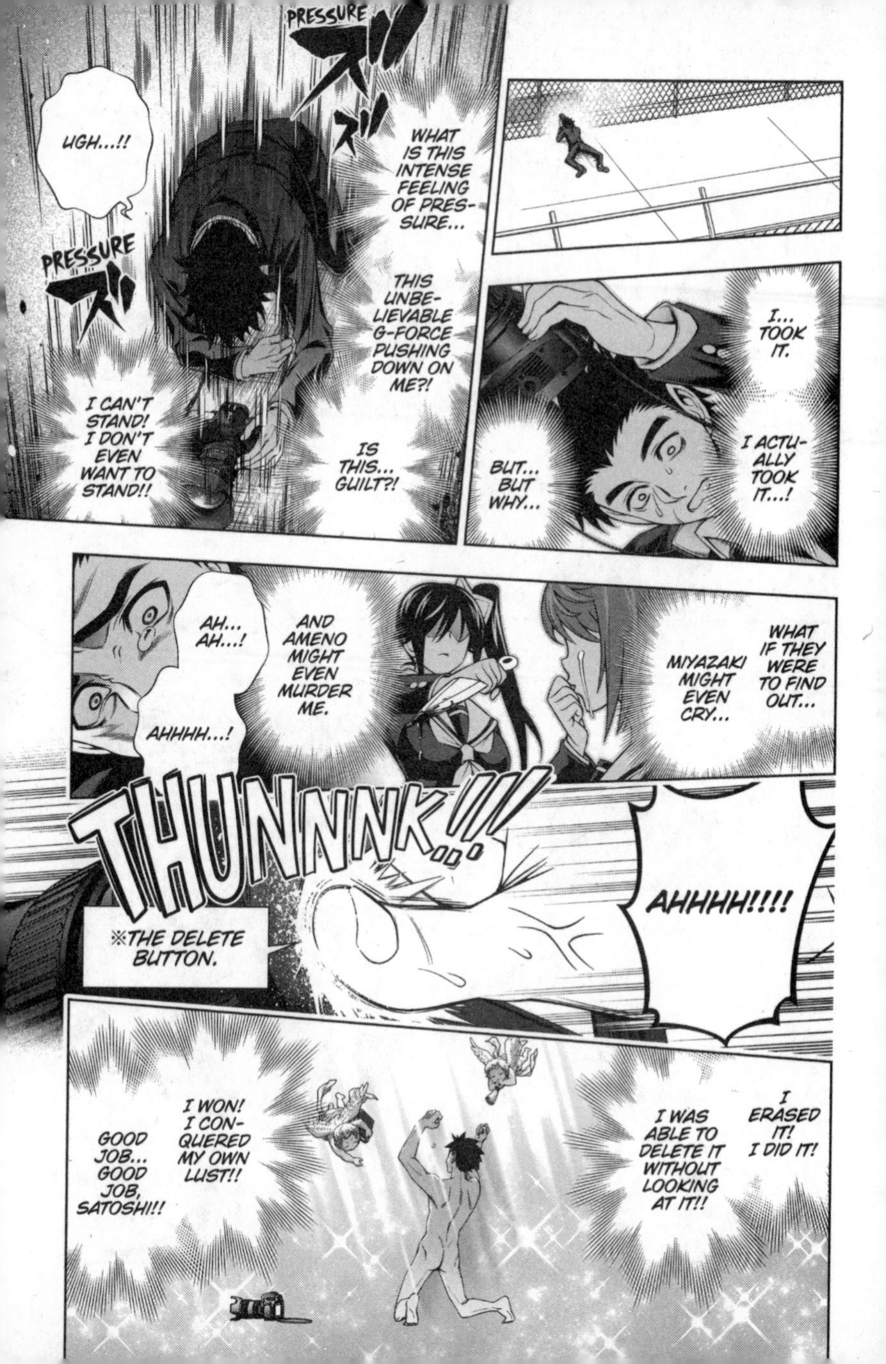
I... TOOK IT.
I ACTU-ALLY TOOK IT...!
BUT... BUT WHY...
PRESSURE
WHAT IS THIS INTENSE FEELING OF PRES-SURE...
THIS UNBE-LIEVABLE G-FORCE PUSHING DOWN ON ME?!
UGH...!!
PRESSURE
IS THIS... GUILT?!
I CAN'T STAND! I DON'T EVEN WANT TO STAND!!
WHAT IF THEY WERE TO FIND OUT...
MIYAZAKI MIGHT EVEN CRY...
AND AMENO MIGHT EVEN MURDER ME.
AH... AH...!
AHHHH...!
AHHHH!!!!
THUNNNK!!!
※THE DELETE BUTTON.
I ERASED IT! I DID IT!
I WAS ABLE TO DELETE IT WITHOUT LOOKING AT IT!!
I WON! I CON-QUERED MY OWN LUST!!
GOOD JOB... GOOD JOB, SATOSHI!!

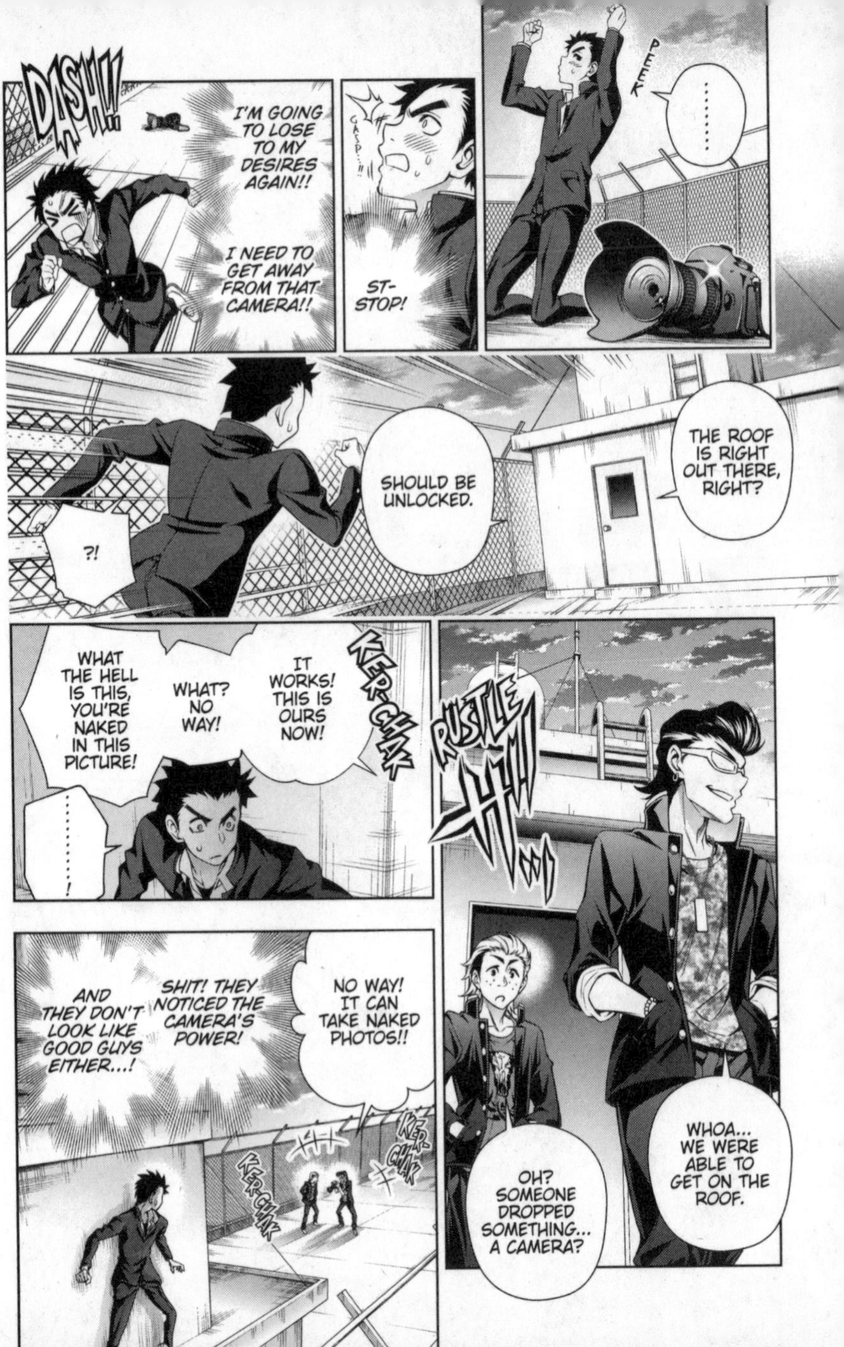
PEEK
......
GASP...!!
ST-STOP!
DASH!!
I'M GOING TO LOSE TO MY DESIRES AGAIN!!
I NEED TO GET AWAY FROM THAT CAMERA!!
THE ROOF IS RIGHT OUT THERE, RIGHT?
SHOULD BE UNLOCKED.
?!
RUSTLE
WHOA... WE WERE ABLE TO GET ON THE ROOF.
OH? SOMEONE DROPPED SOMETHING... A CAMERA?
KER-CHAK
IT WORKS! THIS IS OURS NOW!
WHAT? NO WAY!
WHAT THE HELL IS THIS, YOU'RE NAKED IN THIS PICTURE!
......!
NO WAY! IT CAN TAKE NAKED PHOTOS!!
SHIT! THEY NOTICED THE CAMERA'S POWER!
AND THEY DON'T LOOK LIKE GOOD GUYS EITHER...!
KER-CHAK
KER-CHAK

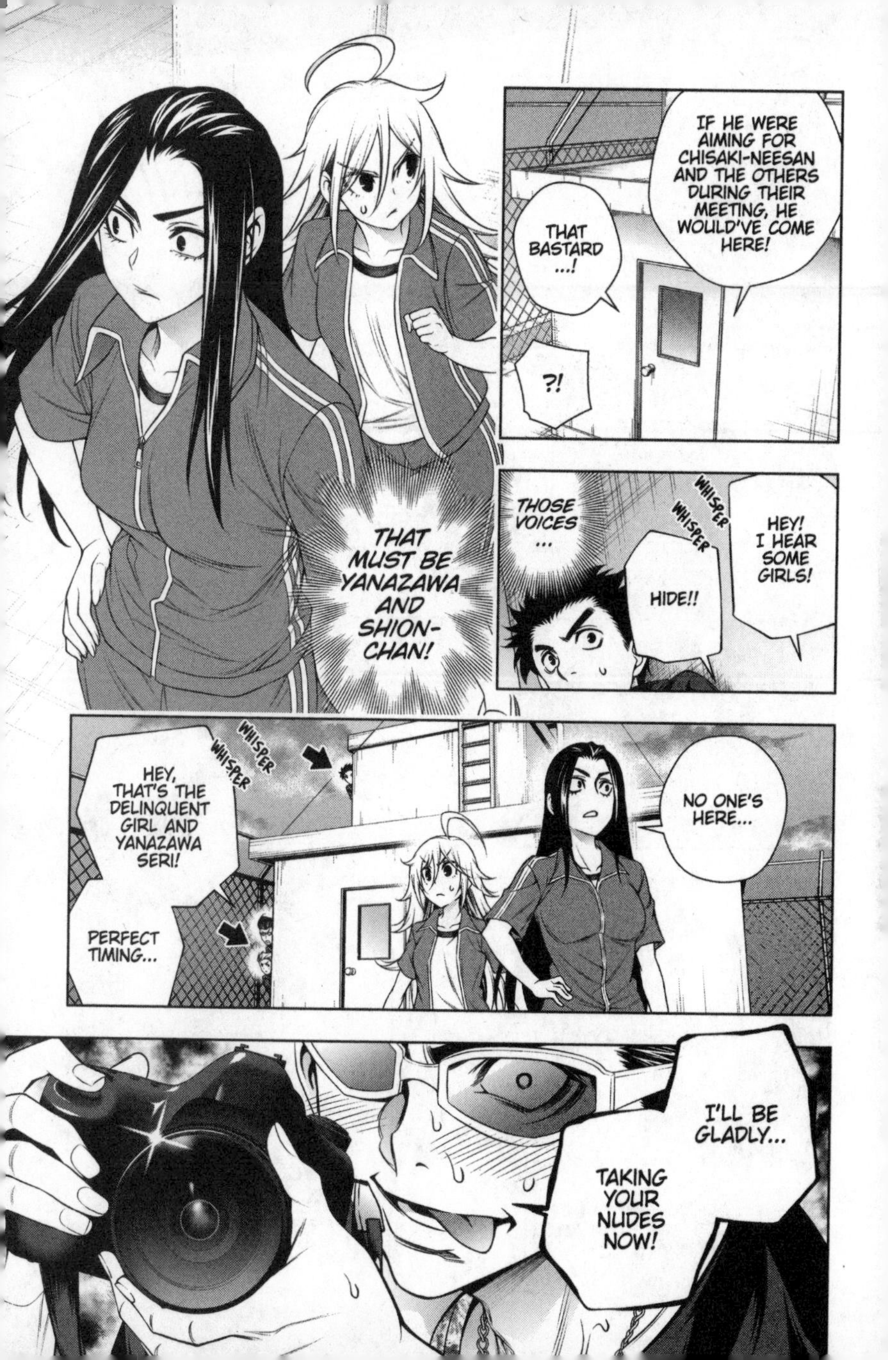
IF HE WERE AIMING FOR CHISAKI-NEESAN AND THE OTHERS DURING THEIR MEETING, HE WOULD'VE COME HERE!
THAT BASTARD ...!
?!
HEY! I HEAR SOME GIRLS!
WHISPER WHISPER
HIDE!!
THOSE VOICES ...
THAT MUST BE YANAZAWA AND SHION-CHAN!
NO ONE'S HERE...
WHISPER WHISPER
HEY, THAT'S THE DELINQUENT GIRL AND YANAZAWA SERI!
PERFECT TIMING...
I'LL BE GLADLY...
TAKING YOUR NUDES NOW!

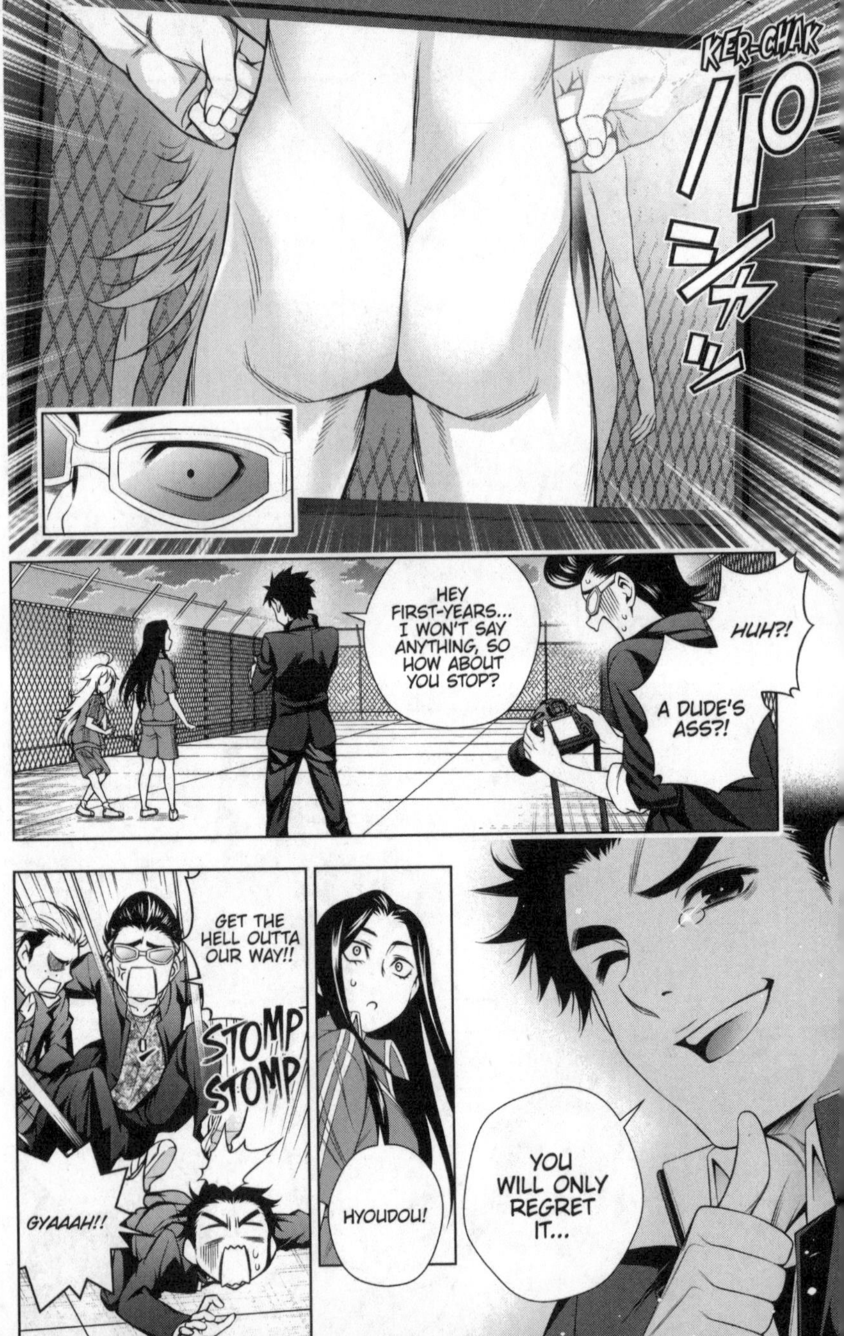
KER-CHAK
パシャッ
HUH?!
A DUDE'S ASS?!
HEY FIRST-YEARS... I WON'T SAY ANYTHING, SO HOW ABOUT YOU STOP?
YOU WILL ONLY REGRET IT...
HYOUDOU!
GET THE HELL OUTTA OUR WAY!!
STOMP STOMP
GYAAAH!!

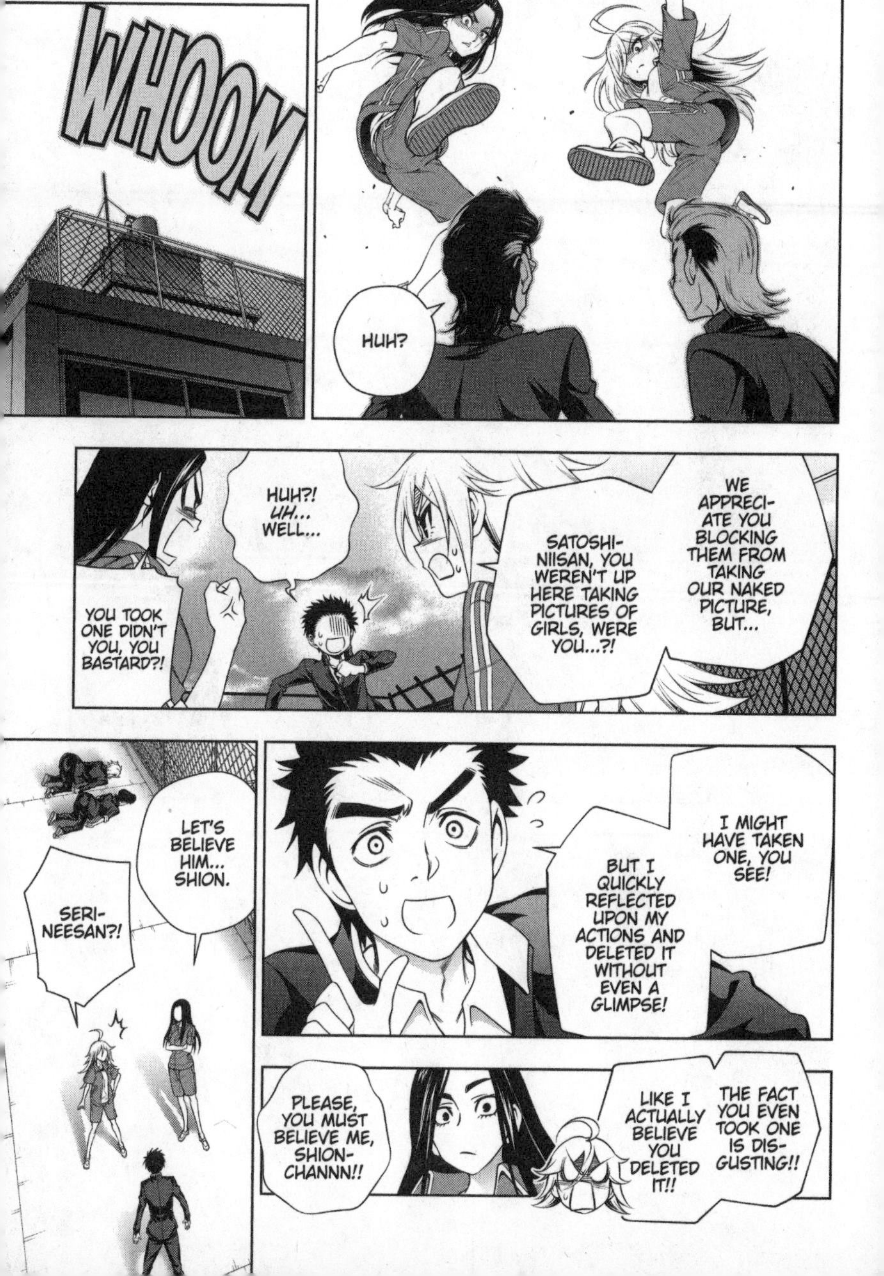
HUH?
WHOOM
WE APPRECIATE YOU BLOCKING THEM FROM TAKING OUR NAKED PICTURE, BUT...
SATOSHI-NIISAN, YOU WEREN'T UP HERE TAKING PICTURES OF GIRLS, WERE YOU...?!
HUH?! UH... WELL...
YOU TOOK ONE DIDN'T YOU, YOU BASTARD?!
I MIGHT HAVE TAKEN ONE, YOU SEE!
BUT I QUICKLY REFLECTED UPON MY ACTIONS AND DELETED IT WITHOUT EVEN A GLIMPSE!
THE FACT YOU EVEN TOOK ONE IS DIS-GUSTING!!
LIKE I ACTUALLY BELIEVE YOU DELETED IT!!
PLEASE, YOU MUST BELIEVE ME, SHION-CHANNN!!
LET'S BELIEVE HIM... SHION.
SERI-NEESAN?!

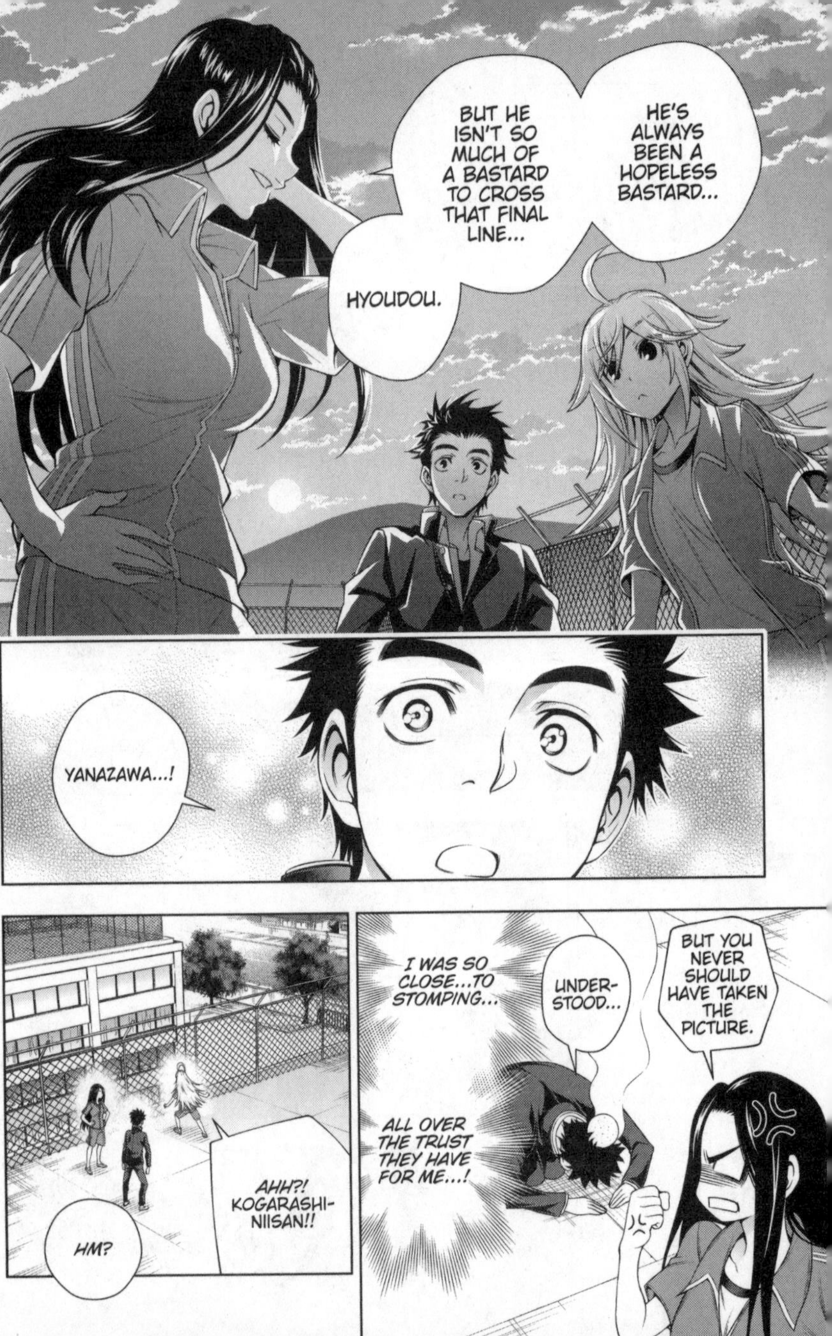
HE'S ALWAYS BEEN A HOPELESS BASTARD...
BUT HE ISN'T SO MUCH OF A BASTARD TO CROSS THAT FINAL LINE...
HYOUDOU.
YANAZAWA...!
BUT YOU NEVER SHOULD HAVE TAKEN THE PICTURE.
UNDER-STOOD...
I WAS SO CLOSE...TO STOMPING...
ALL OVER THE TRUST THEY HAVE FOR ME...!
AHH?! KOGARASHI-NIISAN!!
HM?

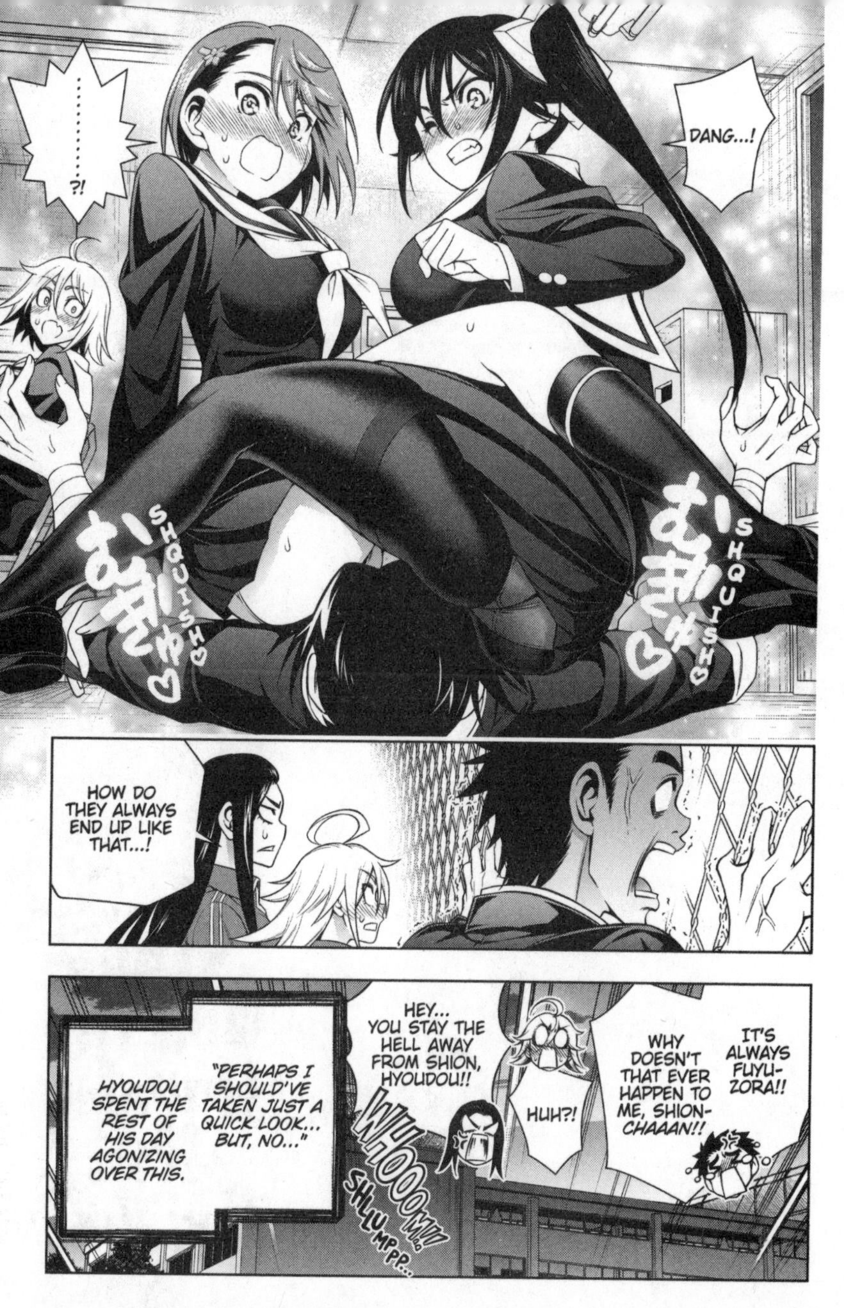
DANG...!
......?!
むぎゅ♥
SHQUISH♥
むぎゅ♥
SHQUISH♥
HOW DO THEY ALWAYS END UP LIKE THAT...!
IT'S ALWAYS FUYU-ZORA!!
WHY DOESN'T THAT EVER HAPPEN TO ME, SHION-CHAAAN!!
HUH?!
HEY... YOU STAY THE HELL AWAY FROM SHION, HYOUDOU!!
WHOOOM!!
SHLUMPPP...
"PERHAPS I SHOULD'VE TAKEN JUST A QUICK LOOK... BUT, NO..."
HYOUDOU SPENT THE REST OF HIS DAY AGONIZING OVER THIS.

Yuuna and the Haunted Hot Springs

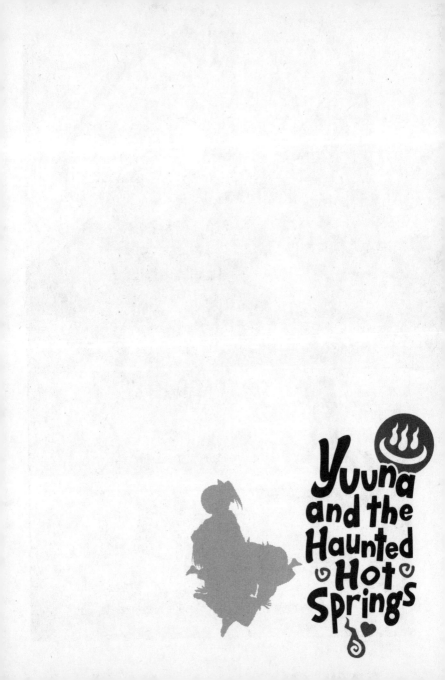

169 Yuragi-sou Strip Rock, Paper, Scissors

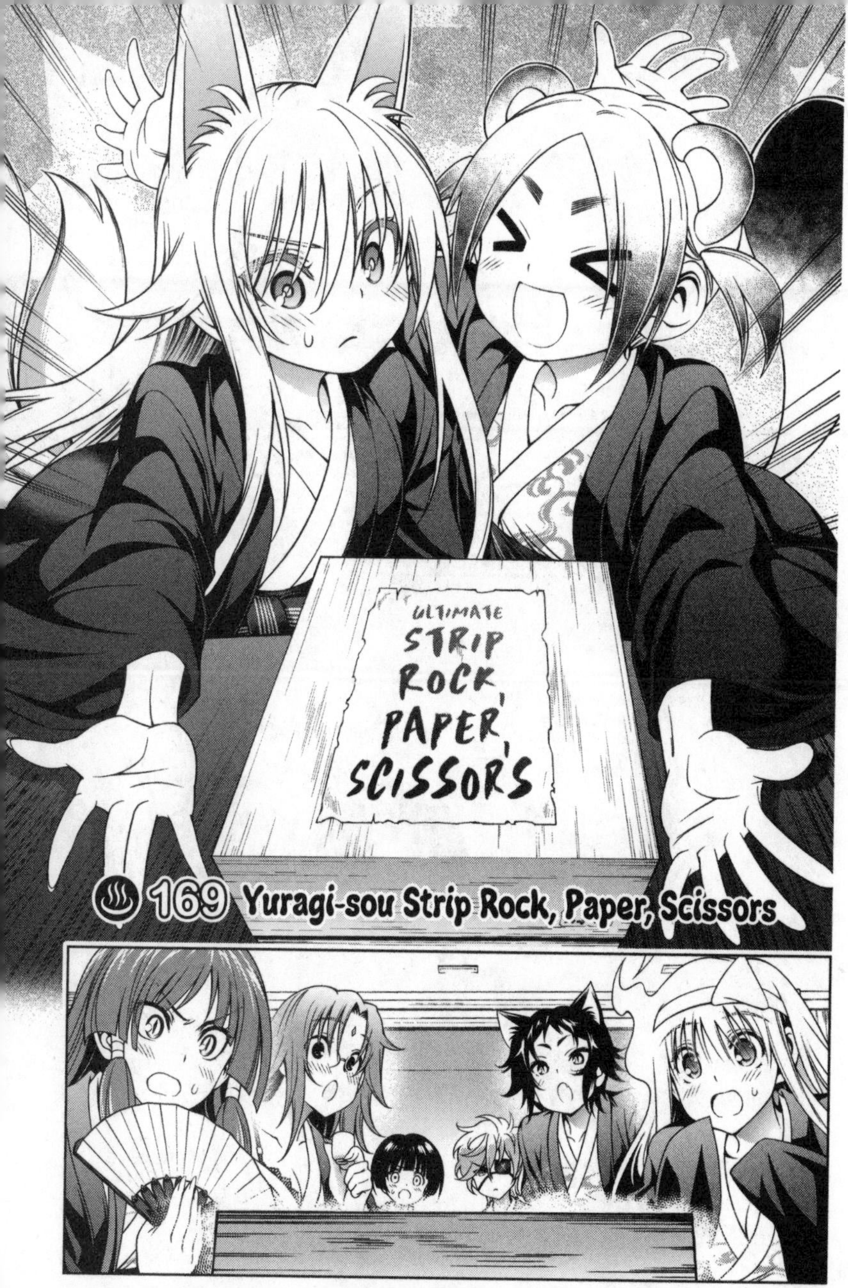
ULTIMATE
STRIP ROCK, PAPER, SCISSORS

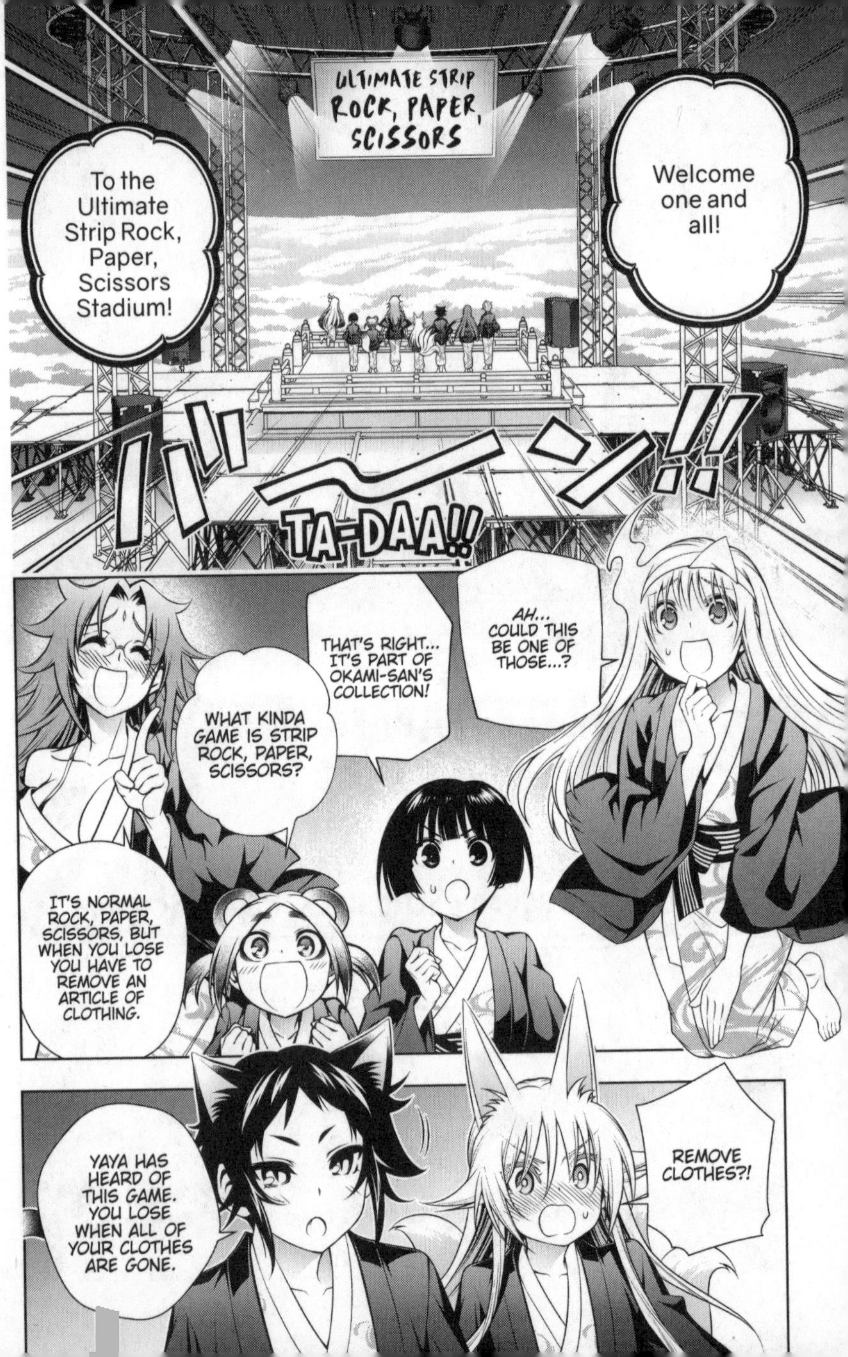
ULTIMATE STRIP ROCK, PAPER, SCISSORS
Welcome one and all!
To the Ultimate Strip Rock, Paper, Scissors Stadium!
TA-DAA!!
AH... COULD THIS BE ONE OF THOSE...?
THAT'S RIGHT... IT'S PART OF OKAMI-SAN'S COLLECTION!
WHAT KINDA GAME IS STRIP ROCK, PAPER, SCISSORS?
IT'S NORMAL ROCK, PAPER, SCISSORS, BUT WHEN YOU LOSE YOU HAVE TO REMOVE AN ARTICLE OF CLOTHING.
REMOVE CLOTHES?!
YAYA HAS HEARD OF THIS GAME. YOU LOSE WHEN ALL OF YOUR CLOTHES ARE GONE.

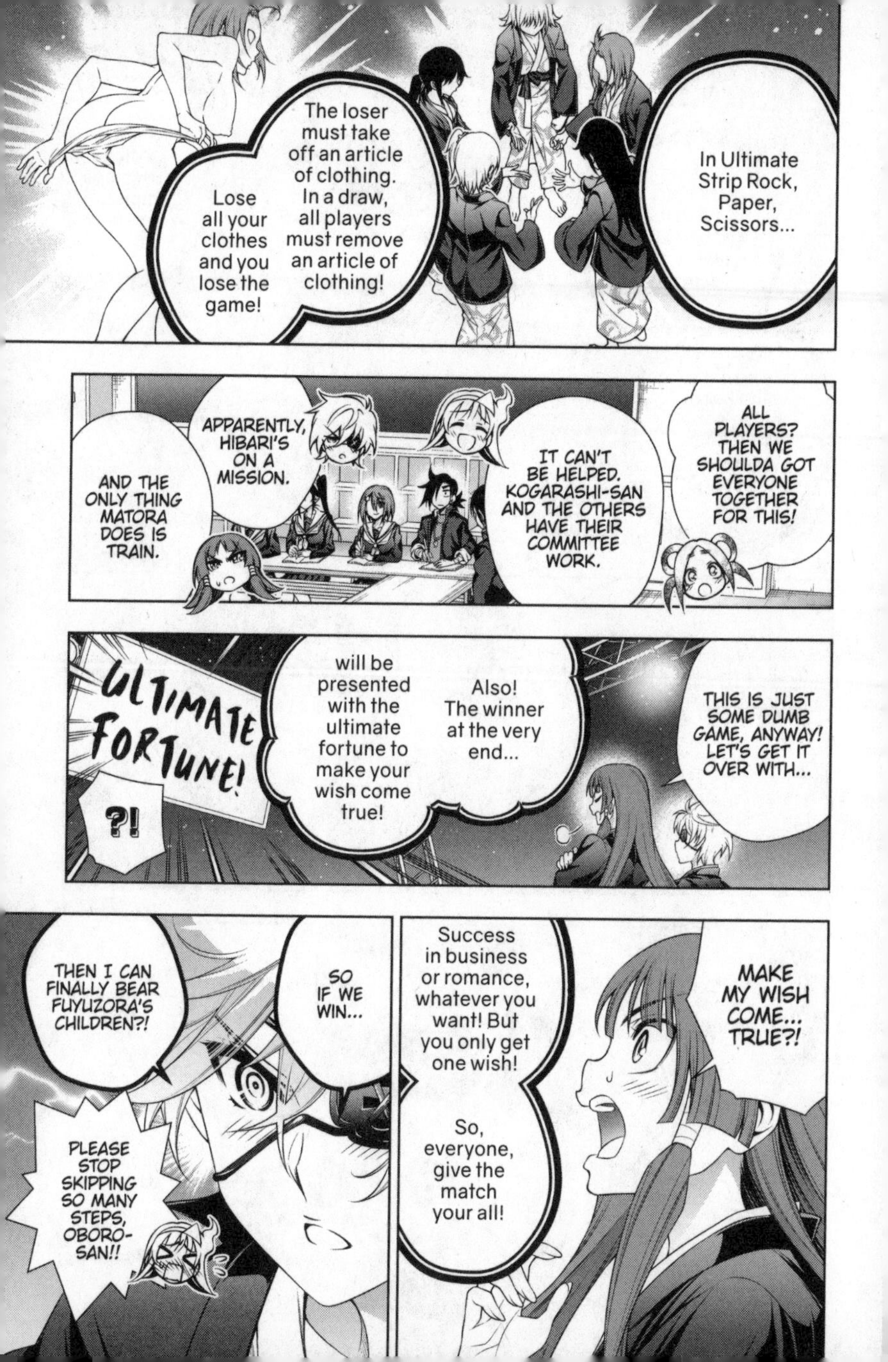
In Ultimate Strip Rock, Paper, Scissors...
The loser must take off an article of clothing. In a draw, all players must remove an article of clothing!
Lose all your clothes and you lose the game!
ALL PLAYERS? THEN WE SHOULDA GOT EVERYONE TOGETHER FOR THIS!
IT CAN'T BE HELPED. KOGARASHI-SAN AND THE OTHERS HAVE THEIR COMMITTEE WORK.
APPARENTLY, HIBARI'S ON A MISSION.
AND THE ONLY THING MATORA DOES IS TRAIN.
THIS IS JUST SOME DUMB GAME, ANYWAY! LET'S GET IT OVER WITH...
Also! The winner at the very end...
will be presented with the ultimate fortune to make your wish come true!
ULTIMATE FORTUNE!
?!
MAKE MY WISH COME... TRUE?!
Success in business or romance, whatever you want! But you only get one wish!
So, everyone, give the match your all!
SO IF WE WIN...
THEN I CAN FINALLY BEAR FUYUZORA'S CHILDREN?!
PLEASE STOP SKIPPING SO MANY STEPS, OBORO-SAN!!

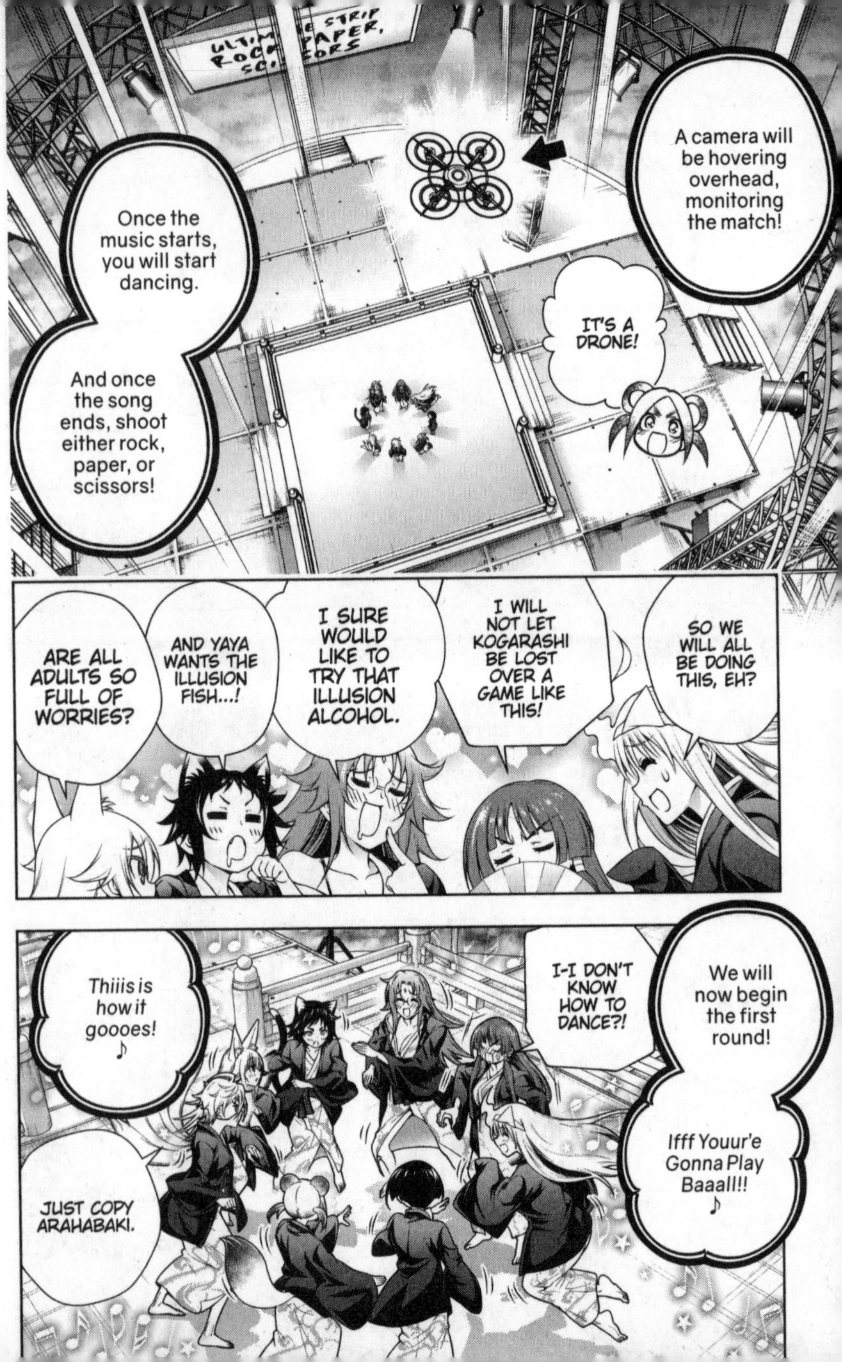
A camera will be hovering overhead, monitoring the match!
IT'S A DRONE!
Once the music starts, you will start dancing.
And once the song ends, shoot either rock, paper, or scissors!
SO WE WILL ALL BE DOING THIS, EH?
I WILL NOT LET KOGARASHI BE LOST OVER A GAME LIKE THIS!
I SURE WOULD LIKE TO TRY THAT ILLUSION ALCOHOL.
AND YAYA WANTS THE ILLUSION FISH...!
ARE ALL ADULTS SO FULL OF WORRIES?
We will now begin the first round!
Ifff Youur'e Gonna Play Baaall!! ♪
I-I DON'T KNOW HOW TO DANCE?!
Thiiis is how it goooes! ♪
JUST COPY ARAHABAKI.

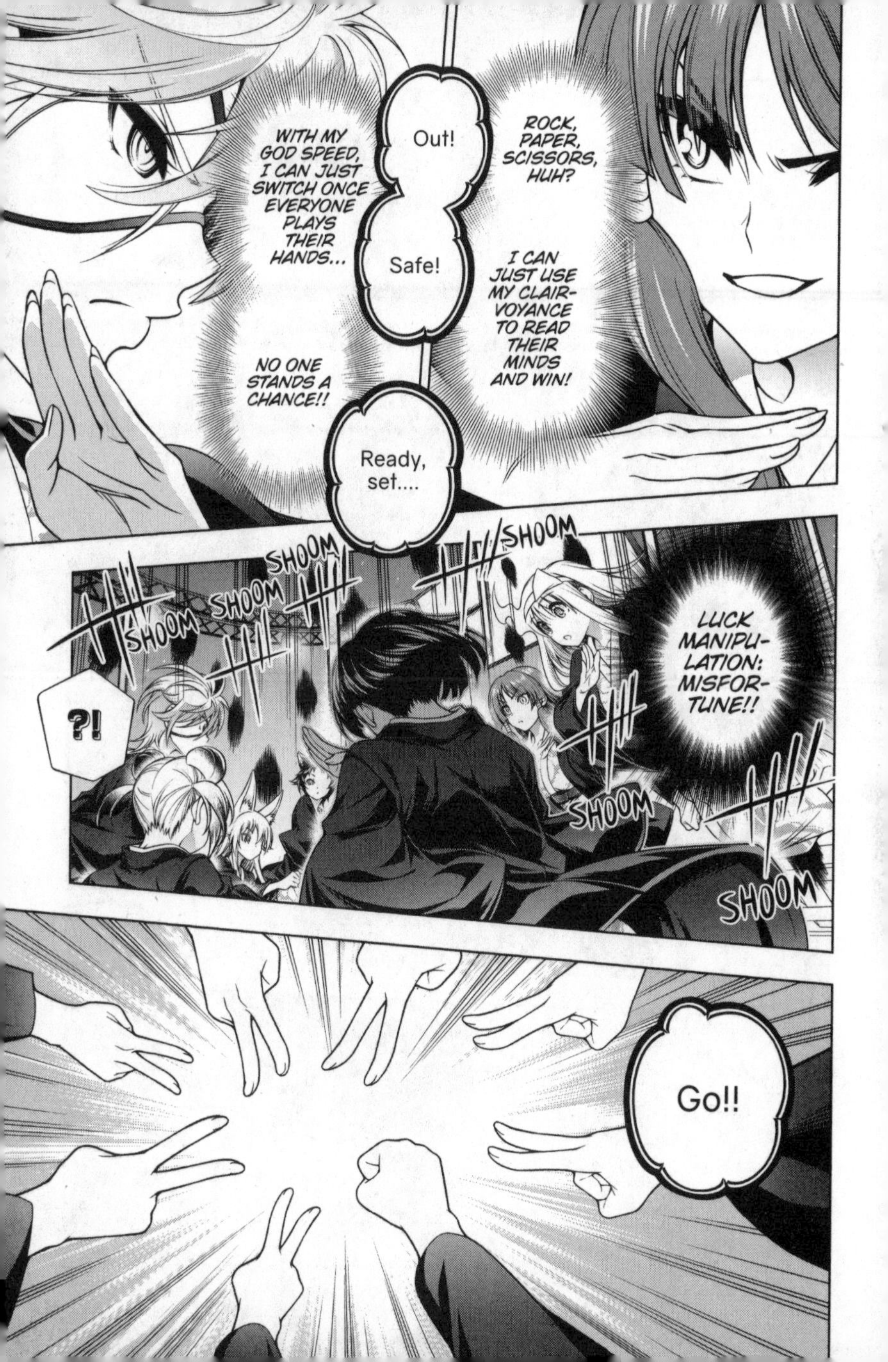
Out!
Safe!
Ready, set....
ROCK, PAPER, SCISSORS, HUH?
I CAN JUST USE MY CLAIR-VOYANCE TO READ THEIR MINDS AND WIN!
WITH MY GOD SPEED, I CAN JUST SWITCH ONCE EVERYONE PLAYS THEIR HANDS...
NO ONE STANDS A CHANCE!!
SHOOM
LUCK MANIPU-LATION: MISFOR-TUNE!!
SHOOM
SHOOM
SHOOM
SHOOM
SHOOM
SHOOM
?!
Go!!

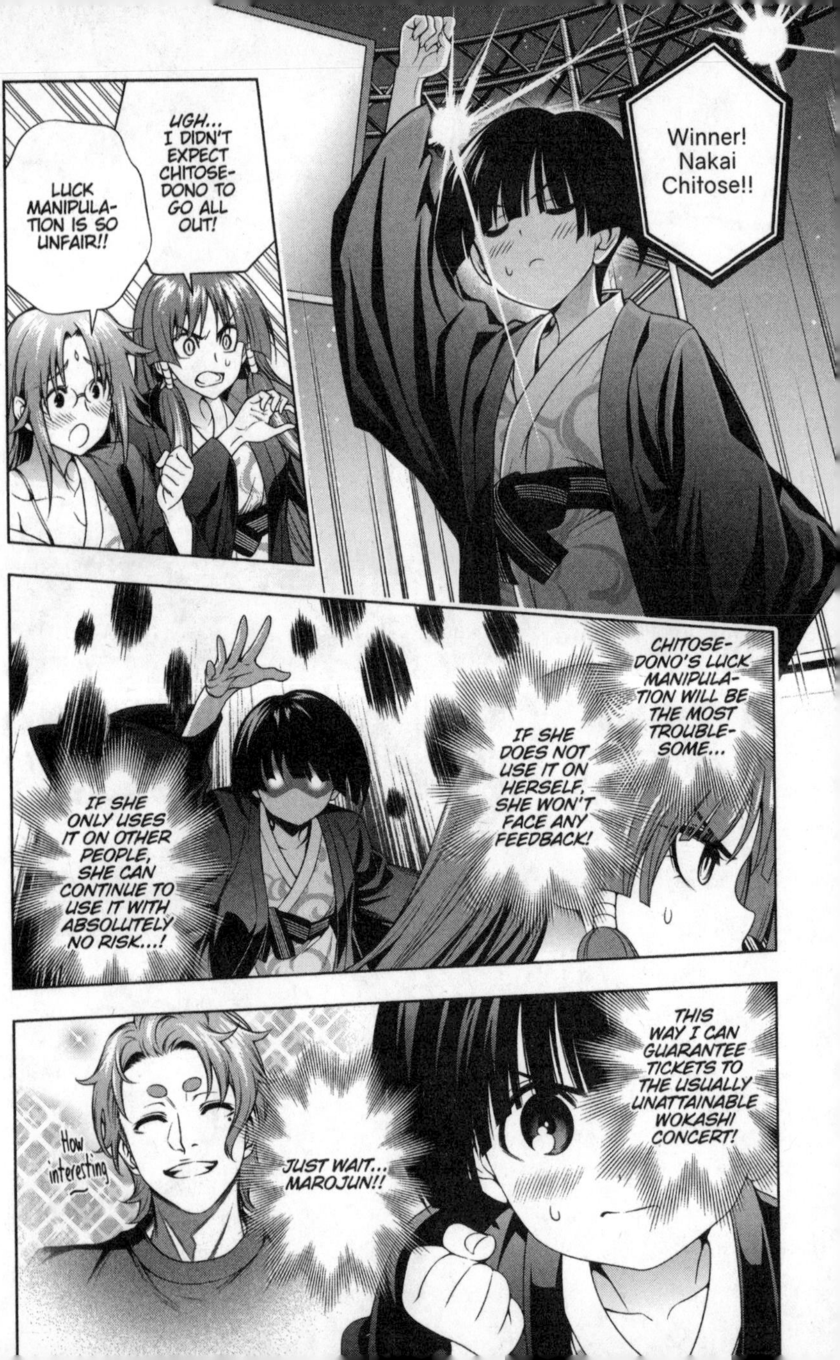
Winner! Nakai Chitose!!
UGH... I DIDN'T EXPECT CHITOSE-DONO TO GO ALL OUT!
LUCK MANIPULATION IS SO UNFAIR!!
CHITOSE-DONO'S LUCK MANIPULATION WILL BE THE MOST TROUBLESOME...
IF SHE DOES NOT USE IT ON HERSELF, SHE WON'T FACE ANY FEEDBACK!
IF SHE ONLY USES IT ON OTHER PEOPLE, SHE CAN CONTINUE TO USE IT WITH ABSOLUTELY NO RISK...!
THIS WAY I CAN GUARANTEE TICKETS TO THE USUALLY UNATTAINABLE WOKASHI CONCERT!
JUST WAIT... MAROJUN!!
How interesting ~

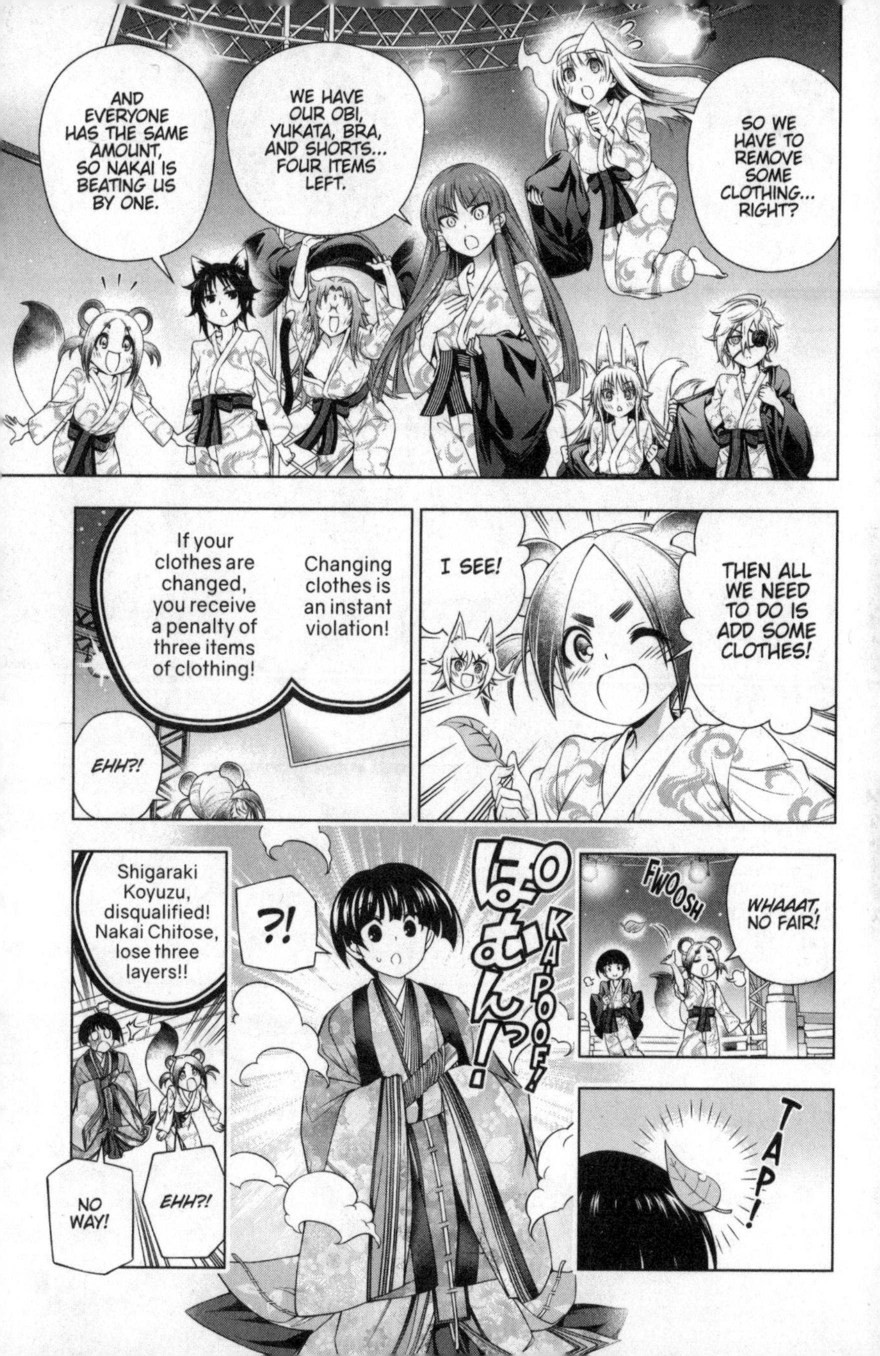
SO WE HAVE TO REMOVE SOME CLOTHING... RIGHT?
WE HAVE OUR OBI, YUKATA, BRA, AND SHORTS... FOUR ITEMS LEFT.
AND EVERYONE HAS THE SAME AMOUNT, SO NAKAI IS BEATING US BY ONE.
I SEE!
THEN ALL WE NEED TO DO IS ADD SOME CLOTHES!
Changing clothes is an instant violation!
If your clothes are changed, you receive a penalty of three items of clothing!
EHH?!
FWOOSH
WHAAAT, NO FAIR!
TAP!
ぼむんっ!!
KAPOOF!
?!
Shigaraki Koyuzu, disqualified! Nakai Chitose, lose three layers!!
EHH?!
NO WAY!

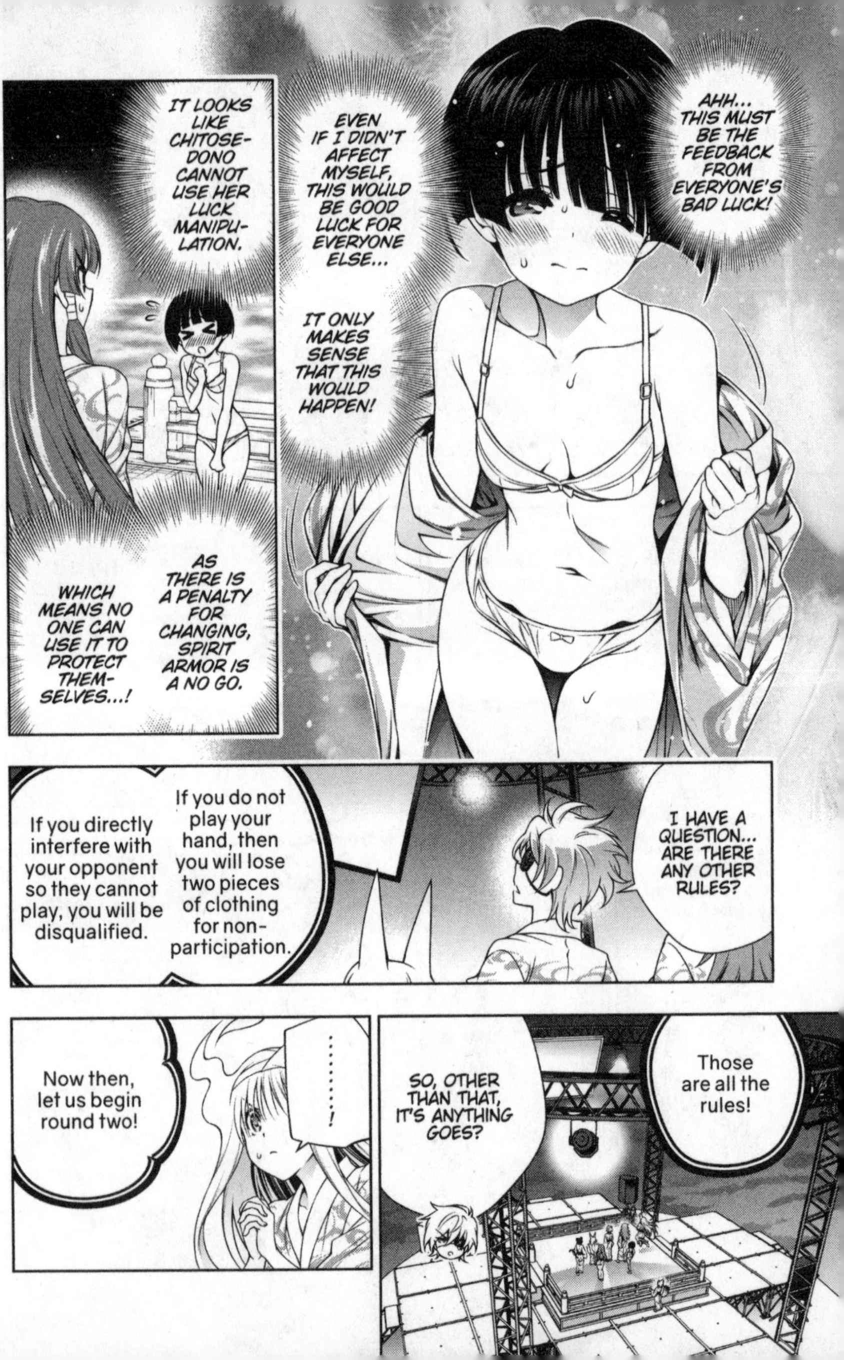
AHH... THIS MUST BE THE FEEDBACK FROM EVERYONE'S BAD LUCK!
EVEN IF I DIDN'T AFFECT MYSELF, THIS WOULD BE GOOD LUCK FOR EVERYONE ELSE...
IT ONLY MAKES SENSE THAT THIS WOULD HAPPEN!
IT LOOKS LIKE CHITOSE-DONO CANNOT USE HER LUCK MANIPULATION.
AS THERE IS A PENALTY FOR CHANGING, SPIRIT ARMOR IS A NO GO.
WHICH MEANS NO ONE CAN USE IT TO PROTECT THEMSELVES...!
I HAVE A QUESTION... ARE THERE ANY OTHER RULES?
If you do not play your hand, then you will lose two pieces of clothing for non-participation.
If you directly interfere with your opponent so they cannot play, you will be disqualified.
Those are all the rules!
SO, OTHER THAN THAT, IT'S ANYTHING GOES?
......!
Now then, let us begin round two!

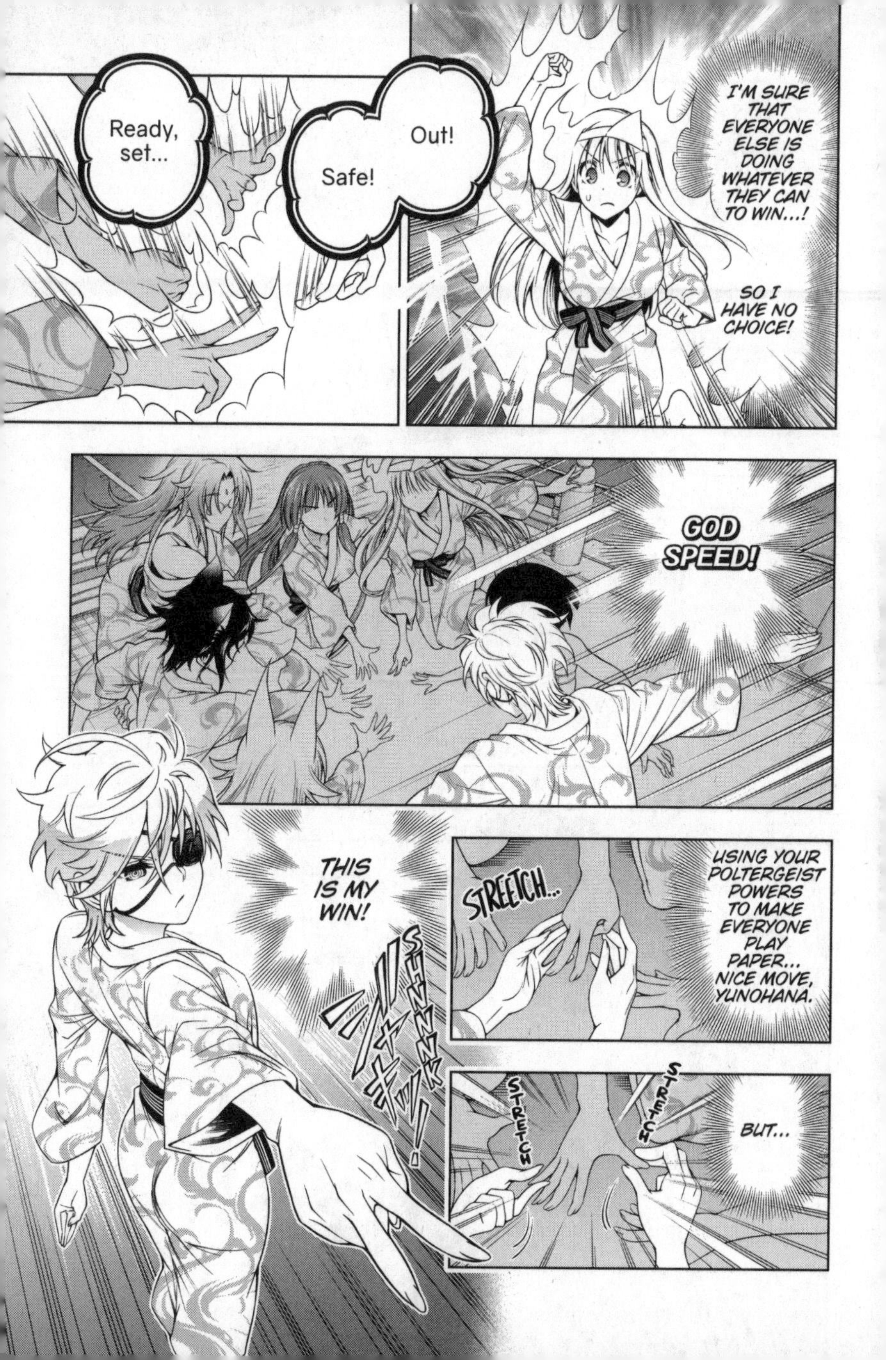

I'M SURE THAT EVERYONE ELSE IS DOING WHATEVER THEY CAN TO WIN...!
SO I HAVE NO CHOICE!
Out!
Safe!
Ready, set...
GOD SPEED!
STREETCH...
USING YOUR POLTERGEIST POWERS TO MAKE EVERYONE PLAY PAPER... NICE MOVE, YUNOHANA.
STRETCH
STRETCH
BUT...
THIS IS MY WIN!
SHNNNK

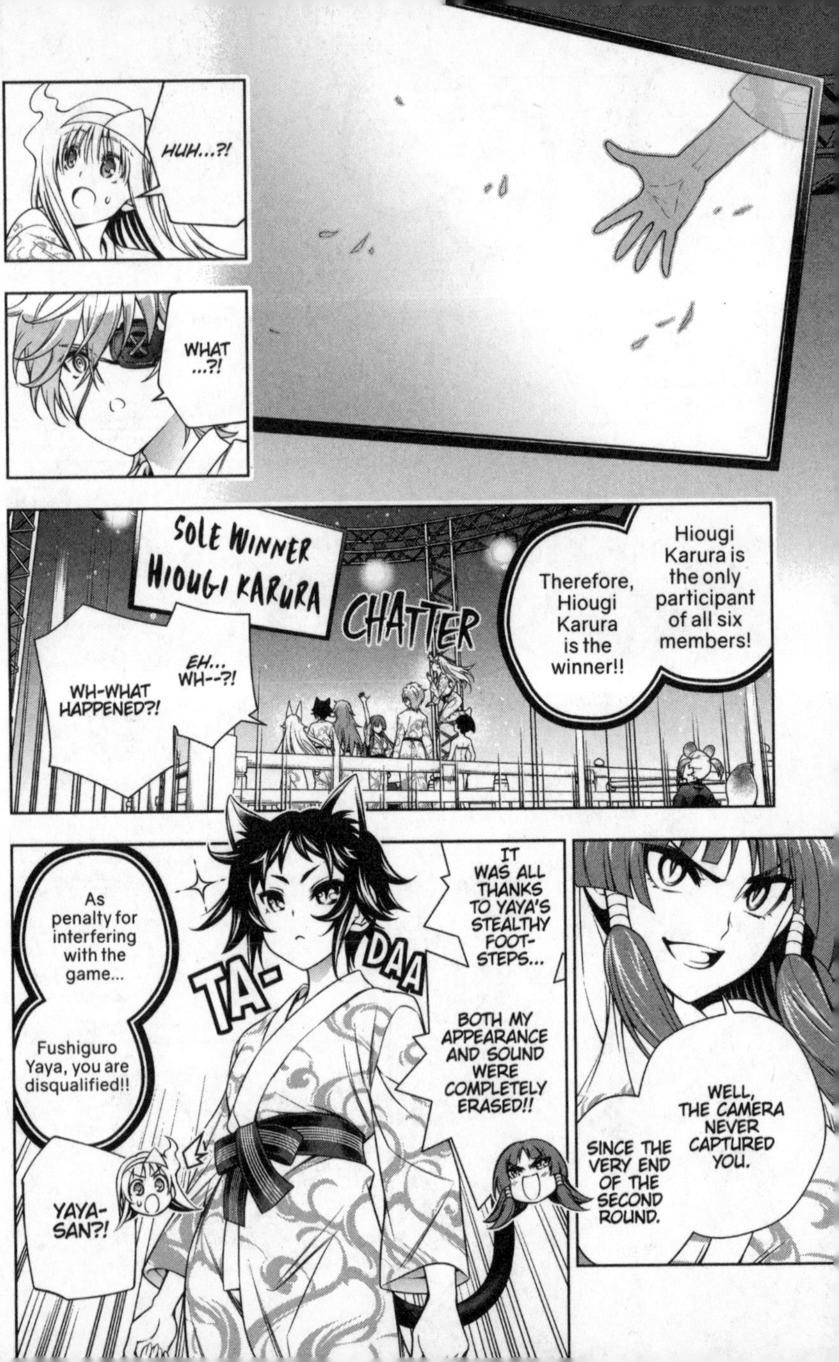
HUH...?!
WHAT ...?!
Hiougi Karura is the only participant of all six members!
Therefore, Hiougi Karura is the winner!!
CHATTER
SOLE WINNER HIOUGI KARURA
EH... WH--?!
WH-WHAT HAPPENED?!
WELL, THE CAMERA NEVER CAPTURED YOU.
SINCE THE VERY END OF THE SECOND ROUND.
IT WAS ALL THANKS TO YAYA'S STEALTHY FOOT-STEPS...
BOTH MY APPEARANCE AND SOUND WERE COMPLETELY ERASED!!
TA-DAA
As penalty for interfering with the game...
Fushiguro Yaya, you are disqualified!!
YAYA-SAN?!

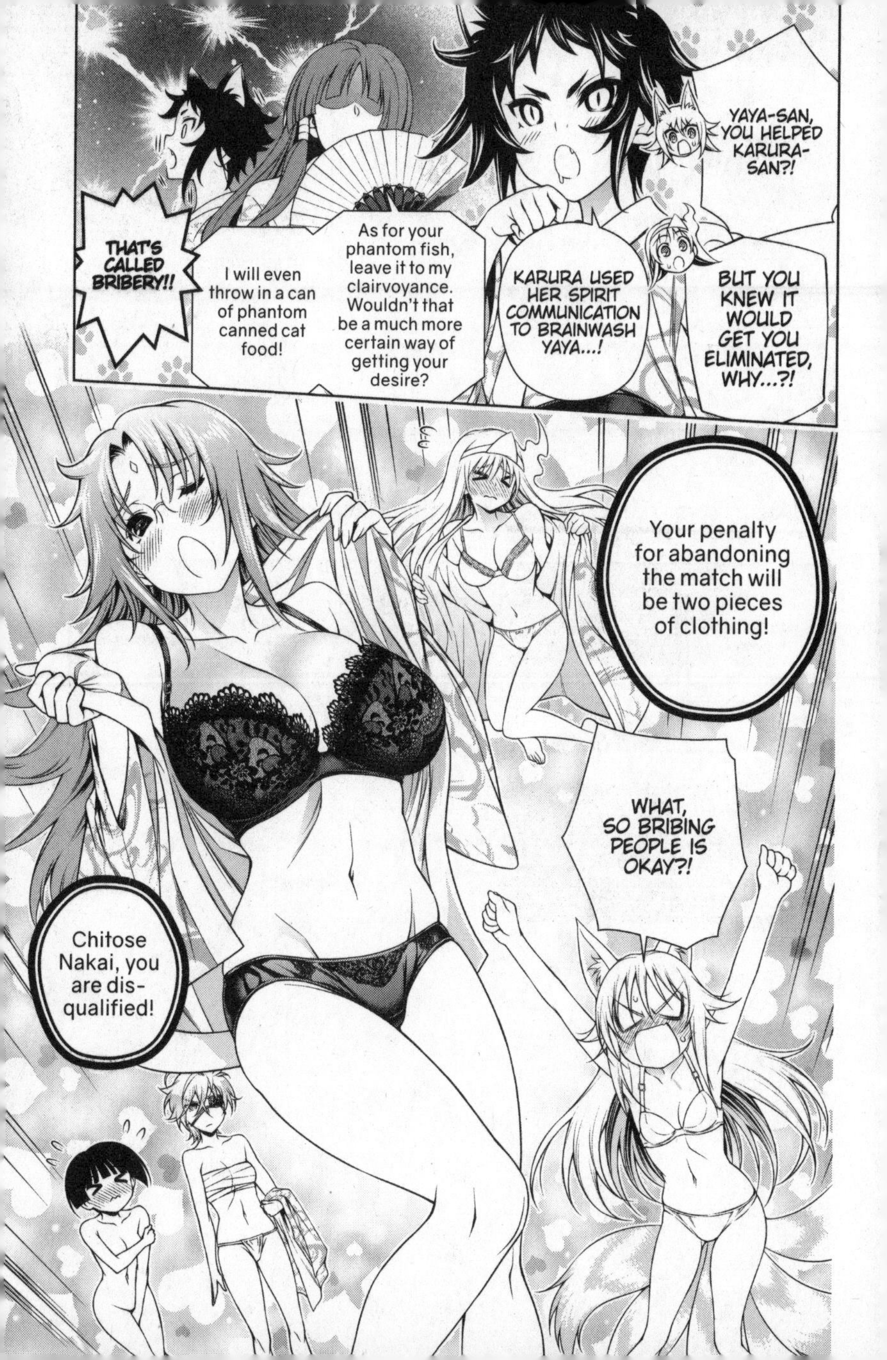
YAYA-SAN, YOU HELPED KARURA-SAN?!
BUT YOU KNEW IT WOULD GET YOU ELIMINATED, WHY...?!
KARURA USED HER SPIRIT COMMUNICATION TO BRAINWASH YAYA...!
As for your phantom fish, leave it to my clairvoyance. Wouldn't that be a much more certain way of getting your desire?
I will even throw in a can of phantom canned cat food!
THAT'S CALLED BRIBERY!!
Your penalty for abandoning the match will be two pieces of clothing!
WHAT, SO BRIBING PEOPLE IS OKAY?!
Chitose Nakai, you are dis-qualified!

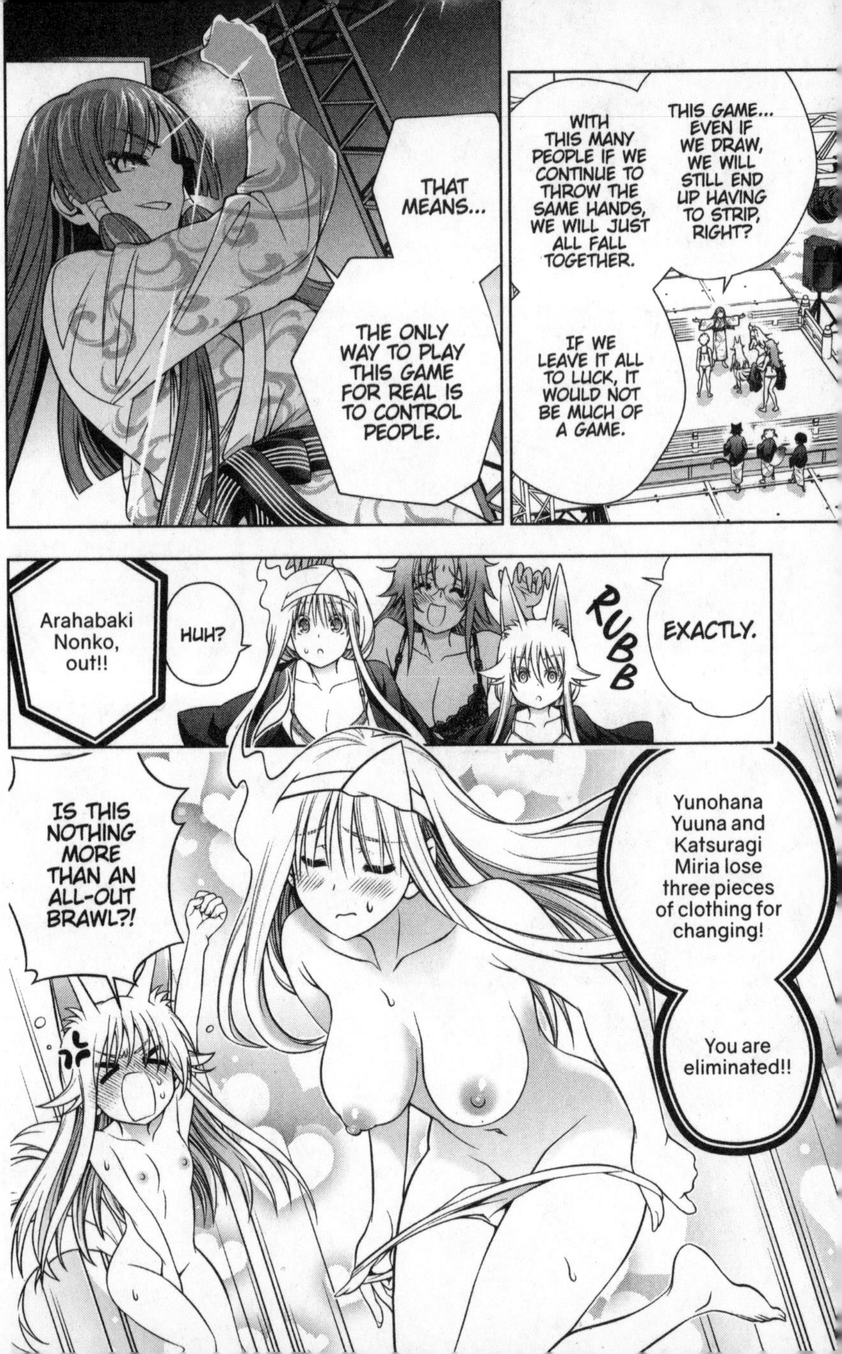
THIS GAME... EVEN IF WE DRAW, WE WILL STILL END UP HAVING TO STRIP, RIGHT?
WITH THIS MANY PEOPLE IF WE CONTINUE TO THROW THE SAME HANDS, WE WILL JUST ALL FALL TOGETHER.
IF WE LEAVE IT ALL TO LUCK, IT WOULD NOT BE MUCH OF A GAME.
THAT MEANS...
THE ONLY WAY TO PLAY THIS GAME FOR REAL IS TO CONTROL PEOPLE.
EXACTLY.
RUBB
HUH?
Arahabaki Nonko, out!!
Yunohana Yuuna and Katsuragi Miria lose three pieces of clothing for changing!
You are eliminated!!
IS THIS NOTHING MORE THAN AN ALL-OUT BRAWL?!

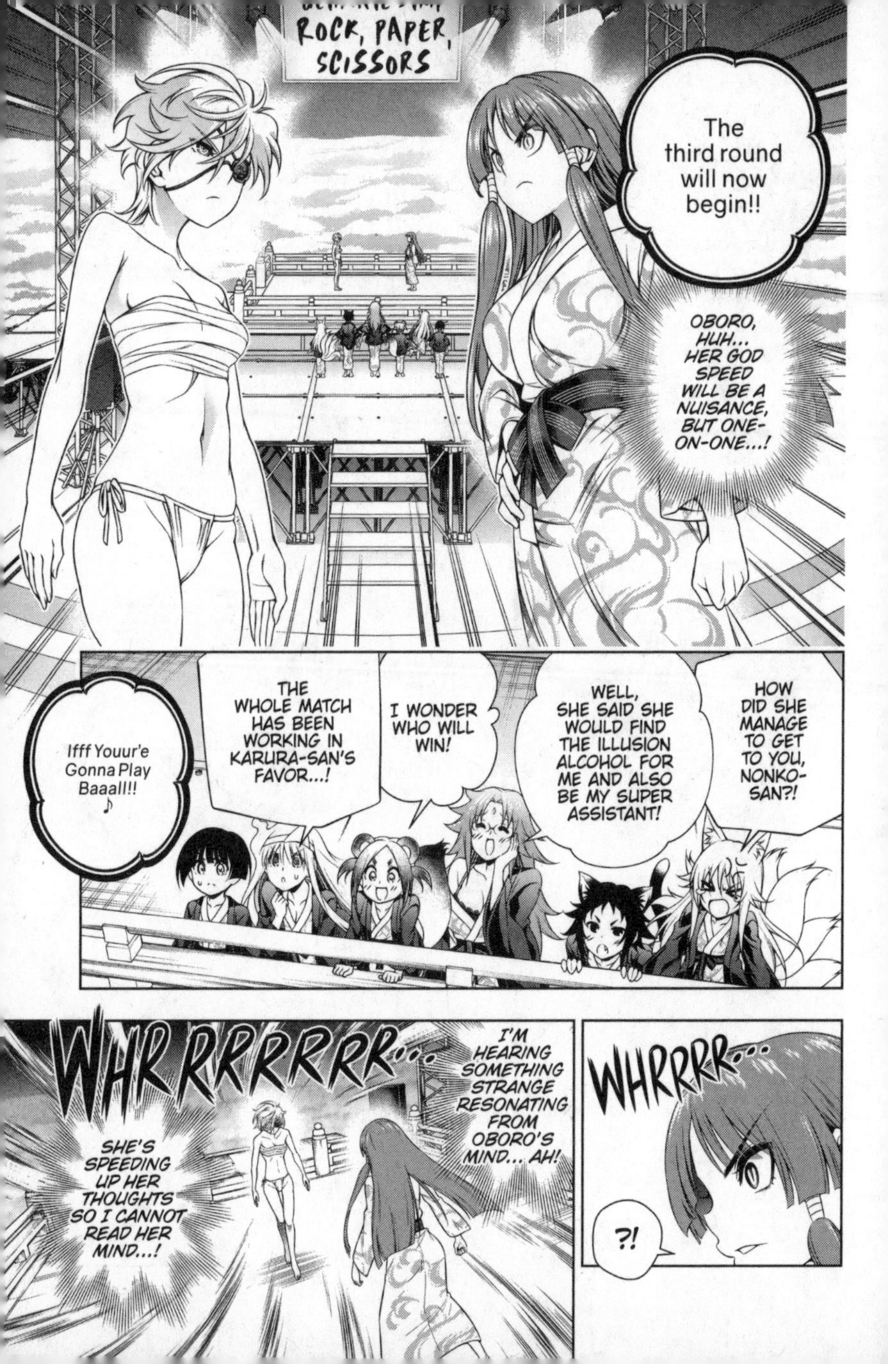
ROCK, PAPER, SCISSORS
The third round will now begin!!
OBORO, HUH... HER GOD SPEED WILL BE A NUISANCE, BUT ONE-ON-ONE...!
HOW DID SHE MANAGE TO GET TO YOU, NONKO-SAN?!
WELL, SHE SAID SHE WOULD FIND THE ILLUSION ALCOHOL FOR ME AND ALSO BE MY SUPER ASSISTANT!
I WONDER WHO WILL WIN!
THE WHOLE MATCH HAS BEEN WORKING IN KARURA-SAN'S FAVOR...!
Ifff Youur'e Gonna Play Baaall!! ♪
WHRRRR...
?!
I'M HEARING SOMETHING STRANGE RESONATING FROM OBORO'S MIND... AH!
WHRRRRRRR...
SHE'S SPEEDING UP HER THOUGHTS SO I CANNOT READ HER MIND...!

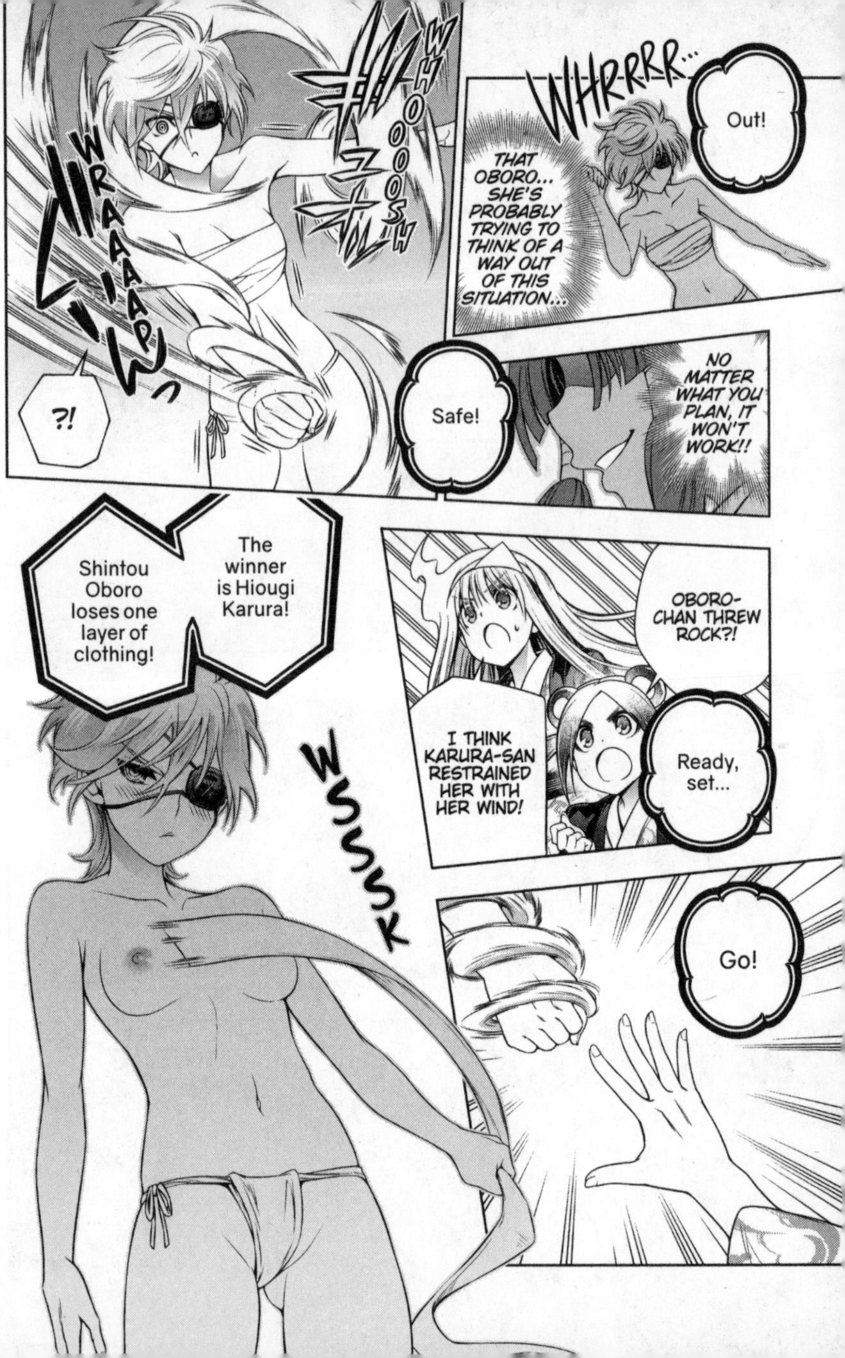
Out!
WHRRRR...
THAT OBORO... SHE'S PROBABLY TRYING TO THINK OF A WAY OUT OF THIS SITUATION...
NO MATTER WHAT YOU PLAN, IT WON'T WORK!!
Safe!
WHOOOOOSH
WRAAAAAP
?!
OBORO-CHAN THREW ROCK?!
I THINK KARURA-SAN RESTRAINED HER WITH HER WIND!
Ready, set...
Go!
The winner is Hiougi Karura!
Shintou Oboro loses one layer of clothing!
WSSSSK

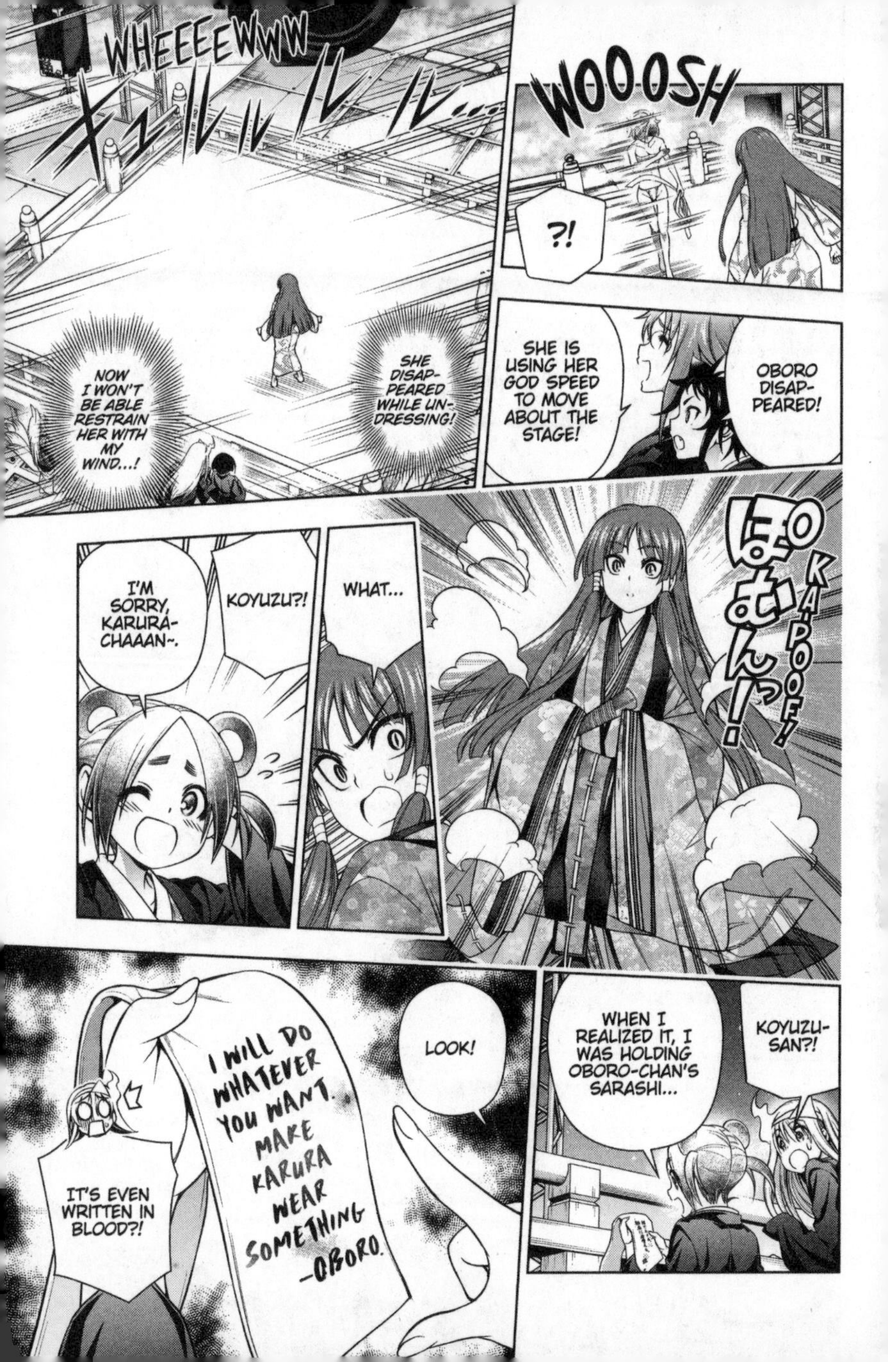

WOOOSH
?!
OBORO DISAPPEARED!
SHE IS USING HER GOD SPEED TO MOVE ABOUT THE STAGE!
WHEEEEWWW
キュルルルル...
SHE DISAPPEARED WHILE UNDRESSING!
NOW I WON'T BE ABLE RESTRAIN HER WITH MY WIND...!
KAPOOF!
ぽむんっ!
WHAT...
KOYUZU?!
I'M SORRY, KARURA-CHAAAN~.
KOYUZU-SAN?!
WHEN I REALIZED IT, I WAS HOLDING OBORO-CHAN'S SARASHI...
LOOK!
I WILL DO WHATEVER YOU WANT. MAKE KARURA WEAR SOMETHING -OBORO.
IT'S EVEN WRITTEN IN BLOOD?!

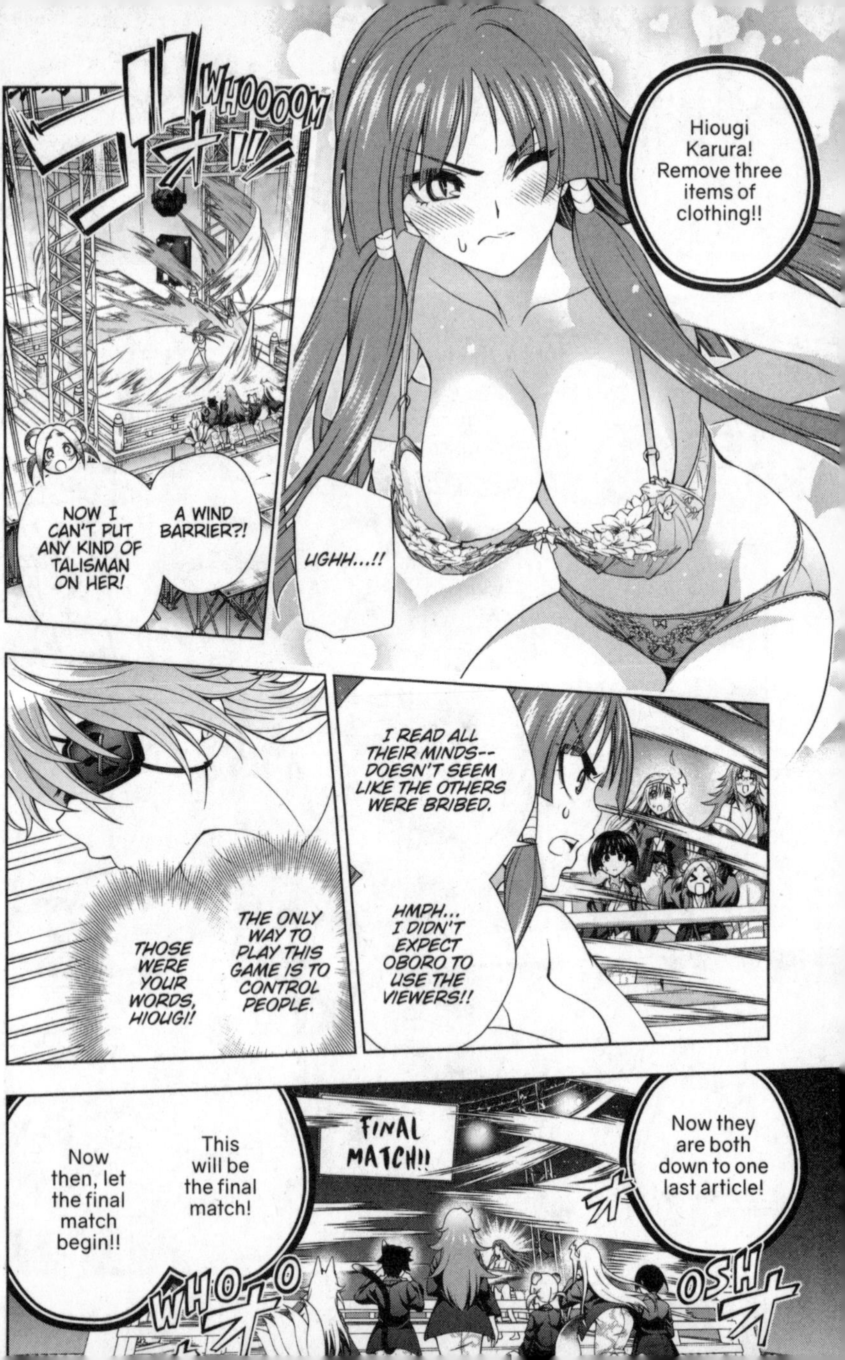
Hiougi Karura! Remove three items of clothing!!
UGHH...!!
WHOOOOM
A WIND BARRIER?!
NOW I CAN'T PUT ANY KIND OF TALISMAN ON HER!
I READ ALL THEIR MINDS-- DOESN'T SEEM LIKE THE OTHERS WERE BRIBED.
HMPH... I DIDN'T EXPECT OBORO TO USE THE VIEWERS!!
THE ONLY WAY TO PLAY THIS GAME IS TO CONTROL PEOPLE.
THOSE WERE YOUR WORDS, HIOUGI!!
Now they are both down to one last article!
FINAL MATCH!!
This will be the final match!
Now then, let the final match begin!!
WHOOOOSH

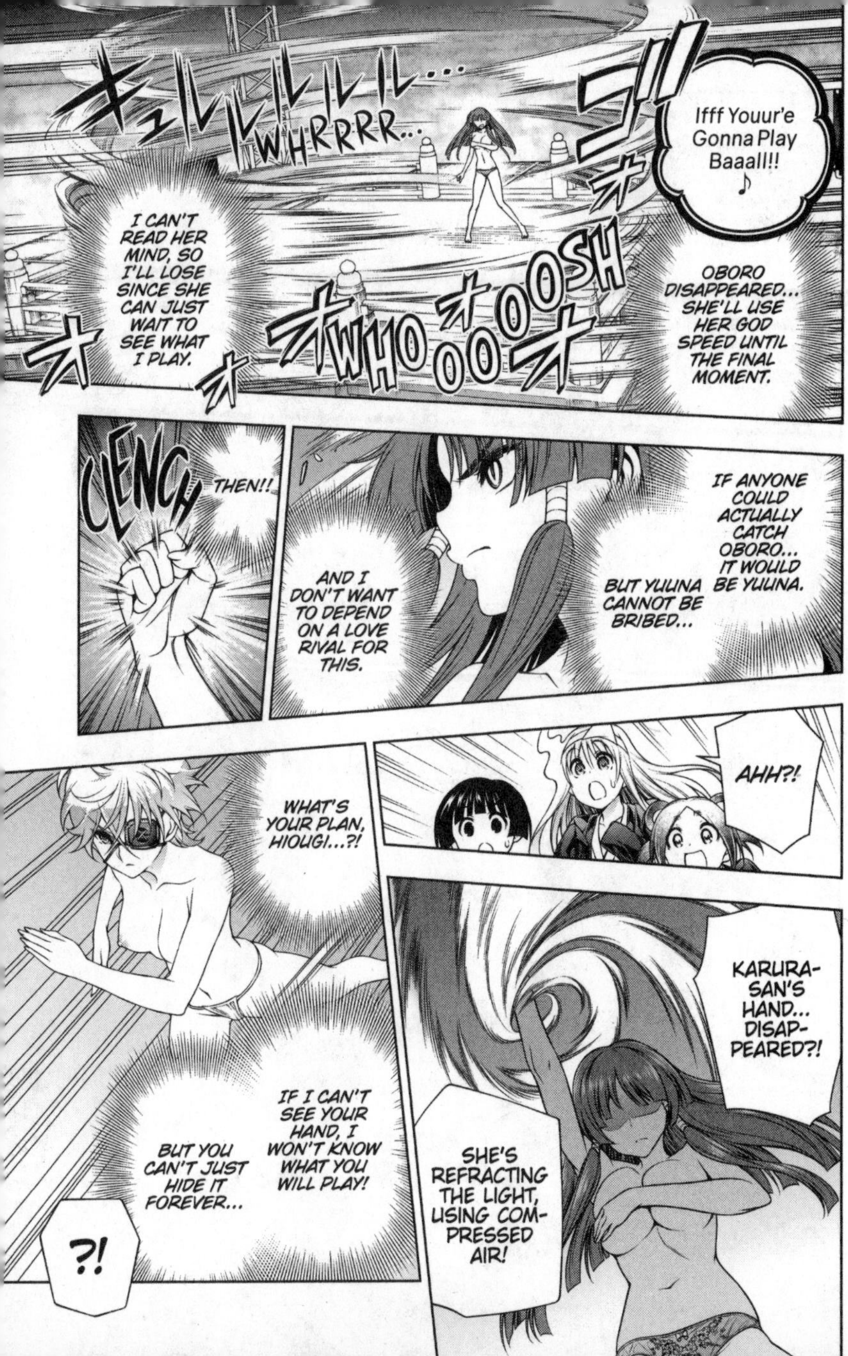
Ifff Youur'e Gonna Play Baaall!! ♪
キュルルルルル…
WHRRRR...
OBORO DISAPPEARED... SHE'LL USE HER GOD SPEED UNTIL THE FINAL MOMENT.
WHOOOOOSH
I CAN'T READ HER MIND, SO I'LL LOSE SINCE SHE CAN JUST WAIT TO SEE WHAT I PLAY.
IF ANYONE COULD ACTUALLY CATCH OBORO... IT WOULD BE YUUNA.
BUT YUUNA CANNOT BE BRIBED...
AND I DON'T WANT TO DEPEND ON A LOVE RIVAL FOR THIS.
CLENCH
THEN!!
AHH?!
KARURA-SAN'S HAND... DISAPPEARED?!
SHE'S REFRACTING THE LIGHT, USING COMPRESSED AIR!
WHAT'S YOUR PLAN, HIOUGI...?!
IF I CAN'T SEE YOUR HAND, I WON'T KNOW WHAT YOU WILL PLAY!
BUT YOU CAN'T JUST HIDE IT FOREVER...
?!

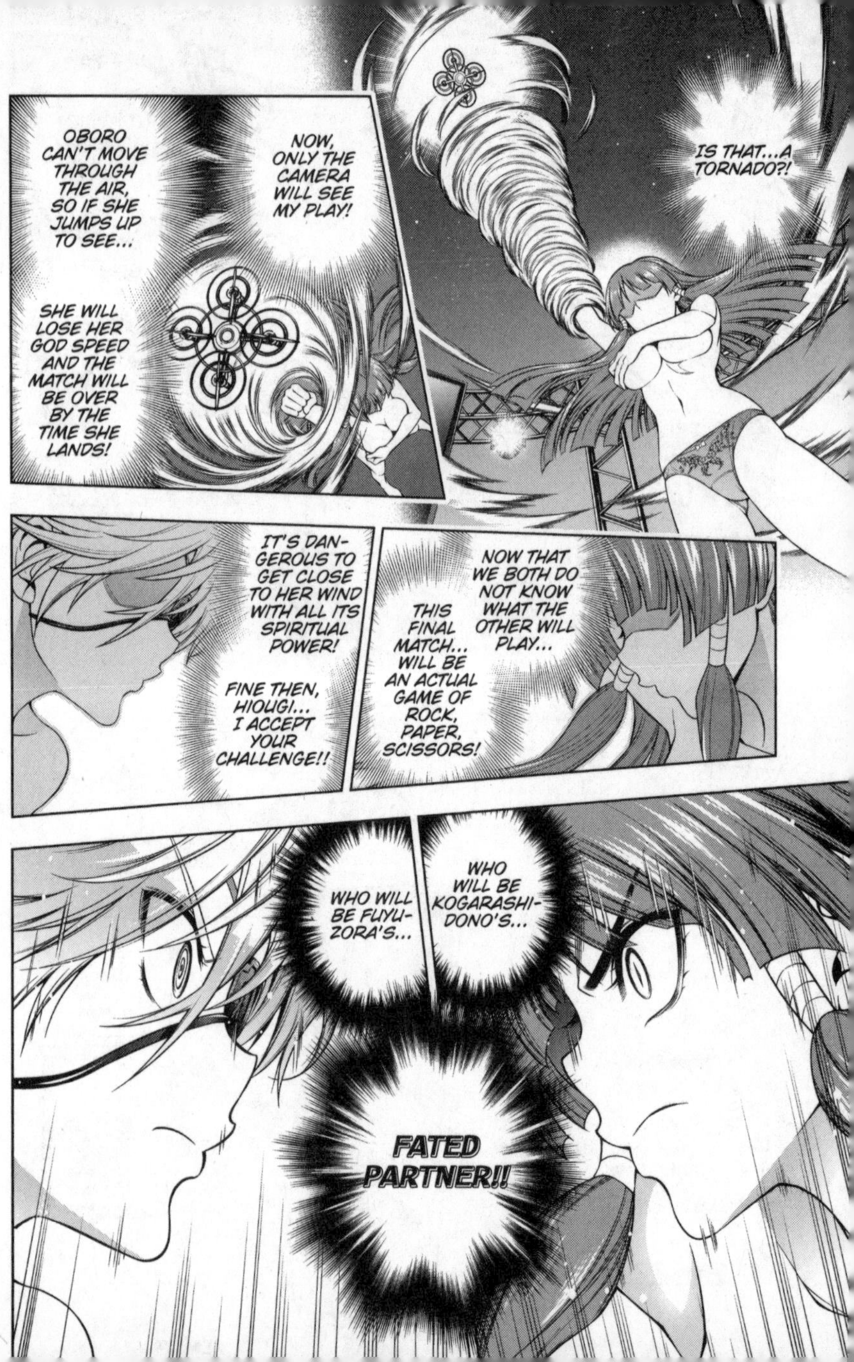
IS THAT...A TORNADO?!
NOW, ONLY THE CAMERA WILL SEE MY PLAY!
OBORO CAN'T MOVE THROUGH THE AIR, SO IF SHE JUMPS UP TO SEE...
SHE WILL LOSE HER GOD SPEED AND THE MATCH WILL BE OVER BY THE TIME SHE LANDS!
NOW THAT WE BOTH DO NOT KNOW WHAT THE OTHER WILL PLAY...
THIS FINAL MATCH... WILL BE AN ACTUAL GAME OF ROCK, PAPER, SCISSORS!
IT'S DANGEROUS TO GET CLOSE TO HER WIND WITH ALL ITS SPIRITUAL POWER!
FINE THEN, HIOUGI... I ACCEPT YOUR CHALLENGE!!
WHO WILL BE KOGARASHI-DONO'S...
WHO WILL BE FUYUZORA'S...
FATED PARTNER!!

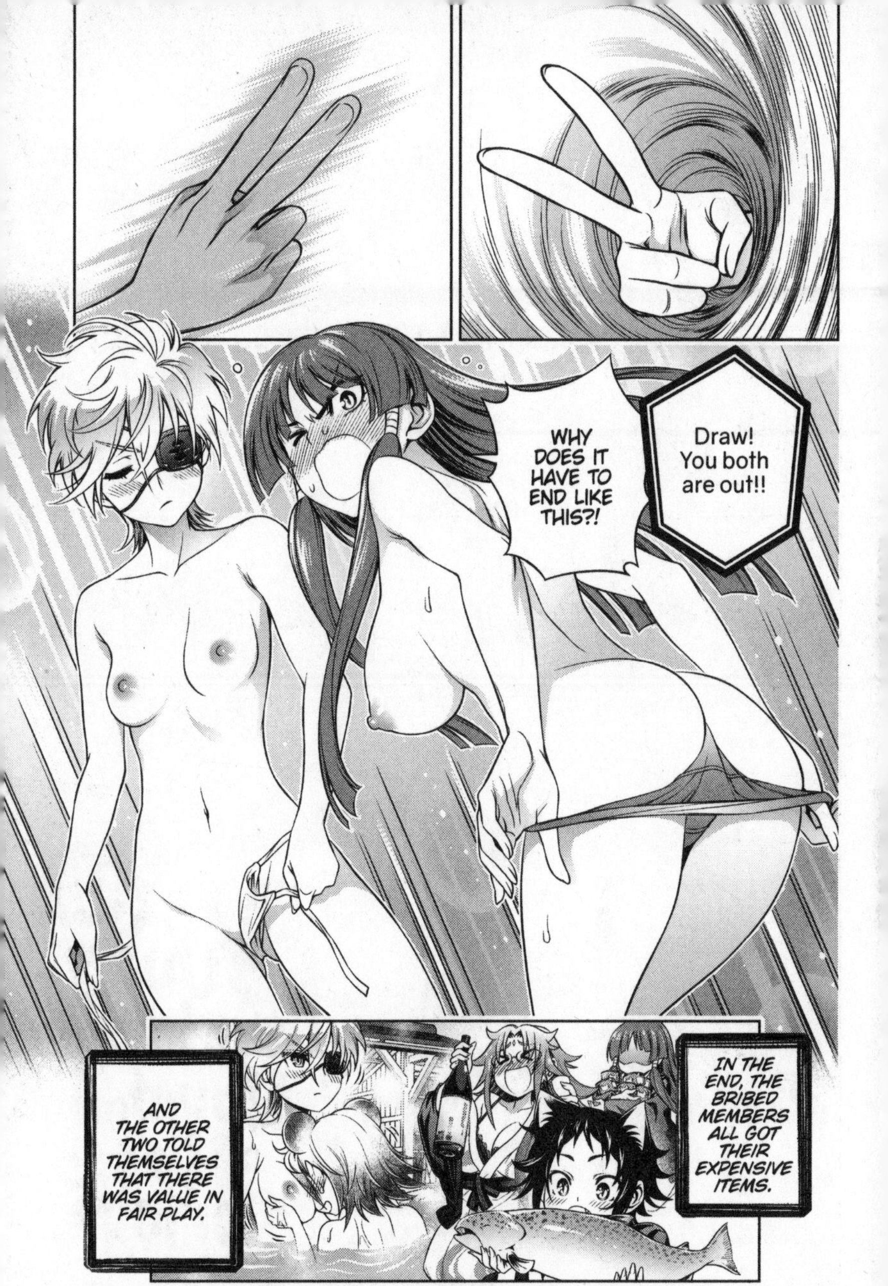
Draw! You both are out!!
WHY DOES IT HAVE TO END LIKE THIS?!
IN THE END, THE BRIBED MEMBERS ALL GOT THEIR EXPENSIVE ITEMS.
AND THE OTHER TWO TOLD THEMSELVES THAT THERE WAS VALUE IN FAIR PLAY.

19 Kogarashi-kun and the Great Danger (End)

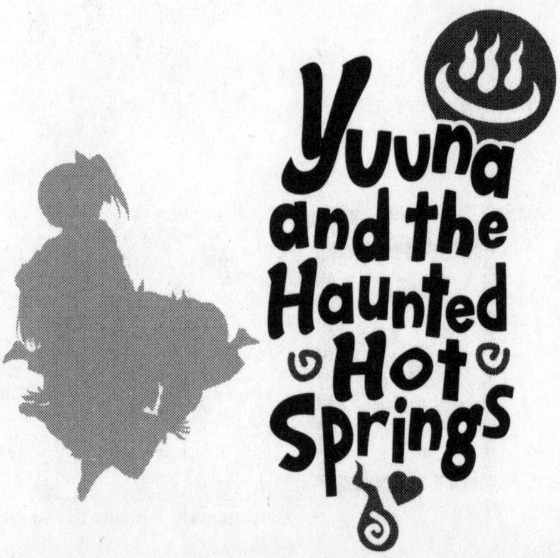

Yuuna and the Haunted Hot Springs

(Yuuna and the Haunted Hot Springs) End of the year extra content.

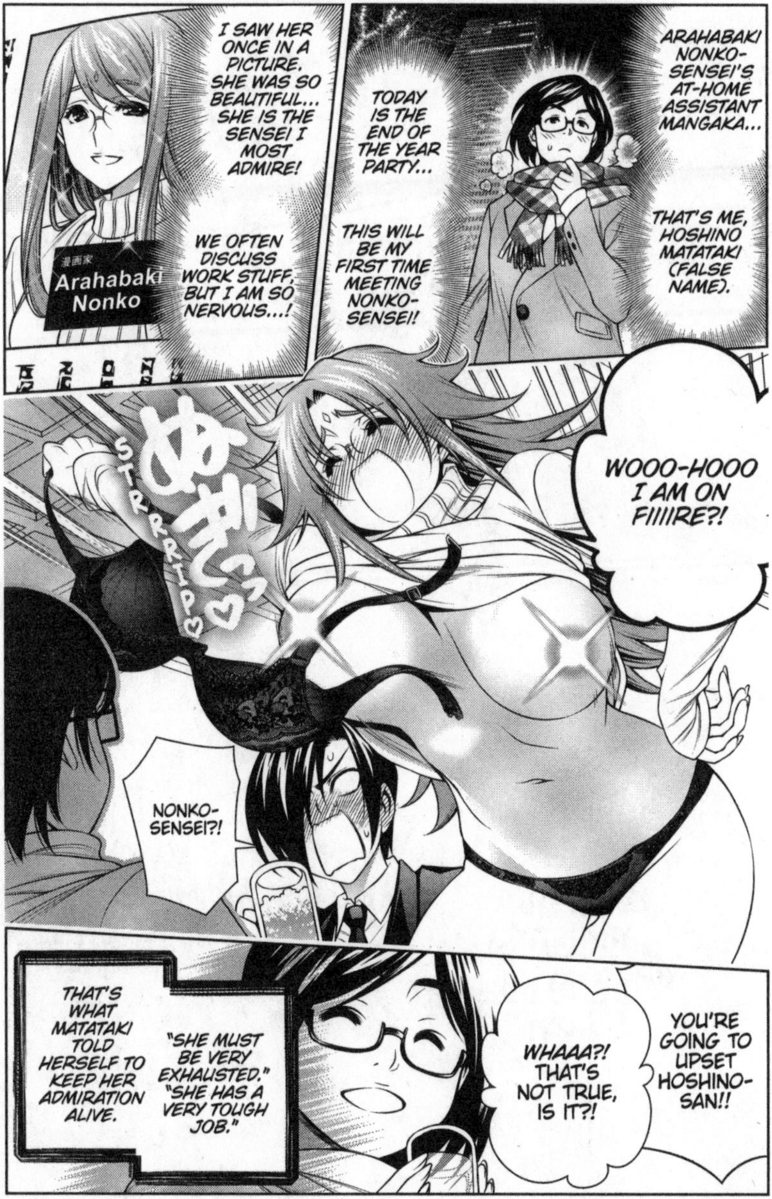
ARAHABAKI NONKO-SENSEI'S AT-HOME ASSISTANT MANGAKA...
THAT'S ME, HOSHINO MATATAKI (FALSE NAME).
TODAY IS THE END OF THE YEAR PARTY...
THIS WILL BE MY FIRST TIME MEETING NONKO-SENSEI!
I SAW HER ONCE IN A PICTURE. SHE WAS SO BEAUTIFUL... SHE IS THE SENSEI I MOST ADMIRE!
WE OFTEN DISCUSS WORK STUFF, BUT I AM SO NERVOUS...!
漫画家
Arahabaki Nonko
WOOO-HOOO I AM ON FIIIIRE?!
STRRRIP♡
NONKO-SENSEI?!
YOU'RE GOING TO UPSET HOSHINO-SAN!!
WHAAA?! THAT'S NOT TRUE, IS IT?!
"SHE MUST BE VERY EXHAUSTED." "SHE HAS A VERY TOUGH JOB."
THAT'S WHAT MATATAKI TOLD HERSELF TO KEEP HER ADMIRATION ALIVE.

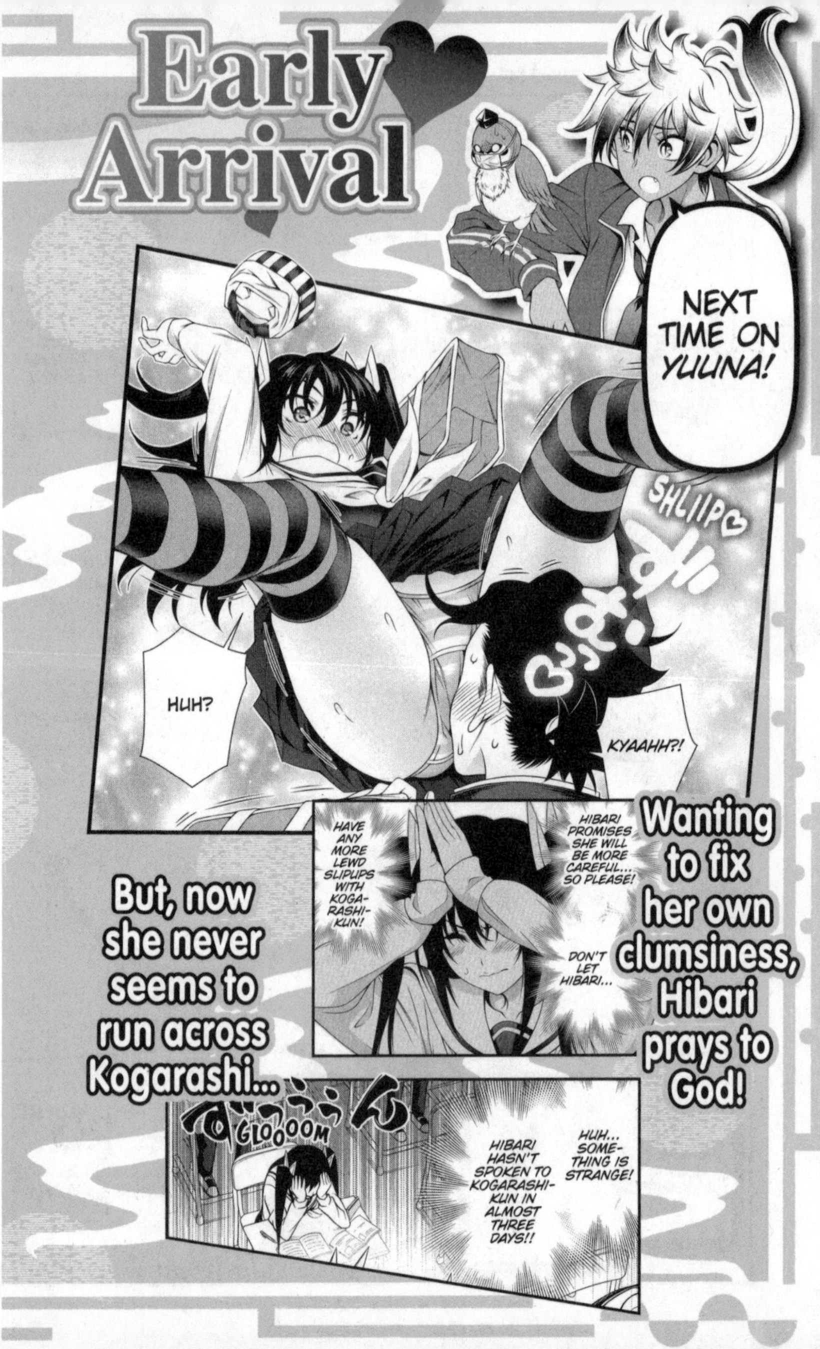
Early Arrival
NEXT TIME ON YUUNA!
SHLIIP
KYAAHH?!
HUH?
Wanting to fix her own clumsiness, Hibari prays to God!
HIBARI PROMISES SHE WILL BE MORE CAREFUL... SO PLEASE!
DON'T LET HIBARI...
HAVE ANY MORE LEWD SLIPUPS WITH KOGARASHI-KUN!
But, now she never seems to run across Kogarashi...
HUH... SOMETHING IS STRANGE!
HIBARI HASN'T SPOKEN TO KOGARASHI-KUN IN ALMOST THREE DAYS!!
GLOOOOM

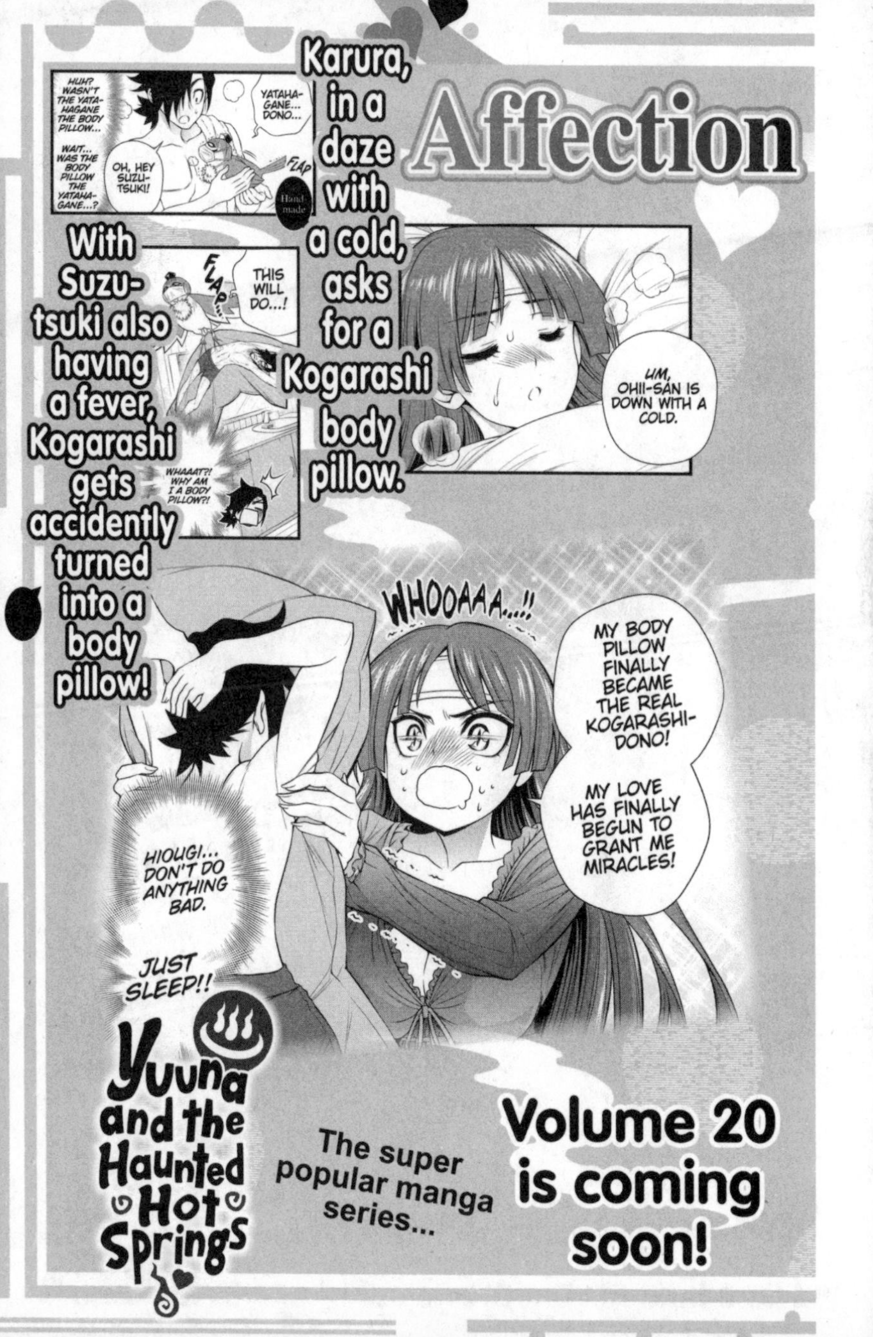
Affection
Karura, in a daze with a cold, asks for a Kogarashi body pillow.
YATAHA-GANE... DONO...
HUH? WASN'T THE YATA-HAGANE THE BODY PILLOW...
WAIT... WAS THE BODY PILLOW THE YATAHA-GANE...?
OH, HEY SUZU-TSUKI!
FLAP
Hand-made
UM, OHII-SAN IS DOWN WITH A COLD.
THIS WILL DO...!
FLAP
WHAAAT?! WHY AM I A BODY PILLOW?!
With Suzu-tsuki also having a fever, Kogarashi gets accidently turned into a body pillow!
WHOOAAA...!!
MY BODY PILLOW FINALLY BECAME THE REAL KOGARASHI-DONO!
MY LOVE HAS FINALLY BEGUN TO GRANT ME MIRACLES!
HIOUGI... DON'T DO ANYTHING BAD.
JUST SLEEP!!
Volume 20 is coming soon!
The super popular manga series...
Yuuna and the Haunted Hot Springs

SEVEN SEAS' GHOST SHIP PRESENTS

Yuuna and the Haunted Hot Springs

VOL. 19

story and art by TADAHIRO MIURA

TRANSLATION
Thomas Zimmerman

LETTERING AND RETOUCH
Phil Christie

COVER DESIGN
Nicky Lim
(LOGO) H. Qi

PROOFREADER
Kurestin Armada, B. Lillian Martin

EDITOR
Nick Mamatas

PRINT MANAGER
Rhiannon Rasmussen-Silverstein

PRODUCTION DESIGNER
George Panella

PRODUCTION MANAGER
Lissa Pattillo

EDITOR-IN-CHIEF
Julie Davis

ASSOCIATE PUBLISHER
Adam Arnold

PUBLISHER
Jason DeAngelis

First published in Japan in 2016 by SHUEISHA Inc., Tokyo.
English translation rights arranged by SHUEISHA Inc.
through TOHAN CORPORATION, Tokyo.

Seven Seas press and purchase enquiries can be sent to Marketing Manager Lianne Sentar at press@gomanga.com. Information regarding the distribution and purchase of digital editions is available from Digital Manager CK Russell at digital@gomanga.com.

ISBN: 978-1-63858-144-4

Printed in Canada

First Printing: April 2022

10 9 8 7 6 5 4 3 2 1

FOLLOW US ONLINE: *www.ghostshipmanga.com*

READING DIRECTIONS

This book reads from ***right to left***, Japanese style. If this is your first time reading manga, you start reading from the top right panel on each page and take it from there. If you get lost, just follow the numbered diagram here. It may seem backwards at first, but you'll get the hang of it! Have fun!!

1
2
3
4
5
6
7
8
9

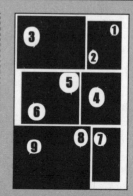